THE SACRED GAME

Cesáreo Bandera

THE
SACRED GAME

The Role of the Sacred
in the
Genesis of Modern Literary Fiction

The Pennsylvania State University Press
University Park, Pennsylvania

A note on the translations: Throughout the text, all translations are by the author unless otherwise indicated either in the text or in the Select Bibliography.

Library of Congress Cataloging-in-Publication Data

Bandera, Cesáreo.
    The sacred game : the role of the sacred in the genesis of modern
literary fiction / Cesáreo Bandera.
        p.   cm. — (Penn State studies in Romance literatures)
    Includes bibliographical references and index.
    ISBN 0-271-01301-X. — ISBN 0-271-01302-8 (pbk.)
        1. Religion and literature.   2. Literature—Philosophy.
    I. Title.   II. Series.
    PN49.B137   1994
    809.3'9382—dc20   93-6295
                                                                 CIP

Published by The Pennsylvania State University Press,
Barbara Building, Suite C, University Park, PA 16802-1003

It is the policy of The Pennsylvania State University Press to use acid-free paper for the first printing of all clothbound books. Publications on uncoated stock satisfy the minimum requirements of American National Standard for Information Sciences—Permanence of Paper for Printed Library Materials, ANSI Z39.48–1984.

Angela, Nicole, Carlos,

futurisque pueris dilectis

This is the peculiarity of the West: not that of having discovered the beautiful, but of having left it hovering in a state of suspension, of having untied the slipknot that strangles the victim. . . . What speaks in art is the voice of the victim who escaped the killing *in extremis*—and forever—when the ritual had already caused all the sacred to flow back into that victim.

—Calasso, *La ruine de Kasch*

CONTENTS

INTRODUCTION

1. On "Sacred Allergy" in Its Modern Form

It happened some twenty-odd years ago. I had just finished the manuscript of my book on the *Poem of El Cid* and was waiting for the critical opinion of a distinguished scholar at the University of Madrid. He had had the manuscript for several days. I came into his office and waited, nervously. He paced up and down for a moment, finally stopped, turned toward me and, visibly embarrassed, spoke: "This sort of thing gives me allergy. I just can't help it." (*Esta cosa me da alergia. No lo puedo remediar.*) It had nothing to do, he explained, with the scholarly quality of my work, which he found above reproach. It was simply that that "sort of thing" gave him allergy.

The "sort of thing" that triggered such an allergic reaction was my premise that the epic hero of the poem, in addition to being a typical epic warrior, was also a Christian model, patterned on the majestic figure of Christ that one can see, for example, on the tympanum of Romanesque cathedrals; that is to say, a kingly, lionlike Christ; similar to those sculptures that represent Charlemagne in a manner practically indistinguishable from the figure of Christ the Pantokrator, the universal lawgiver. It was this conjunction or mixture of the sacred and the profane in my thesis that the distinguished scholar found painful, a deep source of scholarly embarrassment.

It would be difficult to decide whether this type of reaction is caused by the unexpected presence of the sacred in the profane, or the other way around, the intrusion of the profane in the realm of the sacred. Ultimately it does not matter. It is safe to assume that contemporary scholars feel and interpret the reaction the first way. But if we go back in history, or move out of our own cultural environment, we can see that similar reactions are experienced and interpreted the second way. In either case, the active ingredient, the catalytic agent of the reaction, is the sacred. In fact, as soon as the sacred comes in contact with the profane, it appears that the latter loses its independence and cultural specificity. In the experience of the scholar it becomes embarrassingly self-conscious: it stands, as it were, accused; it becomes profanity. The modern lay scholar, the representative of the profane or the secular, senses this danger with a certain amount of anxiety, and vigorously protests against it. Therefore, it is only appropriate to refer to this type of reaction as some sort of "sacred allergy."

The phenomenon in question is, of course, something automatic and unreflective; one might even say instinctive. All self-reflecting scholarly thinking comes after it, not before. Whatever the explicit object of such thinking may be, it is more than likely that it is also a way of avoiding the sacred, of skirting the allergic reaction. But such a sacred embarrassment, as I have indicated, is nothing new. There is a long history behind it, about which we know practically nothing—as would be expected, since the sacred character of such a topic makes it automatically taboo, the unscholarly topic par excellence.

Insofar as it concerns poetic activity, the specifically Western and modern form of this sacred reaction to the mixing of the sacred and the profane, that is to say, to the spread of sacred contamination, can be dated with a fair degree of precision. It did not exist in the fourteenth century, but was already clearly visible by the middle of the sixteenth. One might propose as a symbolic date that of 17 November 1548, when the Paris parliament issued an order prohibiting the Confrérie de la Passion from staging "the mysteries of the Passion of Our Saviour [which, of course, had been the traditional performance of the Confrérie], or other sacred mysteries," although it could continue to play "mystères profanes, honnestes et licites" (Loukovitch, 2). Thus the phenomenon in question seems to emerge as an integral part of the genesis of modern man—a fact that, if proved correct, would have important consequences for today's scholarship. For example, it would render suspect and unreliable any interpretation of the Middle Ages grounded in and guided by specifically modern fears of sacred contamination; it would rule out any interpretation failing to take into account the fact that what appears to modern man as an intolerable mixture of "the human and the divine" did not appear as such to medieval man and, therefore, did not trigger any sacred allergy attack in his mind. "Mixing the human and the divine" are Cervantes's words, and I shall refer to them many times in the course of this book. In Cervantes they are already used to express his profound displeasure: "mixing the human and the divine . . . is a kind of motley in which no Christian understanding should be dressed" (Prologue to *Don Quijote*, Cohen trans., 30). Cervantes is already a modern man. It is also important to notice that in Cervantes's mind keeping the "human" and the "divine" separate is felt to be a Christian demand.

It is only logical to assume that this "allergic" reaction to the mixing of "the human and the divine" must have something to do with the generally acknowledged process of desacralization that took place in the transition from the Middle Ages to the modern era. But this is where we find the problem that, either explicitly or implicitly, will occupy our attention throughout this book. For these two things, desacralization, on the one hand, and "allergic" reaction to the mixture of the sacred and the profane, on the other, are not only *not* the same thing, but are in principle opposites, in spite of the fact that both appear to converge toward the same goal of keeping the "human" separate from the "divine."

The process of desacralization that happened in European society at that time, was something unique and unprecedented, both in its scope and in its lasting effects; a genuine, irreversible, break with the past that set the Western world apart from all other human societies. The "allergic" reaction to the mixing of the sacred and the profane, on the other hand, is a form of experience probably as old as humanity itself, a defensive mechanism triggered when the sacred threatens or—what amounts to the same thing—is threatened. And yet this time things happened differently. The old defensive "allergy," which had always been a conservative reaction aimed at reestablishing the old traditional distinctions (distinctions based on the primary one that keeps the sacred at a safe distance from everything else) became, this time, an emulator of the new, and, putting on an unprecedented disguise, passed itself off successfully as the agent and herald of the modern time.

What the old sacred "allergy" had always hoped for but had never been able to accomplish, namely, a stable, peaceful, nonconflictual, nonallergic separation between the "human" and the "divine," was now actually taking place underneath the misleading "allergic" surface. Covered by this deceiving appearance, the nonconflictual desacralizing process was largely, though by no means completely, invisible, known mostly a posteriori, by its profound and lasting effects.

What is important is that the lasting and increasingly stable desacralization that occurs at the threshold of the modern era, could not be caused by the "allergic" reaction to the mixing of the sacred and the profane that accompanied it. Rather, I shall argue, it had to be the other way around. The strength of the desacralizing process triggered the old sacred "allergy" and, at the same time, modified it, lessened its impact, and thus made it capable of becoming an instrument, no matter how imperfect or ambiguous, of the new. What we shall have to find out is the internal logic of this triggering mechanism.

What happened, therefore, cannot be properly described as a process of substitution or replacement of one thing for another. The new did not make its way by simply destroying the old or pushing it aside. Rather, it appears that, to a large extent, it changed the old from inside and set before it unprecedented opportunities. We are used to thinking of historical progress as a violent process in which new forms emerge from the ruins of the old, but that is probably not a very accurate model.

In the case at hand, a very complex relationship developed between the new and the old, a relationship that extended over the entire sociocultural horizon. Our attention, of course, will be centered on the effects of such a relationship in the field of poetic fiction, even though we shall have to venture beyond this center in order to put things in their proper perspective. But I believe that when we are dealing with the historical effects of the desacralizing process, poetic fiction is not merely one possible field of study among many. I think it is an especially appropriate field, because it was especially sensitive to the mixture of the "human and the divine." This sensitivity, I believe, was highly developed in the case of the best poets, those whose work had a clear future.

But what exactly was the object of this sudden historical "allergy"? How did it manifest itself? And how pervasive was it? We have already mentioned the attitude of the Parisian parliament with regard to the, until then, enormously popular mystery plays. It was by no means an isolated case. Similar prohibitions were issued by other city parliaments in France, for example, those of Bordeaux (1556) and Rennes (c. 1565), even though mysteries continued to be played occasionally in many parts of the country. The same attitude was found in the Spanish Netherlands, where a 1559 edict declared it indecent "to profane the divine mysteries and abuse Holy Scripture by mixing it with things profane and ridicule" (Lebègue, 55). Lebègue mentions the attitude of Boucher, a member of the Catholic League during the religious wars in France, who "takes the general opinion even further: he attributes part of France's misfortunes to the *Passion*, 'played in Paris and elsewhere in France, because of the irreverence committed there'" (55).

Meanwhile, across the Channel, a rich tradition of religious parish drama was coming to an end in England: "Judging by the extant records, this parish dramatic activity reached its height in the 1520's. Just as the tradition achieved full bloom, however, the Reformation, the Dissolution, and the new Anglican Church's rejection of post-biblical saints resulted in a sudden curtailment of these productions. . . . In short, beginning at the Reformation and continuing until the actual banning of parish drama in the 1590's, a very widespread tradition of parish drama in England died a rather rapid and painful death from its height in the 1520's" (Wasson, 73–74).

Without denying that specific national or local circumstances may have played a role in the sudden scandalized opposition to public displays of sacred "mixtures," it is important to realize that the phenomenon appears to be pan-Western, transcending local and national boundaries. In the arch-Catholic Spain of Philip II, Lupercio Leonardo de Argensola, a playwright who had turned against the theater, wrote to the king in 1598 in the following terms, to ask him not to lift a temporary royal ban on the performance of *comedias*, as had been requested in a previous plea by the Madrid municipal council. To understand the passage, we should note that the council had pleaded in particular for permission to stage *autos sacramentales* (sacramental plays):

> Even if Your Majesty were to permit them [i.e., *comedias*] it ought to be by maintaining absolutely the prohibition against these representations of sacred figures and things. Because in their dressing rooms [the actors] engage in drinking, swearing, blaspheming and playing while still wearing the clothes and exterior forms of Saints, Angels, Our Lady the Virgin, and of God Himself. . . . Certainly Your Majesty would not permit an actor to imitate your

figure on the stage. Furthermore, you have justly forbidden them to represent the persons of noble members of the Military Orders by wearing crosses on their stage clothes, as they used to. And yet on these holidays called Corpus Christi and other days in their regular plays, they come on the stage in priestly vestments, and what is more, with the wounds of our Redemption painted on those hands that only a moment before were dealing cards or playing the guitar. (Cotarelo y Mori, 67)

In spite of the *autos'* popularity at the time and during much of the seventeenth century (thanks, in large measure, to the exquisite mastery of Calderón, whose *autos* came to be almost the only ones in demand), the "allergic" opposition to them was there from the beginning, increased with time, and eventually won out. In this regard, it is interesting to compare Argensola's argument with another one, made almost two centuries later, by Clavijo y Fajardo, an influential publicist of the eighteenth-century enlightened and francophile establishment. Clavijo y Fajardo wrote the following in 1762, three years before King Charles III issued the decree that put an end to the traditional *autos*:

> What Catholic with an average capacity for reasoning will fail to be disgusted at seeing the Host painted on the stage curtain as soon as he enters the playhouse? Without having a very low idea of his religion, who would suffer that such profane people represent the persons of the Holy Trinity? Or that a woman, who sometimes is probably not very chaste, represent the Immaculate Virgin? Another of the most common defects in the autos is the mixture of sacred and profane things. (Menéndez Pelayo, *Historia*, 3:279)

The two texts are using basically the same argument. Only its scope has changed. The 1598 text is against the performance of public plays in general, but is especially concerned with the performance of sacramental plays. Thus it is already anticipating the historical narrowing of the attack, focusing in the end on those plays in which the mixture of the sacred and the profane was particularly obvious. In spite of the comparatively longer life of sacramental plays in Spain, the sacred allergy phenomenon was no different there from elsewhere. It should also be pointed out that this longer life has nothing to do with Spain being more "Catholic" than other places, but rather, perhaps, with its popular, tradition-bound culture's tending to be—for whatever reasons—more resilient and difficult to change than elsewhere. For the sacred allergy of which we are speaking appears to develop particularly well among the better educated classes of society. What Raymond Lebègue said about the situation in France regarding the mysteries, should be taken into acount when considering the comparatively longer life of poetic "mixtures" of sacred and profane in Spain (to the best of my knowledge, detailed research on this topic does not exist):

> Autrefois les lettrés aimaient composer des mystères ou assister à leur représentation, et dans leur loges les princes et les nobles y prenaient autant de plaisir que la foule. Au XVIe siècle, l'élite de la population conçoit peu à peu du dédain pour ce genre dramatique: on lui reproche d'être mal joué, d'être un spectacle populaire, d'émouvoir et d'amuser les foules par des moyens grossiers, et de ne pas ressembler au théâtre antique. (48)[1]

> (In the old days men of letters delighted in composing mysteries or in going to their representation; in their boxes princes and nobles took as much pleasure as the crowd. In the sixteenth century, the elite of the population gradually began to look down on this dramatic genre: it was accused of being badly played, of being unsophisticated, of moving and entertaining the crowds in unrefined ways, and of not resembling ancient theater.)

Both the church and the civil authorities had frequently legislated against abuses in the performance of liturgical drama throughout the Middle Ages. But the modern opposition to sacred theatrical performances perceived a fundamental incompatibility between the Christian sacred and the non-Christian theater inherited from antiquity.

This perception existed not only among those moralists and theologians who were totally opposed to the theater, but also among many enthusiasts of modern drama. Saint-Evremond, for example, "asserts that 'de la doctrine la plus sainte, des actions les plus Chrétiennes et des

---

1. Cf. Delumeau, *Le Christianisme*, p. 191: "Longtemps l'Eglise médiévale répugna donc à l'élitisme et ferma les yeux sur une certaine 'folklorisation' du christianisme qui ne semblait pas faire obstacle à la grâce." (For a long time the medieval Church rejected elitism and closed its eyes at a certain 'folklorization' of Christianity which did not seem to be an obstacle to grace.)

véritez les plus utiles, on fera les Tragédies du monde qui plairont le moins [from the holiest doctrine, the most Christian actions and the most profitable truths, only the least pleasing tragedies can be made]'" (Phillips, 220). Even Corneille expresses similar views referring to his own *Théodore* (Phillips, 220). Another defender of modern drama, the Abbé d'Aubignac, concurs (Phillips, 231).

The same can be said regarding other poetic genres, in particular the epic and the romances. Bernard Lamy's *Nouvelles réflexions sur l'art poétique* deals with the rules of both epic and dramatic poetry, "which are also common to those poetic stories called romances" (8). There are no essential differences between different poetic genres. In the eyes of many religious moralists there were no differences at all, "a maker of romances or a poet of the theater is a public poisoner" (Loukovitch, 375).

Consider, for example, the following: in 1554 an obscure Valencian author, Jerónimo Sempere, published a book of chivalry *a lo divino* with the title, *Caballería celestial de la Rosa Fragante.* His purpose is explained in the prologue: "Realizing that those whose taste is accustomed to such lessons [as provided by fictitious books of chivalry] would not come willingly to the banquet of these other [profitable] lessons, [and] having to cross from one extreme to the other, I decided to feed them the delicate morsel of this story spiced with the artifice of those to which they are used, so that they may be lured to liking these and lose their taste for the feigned ones" (Menéndez Pelayo, *Orígenes*, 449). Try to imagine the main characters in Sempere's book: Christ becomes the Knight of the Lion; Lucifer, the Knight of the Serpent. Other characters include the old sage Alegorín and the wise maiden Moraliza.

The author's intention could not be blamed. Nevertheless, the inquisitorial reaction was not late in coming. Sempere's book is already included in the 1559 Index of Forbidden Books. What is even more interesting is that the Inquisition never banned any secular book of chivalry, and this in spite of a widespread clamor against this type of literature, which enlisted some of the most illustrious names of sixteenth-century Spain. Obviously the inquisitors were not amused by such a clumsy poetic attempt to play with the sacred, even with the best of intentions. It was one thing to use poetry strictly as a servant of the sacred, and quite another to dress the sacred in the servant's clothes to make it attractive and, thus, in some way, to bring it down to the servant's level. Two very different things indeed, both from the point of view of doctrine and of poetry, but the line between the two was, nevertheless, rather thin, and the danger of a faux pas high. It took an excellent poetic intuition (such as Calderón's) to walk on so dangerous a high wire without falling. For in this particular respect, the sharpest doctrinal instinct of the stern inquisitors totally coincided with that of the best poets; an amazing coincidence that to the best of my knowledge, has never been given the attention it deserves.

When two hundred years later freethinking Voltaire said that "our saints, who make so good a figure in our churches, make a very sorry one in our Epic Poems" (Le Bossu and Voltaire, *Le Bossu and Voltaire*, 129), he probably did not suspect that his poetic sensitivity echoed the religious sensitivity of sixteenth-century Spanish inquisitors. On the other hand, the dustbin of literary history is full of poetic specimens that were not lucky enough to have found the merciful cutting hand of an old inquisitor. Boileau had put it rather graphically in his Ninth Satire:

> Laissez mourir un fat dans son obscurité:
> Un auteur ne peut-il mourir en sureté?
> Le *Jonas* inconnu sèche dans la poussière;
> Le *David* imprimé n'a point vu la lumière;
> Le *Moïse* commence a moisir par les bords.
> Que mal cela fait-il? Ceux qui sont morts sont morts.
>
> (lines 89–94)

> (Let a fool die in his obscurity:
> Can't an author die in peace?
> The *Jonas,* unknown, is drying in the dust;
> The *David,* printed, has never seen the light;
> The *Moïse* is beginning to rust at the edges.
> What damage does that do? Those who are dead are
>   dead.)

His friend Racine, the author of two of the few successes attained by biblical tragedy in France, *Esther* and *Athalie,* would have agreed; even in the preface to *Esther*, he pointedly remarks that he "has carefully avoided mixing the profane with the sacred" (Loukovitch, 418).

Indeed, this problem of mixing the profane and the sacred, which lay at the root of Sempere's clumsy attempt, was still a problem in the eighteenth century, when Samuel Johnson wrote that "poetry loses its lustre and its power, [when] it is applied to the decoration of something more excellent than itself. . . . The ideas of Christian Theology are too simple for eloquence, too sacred for fiction, and too majestick for ornament; to recommend them by tropes and figures, is to magnify by a concave mirror the sidereal hemisphere" (297). What the Spanish inquisitors saw as bad for doctrine, Johnson sees as bad for poetry, as seldom since the beginning of the modern era have the two been successfully combined: "It has been the frequent lamentation of good men, that verse has been too little applied to the purposes of worship, and many attempts have been made to animate devotion by pious poetry; that they have very seldom attained their end is sufficiently known" (296).

This resistance to the mixing of poetry and religion has continued to be experienced to our own time, in particular by people of great religious sensitivity. "It was Lord David Cecil, introducing the *Oxford Book of Christian Verse,* who declared that in 'Christian Europe' religious emotion 'has not proved the most fertile soil for poetry'" (Gardner, 122). Perhaps the most illustrious example is the Christian poet T. S. Eliot, who wrote that he "could easily fulminate for a whole hour against the men of letters who have gone into ectasies over 'the Bible as literature,' the Bible as 'the noblest monument of English prose'" ("Religion," 225). He further wrote that "for the great majority of people who love poetry, 'religious [i.e., 'devotional'] poetry' is a variety of *minor* poetry. . . . What is more, I am ready to admit that up to a point these [people] are right" ("Religion," 225).

Up to the eighteenth century much of the theoretical argument against mixing poetry and the Christian sacred remained basically unchanged. Johnson was still arguing that the "essence of poetry is invention; such invention as, by producing something unexpected, surprises and delights. The topics of devotion are few, and being few are universally known . . . they can receive no grace from novelty of sentiment, and very little from novelty of expression" (296).

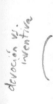

The same argument had been used by Tasso in his *Discourses on the Heroic Poem*:

> The argument of the epic poem should be drawn, then, from true history and a religion that is not false. But histories and other writings may be sacred or non-sacred, and among the sacred some have more and some have less authority. Ecclesiastical and spiritual writings command greater authority. . . . The others doubtless have less authority. The poet had better not touch histories of the first type; they may be left in their pure and simple truth, since

with them discovery takes no effort and invention seems hardly permitted. And whoever does not invent or imitate . . . would be no poet but rather a historian. (39–40)

Clearly the *Divine Comedy* could not have been even conceived from such a perspective. In fact, everything we have been saying about the characteristically modern allergy to the mixing of "the human and the divine" may acquire special significance when set it in relief against the background of Dante's poem, the poetic Christian masterpiece of the Middle Ages. Let us therefore reflect for a moment on this contrast.

2. The *Divine Comedy* as a Contrasting Background

Erich Auerbach writes:

[The] *Divine Comedy* [is] a vision of the divine order of the universe, and into that transcendent order [Dante] gathered the entire living reality of his time, the here and now of Florence and Italy in 1300, with all its passions and tragic involvements. . . . [This] does not apply to the *Inferno* alone. . . . Many of those atoning for their sins in Purgatory . . . move the reader because of their lot on earth, Sordello's greeting of Virgil, the recognition scene between Dante and Forese Donati, and many other passages. . . . Even in many of the blessed, the earthly drama is still discernible. (306–7)

Auerbach cannot but wonder:

It is strange . . . that this triumph of autonomous humanity and of a specifically human will should in all sincerity have represented itself as a vision of the divine order of the world. . . . Many Christian visionaries have proclaimed God's will, but they have neither given so comprehensive a view of it, taking in the whole universe, nor given so concrete a version of divine judgement, applied so closely to concrete historical happenings. (310)

Dante's achievement was, indeed, unique. But being unique does not mean being out of place or time. The *Divine Comedy* fully belongs in the historical context of fourteenth-century Christian Europe. It is its highest poetic expression. The point is that approximately two centuries later such an extraordinary "mixing of the human and the divine"—striking in Dante only for the vastness of its scope—would be totally out of place, indeed shocking and unacceptable. What was perfectly possible for Dante would be impossible, an intolerable embarrassment, for Tasso, and even more so for Milton, whose choice of subject for *Paradise Lost* automatically eliminated the explicit inclusion of the living reality, the here and now of Puritan England, in the poem.

Auerbach tries to explain:

> [This] direct association of historical existence with the kingdom of God is also a Christian heritage: from the outset Christianity was never a mere doctrine or myth but was deeply involved in historical existence. . . . On the one hand Christ became flesh in a definite historical situation, an earthly here and now . . . while on the other hand, by thus atoning for Adam's guilt, he restored man's share in the kingdom of God, which Adam had lost. . . . [It] was no longer so easy to look upon earthly concerns with the indifference that had been so dear to the philosophers of late antiquity, or even to strive for their equanimity. (307–8)

Quite true, but Tasso and Milton were as Christian as Dante, and yet they could no longer do what he did. Indeed, it could be said that, regarding the poetic possibility of "mixing the human and the divine" without scandal, there was less difference between Dante and Virgil, for example, than between Dante and the Christian poets from the sixteenth century on.

The problem is even more puzzling, because the Christian consciousness of the author is deeply involved in both cases. What made it possible for Dante to link his "vision of the divine order of the universe" to the here and now may have been his profound understanding of the meaning of Christianity, as Auerbach suggests. But it was also the Christian consciousness of the sixteenth- or seventeenth-century poet that prevented him from doing the same thing.

One cause, two apparently opposite effects. However, since these effects do not occur at the same time but in historical sequence, it should

be possible, at least in principle, to postulate some sort of logical development between the first and the second. For example, it is generally acknowledged that the transition from the Middle Ages to the Renaissance
involved an increase in historical awareness. In fact Dante has been
placed at the start of this process. Thomas M. Greene has said that Dante
was the first medieval poet fully aware of the gap, the cultural discontinu-
ity, between his time and the Graeco-Roman past (17). This awareness
continues to deepen in Petrarch, Valla, and the humanist movement in
general, and then in the Renaissance.[2]

This being the case, it is not impossible to imagine that such a progressive deepening of the historical consciousness could have resulted in, or
simultaneously fostered, the realization that historical events in general
are fundamentally human events, that human history is the responsibility
of man. That is to say, the realization that God does not intervene directly
in those events, that it is not proper for man to mix "the human and
the divine."

Nonetheless, something is clearly missing in this realization. In a sense,
the problem is its own strictly rational character. It contemplates a logical, basically unproblematic evolution of the historical consciousness;
the change in attitude, however, was rather quick and radical. Poetry's
old, sincere mixing of the human and the divine becomes, almost all of a
sudden, a source of profound uneasiness. What had been accepted as
being in accordance with a Christian vision of the world becomes a scandal, an embarrassment, the "kind of motley in which no Christian understanding should be dressed."

So it was not as if people finally realized that it was illogical or contrary
to reason to mix the human and the divine and then, as a result of that
realization, developed an allergy to such a mixture. It was clearly the
other way around. What brings together on this issue such a diverse array
of people as Parisian parliamentarians, Spanish inquisitors, novelists,
dramatists, English Puritans, Roman Catholics, freethinkers, poetic theoreticians, etc., generation after generation, across national boundaries, is
not their powers of logical deduction, but something far more primary,
even primeval. Nevertheless, it is important to note how easily logic follows in the wake of such sacred allergy, how irresistibly easy it is to perceive the scandalizing mixture of the sacred and the profane as something
fundamentally illogical. We recall Clavijo y Fajardo's, "What Catholic

---

2. See, for example, Seznec and Delumeau.

with an average capacity for reasoning . . . ?" In this respect the rationalism of the Enlightment is no different from sixteenth-century Scholastic
rationalism.

The increasing rationalism of the age, usually associated with the
dawning of the "secular" spirit, in no way diminishes the intensity of the
sacred allergy. What changes is the size, that is, the extension of the sacred field. At the beginning, as we will see in Chapter 1, the allergy-
producing object could be almost the entire literary field, all plays, romances, love lyrics, etc., even those that did not have any explicit, literal
connection with sacred themes or objects. As time goes on, the sacred
field narrows and the allergic reaction acquires a sharper focus. But that
is all. The sacred character of the reaction does not change. Between
the sixteenth-century moralist's condemnation of all poetic fiction and
Voltaire's displeasure with the use of explicitly religious subjects in literature, there is a direct, unbroken continuity. As we shall see in Plato, anxiety in the presence of an unstable sacred and the appeal of rational
thinking can easily be two sides of the same phenomenon. The history of
the old sacred has been to a large extent the history of the flight away
from the sacred, of the expulsion of the sacred; a paradoxical expulsion,
through which the old sacred perpetuates itself. And reason has often
played an important role in this effort to keep the sacred at a distance.

It is an error to imagine that those in the sixteenth and seventeenth
centuries who bitterly attacked poetic fiction in general and the theater
in particular as a threat to morality and religion, were fanatic holdovers
from a medieval past and essentially out of place in a new era increasingly
ruled by reason. On the contrary, as Russell Fraser has pointed out, "it
is . . . in the Renaissance, and not the Middle Ages that the artist . . . is
driven from the commonwealth" (39).[3] It is then that the "war against
poetry" (Fraser's term) intensifies to fever pitch.

And yet, the same allergic reaction to the mixing of the sacred and the
profane that prompted those bitter attacks to drive poetic fiction out of
the city, once modified, lessened, experienced in a less violent way, also
became the very historical condition and the motivation for the development of a new, modern kind of fictional literature.

We must understand that the rabid attackers of traditional fiction and
those who were discovering new possibilities for it belonged together.

---

3. Occasionally this expulsion can become quite literal, as when comedians were expelled
from Venice in 1577 (Loukovitch, 20).

They both agreed on the need to keep poetic fiction away from the sacred. Their difference was merely one of degree—although, with regard to the future of poetry, that difference of degree made all the difference in the world.

It should be clear, then, that we are dealing with a problem that far transcends any kind of ideological definition, one that cannot be investigated within the parameters of traditional intellectual history. It is not a question of studying the relationship between theology and literature, for example, or even between religious and poetic expression.[4] The experience of the sacred precedes and grounds all ideology as well as all theology and poetry.

3. What Is the Sacred?

To begin this discussion, I must first explain what I mean by "the sacred." Mircea Eliade says, "The first definition that can be given of the sacred is that it is opposed to the profane" (14). These are "two modes of being in the World," immensely different from each other; "a precipice separates the two modalities of experience, the sacred and the profane" (17). It appears that this difference has existed between the "non-religious modern man" of Western societies and every other human society throughout history. For even though "the other great cultures of the past have also known non-religious men [and] it is not impossible that they may have existed even at archaic levels of culture, although there is at the moment no documental proof of that . . . it is only in modern Western societies that non-religious man has flourished completely." To this unique, nonreligious modern man "the sacred is the obstacle par excellence before his freedom. . . . He will not be truly free until the moment when he will have killed the last god." And yet, this modern man, "whether he likes it or not," is a direct descendant of the *homo religiosus,* the outcome of "a process of desacralization." "But that implies that the non-religious man has constituted himself through opposition to his predecessor, struggling to 'drain' all religiosity . . . from himself. He recognizes himself to the extent that he 'delivers' and 'purifies' himself from the 'superstitions' of his ancestors. In other words . . . he constitutes him-

---

4. See, especially, Buckley, Gardner, and Wright.

self by a series of negations and refusals, but he still continues to be haunted by the realities he has renounced" (172–73).

Recent thought on this subject extends this type of argument. As John Milbank writes, "[Secular] discourse does not just borrow . . . modes of expression from religion . . . , but is actually *constituted* in its secularity by 'heresy' in relation to Christianity, or else a rejection of Christianity that is more 'neo-pagan' than simply anti-religious" (3). And, in fact, Milbank continues, it may be true that "[Postmodern, post-Nietzschean] social theory increasingly finds secularization paradoxical, and implies that the mythic-religious can never be left behind" (3).[5]

I would like to take this line of thought even further. By struggling to free himself from the sacred, modern man unwittingly repeats the immemorial gesture of his ancestors. As I have indicated, the history of the old sacred is to a large extent the history of the flight away from the sacred. The old sacred is not only beneficent and protecting, but also terrifying and threatening, and above all extremely elusive. I do not deny in the least the difference between modern man and his predecessors. Nonetheless, I do not think there is such a thing as going beyond the old sacred in a violent way, that is, by struggling against it or running away from it. To the extent that modern man truly lives in a desacralized environment, it is not because of his struggle against the sacred, or his allergic reaction to it, but rather because of the way in which the nonviolent spirit of the Christian text has influenced his historical development. In other words, at the basis of this study lies the conviction that there is no such thing as a conflict between Christianity and a purely "secular," nonreligious man, but only between Christianity and the old sacred. As Milbank suggests, modern rejection of Christianity "is more 'neo-pagan' than simply anti-religious." In fact, I see no fundamental reason to use the word "neo-pagan" in quotes, in spite of the fact that "the secular *episteme* is a post-Christian paganism" (280).

Is this difference between the sacred and the profane, however, more appearance than reality? Certainly Emile Durkheim maintained the distinction, placing this opposition between the sacred and the profane at the center of his classic work *The Elementary Forms of the Religious*

---

5. Cf. Gauchet: "[Nous] ne sommes pas simplement passés au dehors de la religion, comme sortant d'un songe dont nous aurions fini par nous éveiller; nous en procédons; nous nous expliquons encore et toujours par elle" (137). (We have not simply passed beyond religion, as if coming out of a dream from which we would have finally awakened; we proceed from it; we still and always explain ourselves by it.)

Life: "All known religious beliefs, whether simple or complex, present one common characteristic: they presuppose a classification of all the things, real [or] ideal, of which men think, into two classes or opposed groups, generally designated by two distinct terms which are translated well enough by the words profane and sacred [*profane et sacré*]" (52).

What do these words mean? Durkheim continues:

> One might be tempted . . . to define [sacred things] by the place they are generally assigned in the hierarchy of things. They are naturally considered superior in dignity and power to profane things . . . and surely this conception is not without some truth. Only there is nothing in it which is really characteristic of the sacred. It is not enough for one thing to be subordinated to another for the second to be sacred with regard to the first. . . . But if a purely hierarchic distinction is a criterium [*sic*] at once too general and too imprecise, there is nothing left with which to characterize the sacred in its relation to the profane except their heterogeneity. However, this heterogeneity is sufficient to characterize this classification of things and to distinguish it from all others, because it is very particular; *it is absolute*. In all the history of human thought there exists no other example of two categories of things so profoundly differentiated or so radically opposed to one another. The traditional opposition of good and bad is nothing beside this; for the good and the bad are only two opposed species of the same class, namely morals, just as sickness and health are two different aspects of the same order of facts, life, while the sacred and the profane have always and everywhere been conceived by the human mind as two distinct classes, as two worlds between which there is nothing in common. (53–54)

There is a telltale sign, a clear indication that we are in the presence of this most basic human differentiation. I have called it "sacred allergy"; Durkheim spoke of an "irresistible" refusal of the mind:

> The opposition of these two classes manifests itself outwardly with a visible sign by which we can easily recognize this very special classification, wherever it exists. Since the idea of the sacred is always and everywhere separated from the idea of the profane in the thought of men, and since we picture a sort of logical chasm

between the two, the mind irresistibly refuses to allow the two
corresponding things to be confounded, or even to be merely put
in contact with each other; for such a promiscuity, or even too
direct a contiguity, would contradict too violently the dissociation
of these ideas in the mind. The sacred thing is par excellence that
which the profane should not touch, and cannot touch with impunity. (55)

And yet, strangely enough, this most basic of all distinctions is also the
most fragile. It can disappear instantly; as soon as anything touches the
sacred, the sacred flows into it, and it becomes sacred itself. Therefore,
extraordinary precautions must be taken at all times to prevent the
spread of the sacred, to keep it within its own bounds. "What makes
these precautions necessary," said Durkheim, "is the extraordinary con-
tagiousness of a sacred character. Far from being attached to the things
which are marked with it, it is endowed with a sort of elusiveness" (358).
   This being so, the following conclusion is unavoidable: the sacred, that
which is worshiped or revered as the ultimate guarantor of stability in
the community is also the very source of instability or undifferentiation.
The sacred is only good if it can be kept at a distance from everything
else; otherwise, it becomes a terrifying danger. The sacred is irreducibly
ambiguous; it is a remedy and a poison. Durkheim reminds us, "One of
the greatest services which Robertson Smith has rendered to the science
of religions is to have pointed out the ambiguity of the notion of sacred-
ness" (455).
   But, clearly, this is just another way of saying that the power of the
sacred is the power of undifferentiation itself. If you manage to keep the
sacred away from everything else, that is to say, to differentiate it from
everything else, everything is differentiated; there are clear differences
everywhere. If you do not, "impurity" spreads all over; all cultural differences are threatened with imminent collapse. What can this mean, in
purely rational terms, except that the notion of the sacred is inseparable
from that of chaotic undifferentiation, or that the only thing that can
contain the spread of undifferentiation is the fear of undifferentiation,
something like a primitive but effective version of our own nuclear deter-
rence strategy? In the last analysis, the primitive worships that which can
destroy him if he fails to keep it at a distance. Durkheim, I think, discarded too quickly "the famous formula *Primus in orbe deos fecit timor*
[Fear first created gods in the world]" (255), although his central idea

about the intimate connection between the social and the sacred still stands.

Durkheim saw clearly that the sacred emerges from a certain collective "effervescence": "[It] is in the midst of these effervescent social environments and out of this effervescence itself that the religious idea seems to be born" (250). In the light of later anthropological reflection, what Durkheim did not take into account properly was the explicit or implicit violence of such "effervescence."

It can be said that René Girard's theory of the sacred starts where Durkheim's left off. Girard's theory involves the collective mechanism (the word "mechanism" is appropriate because it is a violent process whose violence is not controlled by anybody, thus operating with a very high degree of automatism), whereby the sacred as the fundamental principle of differentiation in human society is generated out of violent undifferentiation; the mechanism whereby that which is on the verge of destroying the community becomes the means to save it. Girard's is, to the best of my knowledge, the only theory that can account rationally for that irreducible ambiguity of the sacred of which I just spoke.

At the risk of oversimplification, I shall attempt a brief summary of Girard's theory of the sacred, on which my own study is based. It should be said at the outset that in Girardian theory the generative process that produces the sacred is also the process that makes it possible for symbolic thought itself to emerge. In other words, the birth of the sacred coincides with the birth of language or meaning in human terms. Therefore, it can be said that if in Durkheim the social is the soul of the sacred, in Girard the sacred is the very soul of the social.

At the center of the religious community stands the sacred-making institution par excellence, ritual sacrifice. There is a great variety of sacrificial rituals, but they all have something in common: an act of violence, either real or symbolic, perpetrated on a sacred victim, or rather on a victim that is made sacred in the very act of being sacrificed. Ritual sacrifice is in a very fundamental sense a process of victimization.

Girard tells us that "Sacrifice has often been described as an act of mediation between a sacrificer and a 'deity'" (*Violence*, 6). But this belief is by no means universal. Belief in the sacred is not necessarily linked to any clear belief in an independent god or gods. There are sacrifices without divine participation. Sacrifice is "an act of violence inflicted on a surrogate victim" (7). Girard continues:

This notion [of the victim as a substitute] pervades ancient literature on the subject . . . and has recently been advanced once again. Godfrey Lienhardt (in *Divinity and Experience*) and Victor Turner (in a number of works, especially *The Drums of Affliction*), drawing from fieldworks, portray sacrifice . . . as a deliberate act of collective substitution performed at the expense of the victim and absorbing all the internal tensions, feuds, and rivalries pent up within the community. . . . The victim is not a substitute for some particularly endangered individual, nor is it offered up to some individual of particularly bloodthirsty temperament. Rather, it is a substitute for all the members of the community, offered up by the members themselves. The sacrifice serves to protect the entire community from its own violence. (5, 7–8)

But how did humanity ever hit upon such a device to rid itself of its own violence? In order to answer this question, one must understand that behind the highly ritualized killing of the sacrificial surrogate victim lies an empirically spontaneous process of victimization that, in Girard's theory, can in fact account for the origin of human culture, the leap from animal to man:

JEAN-MICHEL OUGHOURLIAN: We are at the point of asking just how far back in human or pre-human history the victimage mechanism should be situated. If this mechanism is the foundation for everything that is human in man, for humanity's most ancient institutions, such as hunting or the incest prohibition, the question then becomes the process of hominization, or in other words the transition from animal to man.

RENÉ GIRARD: We are indeed moving toward that question. . . .

JEAN-MICHEL OUGHOURLIAN: All the basic elements present at the origin of human culture, considered together, seem more than capable of assuring the destruction of previous systems of behaviour; yet none of them seems at all promising as elements facilitating the creation of a new system. This is the case with stones and weapons as well as with the increased aptitude for violent action necessitated by hunting and warfare, to say nothing of the prolonged and more vulnerable period of infancy. . . . [We] confront an ensemble of factors each of which, in itself, could easily have de-

stroyed the species. It must be that each of these impossibilities
was in one way or another transformed into a resource, because
together, by some "mysterious alchemy," they brought about progressively humanized forms of culture and biological processes.

At the moment when the propensity for rage is systematically
cultivated and developed on the outside by an animal that arms
itself with stones and tools, it becomes more and more necessary
to master this rage on the inside, where this same animal is confronted with familial and social tasks that become constantly
more delicate and absorbing. Instinctual inhibitions are unable to
account for this double, contradictory evolution. . . .

RENÉ GIRARD: Many of these problems are so perplexing that contemporary science has adopted the habit of treating the statement of the
problem as if it were the solution. . . . Evolutionists answer the
supreme confidence of the creationists with their own supreme
confidence. . . . Much like the legendary good fairy, Lady Evolution surmounts all obstacles with such ease and so predictably
that we soon lose interest. . . . Just as the crab needs its pincer and
the bat its wings, which the always benevolent and attentive Lady
Evolution has provided for them, so man has need of culture,
which he duly receives served on a silver platter from this new,
universal Great Mother. (*Things Hidden*, 84–88)

At this point we have to mention another basic aspect of Girard's theory, having to do with the mimetic character of the human mind. By
comparison with animals human beings are extremely mimetic creatures.
The human capacity for imitative behavior is enormous. On the one
hand, this capacity signifies a vast learning capability; on the other, it
amplifies human rivalries and conflicts well beyond the threshold where
they can be contained by instinctual animal mechanisms of survival. In
other words, it makes intraspecific violence extremely contagious and
open-ended: "Beyond a certain threshold of mimetic power, animal societies become impossible. This is the threshold corresponding to the appearance of the victimage mechanism" (*Things Hidden*, 95).

In Chapter 3, as I reflect on the internal logic of the sacrificial principle
that prescribes that "one head must be given up for many," I shall have
the occasion to quote Girard more extensively on this particular point.
All I need say now in order to finish my summary is that the very mimetic
character of human violence, which increases in direct proportion to its

intensity, makes it, statistically speaking, highly probable that all the violent participants in a collective crisis will eventually end up agglutinated against one.

> Except in certain cases, there is no telling what insignificant reason will lead mimetic hostility to converge on one particular victim rather than on another; yet the victim will not appear to be any less absolutely unique and different, a result not only of the hate-filled idolatry to which the victim is subject, but also and especially of the effects of reconciliation created by the unanimous polarization.
>
> The community satisfies its rage against an arbitrary victim in the unshakable conviction that it has found the one and only cause of its trouble. . . . The return to a calmer state of affairs appears to confirm the responsibility of the victim for the mimetic discord that had troubled the community. The community thinks of itself as entirely passive *vis-à-vis* its own victim, whereas the latter appears, by contrast, to be the only active and responsible agent in the matter. Once it is understood that the inversion of the real relation between victim and community occurs [also] in the resolution of the crisis, it is possible to see why the victim is believed to be *sacred*. The victim is held responsible for the renewed calm in the community [as much as] for the disorder that preceded this return. It is even believed to have brought about its own death. (*Things Hidden*, 26–27)

The crucial difference between Durkheim and Girard is the latter's introduction of the sacrificial victim in what might be called the sacred equation. That victim is the basis on which the entire construction of the sacred rests.

We can now understand that the radical, "absolute," difference between the sacred and the profane is itself a result of the violent expulsion of violence through the victim, which is perceived as the embodiment of the undifferentiated, that is to say, of the violent crisis itself. If the difference between the sacred and the profane is, as Durkheim said, the first, the "absolute," the irreducible difference, then, phenomenologically speaking, prior to or apart from that difference there is only unnameable, unspeakable undifferentiation. The elimination of the victim is the event capable of accounting for the original gap, the breathing space necessary to make the first and most important difference: the difference, literally, between life and death.

The expelled victim, and anything immediately associated with it in the collective representation of the group, becomes the untouchable, that is, the sacred. The "absolute" difference between the sacred and the profane is but the gap created in the midst of internally uncontrollable, undifferentiating violence by the elimination of the victim. Outside the violent, sacred-making mechanism of the victimizing expulsion, the desperately needed separation, difference, between the sacred and the profane collapses, for they have no independent existence. In principle anything at all can play the role of the sacred or, in consequence, of the profane. Such roles are as violently incompatible as they are exchangeable. The only thing necessary for such an "absolute" difference between them to take hold of the human mind, thereby instilling in it an "irresistible refusal" to merge the two, is the victimizing process. No victim, no difference between the sacred and the profane.

Thus, if we accept that the "absolute" difference between the sacred and the profane is a result of the victimizing process, we know where to look when we are confronted by an outbreak of sacred allergy. For such an allergy is only the existential manifestation of the sacrificial mind. A sudden heightening of the sensitivity to the "mixing of the human and the divine," as happened during the Renaissance, could only mean that the sacrificial mechanism was not working as smoothly as it used to. When the breathing space between the sacred and the profane is felt to be in need of restoration, we must assume that the effectiveness of the sacrificial expulsion of the danger is also at stake. The process no longer commands the solid unanimity it used to. The implicit assigning of blame may have become less sacred, less untouchable; blame, instead of being clearly concentrated on the victim, spreads dangerously over everybody.

I believe this the social and existential context in which the following observation by J. Delumeau should be understood: "It might easily be thought that any civilization—in this case Western civilization from the fourteenth to the seventeenth centuries—which was besieged (or believed itself to be besieged) by a multitude of enemies—Turks, idolaters, Jews, heretics, witches, and so on—would not have had time for much introspection. This might have been quite logical, but exactly the opposite happened. In European history, the 'siege mentality' was accompanied by an oppressive feeling of guilt, an unprecedented movement toward introspection, and the development of a new moral conscience. The fourteenth century witnessed the birth of what might be called a 'scruple sickness,' a global phenomenon that soon reached epidemic proportions. It was as if the aggresivity directed against the enemies of Christendom had not entirely spent itself in incessant religious warfare, despite constantly renewed battles and an endless variety of opponents. A global anxiety discovered a new foe in each of the inhabitants of the besieged city, and a new fear—the fear of one's self" (*Sin and Fear*, 1). From our point of view these can only be the two sides of the same phenomenon, the erosion of the sacrificial mechanism, which is supposed to channel "aggresivity" toward the outside. What makes this erosion specifically Christian in character is that it leads to individual introspection, to the turning of the blame from the publicly recognized enemy toward the questioning self.

4. Christian Desacralization

In Western society there was only one force strong enough, constant enough, to shake the sacrificial mechanism at its victimizing core, and, at the same time, to offer a different kind of logic, the possibility of breaking the vicious circle of sacrificial violence: the Christian text or revelation, or rather, its essentially nonsacrificial, nonvictimizing, dimension, that basic dimension that runs counter to the old sacrificial system, by revealing its profoundly hidden and fundamental injustice. In other words, it is the Christian text that desacralizes the sacrificial expulsion by making human beings, not God, responsible for it, while, at the same time, transferring the responsibility from the social, the communal, that which is not controlled by any single individual, to the very core of the individual.

Let me try to describe the role that nonvictimizing Christianity plays in the context of a Girardian theory of the sacred. Let us imagine the following: in the course of an immemorial sacrificial history, at a given moment, the sacrificers come upon a victim who refuses to play the sacrificial game. This victim does not refuse to be killed, but he reveals to the sacrificers in no uncertain terms the truth of what they are doing. He tells them they are hypocrites; they claim innocence but their hands are bloody with the killing of all their victims "since the foundation of the world." He tells them they have been doing nothing but hiding their own

the sacred as the space that makes possible the violent death of the truth of violence. (through the sacrificial game)

Christ as the sacrificial victim that reveals to the sacrificers the truth of the game, the truth that is being killed through him. → Christ the desacralizer

dead, their own death. Therefore they are like whitewashed tombs, clean on the outside but full of corruption inside. He announces to them that their sacrificial game is no longer working, because the truth can no longer be hidden. In fact he is the living proof of what he is saying, because he is right there telling them about it. He is the un-coverer or discoverer of the sacrificial truth, the one who breaks the doors of hell, the hiding place of the truth that must be hidden.

They will, of course, kill him, for they have never been able to handle their sacrificial truth in any other way. But in so doing they will inevitably prove him right. Such a victim is indeed the only victim that from a sacrificial perspective, is not arbitrary, since the sacrificial system must expel the truth about itself in order to keep itself in existence. All the other victims could have been spared. Each one of them could have been replaced by something else, leaving the system intact and fully operational, that is, as incapable as ever of facing up to the unspeakable truth. The only victim the sacrificial system cannot spare without immediately running the risk of self-destruction, is the one who reveals, exposes, the truth. And that means that this exceptional victim was always the implied one whenever they killed one of the others. In this sense, the new victim stands for all the other victims in the world.

Of course this is only half the story. The other half has to do with sustaining or upholding the truth thus revealed through the sacrifice of the blameless victim. That is the part for which nobody has yet found any scientific explanation. Precisely because the very survival of the sacrificial system is at stake unless its own truth is sufficiently hidden, the pressures on the nonsacrificial revelation must be enormous; not only the physical pressures, the silencing of any witnesses to the truth, but the pressures on the truth itself, ranging from honest failure to understand it (which can be seen even in Christ's disciples at the beginning) to the scandalized and urgent need to distort it—that is, to drain it of its uniquely devastating power by reinterpreting it in sacrificial terms. This latter possibility is inherent in the sacrificial system itself, which must have at least a basic operational or pragmatic knowledge of the truth in order to function effectively; it must know enough of the truth in order to be able to manipulate it or interpret it to its advantage.

Revealing and upholding the truth hidden by the sacrificial system is an extremely complex enterprise, conducted against formidable odds. This is why the Christian revelation was first and foremost felt and understood as Christ's *victory* against the overwhelming power of sin,

death, and the Devil, the deceiver, the father of lies. This is, according to
Gustaf Aulén, the "classic" Christian view of the atonement (Aulén, 154
and passim). What Girardian theory can contribute to this classic view
is a better understanding of how these three things—sin (man's own violence), death (everything converges toward the killing of the victim), and
the Devil (the deception, the cover-up)—become integrated with one another into a working historical system, the power of which can keep human beings chained to a violent vicious circle.

As we shall see in Chapter 5, it is also important to note that this
original, classic, view of the atonement, in which the emphasis is on
God's active participation on behalf of a humanity kept in hopeless fet-
ters, gradually changes toward one in which the emphasis will shift in
the direction of man's basic responsibility before God for his own entrap-
ment in death's system. The change from the classic view to that of Anselm's *Why God Became Man* is a clear step in that direction. And, again,
a better understanding of the sacrificial system from an anthropological perspective may help soften the old theological controversy
among different atonement theories.

At any rate, from the point of view of the Christian believer, I do not
see how any of this could be seen as dangerous or in conflict with traditionally accepted ideas. And yet, Girardian theory has met with some
determined resistance from such quarters. It may be worthwhile, therefore, to clarify my own understanding of the theory.

It is true that Girard establishes a fundamental, indeed, literally, a crucial, connection between violence and the sacred. But that has nothing to
do with establishing the "ontological" priority of violence, or turning
violence into some sort of metaphysical absolute. From an empirical and
historical perspective, the only absolute priority for the existence of human beings and human culture is that they manage to survive in their
environment for a sufficiently long period of time. And that survival includes, not only food and shelter, as Marx said, but also an equally primary mechanism of defense against intraspecific violence.

John Milbank writes:

> [By] positing a real pre-religious phase of unlimited and anarchic
> conflict Girard falls victim to a component of the pagan *mythos*
> as diagnosed by Augustine. For it is the claim of the legality of the
> *civitas terrena* to have suppressed an anarchy that is necessarily
> ontologically prior. Augustine concedes that this may have been

historically the case, but denies any necessity to sinful confusion. And we should go further than Augustine to suggest that every legality has always claimed validity by virtue of its keeping at bay an essentially imaginary chaos. What came "first" was not anarchy, but this legal, coercive and itself "anarchic" assertion, meeting always a partial resistance from nomadic forces outside its city gates. (394–95)

First of all, it is simply inaccurate and misleading to say that Girard posits "a [human] pre-religious phase of unlimited and anarchic conflict." Any such "pre-religious phase" would not be human yet. But it could not be animal either, because if it were, it would not be unlimited and anarchic; it would be governed by some kind of instinctual mechanism. As soon as this purely animal mechanism breaks down, two possibilities coincidentally emerge: the possibility of unlimited conflict and the possibility of the victimizing expulsion, which effectively prevents the first possibility from becoming a reality and destroying the primitive community. The seed of the sacred is planted as soon as intraspecific violence becomes, in principle, open-ended due to the breakdown of instinctual safeguards. There is no ontological priority of violence over anything. Human culture consists of many things, that are not necessarily violent. But they are all in constant need of protection from violence.

And there is no metaphysical necessity to violence either, which apparently, in Milbank's view, gives the lie to real historical violence. Not being metaphysically necessary, violence is reduced to the status of, well, one of those things that, of course, do happen, but about which one should not become too concerned because, after all, lacking metaphysical necessity, it is not really essential to anything.

Only sinful man, Milbank seems to be saying, can make such a big deal out of human violence. Sinful man builds it up into something that does not really exist, an "imaginary chaos," a bogeyman to scare people into submission to sinful laws. Well, this may very well be, but the critic should add that such a bogeyman is a sacred one. Now, what Girardian theory argues is that this sacred bogeyman is extremely effective in drawing attention away from what is really going on, which is not truly sacred but merely human violence. And this sacred ruse, this incredibly cunning operation, works so well that it can fool even the modern demystifier. Desacralization does for Milbank what sacralization had always done for primitive or pagan man. Primitive man could not quite see the significance of his own violence because it was covered with a sacred veil; demystifiers like Milbank cannot see it either because it is *no longer* covered with a sacred veil. In both cases the significance of human violence is seen through the mediation of the sacred. In fact, in this particular regard Milbank's position is nothing new, as we shall see when we examine some Gnostic texts.

I think Milbank is right in affirming that "Christianity is unique in refusing ultimate reality to all conflictual phenomena" (262). But that cannot mean that such violent phenomena are not fully real; it can only mean that they will not prevail in the end, that they will not have the last word. Christ forgave human beings because they did not know what they were doing, but they were certainly doing it. Otherwise, why Christ at all?

Milbank does not want theology to be contaminated by any anthropological theory claiming scientific status:

> [One] must refuse to give a scientific, explanatory account of the sacrificial character of most human cultures. As Wittgenstein intimated, in his remarks on Frazer, their speaking of a common, sacrificial language must simply be accepted as a surd coincidence. If any discipline can elucidate this coincidence further, it is theology, which deciphers it as the dominance of original sin, the refusal of the true God. But this is not really an explanation (sin, in particular, cannot be explained) but only a conceptual redescription, which arises from the contrast with Christianity as a "counter-sacrificial" practice. (395)

Once again, it seems, we are witnessing a refusal to mix the human and the divine. It is a pity, because Milbank's book is in many respects admirable; and I have profited greatly from his insights.

Historically speaking, it is perfectly clear that the nonsacrificial, Christian revelation did not just drive the old sacred out of existence. Such an event, if it could have come about at all, would probably have brought about an apocalyptic catastrophe. If ultimately human society, left to its own devices, owes the very historical possibility of its existence to the victimizing expulsion, it can only assimilate so much of the nonsacrificial truth at any given time without risking cultural suicide. My thesis is that Western society at the time called the Renaissance assimilated the nonsacrificial truth at an unprecedented rate, giving itself unprecedented opportunities and also aggravating very old problems. Why it happened at that time and not before, we do not really know, but in Chapter 5 I shall try to show that a visible change in the religious spiritual life of the late Middle Ages and early Renaissance points in the direction of an increased awareness of Christ's Passion, the victimizing of Christ, as the central element in the Christian revelation.

5. Christianity and Modern Poetic Fiction

The study of the way in which the new, nonsacrificial, awareness historically influenced the old (though continuing) sacrificial system and mentality, forcing it to look at itself and to find new accomodations with the truth, far transcends the limits of this investigation. I shall limit my demonstration to the following: there would have been no such thing as modern poetic fiction without Christianity. But I maintain from the start that that does not mean that modern poetic fiction is necessarily or specifically Christian in spirit or inspiration. What it means is that modern poetic fiction owes the historical possibility of its existence to the profound transformation that the old sacrificial spirit was compelled to undergo under the influence of nonsacrificial Christianity.

I am not merely saying that modern poetic fiction consists of a pre-Christian, pagan, base as modified by Christianity. One could say that of *Beowulf*, for example, and *Beowulf* is not modern poetic fiction. At the root of modern poetic fiction lies the realization that the spirit of Christianity cannot be mixed with anything deriving from the old sacred. The Middle Ages knew the difference between pagan antiquity and Christianity, but there was no sense of the profound incompatibility between the two. It was precisely in the wake of the great revival of pagan classical learning that such incompatibility was felt at its keenest. The modern era does not begin with tolerance. But before one laments the sudden stiffness, the symptomatic intolerance, one must also understand that the possibility of a more lasting and unprecedented tolerance lay hidden in the midst of the intolerance.

The incompatibility between the nonsacrificial spirit of Christianity and the old sacred is crucial to the development of modern poetic fiction. Modern poetic fiction was born of a profound self-analysis, a turning of the old fiction mode back upon itself, to discover its sacrificial, victimizing, core, without the protection of the old sacred veil; that is, as seen in the mirror that the nonsacrificial spirit held up to it.

Of course, in front of such a mirror two things could happen, either a genuine self-analysis or a rush for the leaf to cover the shame, to put on a new disguise, to simply look for survival. Both possibilities, the genuine and the fake, are, nevertheless, modern. And, needless to say, in practice the difference between the two is not always clear.

But there was not only a question of self-analysis and self-responsibility; there was also a profound sense of liberation involved. The fundamental incompatibility between the old sacred and Christianity provided, for the first time in Western civilization, a genuine nonfictional perspective on fiction; or, to paraphrase and modify Adorno's definition, "Art is magic liberated from the lie of being the truth" (quoted in Calasso, 198), it liberated the old fiction from its sacred need to substitute for the truth or to pose as truth.

This liberation, while revealing the old sacred-bound fiction as fiction, that is, as arbitrary and unnecessary in the most fundamental sense, can also become the liberation of fiction itself, which does not have to hide its fictional character any longer. It should no longer be afraid of the truth about itself; it no longer has to substitute for or hide anything.

It does not take much effort to see how important this liberation of fiction was in the development of the modern novel and theater. Cervantes's outrageous, irreverent irony and endless play with his own fiction in the *Quijote* can only be fully understood in a relatively desacralized historical environment. For the same reason, one can hardly think of a more significant symbol at the threshold of the modern novel than mad Don Quixote, who mistook fiction for reality, a most un-Christian thing to do in Cervantes's eyes.

But this undermining of the old sacred, which liberates fiction from its lingering sacred attachment, can easily be reinterpreted in non-Christian terms. For example, if, as Cervantes discovered, behind the historical pretense of the old narrative there was only the wishful thinking, the daydreaming, of human desire, then the new liberated fiction, free from sacred fears, could become even more seductive and dangerous to all the Alonso Quijanos of the world than the old sacred fiction had been. In other words, a fiction liberated from its sacred need to appear as truth could in fact turn its newfound freedom into a new form of self-delusion, an ever-present temptation to ignore its own fictional character. A fiction without sacred fears, coextensive with and practically indistin-

guishable from human desire, is also a fiction without a sense of boundaries, especially of the boundary between reality and fiction. It would not
take long for such a "liberated" desire to create its own sacred idols, or
to turn itself into one.

We can also put it as follows: as the process of desacralization exposes
the old sacrificial game and makes it increasingly unnecessary, the game
also becomes much easier and safer to play. Desacralization can actually
be turned by an unrepentant old sacred into a new way of keeping itself
alive. Art, and in particular poetic fiction, can become an ideal refuge
for the old spirit. Once again, a secular appearance is no guarantee of a
desacralized heart.

A Christianly tamed sacred becomes much easier to deal with and to
keep within bounds. It was probably an inevitable result of the desacralizing process, that with a sacred significantly drained of its former terrifying violence, a radically new historical possibility would arise within
the logic of the sacred game. In the eyes of the sacred players, it would
eventually seem quite possible to expel the sacred—now appearing to
them in Christian attire—without having to adore it in fear, as had always been the case before. All of a sudden, the sacred players noticed, it
was incredibly easy to get rid of the sacred! They could not understand
why humanity had been in the grip of religious obscurantism and fear
for so long. At any rate, it would eventually appear obvious that Christianity was the last, weakened, remnant of the old sacred, soon to be dis-
posed of; in spirit or in principle already vanquished, since clearly it
offered relatively little resistance to attack.[6]

At the same time the growing ineffectiveness of the victimizing mechanism uprooted the radical difference between the sacred and the profane.
As we have seen, the only thing that creates and maintains that difference
is the unanimous expulsion of the victim. Thus another unprecedented
possibility arose: the sacred and the profane appeared to exchange roles.
It did not take long before the inquisitorial allergy to the contamination
of the sacred by the profane found its perfect counterpart in the more

6. Significantly, it never occurred to these sacred players that the alternative to a weak, Christianly tamed, sacred could very well be a healthy, old, strong one. On the contrary, without
knowing why or ever reflecting on it, they nevertheless "knew," or took for granted, that Christianity was not really one among other sacred alternatives, but the last one, the end of the
sacred. In spite of themselves, they "knew" that a post-Christian society, whenever such a thing
would ever come to pass, would be a society finally liberated completely from the old sacred.
Cf. Gauchet's words, "[Le] christianisme aura-t-il été *la religion de la sortie de la religion*" (II).
(Author's emphasis) (Christianity will have been the religion of the passage from religion.)

modern, "secular" allergy to the contamination of the profane by the sacred.

I think that modern irreligious secularism is just a way of deluding oneself with the truth. There is something farcical about it. It all looks like a theatrical plot played mostly in the dark, with the automatism of puppet characters unaware of the sacred strings that make them move one way or another (strings, of course, not pulled by anybody other than the players themselves, as soon as they yield to the underlying violence of the sacrificial play), who march confidently in one direction while thinking they are going exactly in the opposite one.

This brings to mind Plato and the poets. For nobody knew better than Plato how playful, elusive, protean, the sacred can be, capable of putting on the most unsuspected disguises. "Man," said Plato, "has been devised as a certain plaything of God." Therefore, "One should live out one's days playing at certain games—sacrificing, singing, and dancing—with the result that one can make the gods propitious to oneself and can defend oneself against enemies" (Laws, 803e).

There is a profound affinity between homo sacer and homo ludens (among the latter, we must include, of course, the poets; see Huizinga). Profoundly aware of living in the immediate presence of the sacred, Plato's man dances the dance of life, not with random steps, but most carefully and reverently, skirting the sacred presence, meticulously avoiding any direct encounter, any contamination, fearful that any false step may bring about disaster, rejoicing when everything happens according to plan.

Our modern, so-called secular dancer still dances the same sacred dance, as allergic as ever to the presence of the sacred, still avoiding any direct encounter. But he can now take liberties that would have horrified Plato, because the sacred dance he is dancing has become largely irrelevant. The thunder of Jupiter, with which our brave secular dancer loves to believe he is dealing, is only a faint echo of the old one. It really does not make much sense to tiptoe around a sacred presence that has lost most of its bite.

Naturally our secular dancer is not fully aware of that. In fact, he no longer even knows why he is dancing the poetic dance. All he perceives is that his daring steps do not bring about any great disaster; a perception that prods him on to even higher levels of unnecessary though fascinating daring. He therefore comes to the conclusion that he is engaged in something where there are no limits to his creativity. He is filled with the emotion of having found a privileged realm of boundless freedom. He knows nothing about the source of his creativity or the logic of his newfound freedom. In his ignorance he sees everything in reverse: creativity and freedom become a result of his daring, a conquest of his defiant, boundless spirit.

He fools himself, and yet there is a logic behind such foolishness. If our understanding of the desacralizing process is correct, then it is no accident that the realm of human activity described by Plato as "sacrificing, singing, and dancing"—that is, the ludic, the poetic, and in general the realm of the mimetic, traditionally holding a particularly intimate relationship with the sacred—should now appear as being a special, privileged realm of freedom. For the absence or the inactivity of the sacred should be especially obvious and felt with special relish there. One would expect precisely such a perception of the historical effects of desacralization, in sacrificial eyes accustomed to seeing with sacrificial logic. From a genuinely desacralized point of view, on the other hand, there cannot be such a thing as a privileged realm of freedom different (in the character or quality of its freedom) from other realms of human activity.

In other words, what we see gradually developing from the late sixteenth century on is a rather curious phenomenon. On the one hand, poetic fiction becomes anathema, or is increasingly perceived as being nothing but fiction, at best a beautiful ornament to the res publica, but basically unconnected with anything central or of real historical relevance. On the other hand, one can also perceive a growing glorification and exaltation of that beautiful ornament, to the point where the traditional discourses of poetry and rhetoric merge into a new and more comprehensive notion, that of "literature," which is perceived by many as "a main element in the formation, consolidation, and order of something like a new social compact" (Reiss, 227). In fact, by the time we get to the nineteenth century we can see this literary discourse explicitly turned into a new religion by critics like Matthew Arnold, whose influence continued well into this century.

This more recent, secular, resacralization of poetry, as we shall see in Chapter 4, is a direct descendant of the equally boundless praise of that noblest of all poetic genres, the epic, by critics like J. Peletier du Mans in the sixteenth century, or René Rapin, Sir William Davenant, or Richard Blackmore in the seventeenth.

When Matthew Arnold says that "the future of poetry is immense, because in poetry, where it is worthy of its high destinies, our race, as time goes on, will find an ever surer and surer stay," or when he says that "[more] and more mankind will discover that we have to turn to poetry to interpret life for us, to console us, to sustain us. [For] without poetry our science will appear incomplete; and most of what now passes with us for religion and philosophy will be replaced by poetry. . . . For finely and truly does Wordsworth call poetry . . . 'the breath and finer spirit of all knowledge'" (65), we hear the unmistakable echoes of the enraptured enthusiasm those earlier critics felt in the contemplation of poetry at its best, the epic. The following words, in Rymer's translation of Rapin, are a good illustration:

> The Epick Poem is that which is the greatest and most noble in Poesie; it is the greatest work that humane wit is capable of. All the nobleness, and all the elevation of the most perfect genius, can hardly suffice to form one such as is requisite for an Heroick Poet. . . . [There] must be a judgement so solid, a discernment so exquisite, such perfect knowledge of the language . . . such obstinate study, profound meditation, vast capacity, that scarce whole ages can produce one genius fit for an Epick Poem. And it is an enterprise so bold, that it cannot fall into a wise man's thoughts, but affright him. (72–73)

The glorious, the "immense" value of poetry, that Arnold projected into the future, was seen in the past as a halo surrounding the classical masters:

> [By] the great performances of such an extraordinary genius as animated Homer and Virgil, many great, extraordinary and almost miraculous effects were produced. Love, admiration, and esteem were the common tributes which the vulgar paid to the venerable name of Poet. They were so charmed with the sweetness of all poetical composures, that they looked upon what the poet said as divine, and gave the same credit to it, as to an oracle. . . . Nor is it unreasonable to imagine that even the refinedness of Athens was owing more to the poets, than to the philosophers' instructions. (Le Bossu and Voltaire, English preface to Le Bossu's *Treatise*)

Similar sentiments are expressed in Davenant's preface to his own epic,

Gondibert, and in Richard Blackmore's to his *Prince Arthur*. And yet, what could be more revealing than to see such encomiastic rhetoric about "the greatest and most noble in Poesie"—the immediate precursor of Arnold's poetry "worthy of its high destinies"—as an introduction to such pathetic failures as *Gondibert* and *Prince Arthur*? According to *Gondibert*'s editor, David F. Gladish, "[by] 1653 there had been time for the humorists to get the flavour of *Gondibert*. . . . [They mocked] his style and his language and [recommended] a most unliterary use for the pages of *Gondibert*" (ix). We need no further comment.

Although written before Arnold's sacralizing encomium, the following words by Edgar Allan Poe can be taken as a direct reply to it:

> While the epic mania . . . [has been] gradually dying out of the public mind . . . we find it succeeded by a heresy too palpably false to be long tolerated. . . . I allude to the heresy of *The Didactic*. It has been assumed, tacitly and avowedly, directly and indirectly, that the ultimate object of all Poetry is Truth. . . . With as deep a reverence for the True as ever inspired the bosom of man, I would, nevertheless, limit in some measure its modes of inculcation. I would limit to enforce them. I would not enfeeble them by dissipation. The demands of Truth are severe; she has no sympathy with the myrtles. All *that* which is so indispensable in Song is precisely all *that* with which she has nothing whatever to do. . . . In enforcing a truth we need severity rather than efflorescence of language. We must be simple, precise, terse. We must be cool, calm, unimpassioned. In a word, we must be in that mood, which, as nearly as possible, is the exact converse of the poetical. He must be blind, indeed, who does not perceive the radical and chasmal differences between the truthful and the poetical. . . . He must be theory-mad beyond redemption who, in spite of these differences, shall still persist in attempting to reconcile the obstinate oils and waters of Poetry and Truth. (375–76)

Poe's words are indeed a welcome antidote against the enthusiastic and neo-pagan excesses of a Romanticism that had lost all restraint. But a radical separation of poetry from truth (whether intellectual or moral, to use Poe's categories) carries its own danger. It can lead to a state of debilitating poetic isolation or to what, more recently, has been called an "epistemological cut" (*coupure épistémologique*) between the sciences and the liberal arts, from which we are only now beginning to recover.

Our point is, however, that it would be silly to choose between the antipoetic attitude of suspicion and rejection on the part of the moralist, and its symmetrical opposite, the worshiping admiration of the epic enthusiast, whether the enthusiast be a Davenant or an Arnold. Both attitudes react to the perceived sacred character of poetry. The reason why the moralist sees the spirit of traditional poetry as fundamentally pagan, anti-Christian, is the same reason why poetry would eventually be perceived as a substitute for religion, as something "capable of saving us," to use I. A. Richards's phrase (Mulhern, 27; Buckley, 30). It is not that they are wrong in what they perceive. Poetry, as just said, like art in general, is directly linked to the old sacred. But both attitudes are equally trapped in what they see. Their antithetical reactions spring from the same cause. In spite of their irreconcilable character, each confirms the other.

This radical ambivalence, we know, has always attached to the old sacred. And this is the ambivalence that was stirred up, as it were, by the desacralizing process. However, this process did more than stir up the old ambivalence. It also influenced the manner in which the ambivalence manifested itself. It weakened the immemorial link between the two sides of the ambivalence, the fearful and the venerable, the two sides of the sacrificial victimization. The desacralizing process, indeed, weakened the victimizing process itself.

As the centrality of an untouchable victim, which was both a source of pollution and of safety and reassurance, recedes into an increasingly forgotten past under the impact of the blameless and loving Christian victim, so does the sacred link between the two antithetical sides of the victimizing process. As a result, we end up with two enemy twins who can no longer recognize their underlying family ties.

Caught between scandalized hostility, on the one hand, and the impossible task of retrieving or continuing the poetic glory of an epic past hopelessly tied to the old sacred, on the other, modern literary fiction would not have had much of a future, even assuming it could have come into existence at all as something specifically modern. There had to be something else, something allowing for the possibility of a Cervantes, a Shakespeare, a Calderón, a Racine, etc. That is the historical possibility to be explored in this book. It was a new possibility, not only in reference to the immediate medieval past but, most important, in reference to classical antiquity.

The special importance of this classical reference is evidenced by the many ways in which the Renaissance chose the works of that world as models. The idea of the superior human wisdom of the ancients was very powerful in the sixteenth century; a curious self-delusion that has, in turn, misled generation after generation of critics and historians for the past two hundred years even to this day. Indeed, I think Hans Blumenberg may be too optimistic when he says that "[hardly] anyone can still be inclined to join in the Renaissance's misunderstanding of itself as a reappearance of the old. . . . That the modern age is neither a renewal of the ancient world nor its continuation by other means no longer needs to be argued" (125–26). It was precisely at that time that such superior wisdom was about to become largely obsolete and abandoned in the praxis of almost every discipline of the arts and sciences. One has only to think of what was about to happen in physics and astronomy with Galileo (who accused Aristotle of being "ignorant not only of the profound and abstruse discoveries of geometry, but even of the most elementary principles of that science" [quoted in Schmitt, 112]) and then with Newton; or in philosophy with Descartes.

This new historical possibility was not known to Plato, Aristotle, or Virgil. It came about in the wake of an extraordinary transformation in the historical experience of the sacred, which revealed the human being as alone responsible for his own violence against a foundational victim who, amazingly, instead of pointing an accusing finger, offered the possibility of a nonviolent rescue from violence.

But we still must go back to Plato, Aristotle, and Virgil to learn from them what desacralization has caused us to forget. They were much closer to the frightening ambivalence of the old sacred. They had to deal, either frontally or cunningly, with a sacrificial environment, at the very center of which stood a founding victim who cast over everything a very different shadow from that of Christ on the cross.

6. The Trajectory of This Book

The structure of this book will be, first, to go back to Plato, Aristotle, and Virgil in order to understand precisely how the dawning of the modern era went *beyond* them. Of course, going *beyond* them does not necessarily mean doing *poetically* better than they did, as is strikingly clear in the case of Virgil; nobody in the Renaissance or later could equal Virgil's epic achievement. Not even a resurrected Virgil could have repeated himself; such a thing was no longer possible. In fact, after studying Virgil, I shall discuss the amazing paradox of an age that, as we have already indicated, elevated the epic to an unprecedentedly high pedestal precisely at the moment when it had become impossible to produce anything that would measure up to its own expectations.

I shall then explore the human spectacle that came into view for the great masters, those in whose hands lay the future of poetic fiction, as the sacred epic veil fell to the ground. And that view will not be that of the lonely hero, so dear to our Romantic desires, facing an alien world abandoned by the gods; a single heroic figure, the victim of formidable forces beyond its control, who, alas! must suffer while a faceless crowd of readers or spectators looks on and mourns the victim's fate. Such is the typical sacrificial scenario. Instead, the light will shift from the fiction of that lonely heroic victim to the faceless crowd, which will be revealed as a persecuting crowd. And yet, it will not be the crowd as such that will be interpellated, but the individual member of the crowd, addressed, as it were, by name, who, revealed as a persecutor in his heart, will no longer be able to hide among the faceless many. As Calderón said, every time a man comes to look at a spectacle, "he is looking on his own shamelessness" (*La vida es sueño,* act 2).

What will come into view will be an extremely fluid network of human interrelations, a criss-cross world of intentions and desires in which, through reciprocal attractions and repulsions, the individual may lose his freedom and become alienated with frightening ease. A world in which, as Cervantes knew so well, reality and fiction can look alike; where good and evil, "beginning from vastly different points, can converge toward each other" (Persiles, *Obras Completas,* p. 1983), a "confusing abyss" *(La vida es sueño)* to use Calderón's terminology, where life becomes a dream, or rather, one does not know for certain whether it is reality or a dream. A world, therefore, of pure immanence; yet, in radical contrast to the sacrificial vision, what this new vision reveals is that it is totally arbitrary and unjustified for anybody to throw the first sacrificial stone, a terrifying thing to discover in the midst of a sacrificial world that had always survived by sacrificing somebody. And terrifying because this is a mirror image of that sacrificial world *minus the victim*, because no

victim can be found credible enough, different enough, to rally everybody's violence against it. Cervantes and Calderón will provide the textual evidence.

The general trajectory of the book will be, then, from the old sacred,
the old spirit of the social, through the process of desacralization and the
de-construction of the persecuting crowd, to the individual, as conceived
by those two masters, who have been chosen here for their paradigmatic
value; an individual now discovered as bearing an unprecedented,
unique, and nontransferable responsibility, who, nevertheless, may become alienated, may abdicate his or her responsibility and freedom at
the feet of another individual. At this point, as the texts describe the
alienation of this unprecedentedly responsible individual, as they medi-
tate on the erosion or disintegration of this newly discovered freedom,
we get a view of the intersubjective, social crisis from which the sacrificial
or victimizing system emerges.

Chapter 5 will then provide an overview of the historical evolution
that took place in the Christian experience of the sacred, as it moved
toward the kind of spirituality of the *devotio moderna*, which announces
the immediate coming of the modern era. The goal will be to show the
rapidly increasing awareness of the centrality of the Crucifixion (and its
power of exposure of the victimizing sacrifice) as the Middle Ages come
to an end, a fitting prelude to the nonsacrificial awareness of the great
poetic masters.

The book could have ended at this point without, I think, any damage
to its internal coherence. But a book based on the idea that there is no
such thing as leaving the sacred entirely behind, and, in particular, that
one cannot fight or violently expel the sacred without perpetuating it;
furthermore, a book that says that the causes of human alienation are
not "systemic" in nature, but are rather to be found ultimately in the
ways individuals relate to other individuals, is a book that could hardly
ignore Marx's direct challenge to all such ideas. Thus, the need for a
Marxian epilogue.

Besides, an analysis of Marx's theory can in fact become a test of the
basic assumptions and conclusions of this book. If it is true that the only
genuine desacralizing trajectory moves in the direction of the responsible
individual in his relations to other individuals, beyond the operation of
existing collective social mechanisms, which are the original domain of
the old sacred, then any attempt to go in the opposite direction, that is,
from responsible individual relations back to social mechanisms, should

turn out to be a resacralizing regression. I intend to show that that is precisely the case with Marx.

It is true that Marx abandoned the notion of *Man* in traditional philosophy for the consideration of *men* living and working in a given society. There, at the social level, he discovers the central fact of human alienation. This alienation means that the individual, instead of mastering the products of her own work, is in fact mastered, governed, by them. And this, Marx will repeat incessantly, is precisely what happens with religious or sacred notions, where people are governed by the creations of their own minds.[7]

Marx discovers hidden behind the tenets of liberal economic theory a market world of exchanges, whose internal logic resembles to an amazing degree the logic of a world governed by the sacred. In Marx's eyes, of course, this resemblance is simply a further confirmation of the alienating character of such a world. But I shall show that he actually saw too much for his own good, that the parallelism between the realm of the sacred and that of commodities places a formidable question mark after his idea of the absolute priority of the material over the "ideological."

I am not at all suggesting that Marx's priorities should be reversed. What I mean is that Marx himself proves that, in reference to the sacred, the difference between the material and the "ideological" is totally irrelevant. The logic of the sacred can be, for example, the internal logic of the commodity market or, indifferently, the logic that governs social relations (which are supposed to be a direct reflection of the forces of production). At one point Marx comes very close to saying that the appearance of the sacred coincides with the emergence of human self-consciousness.

Having discovered the social as a collective mechanism where nobody is really in command of his own destiny, Marx is but a small step from seeing it as a victimizing mechanism, a mechanism of exploitation: "one fact is common to all past ages, viz., *the exploitation of one part of society by the other" (Karl Marx: A Reader,* 265). This formula, I shall argue, is a somewhat uneconomical rendering or interpretation of the old sacrificial principle requiring only one head for the sake of many.

---

7. John Milbank writes that Marx "accepts the Hegelian view which sees the state as embodying religious beliefs and practice, and thereby alone establishing itself. Marx tries to show, against Hegel, that the state in reality promotes merely the purposes of capitalism, but this involves him . . . in also arguing that it is the economic base which really operates 'like a religion.' . . . This is clearly indicated by all the coy and knowing metaphors comparing capitalist processes to Christian sacramental practices" (182).

In other words, I shall try to demonstrate that as Marx searches for the material laws governing the collective mechanism of human society, what he in fact finds is the "laws," i.e., the internal logic, of the collective sacrificial mechanism.

I believe Marx saw the terrible human truth that lies behind all "ideological" veils. But like the old blind seer, he became a victim of what he saw. He saw that all previous victims had been unjustly sacrificed, and he understood that what had to be sacrificed was the sacrificial mechanism itself, the system. But then Marx made a fatal mistake: he thought he could beat the old monster at its own game, turn it against itself. In good sacrificial fashion, he realized that for the expulsion to work, it had to be unanimous, which, given prevailing historical conditions, actually meant universal, a condition that had never been fulfilled before. But now, Marx thought, the moment had finally come when the requirements of the system would be fully satisfied and the definitive expulsion would take place, leaving no further need for the system to continue in existence. Again, in good old sacrificial fashion, Marx thought he had discovered the perfect trick to fool the monster. As the monster would swallow its last victim, it would turn out that the expelled victim was the monster itself, that is, the system.

It was important, then, to let the system work itself out. And while it did so, all the sins of the world would adhere to the system, and not just any system, but the one—capitalism—that the scientifically discovered material laws of history had finally revealed as the true, the inescapable, victim, toward which all the arbitrary violence of man against man throughout history finally flowed; the final victim, the one system, whose elimination would restore man to himself, to his fundamental, presacrificial innocence (in this essential regard, Marx's theory is no different from the liberal myth of spontaneous liberation, which also assumes the original innocence of man and his subsequent enslavement by forces beyond his control).

Marx never suspected the intimate connection between "the system" and the old sacrificial victim. He never knew that the sacred victim was always meant to fulfill a "systemic," differentiating, function. It was meant to stand between a human being and another, between enemy twins, like a barrier designed to take upon itself the violent blows that were in fact directed at each other. This barrier, *skandalon*, stumbling block was also designed, therefore, to hide the real source and the real target of the violence; to shield one's eyes from the hate-filled (or even the inquisitive) eyes of the other—in sum, to hide human violence from human eyes; to prevent man from finding himself alone, naked, radically unable to justify himself, in the face of his own violence.

On purely scientific grounds the internal coherence of Marx's theory has been shown to be tenuous.[8] My contention is, however, that what governs the development of his theory is ultimately the logic of the sacrificial mechanism. This sacrificial logic, which tapped so deep a source of conviction in the human mind, gave his theory a formidable power of persuasion, even though it never had a chance of ever reaching its stated goal of salvation for humanity.

To blame the violence on the system is not to renounce violence, but only to believe in the possibility of a system that would justify, and thus hide, the violence better. But in a world of pure collective immanence, from which all "ideological" transcendance has vanished, there is only one way to achieve a fully satisfactory justification of human violence: complete unanimity. Everybody must share in and approve the violence, any dissent becomes a scandal. At the same time, such a state of collective violence would soon run out of control unless it were channeled outside the community. And there has never been any way to achieve such channeling except through some process of victimization. A culprit has to be found at any cost or the system will collapse.

It was no accident that Karl Popper saw in Marxism and other totalitarian movements a clear regression to a tribal past. On the other hand, no pre-Christian sacrificer ever believed in the possibility of one special sacrifice, toward which all previous sacrifices had led, that would be the last sacrifice, the one to do away with the sacrificial system itself. It is not difficult to see how the Judeo-Christian text influenced Marx. But it was not an influence to open his eyes; on the contrary, it only served to make his blindness absolute.

---

8. See Elster, passim.

1

BEYOND PLATO

1. Revisiting Plato's Expulsion of the Poets and the Renaissance "War Against Poetry"

"All Renaissance theorists felt themselves obliged to deal with Plato's banishment of the poets. . . . The defence of poetry in the Cinquecento is largely a reply to Plato" (Weinberg, *A History*, 1:251).

Not only Renaissance theorists, but practically every critic or literary historian for the past hundred years or so has felt obliged to go back to Plato when dealing with the antipoetic attitude in the Renaissance. They have done so from a moral and a philosophical perspective that is clearly justified, but they have paid little attention to the fact that Plato was especially horrified at seeing the poets, both physically and symbolically, close to the sacred. He shuddered at the sight of such an unreliable, ambiguous figure standing, literally, next to the sacred altar. It is precisely there that the need to keep things separate, to avoid mixing the unmixable, confusing the good with the bad, becomes anxiously urgent. His fundamental accusation against the poets is that they do not know what they are doing, that they do not have any reliable criterion to keep each thing in its proper place. And that can be a disaster when dealing with the sacred, for, as he said, they can easily turn a blessing into a curse.

In other words, underlying the elaborate rational argument against poetry, both in moral and philosophical terms, we can find what might be called the sacred argument, which is really no argument, but an automatic, prephilosophical rejection of the mixing of the sacred with the profane, or what amounts to the same thing, a scandalized reaction to the profound ambivalence of the sacred.

Plato's experience of the sacred is still explicitly tied to the old sacrificial altar, where a variety of ritually prescribed victims are regularly immolated. His sensitivity to the fundamental sacrificial mechanism that sustains human society, is very difficult for us to understand because we no longer see or feel the connection between the sacred that protects the city and the immolation of the victim. By comparison, Renaissance society in general was much closer to Plato's experience of the sacred than we are.

I believe it will be worthwhile to recall a few things about European society in the sixteenth and seventeenth centuries that we normally do not take into consideration, or do not know what to do with, when dealing with literary history.

The following, for example, is an important incident in the life of poet and dramatist Gil Vicente. On 26 January 1531 there was an earthquake near Lisbon. A second tremor was feared imminent and the rumor spread, apparently encouraged by the friars of Santarem, that the Jews were to blame. Perhaps a massacre was averted by the enlightened and courageous action of people like Gil Vicente who, in a letter to the king, explains how he preached to those friars and reprimanded them for spreading such rumors against "some who are still strangers to our faith," and how he told them that it was more fitting to the virtue of the servants of God to urge them to convert than "to scandalize them and chase them to appease the deranged opinion of the populace" (Gil Vicente, 2:645). Clearly "the populace," struck with panic, was looking for a scapegoat and the friars were steering it in the direction of the Jews.

We know that accusations of ritual infanticide against the Jews were still being brought to court throughout Europe in the sixteenth century, even though it was becoming increasingly difficult to obtain convictions. The same situation existed with witches, who were still seriously considered a public menace (see Po-chia Hsia and Henningsen).

Let us proceed along literary history. In 1577, London was gripped by the plague. It was then, according to Russell Fraser, that "the first wholesale condemnation of the drama [in England] occurs . . . on November 3 . . . in a Sunday sermon delivered at Paul's cross. . . . The cause of plague is sin [and] . . . 'the cause of sinne are playes: therefore the cause of plague are playes.'" And still another case mentioned by Fraser in connection with the theater:

> On September 2, 1642 Parliament ordains the closing of all theaters in England. "Whereas," runs the edict which puts a period to the Renaissance drama, "the distracted estate of England, threatened by a cloud of blood by a civil war, calls for all possible means to appease and avert the wrath of God . . . it is therefore thought fit and ordained by the Lords and Commons in this Parliament assembled, that, while these sad causes and set times of humiliation do continue, public stage-plays shall cease and be forborne." (13–14)

As late as 1676, this time in Sevilla, "on the occasion of the plague that was approaching from Málaga, a Jesuit preacher, Father Tirso González, publicly announced that the sickness would not enter Sevilla as long as [theatrical] representations were forbidden. The city council petitioned the King for the suspension of dramatic activities" (Arróniz, 49).

Earlier we saw that even the representation of the mysteries, in particular the Passion, seen as an act of irreverence, could be blamed in part for the calamities of the religious civil war in France. And yet, in spite of the widespread prohibition to stage the mysteries, there were places in France where, still in 1598 and 1631, during the plague, the people vowed to play the mystery of Saint Sebastian or that of Saint Etienne as an act of thanksgiving upon the ending of the pestilence (Lebègue, 4).

All these episodes, and many similar ones tell us that European society in the sixteenth and seventeenth centuries was much closer to old sacrificial forms and attitudes than we would like to think. Our forgetfulness, of course, is not without cause. Those sacrificial forms and the attitudes attached to them were rapidly becoming untenable, remnants of a past that would rather be forgotten. But they were there, and the modern historian cannot ignore them.

In terms of sacrificial primitivism there is little difference between the antitheatrical examples linking plays and the plague, and the scapegoating cases mentioned. We would not be terribly surprised if perchance we were to find out that the people who blamed the Jews for an earthquake also blamed the theater—and, of course, theater people, especially actors—for the plague. In both cases we can easily detect the same victimizing mechanism at work: the community is in serious danger and people immediately set out to search for the guilty party. Nevertheless, we must continue to remind ourselves that these historical forms of sacrificiality were only residual, that is, greatly diminished from what can be seen in earlier societies.

Let me emphasize this important point by comparing the antitheatrical cases mentioned, with the episode narrated by Livy in his *Annals* about the plague that struck Rome in 365 and 364 B.C.: "The pestilence lasted this year and the next. . . . When neither human means nor divine help could alleviate the violence of the disease, spirits broken by superstitious fears, they are said to have instituted scenic plays also, among other placating devices, to avert the wrath of heaven, a new thing among these bellicose people, whose spectacles had been of the circus type."

The same situation appears to prevail in Christian London, Seville, or Paris. But there is a significant difference: when the Romans tried the new *ludi scenici* after all their traditional sacrifices to various divinities had failed, they were obviously looking for the right divinity or power to placate, the god or power of the plague, since none of the others had responded. They were, in fact, appealing to the sacred power of the plague to expel the plague. One can imagine perhaps the fearful reverence, the sacred fear with which those *ludi* must have been performed or watched; if they had the power to expel the plague, they must have also been perceived as having the power to unleash it. Those primitive plays were sacred instruments, they had (or were expected to have) in themselves the magic power, the "virtue," to placate the sacred power of the plague, because their power was the same as the plague's power. In other words, those *ludi* were irreducibly ambivalent; they held within themselves the secret of the remedy and of the scourge.

In sixteenth- and seventeenth-century Europe the situation was not quite the same. Plays could still be perceived as sacrificial devices, but their sacred power did not really reside in themselves; they were not magic instruments. They could be instrumental in triggering the plague, but not even in those communities that vowed to play the mysteries at the end of the plague, can it be said that their performance was a remedy against the plague. The old link between the remedy and the poison, the terrifying ambivalence of the old sacred, had weakened almost to the vanishing point. What we see at that time in Christian Europe is a clear remnant from the past, but only a remnant.

Having made this important proviso, I still must say that, as typically sacrificial operations, those illustrative examples reveal a sociohistorical situation in which any serious threat to the community, regardless of its specific objective nature, is experienced—heard, as it were—on a sacred register. That is, any such threat transcends its empirical circumstances and is felt as a direct danger to the whole, or rather to the sacred center that keeps the whole together. Thus, the defensive reaction is always the same, for it is not determined by the specific nature of the threat, but rather by the one and only mechanism that can maintain the integrity of the sacred whole, namely, the sacrificial expulsion. No matter what the threat may be, what is felt to be at stake is total disintegration, and the search for a remedy will always involve more or less explicitly the question of *who* is guilty of the threat, *who* is attempting against the sacred center. By definition, the sacred cannot be threatened by *something*, only by *somebody*.

I believe we have to keep this sacrificial background in mind when we encounter "the fears of impurity, of contamination, of 'mixture,' of the blurring of strict boundaries, which haunted thousands in the Renaissance as they had haunted Plato and Tertullian . . . the fear of total breakdown" (Barish, 87). This fear can account for the violent intensity of the Renaissance attack against poetic fiction. And we must also remember this sacrificial background in order to understand the recurring argument used in those attacks, which is first and foremost of a religious or sacred character. The moral and, occasionally, the psychological aspects of the antipoetic argument are strictly secondary (in time, however, this situation will tend to be reversed). Poetic fiction is perceived as not only useless, but, more important, as a devious challenge to Holy Scripture or even a threat to the purity of the sacred.

The following examples illustrate different degrees of such a sacred fear in their authors, who may otherwise be perfectly reasonable and moderate in their opinions. The first, from Pedro Malón de Chaide

(1530?–89), illustrates the fear of having poetry substitute for Holy Scripture:

> What else are love stories and pastoral romances and the love lyrics of a Boscán and Garcilaso, and those monstrous books, assortments of fabulous tales and lies, the *Amadises, Florisels,* and *Don Belianises,* and the whole array of similar monstrosities as are written today—when placed in the hands of young people— but a knife in the hands of a furious madman? . . . As if Holy Scripture and the books written by the Church Doctors lacked pure truths, without having to go begging for lies; as if we did not have an abundance of famous examples in as many kinds of virtues as we may wish, without having to make up fantastic and unbelievable monsters. (Quoted in Menéndez Pelayo, *Orígenes,* 443–44)

The second is from Melchor Cano (1509–60), an illustrious Dominican theologian and a humanist, who despised books of chivalry and the like, but was specially concerned with the vernacular literary treatment of sacred subjects:

> I do not grieve primarily because of those fables, which I just mentioned, no matter how unlearned they are and not in the least conducive to, I won't say leading a good and holy life, but not even having an informed understanding of human affairs. For, in fact, what profit do they offer, these mere vain frivolities feigned by idle men, produced by corrupted minds? But my grief is most painful and disconsolate, because some (I wish they were as prudent as they are full of fervor), wishing to avoid and eliminate this harm, publish, not truthful and dignified histories instead of fables, which would be most useful to the populace, but books filled with the mysteries of the Church, which should be kept from lay hands; and this is, in my opinion, a most pernicious pestilence. (Quoted in Menéndez Pelayo, *Orígenes,* 442 n. 1)[1]

---

1. Nec de fabulis istis potissimum excrucior, quas modo dixi, quamvis ineruditis, et nihil omnino conferentibus, non dico ad bene, beateque vivendum, sed ne ad recte quidem de rebus humanis sentiendum. Quid enim conferant, merae ac vanae nugae ab hominibus otiosis ficta, a corruptis ingeniis versatae? Sed acerbissimus est dolor, et vix omnino consolabilis, quo quidam (utinam tan prudenter quam ferventer) incommodum hoc rejicere, ac devitare cupiunt non pro

It is not entirely clear to me what exactly is the kind of literature that Melchor Cano has in mind as posing such a serious danger. But the basic argument seems clear enough: secular fictional literature is generally worthless. But that is not the worst of it. There are those who fill such fictional forms with a sacred content, and that is an outrageous pestilence *(pestilentissimum)*, because it steps over the boundaries of what should never be touched by lay hands.[2]

B. W. Ife has studied these antipoetic attacks and some of their consequences in the Spanish literature of the Golden Age. The following examples can give an idea of how virulent those attacks could be: "Jesuit Gaspar de Artete can refer to writers of fiction as cruel, shallow, loud-mouthed, deranged, indecent and without fear of God, or say that their mouths are full of evil blasphemy and obscenity, their throats stinking sepulchres belching forth every kind of foetid putrescence and their hearts sewers of wickedness" (11). Even a man of the high intellectual caliber of Benito Arias Montano speaks of novels of chivalry as "monsters, the offspring of stupidity, excrement and filth gathered together for the destruction of the age" (quoted in Ife, 12).

In spite of their sacred fears (fears for and of the sacred), it may seem odd, even unfair, to suggest that such reputable and widely respected men as Malón de Chaide, Melchor Cano, or Arias Montano should be placed in the company of people like the above-mentioned friars of Santarem or those others who blamed plays for the plague. But of course I am not comparing them as individuals, each responsible for his own actions and opinions. I am not in the least suggesting that Melchor Cano, for example, would have ever done what the Santarem friars did. What I am saying, however, is that such antipoetic texts have little to do with the specific content of either the poetic texts they anathematize or the Christian texts whose integrity they are trying to preserve. Their internal logic, their driving motivation, is grounded in an immemorial experience of the sacred and of the absolute need to maintain its purity or, to put it differently, in the anxiously felt need to keep the sacred free from ambiguity or ambivalence.

---

fabulis veras et graves historias edunt, id quod esset plebi utilissimum; sed libros mysteriorum ecclesiae plenos, a quibus arcendi profani erant: id quod est, mea quidem sententia, pestilentissimum *(De locis theologicis,* Book 10, chap. 6).

2. One should not be surprised to find a symmetrically opposite opinion expressed during the same period: there is something divine about poetry, therefore the proper subject for poetry should be something sacred. Such was the opinion of Fray Luis de León, probably the best religious poet in sixteenth-century Spain (see Jones, 132).

Perhaps it could still be said that preserving the sacred from dangerous ambiguity is one thing and engaging in some sort of sacred victimizing process is another. At the very least, it might be argued, the connection between these two things, sacred victimization on the one hand and avoiding sacred ambivalence on the other, would not be evident to everybody. The purpose of this chapter will be to show that such a connection does exist at the most profound and decisive level; that sacred anxiety is the existential experience of sacred ambivalence; and sacred ambivalence is ultimately the ambivalence of the sacred victim. These things may and do appear disconnected in the historical experience of Christian Europe in the sixteenth and seventeenth centuries. We see clear victimizing processes here, sacred anxiety over there. It is as if the old sacred, having been shattered, is lying about in disconnected pieces. We have to go back in time in order to reconstruct the puzzle. And this is where Plato's testimony can be of invaluable help.

2. Plato's Sacred Anxiety

ATHENIAN: Suppose a sacrifice is taking place and the sacred meats are being burned as the law dictates, and let's say someone in a private capacity, a son or a brother, while standing near the altars and sacred things, breaks out in total blasphemy. Wouldn't we assert that his utterance would fill his father and the other kinsmen with despondency, and a sense of bad omen and prophetic warning of evil?

CLINIAS: How could we not?

ATHENIAN: Well, in our part of the world this happens in almost every city, so to speak. For whenever some official carries out some sacrifice in public, a chorus comes along afterwards—in fact not just one, but a mass of choruses—and standing not far from the altars, indeed sometimes right beside the altars, pours total blasphemy on the sacred things! They use words, rhythms, and very mournful harmoniae to get the souls of the hearers all worked up, and whoever can straightaway make the city that is engaged in sacrificing weep the most is the fellow who wins the victory prize! Won't we vote down this "law"? If it is sometimes necessary for the citizens to hear such wailings, on certain impure and ill-omened days, then there should rather be certain choruses of singers who come, hired from abroad, of the sort that are paid to walk before funeral processions, inspired by some Carian muse. Presumably such would be the fitting occasion for songs of that kind. And presumably it wouldn't be fitting for the garb that goes with the funeral songs to be crowns or golden ornaments, but entirely the opposite—so as to leave off discussing these matters as quickly as I possibly can.

    With regard to such a thing, I ask ourselves once again: should we lay down this first instance as one satisfactory mold for songs?

CLINIAS: Which?

ATHENIAN: Auspicious speech. Shouldn't our species of song be wholly auspicious . . . on every occasion?

CLINIAS: [By] all means. . .

ATHENIAN: What would be the second law of music after auspicious speech? Is it not that there are to be prayers to the gods to whom we are sacrificing on each occasion?

CLINIAS: What else except this?

ATHENIAN: The third law, I believe, should be that poets must realize that prayers are requests to the gods, and they must apply their intelligence to the utmost in order to avoid ever mistakenly requesting evil in place of good. . . . [But] the race of poets is not entirely capable of understanding well what things are good and what things are not. Presumably, if some poet creates, through words or melody, a work that is erroneous in this respect—if he creates prayers that are incorrect—he will make the citizens pray in a way opposed to what we ordain, in respect to the greatest matters. And as we said, we won't find many mistakes that are graver than this. (Plato, *Laws*, VII, 800b–801c)

The Athenian philosopher is horrified. He would rather not even talk about it. He wants "to leave off discussing these matters as quickly as [he] possibly can." But for a moment we catch a glimpse of his profound apprehension, even his emotional disturbance, in the face of an unclear, ambiguous appearance of the sacred. He is embarrassed and scandalized at the implied suggestion that the sacred could be anything but good, a reassuring presence. Why the "mournful harmoniae"? Why "such wailings" and weeping in sight of, nay, even in contact with, the sacred victim that has been just immolated?

If there is some accursed reason why sacrifice should be treated as a funeral, let it be done "on certain impure and ill-omened days," and not ourselves directly; rather, let us hire foreign singers "of the sort that are paid to walk before funeral processions." Coming from abroad, from beyond the protected circle of the city, foreigners are, of course, already impure, contaminated. In any case, it is especially dangerous for the same community that has just killed the sacred victim to mourn before it. That amounts to turning a blessing into a curse, "mistakenly requesting evil in place of good."

Socrates had already said in the *Republic* that "we shall have to reject all the terrible and apalling names [with] which [the poets] describe the world below—Cocytus and Styx, ghosts under the earth, and sapless shades, and any similar words of which the very mention causes a shudder to pass through the inmost soul of him who hears them. . . . And we [shall] proceed to get rid of the weepings and wailings of famous men" (III, 387). The difference is that now, "right beside the altars," what had been treated as psychologically damaging ("there is a danger that the nerves of our guardians may be rendered too excitable and effeminate") appears unmistakably as a sacrilege. It is simply a question of the distance from the sacred at which the philosophical discourse takes place. At a remote enough distance all kinds of rational and psychological explanations are possible and in order. In the immediate, physical presence of the sacred altar the attitude changes radically: the philosopher's reaction is triggered automatically; he becomes scandalized; seized by sacred fear; he cries "blasphemy" in horror.

All mourning and wailing in the presence of the sacrificial victim must be strictly forbidden. The first rule of hymnody to which the poets should adhere, must be that of "auspicious speech . . . our species of song [must] be wholly auspicious." In the presence of the sacrificial victim all signs of "pity and fear"—in the words of Plato's most distinguished disciple—are entirely out of place. In other words, it is of the utmost importance not to look at the victim qua victim. One must avoid even the thought that the victim is being in any way victimized, as we would say today (had Plato had his way, the modern notion of "victimization" would have never existed).

But Plato never asks why ritual sacrifice had always seemed the logical, indeed the required, occasion for the "mournful harmoniae," the wailing and the weeping. What did they think they were mourning? Why did they treat the killing of the victim as something sad? Much later Plutarch will tell us that "[when] they began to make sacrifices . . . they were revolted and terrified by what they did [so that] even now people are very careful not to kill the animal till a drink offering is poured over him and he shakes his head in assent" (quoted in Guépin, 101). The fact is that "they were revolted and terrified by what they did," because the animal victim was only a half-veiled sign of the implied human victim. As Walter Burkert has pointed out, "human sacrifice . . . as a horrible threat, stands behind every sacrifice" ("Greek Tragedy," 111).

There is an elaborate "comedy of innocence" surrounding ritual killing (Burkert, *Greek Religion*, 58):

> A procession escorts the animal to the altar. Everyone hopes as a rule that the animal will go to the sacrifice complaisantly, or rather voluntarily; edifying legends tell how animals pressed forward to the sacrifice on their own initiative. A blameless maiden at the front of the procession carries on her head the sacrificial basket in which the knife for sacrifice lies concealed beneath grains of barley or cakes. . . . The sacrificial knife in the basket is now uncovered. The sacrificer grasps the knife and, concealing the weapon, strides up to the victim . . . (*Greek Religion*, 56)

Understandably, Plato is not interested in such questions. In fact, he is not only not interested, but, from the way he is looking at the problem, the questions themselves would be blasphemous. He wants to look at the sacred in such a way that questions of that nature, questions that relate to the act of killing the victim, could never come up.

He blames the poets for their deviousness, their ambiguity. He blames them for their "mournful harmoniae," that is, for claiming innocence for a crime that, Plato insists, does not exist, thereby indirectly insinuating that there may be something criminal about the most sacred of sacred acts.

But, clearly, it is not the poets that frighten and scandalize Plato. It is rather the suggestion, the implied possibility, that the killing of the victim might not be a sacred act. It is not the fate of the victim that worries Plato, but the fate of the sacred itself. For if the killing of the required, legal, victim is not a sacred act, then no killing is sacred, then all killings are nothing but killings; in which case all barriers break down and there is nothing to stop the killings but more killings, and so on ad infinitum. The poets are not only accused of making a mistake. They are accused of blasphemy, that is, of violating the sacred itself. They must be sacrificed, expelled, in order to save the sacred character of the victimizing process, which, by sacralizing the killing, draws a veil over its violence and, in a sense, puts it out of sight and off-limits.

Plato, therefore, is not really trying to do anything different from what the wailing sacrificers, with their "comedy of innocence" (which to them was a very serious thing), had always done. They, too, were hiding their violence. He is just trying to do the same thing more efficiently.

Of course, this cover-up is the sort of thing in which you cannot miss. If you don't do it right, completely right, leaving no room for questioning, you don't do it at all; any doubt will place the entire sacralizing process in jeopardy. At the same time nobody is more aware than Plato of how easy it is to make a mistake, and this mistake would always be an intolerable one; in sacred matters, "the greatest matters." This is why the new poets in the new city would have to apply "their intelligence to the utmost in order to avoid ever mistakingly requesting evil in place of good." He had already said (Laws, 688c) that "it is dangerous for one who lacks intelligence to pray, [for] the opposite of what he wishes comes to pass." In these matters, making a mistake is not just missing the mark; it is doing exactly the opposite of what one intended to do. And that is precisely what happens, in the eyes of Plato, with all the poetic wailing and weeping.

Perhaps it can be said of sacred matters what the wise Athenian had already said of the difference between just and unjust things in general. They are like "shadow figures" or like things observed from a distance, a phenomenon "[which] produces a dizzying obscurity in everyone" (663c). Their contours change in the eye of the observer. They may look like one thing now and like something else a moment later. One must choose and hold the right appearance, even though the wrong one may appear just as real. This is why the wise lawgiver "will somehow or other persuade [the citizens], with habits and praises and arguments" to look at such things the right way, the way of the just man.

Ambiguity is intolerable because it touches the most sensitive cord in Plato's mind, the sacred one. It is most dangerous because it undermines the sacred foundation of the city. Against it the remedy must be careful differentiation, precise, mathematical calculation, calculation being "the golden sacred pull" of the soul, also "called the common law of the city" (645a).

Once precisely calculated differentiations are established, they should not be allowed to change, to deviate, to waver. Plato abhors change:

> Change, we shall find, is much the most dangerous thing in every-thing except what is bad. . . . It isn't the case that change is safe in some things and dangerous in others. . . . If [people] are brought up under laws that by some divine good fortune have remained unchanged for a great length of time, if they neither re-member nor have heard that things were ever otherwise than they are at present, then the entire soul reverences and fears changing any of the things that are already laid down. Somehow or other the lawgiver must think up a device by which this situation will prevail in the city. (797e–798b)

That kind of "divine good fortune" must be rare, but it is by no means impossible. There is one admirable example of it, the one provided by the immobile schemata of Egyptian art, to which he had referred else-where in the *Laws* as an example of an excellent system of education for the young:

> Long ago, as is likely, this argument which we are now enunciat-ing was known to them [the Egyptians]—the argument which says that it's necessary for the young in the cities to practice fine pos-tures and fine songs. They made a list of them, indicating which they were and what kind they were, and published it in their tem-ples. Painters and others who represented postures and that sort of thing were not allowed to make innovations or think up things different from the ancestral. And they are still not allowed to—not in these things or in music altogether. If you look into this you will find that for ten thousand years—not "so to speak" but really ten thousand years—the paintings and sculptures have been in no way more beautiful or more ugly than those that are being made, with the very same skill, by their craftsmen now. (656d–657a)

The sacred is the ultimate guarantee of stability. Clear, differentiated things, unambiguous, unmixed things, things that do not change, fill the soul with reverence. Stability and the sacred, each one breeds and supports the other. It is not enough for the lawgiver to know what is correct and "boldly to order it in law" (657b). As we have seen, he "must think up a device," use any kind of persuasion to instill in the citizens reverence for the law. If a law is sufficiently sanctified, made sacred enough, it will be observed; it will last. Indeed, the power of the sacred can be amazing. Not only can it guarantee the stability of the law, it can in fact eliminate even the desire to break the law, so that in the case of a truly exceptional breaking of the sacred law, the citizens perceive it as something monstrous, unnatural, and are filled with revulsion and horror. Such being the power of the sacred, there is no law of which observance would be too difficult if endowed with the full force of the sacred.

Among the laws that should govern the Platonic city are those the alteration of which "make no small difference, about which it is difficult to be persuasive, and which are in fact the task of the god, if it were somehow possible to get the orders themselves from him" (835c). Short of direct orders from the god in these very difficult matters, the wise Athenian has discovered an "art," a technique, that would produce similar results. I believe it is worth examining this "art" in some detail. The problem comes up in connection with erotic desires and the extremely difficult decision of what kinds of sexual intercourse should or should not be allowed in the city:

ATHENIAN: When I arrived, in the course of the argument, at education, I saw young men and young women mixing together affectionately. As might be expected, a fear came over me as I reflected on the problem of how someone will manage a city like this, in which young men and women are well reared, and released from the severe and illiberal tasks that do the most to quench wantonnness; and where sacrifices, festivals, and choruses are the preoccupations of everyone throughout their whole lives. How, in this city, will they ever avoid the desires that frequently cast many down into the depths, the desires that reason, striving to become law, orders them to avoid? (835d, e)

How does the lawgiver deal with such powerful desires? How does he subject them to rational legal constraints?

ATHENIAN: In order to establish this law, I have now a certain art, which will be in one respect easy to employ but in another respect extremely difficult in every way.

MEGILLUS: What do you mean?

ATHENIAN: Presumably, we know that even at the present time most human beings, however lawless they may be, nevertheless punctiliously refrain from intercourse with beautiful persons, and do so not involuntarily, but with the greatest possible willingness.

MEGILLUS: When do you mean?

ATHENIAN: When the beautiful person is one's brother or sister. Moreover, with regard to a son or a daughter, the same unwritten law guards in a very effective way. . . . In fact, among the many there isn't the slightest desire for this sort of intercourse.

MEGILLUS: What you're saying is true.

ATHENIAN: And isn't it just a little phrase that quenches all such pleasures?

MEGILLUS: What phrase are you referring to?

ATHENIAN: The phrase that declares these things are not at all pious, but are hateful to the gods and the most shameful of shameful things. Isn't the cause the fact that no one ever says anything else, but from the moment of birth each of us hears people saying these things, always and everywhere? In jokes and in every serious tragedy isn't it frequently said, and when they bring on Thyestes-figures or certain Oedipuses, or certain Macareuses, who secretly have intercourse with their sisters, isn't it seen that they promptly inflict upon themselves the just punishment of death for their crime?

MEGILLUS: You are quite correct to this extent: when no one ever even tries to breathe against the law in any way, then the pronouncement has an amazing power.

ATHENIAN: So . . . when a lawgiver wishes to enslave a certain desire which especially enslaves human beings, it is easy to know, at least, how he should handle it. By having everyone—slaves, free men, children, women, the whole city in agreement together—hold this pronouncement to be something sacred, he will have succeeded in making this law very firm.

MEGILLUS: That's certainly so. But now how it will ever be possible to arrange things so that everyone is willing to say such a thing—

ATHENIAN: —It's fine of you to take me up this way. For this was the very thing I said, that in regard to this law I had an art that would promote the natural use of sexual intercourse for the production of children. . . . But if there were standing here some vehement young man full of a lot of sperm who had been listening to the laying down of the law, he would probably revile us for setting up mindless and impossible customs, and would fill the air with his clamor. It was with a view to such that I made my pronouncement, about a certain art I possessed, in one respect the easiest of all things to apply and in another respect the most difficult, which would promote the permanent establishment of this law. It's very easy to understand that it's possible and in what way: we assert that if this custom is sufficiently sanctified, it will enslave every soul and instill it with a fear that will insure its total obedience to the established laws. (838a–839c)

The reason why it would be "most difficult" to apply this "art" is just the disbelief with which such legal pronouncement would be received, as "[it] occurs in the case of the practice of common meals. . . . It's because of this, because of the strength such disbelief possesses, that I have described both these practices as things that are very difficult to make permanent in the law."

The argument is clear enough. Nothing carries so much unquestioned assent and willing adherence as a sacred taboo. Indeed, Plato is talking about what is perhaps the most universal sacred prohibition, the incest taboo; so universal that it is right on the dividing line between nature and culture. Even modern anthropology could not have chosen a better example. Therefore, all the lawgiver has to do to obtain universal compliance with his law is to give it the same kind of sacred power.

But he mistakes the effect for the cause and in the end the argument becomes circular: "when a lawgiver wishes to enslave a certain desire," he must make everybody "hold this pronouncement to be something sacred." But "how will it ever be possible to arrange things so that everyone is willing to say such a thing?" Answer: by having "this custom sufficiently sanctified," that is, by making it sacred enough. And how does one do that? By having everybody hold this pronouncement . . . , etc.

Something is missing which Plato is afraid to touch. He keeps running in logical circles around it, in an effort to keep the argument on strictly rational and philosophical grounds. What is missing, of course, is the sacrificial scene, with the victim at the center, which is the testing ground and the paradigmatic expression of sacred unanimity. Such unanimity either stands or falls at the sacrificial altar. It is there that any deviation, any form of dissent would fill everybody "with despondency, and a sense of bad omen and prophetic warning of evil"; it is at that moment that the sacrificial community is in the presence of something awesome and terrifying, something capable of unleashing a devastating catastrophe—which is why there is also a victim, a decoy, a so-called peace offering, at the center of that scene.

But Plato does not want to talk about the sacred victim, because the sacred victim is the telltale sign of an unpredictable and violent sacred. Philosophy has no use for a sacred victim. The idea that sacred unanimity is entirely dependent on the elimination of the sacred victim, is profoundly repugnant to Plato and to philosophy in general. Indeed, philosophy would try to turn this proposition around and make the expulsion of the victim the result of a preexisting unanimity based entirely on rational persuasion, which is not how the sacred works at all.

A sacred killing is a very ambiguous affair, and the philosopher wants a very unambiguous sacred. Plato would have no objection to the idea of a sacred "offering," or "present," or any other similar notion. But he has to separate the sacred from the killing in order to keep the sacred pure; not—and this is crucial—in order to stop the killing, but in order to do it unambiguously, that is, without fearing for the sacred. Paradoxically, he must separate the sacred from the killing (or ignore the sacred victim altogether, which is the same thing) for the same reason that the victim had always been considered sacred: to justify the killing, to do the killing and, at the same time, be able to claim innocence. He would desacralize the killing in order to keep the sacred character of the victimizing process running smooth, free from ambiguity. Plato's philosophical avoidance of the sacred victim, qua victim, is a ruse, a new form of expulsion to repair or substitute for the old sacred veil, which was wearing thin and becoming a little too transparent.

The poets, on the other hand, would not exist without the mourning and the wailing around the sacrificial altar. They need the sacred victim at the center. Of course, the poets do not mourn exactly for the animal that has just been killed. They have diverted the ritual pity and fear of the sacrificial "comedy of innocence" onto the tragic fate of characters like those "Thyestes-figures or certain Oedipuses, or certain Macareuses, who—in the opinion of Plato—[should not be mourned at all, but must] promptly inflict upon themselves the just punishment of death for their crime."

There is nothing sacred, Plato would say, about breakers of sacred taboos. It is a sacred duty to dispose of them as quickly as possible. But this sacred duty is something "natural," fully supported by reason and philosophy. It has nothing to do with pity and fear, which are totally out of place here. Plato wants to turn sacred unanimity into a matter of moral, that is, rational and philosophical persuasion.

Quite true, but he also wants the opposite. He wants philosophy to be like the old sacred, to borrow its strength, to work with the same effectiveness. He does not want to substitute philosophy for the old sacred. He just wants to take the sacred victim out of the picture. Philosophy equals the old sacred minus the ambiguous, poetic, victim; because the only victim which philosophy can contemplate, qua victim, must be fully guilty, fully deserving of expulsion. But that formula is not going to generate the sacred fear that he still wants "to enslave every soul [and] insure its total obedience to the established laws." The only rational, scientific, substitute that philosophy could produce for sacred fear would be a generalized state of terror administered by a tyrannical power meting out harsh punishments, which would, in turn, mean the end of philosophy itself. (Is this not an ever-present danger whenever reason wants to substitute for or merge with the sacred?)

But I do not think that Plato is a heartless tyrant. The fear that he wants is not exactly fear of the punishment established by the city for the lawbreaker. To instill that kind of fear alone the sacralizing process to which he refers would not be needed. He is after a more primordial fear, a fear caused, not so much by the punishment for breaking the law, but by the breaking of the law itself (perhaps a primitive antecedent of what philosophy would eventually define as an a priori moral imperative).

He wants to sanctify the laws of the city. But if the laws are truly sacred what threatens the community when they are broken is the sacred itself. The damage done is not to this or that part of the common good easily differentiated, but to the sacred, to that which holds *everything* together. Because of that the lawbreaker, as a differentiated individual, is unimportant except that he is the one who triggers or releases the sacred threat upon the community. He does not threaten the community directly, as an individual, but indirectly, as a carrier of the sacred. He himself is touched, contaminated, by the sacred in the act of breaking the sacred law. And it is not anybody in particular that is threatened by the breaking of the sacred law, but the entire community. Sacred fear of the sacred spreads instantly. It dissolves the fate of any single individual into the fate of the clan, the tribe, the whole community. That is the kind of fear capable of generating the solid, unhesitating, unanimity admired by Plato and required by his ideal system. The kind of fear that, in Plato's own words, can fill the sacrificing community "with despondency, and a sense of bad omen and prophetic warning of evil," when the sacred law is broken; the very same fear that seizes the philosopher himself, when he sees the poets mourning and wailing in the presence of the sacred victim.

The problem, once again, is that Plato cannot have it both ways. He cannot have that sacred fear and not have a sacred victim, or rather, a sacred taboo-breaker. For it is precisely sacred fear that sacralizes its victim and turns every execution into a sacrificial rite; and this sacrificial rite often includes expressions of pity, through which the sacred character of the victim can also be acknowledged.

In this respect it is most instructive to see how Plato's own fear of the poets works in his text. I do not think I am discovering anything new by pointing to the basic ambiguity of Plato's attitude in regard to the poets whom he must expel from the city. The following passage in the *Republic* is well known. In it, half-jokingly, the pantomimic poets are expelled in explicitly ritual fashion from the ideal republic:

> And therefore when one of these pantomimic gentlemen, who are so clever that they can imitate anything, comes to us, and makes a proposal to exhibit himself and his poetry, we will fall down and worship him as a sweet and holy and wonderful being; but we must also inform him that in our state such as he are not permitted to exist. . . . And so when we have anointed him with myrrh, and set a garland of wool upon his head, we shall send him away to another city. (III, 398)

He is ironic, to be sure, but in a way that he obviously considers appropriate to the occasion. Since the poets are ambiguous creatures, living, as they do, in the proximity of the sacred, they should be expelled in properly sacrificial manner. First you consecrate them—anoint them with myrrh and place on their head a garland of wool, as was traditionally done with the sacred victim—then you expel them to protect the community from ambiguous sacred contamination. It was only half a joke.

Yes, the poets are ambiguous creatures. And their ambiguity is especially alarming in the eyes of the philosopher, because they are the traditional spokesmen for the sacred. Nevertheless, their ambiguity is not specifically poetic, it belongs to the sacred victim itself, and the sacred victim precedes the poets. For poetry emerges out of the schematic rigidity of the purely ritual through the fissure, the sacrificial freeplay, fostered by the sacred ambiguity of the victim, a source of sacred fear and pity. Such an ambiguity is poetry's historical and epistemological condition of possibility.

When Plato blames the poets for their ambiguity, he is simply substituting them for the sacred victim. To blame the poets is to shift attention from the evidence, from the ambiguous character of the sacred victim and of the victimizing process itself. It should be clear, then, that not wanting to talk about the victim and blaming the poets are the two sides of the same sacrificial operation, which constitutes philosophy as such.

But there is something else the poets do around the sacred victim that must bother a rational philosopher like Plato, sensitive to all the dangerous implications of the poets' mourning and wailing.

The mourning and the wailing around the sacred meats of the animal that has just been sacrificed is illogical; philosophically it does not make sense. But when such a funereal behavior is poetically diverted toward the traditional fate of such despicable characters as those "Thyestes-figures or certain Oedipuses or certain Macareuses," something else is implied: the possibility that the terrible accusations of parricide and incest traditionally leveled against them may not be what they appear to be, that their guilt may have been manipulated, just as the poets manipulate the feelings of the sacrificing community (which would, in fact, make the poets, as guilt manipulators, the true image, the real representatives of the sacrificing community). And such manipulation is much worse than failing to condemn the guilty unambiguously, without fear or pity. To cast doubt on the guilt of the guilty next to the sacrificial altar, under the aegis of the sacred, is to make the sacred an accomplice in a manipulated setup.

To cast such a doubt, was not, of course, the motivation for the traditional mourning and wailing. But Plato cannot discard any rational implication. He is looking ahead, and there is no telling what one of those irresponsible poets, perhaps too perceptive for his own good, might do if he begins to see what the philosopher himself is already anticipating and trying to push out of sight with the help of his new and more efficient philosophical method. He trembles at the thought.

The idea that a historical experience of the sacred could be instrumental in the revelation of a victim who, in spite of being a scandal to everybody, despised and accused by the crowd, is without guilt, could only appear frightening to Plato. Within the Platonic system it is simply inconceivable that God could be the breaker of collective sacrificial unanimity, that God could be on the side of a victim unanimously found guilty and despicable. That is, of course, the radical, the immense, difference that separates Plato from the Judeo-Christian revelation.

This accused yet innocent victim, the suffering servant of the Old Testament, for example, and above all Christ, stands outside both Plato's philosophical project and the sacred performance of the poets. We must keep this extraordinary revelation in mind in order to understand the profound difference within the similarity between the sixteenth- and seventeenth-century historical situation of poetry and its Platonic background.

3. Similarities and Differences

It is true that the antipoetic moralist of sixteenth- and seventeenth-century Christian Europe reiterates or reactivates to a large extent Plato's ethico-philosophical argument against poetry's dangerous ambiguity, understood from the point of view of philosophy itself: halfway between the true and the false, appearance and reality, etc. But our brief excursus through Plato should also tell us that behind this philosophically feared ambiguity lies an older one, to which both Plato and the Renaissance antipoetic moralist are far more sensitive than has been generally assumed: the ambiguity of the sacred itself, which is ultimately rooted in the irreducible ambiguity of the sacrificial victim. And I hope it is also clear by now that the "old quarrel between philosophy and the poets," in Plato's own words, centers around that victim.

Once we understand the sacrificial spirit, the sacred anxiety that motivates Plato's profound distrust of the poets, the virulence of the antipoetic attack in the Renaissance may become more intelligible.

It has been said that "the source of this [antipoetic] animus is the delight in Naked Truth: the thing itself, undefiled, unaccoutered, for which [poetic fiction] or the vulgar empiric substitute their specious approximations" (Fraser, 28). This concern for the "naked truth," Fraser argues, will become the fundamental characteristic of modern man: "Modern or progressive man is elusive in his politics, and not to be described—or not infallibly—as Royalist or Roundhead. The decisive thrust which moves him, and distinguishes present from past, is the zeal for perspicuous truth" (178).

I think these observations are basically correct; they can acount both for Plato's and the Renaissance moralist's opposition to poetic fiction, but not for its violent intensity, not for the concomitant anxiety. Only a sacrificial, sacralizing, experience of the truth can account for the violent anxiety felt in the presence of the ambiguity or ambivalence that characterizes poetic fiction. The anxious Renaissance moralist feels very deeply that poetic fiction is fundamentally alien to Christianity. And he is objectively right. But his violent anxiety is a reliable indication that his experience of the Christian truth is still basically sacrificial, no different, in this respect, from Plato's experience of his own philosophical truth. In both cases the truth is in need of protection, must be preserved from contaminating ambiguity.

Nowhere is this more evident than in the Christian moralist's attack against the theater. What Fraser said about this attack in England could also be applied to Spain or France, by slightly modifying the dates: "From the 1570's forward, the reformer reserves his fiercest hatred for the drama: not as he hates poetry less but as he fears the drama more" (16). Or, as Henry Phillips has remarked, in reference to the situation in France, "Horace's dictum about what one sees having far greater impact than what one reads was taken at its face value by theorists and moralists alike. For the latter this makes drama by far the most dangerous branch of literature" (9).

From our point of view, the most significant feature of the antitheatrical attack is the use of the same arguments that had been leveled against the pagan theater by the early Church Fathers. Those arguments are revived and reiterated with amazing vigor from the end of the sixteenth century on. Here is a sampling of them:

> Plays being "consecrated to idolatrie, they are not of God; if they proceed not from God, they are the doctrine and inventions of the Devill." (Stephen Gosson [1582], quoted in Barish, 89)

Stage-plays are the Pomps of the devil, which we renounce at baptism, because their original and the materials of which they are composed, is wholly patched up of idolatrie. (Tertullian, quoted in Ridpath, 61)

[Saint Cyprian] tells us further that . . . "Romulus at first did consecrate stage-plays to Consus, as the god of counsel, for the Sabine women that were to be ravished; and whatever else there is in stage-plays . . . if its original be enquired into, hath either an idol or a devil for its founder." (Ridpath, 66)

Are not these plays the subversion of life, the corruption of manners, the destruction of marriage, the cause of wars, of fightings and brawls in houses? (Saint Chrysostom, quoted in Ridpath, 56)

Saint Augustine . . . and Saint Isidore . . . say that the theaters originated in idolatrie and were the invention of the devil for the purpose of entertaining idol worshippers with something pleasurable, so that they could better swallow the cruelties of the sacrifices which the devils demanded of them; and also Saint Cyprian who says, in *De spectaculis, quod spectaculum sine idolo?* (Anonymous, quoted in Cotarelo y Mori, 212)

Theater-houses are nothing other than temples of idols where public sacrifices are offered to the devil. (Father José de Jesús María; quoted in Cotarelo y Mori, 379)

It is true that this type of argument is often repeated without much thinking from author to author. However, after it has been repeated so vigorously for two hundred years, it is difficult to view it from beginning to end as nothing but a senseless act, an unthinking and out-of-place rehashing of old topics, that has nothing to do with the reality of the theater in seventeenth-century Europe. For it is indeed true that the theatrical representation of a work by Shakespeare, or Racine, or Calderón is something very different from the crude pagan spectacles of the late Roman empire, at the time of the early Church Fathers.

The contrast is such between what we see in the theater of a seventeenth-century classic and what those arguments tell us about the theater, that we must suspect that either those antitheatrical moralists were insane or we are missing something very fundamental. I am inclined toward the latter, even though there was clearly an element of sheer irrationality in the way they argued their case. First, it should be noted they were not saying that what they saw on the modern stage was literally a repetition of the "cruelties of the sacrifices which the devils demanded of [the pagans]." They simply recognized in the theatrical performance as such, not in this or that play in particular, the spirit of paganism and old sacrificial rites. And that recognition cannot be discarded as either insincere or gratuitous.

Even today we are moving closer to that very recognition. What Roberto Calasso has recently written about art in general may be especially appropriate to the case of poetic fiction. He begins by quoting Adorno:

> "Art is magic liberated from the lie of being the truth." Of art, elusive by nature, only a genetic definition can be given—and that of Adorno is perhaps the neatest. To escape the power of magic, the magic demanded by sacrifice, is not only a trick by reason to detach itself from [sacred] powers. It is also a gesture which opens up an unheard-of dimension: [the possibility] to play with the sacrificial objects, with the relics and the ruins which the wrecking of the world of magic has abandoned on the shores of the psyche. All of art's characteristics, its absorbing ambiguity, its cathartic function . . . and even its way of being "disinterested," according to Kant's formula, are sacrificial vestiges. In Beckett's "doing that, without knowing what" echoes the original *operari* which was sacrifice itself. The "without knowing what" evokes the hidden powers which act without a name. This is the peculiarity of the West: not that of having discovered the Beautiful, but of having left it hovering in a state of suspension, of having untied the slipknot that strangles the victim. . . . What speaks in art is the voice of the victim who escaped the killing *in extremis*—and forever—when the ritual had already caused all the sacred to flow back into that victim. (198)

The difference is that such sacrificial vestiges, relics, or stranded wreckage were significantly more alive in sixteenth- and seventeenth-century Europe than they are today. In the eyes of those antipoetic and antitheatrical moralists, the play with the sacrificial objects was still something dangerous; it conjured up the kind of sacred fear that Plato felt at the sight of indiscriminating, ambiguous poets in the vicinity of the sacred. They had not fully understood or accepted that liberation of art which is a direct consequence of the liberation of the sacrificial victim.

Henry Phillips has also made an interesting observation regarding the antitheatrical moralists in France:

> [The] threat posed by drama to the Church, coming as it does from outside the latter's sphere of influence, may well resemble in moralists' minds the threat posed by witchcraft, still very much regarded as a danger in seventeenth-century France. In many ways the assimilation is easy to make: both seduce men's minds by casting a spell (in the context of drama *charmer* and *enchanter* retain very much of their literal meaning) and both possess individuals with specialized skills able to conjure up an alternative world. (250)

In fact, the association between witchcraft and the watching of spectacles in general was made by Beda, who is quoted to that effet by Thomas Aquinas in the *Summa Theologica* (2–2. q.167, a.2): "Ut autem dicit Beda, concupiscentia oculorum est non solum 'in discendis magicis artibus,' sed etiam 'in contemplandis spectaculis, et in dignoscendis et carpendis vitiis proximorum.'" (As Beda says, the concupiscence of the eyes does not consist only "in learning the magic arts," but also "in watching spectacles, and in inquiring about and castigating the neighbors' vices.")

The "antitheatrical prejudice," as Jonas Barish has called it, is a sacred "prejudice," reflecting the sacred character of the object to which it is attached. It is as old as the theater itself and it has lasted for more than two millennia, which is proof enough that it is not ultimately dependent on specific cultural or historical conditions (such as the jealousy of the Church, concerned about losing its power over people's hearts). A telltale sign of its sacred character is its inherent instability. Without apparently being aware of it, Barish describes a typically sacred phenomenon, and his is one of the most thorough and convincing investigations on the subject:

> The case of George Moore, capable in one moment of a warm imaginative kinship with actors, and in the next of a cold and contemptuous withdrawal from them, may serve to remind us of the instability of even the protheatrical bias, its frequently conflictive and unresolved nature. Almost inevitably, it seems to con-

tain the seeds of its own opposite. Aside from those renegade
playwrights, like Plato, Gosson, and Rousseau, who abandon the
theater only to denounce it, aside from those who renounce the
stage in the throes of a religious conversion, like Calderón, Racine, and Jean-Baptiste Gresset, we also find renegade patrons like
the Prince de Conti: having energetically furthered Molière's ca-
reer at one time, he went on to become one of the most resolute
and eloquent antitheatricalists of his generation. More strikingly
and disturbingly we see the same ambivalence on a mass scale, in
the theatergoing public of the late Roman Empire or of eighteenth-century France, which mingles hysterical adulation of the
actors with cruel legal proscriptions. Attitudes towards the stage,
quite plainly, come fraught with passion and charged with contradiction. (400)

Moving within this sacred frame of reference, the antitheatrical moralist of sixteenth- or seventeenth-century Europe sees the theater as the
wrong sacred or the sacred gone wrong, sacrifice miscarried—which was
precisely the way Plato saw the participation of the traditional poet in
ritual sacrifice, as we have just seen.

Regardless of the theological convictions of those antitheatrical moralists, or the orthodoxy of their beliefs, in their attitude toward the theater,
Christ's blameless sacrifice ends up playing the same role that philosophy
played in Plato. Instead of being the point outside the sacrificial circle
from which sacrificial circularity itself is exposed, Christ's sacrifice functions for them as part of the sacrificial system by serving as a contrasting
background against which the paganlike, ambiguous sacrifice of poetic
fiction reveals its sinful imperfection and devilish ambiguity. Like Plato,
the antitheatrical moralist of the Renaissance sees the poet as being too
much on the side of the guilty. The poets are accused of making attractive, of displaying in a favorable light, all kinds of sinful behavior.

The accusation is fully deserved. But the moralist, like Plato, finds such
a favorable light objectionable, because it undermines the rationality of
the punishing process, by blurring the distinction between the guilty and
the not guilty. He, like Plato, wants a clear and unambiguous kind of
punishment. What he does not understand is that it is not really a question of guilt or innocence; what is at stake is whether or not one yields
to the sacrificial, victimizing mechanism, whether or not one is still in the
grip of the devil's system, to put it in the moralist's own terms. For, as

we saw in Plato, a rationally controlled system of punishment is in the final analysis only a cultural improvement on the devil's system, on the old mourning and wailing, that is, on the system that puts a beautiful glitter, an attractive and beguiling appearance, on the victim who is about to be sacrificed. Carried away by his scandalized indignation, the moralist tends to forget that if the theater is the devil's sacrifice, the glitter that the devil puts on the guilty cannot possibly be for the purpose of saving them. There's more than one way to skin a cat, one might say. And theater's way is both more primitive and, in a sense, more subtle than philosophy's.

Intellectually speaking, the Renaissance moralist's argument against poetic ambiguity in general is much more complex and philosophically sophisticated than the antitheatrical attacks, all by themselves, would lead one to believe. Because of their extreme and radical character, those attacks appear to us as a historically marginal phenomenon, in spite of their being more widespread than literary critics would like to admit. But from the point of view of a historical phenomenology of the sacred, those violent attacks are only an intensification of what underlies the antipoetic argument in general, namely, the experience of the sacred. That argument is above all a religious argument.

It could be said that the difference between a reasonable and learned moralist like Luis Vives, for example, and those attackers of the theater who see it, literally, as the work of the devil, is analogous to the difference between the Plato of the *Republic* or of *Phaedrus,* for example, and the scandalized Plato we have just seen in the *Laws.* The ethico-philosophical disapproval of poetic ambiguity deepens and turns into scandalized anxiety as it gets closer to the sacred altar. In the immediate vicinity of the sacred, everything may appear a little irrational. Moral philosophy, with its carefully built rational arguments, is a yardstick measuring the distance at which the philosopher has been able to displace the sacred presence. We should not, then, be surprised to see a little sacred "irrationality" flaring up on the margins of the ethico-philosophical argument during the Renaissance. What is important to remember is that the roots of such an "irrationality" are the same as those of its more philosophically rational contemporary.

The problem with the radical antipoetic moralist of the Renaissance and beyond is not that he is wrong in what he sees behind the attractive poetic facade, be it that of narrative or of dramatic fiction, but that he is, in fact, a man of little faith. He misjudges the social and historical strength of what he calls the devil's work, the old sacrificial mechanism. Plato's anxiety was fully justified. Poetry was by no means a marginal activity. The poets' ambiguous play with the sacred affected the very cornerstone of the social order. They had been and continued to be the traditional spokesmen of the sacred. In fact, Plato's expulsion of the traditional poets was a purely theoretical exercise. It did not change anything in its sociohistorical environment. In this sense, his philosophical project was purely self-referential. It only appeared to work to the extent that it could abstract itself from the historical reality of its time.

The situation in the new Europe could not be more different. There was no longer a "quarrel" between philosophy (or theology) and the best of poets regarding the need to keep poetry separate from the sacred. As we saw in the Introduction, they all agreed on that. But their agreement had nothing to do with mutual persuasion or the reaching of any kind of historical compromise. They were simply acknowledging the reality of what had already happened; an extraordinary event that shook the very relationship between the sacred and the profane, and of which their allergic reaction to the "mixing of the human and the divine" was merely a symptom. That separation, which in Plato was a purely theoretical goal, fervently desired but never actually reached, had now become largely a reality, an unavoidable reality.

And yet, it was not as if Plato's expulsion had finally succeeded. On the contrary, what happened is that such an expulsion was now largely unnecessary. It was no longer imperative to throw poetry out of the city altogether in order to keep it away from the sacred. A new, largely desacralized, space could be found inside, even though it was still felt to be somewhat marginal, a mere ornament to the res publica (an indication that desacralization had indeed its limits).

In Spain there is an exceptional historical witness to this poetic marginality: the Inquisition. To the dismay of the many enemies of poetic fiction, both laymen and ecclesiastics, the Tribunal of the Holy Inquisition, charged with maintaining the doctrinal purity of the faith, did not think that poetry was relevant to that doctrinal core or posed any real danger to it—a definitely non-Platonic attitude.

This indifference has become increasingly obvious in recent years. At the end of his study, "Literatura e Inquisición en España en el Siglo XVI," Jesús Martínez de Bujanda declares: "In conclusion, our findings show that the Spanish inquisitorial censorship in the sixteenth century does not attribute much importance to writings of a literary character. Of a total of more than 2000 prohibitions, hardly ten percent are written in Spanish, and of this group of fewer than 200 . . . some twelve percent are works of a literary character" (in Pérez Villanueva, *La Inquisición Española*, 591).

In the eyes of the Inquisition, poets were in a very different category from doctrinal or religious writers. Antonio Márquez, who studies the Renaissance theater in particular, writes: "Even though it is never stated in any of the numerous inquisitorial directives, the author of an artistic work, the literary writer as such, is in fact treated with a different criterion than the doctrinal author specifically didactic and sectarian. In this sense, it can be stated categorically that no dramatic author was ever indicted for his work, even when his work or part of it may have been censored, expurgated, or prohibited during his lifetime" (*La Inquisición Española*, 602).

In fact, the entire Golden Age of Spanish literature happened under the watchful eye of the Inquisition. Marginality, therefore, meant freedom. But this relative freedom from inquisitorial intervention was only symptomatic of a deeper poetic freedom from poetry's own ancestral attachment to the sacred. In other words, freedom from itself. Poetry could now reflect upon itself, analyze itself, and experiment with itself to an unprecedented degree. One of the results of this newly acquired freedom was an extraordinary theoretical interest in poetry. A wave of new treatises on poetics appeared, first in Italy and then spreading over the rest of Europe. This is the age that "discovered" Aristotle's *Poetics*, as we shall see in Chapter 2.

All of which could only mean that the experience of the sacred had changed. It was now much less affected by the ambiguous fiction of the poets. The danger of turning a blessing into a curse was now much more remote than in Plato's time. The good had become more stable, less affected by the proximity of the bad. A new historical possibility had arisen to break the sacred circularity between the good and the bad, the remedy and the poison: a possibility to give the good a better opportunity to be truly different from the bad, to be more than just the other side of the bad; that is to say, the bad violently expelled, or more precisely, hidden from view.

Indeed, only to the extent that such a *nondialectical* differentiation became historically possible can we speak of a real process of desacralization. Such a phenomenon could have never been brought about by any form of sacred allergy alone. In fact, when we speak of desacralization we speak of the possibility of a world governed to some degree by non-scandalized reason, a reason not driven by any kind of sacred allergy, whose logic would not be the logic of the sacred expulsion of the sacred. In other words, we speak of the dawning in human consciousness of the possibility of a world where the divine cannot really contaminate the human or vice versa, because they no longer threaten or repel each other; the only world in which the human can be fully the human, in the sense that no external, arbitrary, barriers are placed on its path.

4. The Role of Poetry in an Increasingly Desacralized Reality

This new situation, in which it was no longer of the essence to expel poetry to keep it away from the sacred (a futile gesture anyway), posed a new problem for the meaning and the future of poetic fiction. What could be the role and the relevance of ambiguous poetic fiction detached from the old sacred, and irrelevant to a new, largely unambiguous experience of the sacred? How could such a deceiving thing as poetic fiction, the beautiful creature so deeply mistrusted by Plato, have a future in the new era? In what way could it accurately reflect, echo, or truthfully acknowledge a largely desacralized reality? In other words, would desacralization condemn poetry to utter marginality, to be no more meaningful than it was in the eyes of the Spanish inquisitors, forever relegated to be purely ornamental, a museum piece?

The answer, gleaned from the texts of poetic fiction itself, could be summarized as follows: it could tell the truth of what was happening to itself; it could look at its own sacrificial character and the human condition that makes it possible, as never before.

Such a self-reflection and meditation would not be totally unprecedented, as we will see when we study Virgil. What was new was the degree of freedom with which it could be carried out. But that freedom carried a heavy price of uncertainty. Standing at the threshold of the modern era, without sacred protection or any of its reassuring benefits—security, respectability, a sense of belonging, etc.—poetic fiction cut a rather sorry and unsteady figure, looking very much an outcast.

What kind of a character would fit such poetic attire? Certainly not a hero. A clear possibility was an antihero, a *pícaro*. It could also be an illusory, a make-believe hero, in other words, a Quijote. But whatever the specific form that uncertain figure would take, given the desacralizing indirect reasons for its uncertainty and lack of respectability, the fundamental question regarding its fate was the following: Would this unprotected figure, who looked very much an outcast, be finally thrown out of the city, marginalized without hope, ridiculed out of existence, expelled forever from the company of respectable persons? Or would it be rescued from its marginality, forgiven for its sacrificial past, and shown to be fully human, no different from anybody else? And, since this figure embodied the new situation in which poetic fiction found itself, the question can be reformulated as follows: Would poetic fiction, upon discovering its sacrificial, idolatrous, devil-inspired underpinnings, turn against itself in the spirit of the antipoetic moralist attackers? Or would it try to renounce its old victimizing spirit and, more in keeping with the spirit of the nonvictimizing, desacralizing process, find a way to become reconciled with itself, to become a medium of reconciliation rather than of expulsion?

This question can be given a very specific reference in the context of Golden Age Spanish literature. To put it very succinctly, Whose path would literary fiction take, Quevedo's or Cervantes's? What character would have a clearer future ahead of him, Pablos the *pícaro,* or Don Quijote? Of course, we already know the answer. Quevedo's path would have led rather quickly to a dead end.

B. W. Ife has probably seen better than anyone the unsettling and destructive potential of the picaresque novel as a genre and of Quevedo's *Buscón* in particular. It is worth quoting him at length:

> With the advantage of hindsight it is now possible to gauge how definitive a blow the author of *Lazarillo de Tormes* dealt to traditional assumptions about the related hierarchies of style and subject matter. . . . The mixture of informality and sententiousness in Guzmán's narrative results in a style that is challenging and provocative, one which implicitly rebukes the reader for his allegiance to high art in the very act of showing him what riches there are to be found in a narrative of low life. . . . Quevedo's *Buscón* pushes the disturbing potential of these issues to their furthest limits. . . . It is as if the moral and social misrule that the book documents has spread to the medium itself, so that one no longer knows what a work of fiction is supposed to be, what purpose it

is supposed to have, or how to judge whether it is any good. On top of this, the central character of the book, a creature drawn from the very dregs of contemporary society, narrates its infamous progress in the unmistakable language of one of the foremost writers of his time. (148)

And again:

Quevedo made use of the picaresque in a way which suggests that not only did he wish to outdo the opposition in satire but by parodying them to the point of travesty, he intended to destroy the genre along with the society it depicts. (150)

Cervantes, on the other hand, did not want to destroy anything; not even books of chivalry as a genre, if they could be reformed and made verisimilar. And yet, he was fully aware of the novelty of what he was doing. He knew he was sending out into the world, as he tells us in the Prologue to the First Part, a strange brainchild, "the story of a lean, shrivelled, whimsical child, full of varied fancies that no one else has ever imagined" (all translations those of J. M. Cohen). And what is even more significant, he knew that this new child, never imagined before, for that very reason, had to go out entirely unprotected. It could bear none of the traditional marks of introduction and identification (marks of genre, for example); marks that not only protect the traditional work by signaling its progeny and, therefore, its own identity, but also offer protection to the receiving audience, an audience easily troubled by the unfamiliar, into the midst of which the naked creature must be launched: "I would like to present it to you naked and unadorned, without the ornament of a prologue or the countless train of customary sonnets, epigrams and eulogies it is the fashion to place at the beginning of books. For I can tell you that, much toil though it cost me to compose, I found none greater than the making of this preface you are reading." We must remember also that, insofar as they have a social function, these poetic marks of introduction and identification operate in the same way as any other protective, differentiating, identifying marks in a traditional society. In such a society, as was still to a large extent the case with Spanish society at the time, everything must bear identifying marks, because everything is interconnected by a sacred bond, and therefore extremely sensitive to the threat of rampant undifferentiation (the importance of genre or poetic type, for example, tends to increase as we step back into earlier and more traditional stages of society).

So "naked," so unprotected is this "lean and shrivelled" child that not even his "father" is going to stand by his side. He is acting more like a stepfather. He denies his paternity: "It may happen that a father has an ugly and ill-favoured child, and that his love for it so blinds his eyes that he cannot see its faults, but takes them rather for talents and beauties. . . . But I, though in appearance Don Quixote's father, am really his step-father, and so will not drift with the current of custom, nor implore you, almost with tears in my eyes, as others do, dearest reader, to pardon or ignore the faults you see in this child of mine."

There is a direct connection between the lack of protecting identity marks and the state of dereliction and defenselessness in which the strange-looking creature finds himself. This creature really is an outcast. He has no place he can call home. He stands out in jarring disharmony with his environment. No wonder it was not "a quiet place, the pleasantness of the fields, the serenity of the skies, the murmuring of streams and the tranquility of the spirit" that engendered him, but "a prison [whether real or symbolic], where every discomfort has its seat and every dismal sound its habitation." What else but a prison could be the proper place of birth for an outcast?

But this creature is, of course, a double one. It is the narrative that tells the story of Don Quixote and it is Don Quixote himself. Now, a book unprotected by any of the traditional marks of introduction and identification is a book that offers no protection to its own protagonist; it leaves him exposed as an outcast and entirely at the mercy of whatever anybody wants to do to him. When Cervantes tells the reader, "you are no relation or friend of his [the book's]. Your soul is in your own body, and you have free will with the best of them . . . all of which exempts and frees you from every respect and obligation; and so you can say anything you think fit," he is also speaking in reference to Don Quixote. The book, therefore, is not only an outcast but an outcast-making mechanism as well. It produces an outcast and knows itself as an outcast-producing instrument. It does not hide its sacrificial character. That is what it means for the book to be utterly exposed, totally unprotected. Or, what amounts to the same thing, that is what it means for the book to be radically new (see Anthony Close's interesting observations on this prologue in "A Poet's Vanity," especially p. 40ff.).

In other than Cervantes's hands the story of Don Quixote could have easily become another victimizing story of a fool trying to be, pretending to be, something that he is not, a story to satisfy the victimizing proclivities of a crowd. That is exactly what Quevedo did with Pablos de Segovia in *El Buscón,* the story of a *pícaro* of low and infamous origin, who keeps trying to imitate his noble companions, be one of them, but who is mercilessly rejected, unceremoniously thrown out, every time he tries; a story fittingly full of scenes of criminals and others being exposed to public shame and humiliation, including one with clear references to Christ's Passion, when Pablos is being spat upon by a crowd of fellow students, the association probably meant to make Pablos's predicament even more laughable by contrast.

Nevertheless, we should think twice before we, in turn, expel Quevedo from the company of respectable picaresque classics. For he was not just writing another picaresque novel. He was also writing the hidden story of the picaresque novel as such; that is, he was following the inner logic of the antihero type. An antihero is only a hero in disguise. It is what a hero looks like as she becomes the object of expulsion. It is the hidden face of the hero. When the hero falls from the pedestal (as they started to do in the sixteenth century), when her heroic quality crumbles, the victimizing crowd reaches for a ready-made explanation: she was not a real hero; now we see her ridiculous true nature; how could she ever pretend to be a hero? In other words, in the eyes of the victimizing crowd the hero will undergo a rapid transformation into antihero (with appropriately identifying marks and circumstances, which are also ready-made, generic, ritual formulas) as she is chased away. A metamorphosis takes place that only reverses the direction of a much older, much more primitive, expulsion that transformed its victims into mythical gods and heroes. We could also put it this way: in good Platonic fashion, Quevedo does away with all the disguising "mourning and wailing" with which the poets have always, in one way or another, disguised their victimizing intention. He does it, so to speak, straight. I think Ife is right; Quevedo's picaresque novel is essentially an attack on the picaresque. But even this difference between *El Buscón* and the other picaresque classics, *Lazarillo* and *Guzmán de Alfarache,* is ultimately unimportant. They all do the same, whether straight or on the sly, or even with apologies, like *Guzmán.*

Cervantes also begins by sketching the basic features of a victimizing scenario. But, in a way, he catches himself in the act, becomes fully conscious of what he is doing, and reacts to it.[3] He will not turn the shattered image of the chivalric hero into a victimized antihero. Instead, the story of Don Quijote will turn out to be the story of a fool, whose foolishness is gradually revealed as an emblem or a symbol of a like foolishness existing all around him. The difference between the sacrificial uniqueness of the outcast and the rest of the people around him will decrease, until eventually the strange creature who left home derelict and unprotected, bearing the negative marks of the victim, comes home in every sense of the word. Everything was ready for the sacrifice of the victim by the crowd, but neither the victim nor the crowd were sacrificed by Cervantes.

This nonsacrificial attitude may give us the most revealing clue to Cervantes's lasting admiration for Heliodorus's *Aethiopian Story.* For Cervantes's poetic debt to the Hellenistic author is very substantial. It is not only in the *Persiles,* the book in which Cervantes "dares to compete with Heliodorus," the book for which he would have liked to be remembered; it is also present in the *Novelas ejemplares,* and even in the *Quijote.*

Heliodorus's story could suggest to Cervantes much more than the commonplace idea that virtue triumphs over adversity. Even things that might not look particularly admirable to us today, could be extremely suggestive to Cervantes: for example, that the fate of the protagonists, the chaste lovers Theagenes and Chariclea, is explicitly governed at all times by some kind of divine power (whose identity, however, is never clear), who is ready to rescue them time and again from the very edge of deadly misfortune; especially because all of these misfortunes are but a prelude to the final one, when they are both captured and destined to become human sacrifices. To make it even more admirable in the eyes of a Christian writer, the final rescue and recognition that will turn them from sacrificial victims to legitimate heirs of a kingdom, is accompanied by a priestly declaration that human sacrifice is not pleasing to the gods:

> [And] now, to consummate their beneficence and, as it were, bring the drama to a joyous climax, [the gods] have produced this foreign youth [i.e., Theagenes] as the betrothed of the maiden [Chariclea] . . . ; come, let us recognize the divine miracle that has been wrought, and become collaborators in the gods' design. Let us proceed to the holier oblations, and exclude human sacrifice for all time. (in Heiserman, 199)

3. See my *Mímesis conflictiva,* chapter 1, "Cervantes frente a Don Quijote: violenta simetría entre la realidad y la ficción."

In a sense, it could be said that the *Persiles* begins by picking up the sacrificial theme at the end of the *Aethiopica*. It begins in a primitive dungeon where human victims are kept to be sacrificed to a deity. From there, the symbolic itinerary of the two chaste lovers will proceed to its final destination, Rome.

This is not the place to engage in what would have to be a lengthy comparative analysis of the two works. The analysis would surely reveal striking differences, the most important of which would be that in Cervantes the road to salvation is fundamentally an inner road; the external obstacles that the lovers have to overcome are also symbols of the inner ones, obstacles of their own making that threaten their desired union and put their own relationship in jeopardy. The road to Rome is also a difficult road from one lover to the other.

Nothing of the sort exists in Heliodorus's novel. As the French critical editor and translator of *Les Ethiopiques* noticed, "psychologically speaking, [the characters] do not present any interest" (Heliodorus, xxii). Heliodorus's novel is constantly alluding to the role of the characters as toys in the hands of some god who takes pleasure in playing with them. On their part, the best they can do is just play along and hope for the best. As Chariclea said on one occasion, "let us feast the demon who pursues us, as is proper. Let us offer him the song of our lamentations and the pantomime of our sorrow" (VI. 3, p. 97).

What I emphasize here is Cervantes's demonstrated preference for what may be described as the *providential rescue* model or pattern (an almost unthinkable preference in Quevedo). A providential rescue may look sometimes like an arbitrary, deus ex machina, solution (as in the accumulation of providential coincidences in Juan Palomeque's inn in the *Quijote*) until one realizes what the persons involved are ultimately being rescued from. For at the bottom of a bewildering network of ambiguous human relationships, Cervantes discovers a "primeval confusion" *(confusión primera)* from which, he clearly believed, humanity had been rescued by Christ. In contrast to Quevedo's unabashed preference for the victimizing pattern in his novel, Cervantes does not establish fixed, unalterable, distinctions between good and bad guys; on the contrary, he seems intent on demonstrating that the primeval confusion can and does happen to everybody, even to the best, such as Periandro and Auristela in the *Persiles*. This is why the "providential rescue" becomes absolutely necessary, as I will explain further in Chapter 4.

Because we have paid special attention to the theater in this chapter, I would like to offer further illustration of what I am saying with an example from Calderón's famous *La vida es sueño* (Life is a dream). Because the "providential rescue" is the Cervantine equivalent of Calderón's "acudamos a lo eterno" (let us [therefore] appeal to the eternal). In Calderón there are no fixed boundaries between the good guys and the bad either.[4]

The following passage has a certain emblematic quality. It puts the entire complex relationship between Calderón and his own theater in a nutshell. The words, an aside addressed to the spectators, are spoken by Clarín, the *gracioso* or jester, who—as I have written elsewhere ("La muerte")—is the very symbol of the stage.

> A costa de cuatro palos
> que el llegar aquí me cuesta
> . . . .
> tengo de ver cuanto pasa;
> que no hay ventana más cierta
> que aquélla que, sin rogar
> a un ministro de boletas,
> un hombre se trae consigo;
> pues para todas las fiestas,
> despojado y despejado
> se asoma a su desvergüenza.
> (lines 1166–77)

(Four whacks I had to take to get inside here, but I have to see what's going on; for there is no window on the stage offering a better view than that which, without pleading with a ticket seller, a man brings along with himself; for at all spectacles, naked and in the open he is looking at his own shamelessness.)

This passage is much more than another version of the old Horatian device, *de te fabula narratur* (the story is about you). The act itself of looking on the spectacle exposes the prying spectator. It reveals his nakedness, his shame. The window through which he sees is the window through which he is seen. As he focuses on the stage the stage focuses on him.

4. Calderón was also attracted to the *Aethiopica*, which he adapted to the stage in *Historia de los amantes Teágenes y Cariclea*. Unfortunately, it is not one of his best plays.

Clearly there is nothing innocent or neutral about the stage spectacle, or in more general terms, the feast ("todas las fiestas"), just as there are no innocent onlookers. Calderón is not thinking of the stage or the feast as mere entertainment. If a man brings within himself a "window" on the feast everytime he goes to one, then the feast belongs to him organically. This does not define him exactly as *homo ludens*. In Calderón's eyes, he is above all a spectator, and more precisely, like Clarín, the jester, a curious Peeping Tom.

But all of this does not tell us yet why such an original or essential curiosity is something shameful. It only tells us that the spectacle does not exist by accident but is required and constituted by man's essential curiosity, his spectatorlike nature; an observation that may simply confirm Aristotle's unproblematic definition of human nature as mimetic. What does Calderón see in the spectator qua spectator? Clarín has the answer, for Calderón makes him the spokesman for the human spectator. He is the prototypical one, the one every human being brings inside herself, the one whose face shows up at the human window through which the spectacle is watched.

Therefore, who is Clarín? At one point, shortly after violent Segismundo wakes up in the palace after taking the narcotic in the tower, he turns toward Clarín and asks, "who are you? In this strange world, you are the only one who pleases me." To which Clarín responds: "Sir, I am a great pleaser of all Segismundos." He is nobody in particular, because he can be anything that anybody wants him to be as long as it is necessary to keep himself just barely alive and breathing. Morally empty, without a shred of dignity, he is a nonentity. He can pretend to be anything or anybody. He is pretense incarnate, so to speak, pure spectacle. He is what man sees through the hidden window, which he brings along with himself to all feasts.

But of all the angles from which Clarín's personality, or lack of it, can be observed, one is of special significance to Calderón: Clarín is above all the prototypical evader of responsibility. If he can help it, at whatever the cost, he will not face up to anything or ever put himself at risk. This is why the death of Clarín by a stray bullet, as he tries to hide from a civil war that makes the kingdom "swim in scarlet waves" of blood, is so important for a proper understanding of the play. In fact, of all the dramatis personae involved in the horrendous civil war, Clarín is the only one to die; his death is the only one that Calderón cares to describe. And it is at the moment of death that he tells the truth:

Soy un hombre desdichado,
que por quererme guardar
de la muerte, la busqué.
Huyendo della, topé
con ella, pues no hay lugar
para la muerte secreto;
de donde claro se arguye
que quien más su efeto huye,
es quien se llega a su efeto.

(lines 3075–82)

(I am an unlucky man. Trying to hide from death, I was, in fact, looking for it; fleeing it I run into it. There is no secret place for death. From this you clearly may conclude that he who runs from it the most, is the one who finds it quickest.)

This is really unprecedented. Heroes are supposed to die, not jesters. To kill the jester is to steal the show from the hero, to pull the rug from under his feet. When the hero dies the show reaches its appointed, its "natural," conclusion. It fulfills itself. To kill the jester, on the other hand, is to kill the show, to frustrate its fulfillment, to cry out, Enough! The show's over!

The death of the hero confirms him as hero. The death of the jester is just death. It reveals the deadness of death hidden behind the tragic glory of the hero, and thus exposes this tragic glory as a cover-up, a spectacular decoy, a form of fleeing from the sight of death. But "there is no secret place for death," as the dying Clarín says. It is the spectacle itself who speaks. And it says even more: not only will it not protect you from death, but in fact you will hasten it, you will be the direct agent of its coming and make your worst fears come true, precisely by looking for such an illusory protection.

This last statement, however, deserves further comment. Why will I be the direct agent of my own tragic fate precisely by trying to run away from it? Are we back in some kind of Oedipal situation where one simply cannot fight or trick one's appointed, oracular destiny? Not at all. In Calderón's world there is nobody on Olympus spinning the wheel of destiny for any individual. The secret, once more, is in Clarín, for he is, paradigmatically, the one who runs from death. But we have to make a distinction. It is one thing to see this ridiculously undignified, amoral, infinitely pliable nonentity out there, on the stage—that is to say, as a figure of fiction—and quite another to experience the hidden Clarín inside every human being. All of a sudden the laughable emptiness becomes a terrifying void from which the individual tries to flee in panic, a secret voice telling him he is worthless—which is why the Calderonian character, like King Basilio, always "da crédito al daño," always believes a prediction if it is bad for him, because he cannot avoid feeling that he deserves it.

However, the real problem is that this panicky, Clarín-like individual, incapable of accepting responsibility, is totally dependent on somebody else. He always lives at the feet of an other on whom he shifts responsibility for everything. Only the other can grant him honor, by accepting the show of dignity with which the individual hides the inner void from his own eyes; and only the death of the other will cover the void or silence its voice whenever the individual is faced with it (which will happen every time he is tested or challenged in any way). He will kill the other because he is totally incapable of doubting the other as a witness to his own inner shame.

When the protagonist, Segismundo, "a man among beasts and a beast among men," is first surprised in his helpless condition in the tower by the intruding Rosaura (who appears disguised as a man), his immediate reaction is to move to strangle the intruder:

> Pues la muerte te daré
> porque no sepas que sé
> que sabes flaquezas mías.
> (180–83)[5]

5. Almost immediately, as soon as Rosaura throws herself at his feet in complete surrender, Segismundo changes radically and becomes fascinated by that human being, that other, whom he encounters for the first time:

> Con cada vez que te veo
> nueva admiración me das,
> y cuando te miro más,
> aún más mirarte deseo.
> Ojos hidrópicos creo
> que mis ojos deben ser,
> pues cuando es muerte el beber
> beben más, y desta suerte,
> viendo que el ver me da muerte
> estoy muriendo por ver.
> (lines 223–32)

(I will kill you, that you may not know that I know that you know my weakness)

Alone, Segismundo can hide the truth from himself (or rebel against it, which can be a form of closing one's eyes to the truth). Even if the other knows the truth, conceivably he could still pretend to be unaware of the other's knowledge. But if he knows that the other knows that he is pretending, then he will no longer be able to hide the truth from himself under the gaze of the other and will either have to face the shameful truth or kill the other.[6] Therefore, what is really at stake here is not so much the possibility of knowing the truth, but rather the possibility of hiding it, or better still, of pretending that it is not there, of putting on a show, first of all, for one's own benefit. If only everybody cooperated! If only they were all convinced that it was for real!

This is a world of pure intersubjective immanence. Unable to face the truth that the interconnectedness of everybody inevitably reveals, this world can only survive by putting on a big show *(totus mundus agit histrionem)*. It maintains a semblance of order, by fabricating its own transcendance, by paying homage to its own disguising, decoying idols. But, as we have just seen, these idols can only be maintained on their pedestals, by constantly sacrificing victims—intruders upon the truth—to them.

This is the show that Calderón sees through the shameless window that every human being brings with himself to the show. This is Clarín's show, rooted in fear and evasion, and erected by a victimizing shifting of responsibility. This is also the show that would collapse like a house of cards if Clarín—literally, the Clarion—were to sound, were to reveal his secret—which is the explicit reason given in the text to lock him up in the same tower with victimized-victimizing Segismundo:

CLARÍN: ¿Por qué a mí?

(Each time I look at you my admiration increases, and the more I look the more I yearn to look. My eyes must have the dropsy, to go on drinking more and more when drinking means death, in such a way that seeing that vision is fatal, I'm dying to see more.)

6. An excellent logician, Jean-Pierre Dupuy, has pointed out to me that in situations of this kind it is logically possible to keep on pretending ad infinitum. If this is so, it can only prove that existentially things are not always or necessarily governed by pure rational logic. It is simply inconceivable that the Calderonian subject we are discussing could withstand the knowing, perhaps ironic, look on the other's face for long.

CLOTALDO: Porque ha de estar
                    guardado en prisión tan grave,
                    Clarín que secretos sabe,
                    donde no pueda sonar.
                                        (lines 2033–37)

(Why me? Because a Clarion who knows secrets, must be kept in heavy prison, where he cannot sound.)

Of course, if the existential show that Calderón sees behind the theatrical show, were to collapse, the theatrical show itself would also collapse. Clarín's secret works at both levels. The theatrical show as such is only an expression and an extension of the idolatrous victimizing show behind. The spectator at the theater house comes to pay homage to the same idols that sustain the semblance of order that allows the theater house to exist.

One of the Renaissance moralists quoted earlier was in turn quoting Saint Cyprian on the theater: *Quod spectaculum sine idolo?* (What spectacle can exist without idols?) Calderón's *La vida es sueño* can be seen as a long meditation and an answer to that rhetorical question.

Finally, we should also consider the following: when Renaissance moralists said that their theater was idolatrous in spirit, they meant it not only in a moral but also in a historical sense. They saw in the theater the spirit of the pre-Christian, pagan past. Does Calderón have a similar historical awareness when he meditates on the idolatrous existential problematic we have just seen in reference to *La vida es sueño?* I believe he does.

His awareness has to do with the role that rational scientific knowledge (which included, not only the natural and physical sciences but all the liberal arts as well, such as the art of government) can or cannot have in a given state of social, interpersonal relations. From the point of view of rational scientific development the existential world of pure immanent relations, is a very primitive one, because in such a world scientific knowledge is useless. What an individual does or does not do is entirely governed by the experience of his relationship with other individuals and not by any objective standard of truth transcending this relationship. To put it in the words of Rosaura in one of her moments of doubt, regarding her relationship with Astolfo:

¿Qué haré? Mas ¿para qué estudio
lo que haré, si es evidente
que por más que lo prevenga,
que lo estudie y que lo piense,
en llegando la ocasión
he de hacer lo que quisiere
el dolor?, porque ninguno
imperio en sus penas tiene.

(lines 1868–75)

(What shall I do? But what's the use of planning what to do when it is obvious that, no matter how much I look ahead and study it and think about it, when the time comes, I will do as my sorrow dictates, because no one has power over his grief.)

In such a world, consulted for a prediction, scientific rationality can only anticipate in a scientific way its own breakdown, in other words, disaster. Which is precisely what it does when King Basilio, universally acclaimed for his scientific knowledge, consults the stars with his "matemáticas sutiles" for a scientific reading of his son Segismundo's horoscope. In such a world, every objective sign, in the sky and on the earth, is an ominous one, as Basilio's counselor, Clotaldo, remarks, "en tan confuso abismo, / es todo el cielo un presagio / y es todo el mundo un prodigio" (lines 983–85).

This world of radical intersubjectivity, where everything is taken ad hominem, where rational, objective transcendance is not yet possible, being governed instead by a fictitious transcendance, a simulacrum posing as knowledge, is a world explicitly described as barbarous or primitive by Calderón in another important drama, *La estatua de Prometeo* (Prometheus's statue): Prometheus, a knowledge-loving man born among the primitive and violent Caucasians, guided by "la lógica natural" infused in the soul, goes out in search of knowledge among the learned Syrians. He returns to his people desiring to give them "preceptos de político gobierno," because he is hurt by

la ruda
barbaridad que os mantiene
sin leyes que os constituyan
racionales.

(*Obras Completas*, 1:2084)

(the rude barbarism that keeps you without laws that would make
you fully rational.)

They are not ready for it. Misinterpreting his intentions as an attempt
to set himself as a tyrant over them, they rebel violently. Prometheus
then withdraws into a cave and fashions a beautiful statue, an image
of Minerva, the goddess of wisdom, which he presents to the violent
Caucasians with these words:

> Llegad, pues, llegad, vereis
> su efigie; y pues mi cordura
> ya no os da leyes, sino
> simulacros, substituyan
> a políticos consejos
> sagrados ritos.
> (*Obras Completas*, 2085)

(Come, then, come. You will see her effigy. And since my judi-
ciousness no longer gives you rational laws, but simulacra, let political counsel be replaced by sacred rites.)

We have the germ of an anthropological theory of culture here. "Sacred rites" or more precisely, the worship of simulacra, idols, effigies—
which are worshiped not as symbols, but as having a reality of their own
(in the drama, intense desire gives life to the statue, and this, in turn,
brings havoc to the Caucasians)—is not something merely fanciful or
arbitrary. Rather, it corresponds to a state of sociability, of human interconnectedness, characterized by intense, violent desires and suspicions.
Idol worship brings a semblance of order, no matter how precarious, to
that kind of society. It is a beginning. Prometheus's fire is, after all, a gift
from heaven. But it is the kind of gift that, in the beginning, looks more
like a disaster. To put it in the terms of the drama itself, when Minerva's
statue comes alive she is also known by the name of Pandora.

This anthropological background, to which Calderón gave dramatic
expression in *La estatua de Prometeo,* must be kept in mind when we
encounter the kind of existential state of intersubjectivity found in *La
vida es sueño* and other Calderonian dramas. This is the background
that gives the human problematic of Calderón's most famous work a
historical dimension. In Calderón, lack of transcendance, intersubjective

victimizing violence, idolatry, and primitive or uncivilized status are intimately related notions.

All of this is what lies behind the theatrical simulacra and can be seen through the "window which a man brings along with himself; for at all spectacles, naked and in the open he is looking on his own shamelessness"—both present and past, we may add now.

Therefore, it can be said that Calderón's view of the theater is no more flattering than the one held by those stern moralists, heirs to Plato's legacy, who saw the theater as the sacred gone wrong, and wanted to eliminate it altogether. But there is a difference: they were scandalized by what they saw and Calderón was not. In other words, they were still looking at the theater and reacting to it in a sacrificial way; they saw the sacrificial character of the theater and reacted to it in like manner. Calderón, on the other hand, while seeing the sacrificial character of the theater just as clearly, was not overpowered by it, drawn into its victimizing, expelling orbit. And this capacity to withstand the victimizing sacred gave him an extraordinary opportunity to see through it.

But, as said previously, not only the possibility of a view like that of Calderón, but the antitheatrical moralist's reaction as well, should be seen as a result of the historical weakening of the sacred. This weakening can either trigger the defensive scandalized reaction of the moralist—a recrudescence of the old—or become an unprecedented opportunity (or indeed, in the concrete experience of any individual, any combination thereof). Calderón's theater (and by extension the modern popular theater that begins in the fourth quarter of the sixteenth century) is a weakened sacrificial form that reflects upon itself. That is to say, weak enough sacrificially to be able to see the arbitrary character of its own sacrificiality.

Everything is a result of the desacralizing power of the Christian text, which afforded the Renaissance poet a nonsacrificial and, therefore, nonfictionalizable perspective. It was this perspective that allowed the new poet to explore the connection between his own poetic fiction and the sacrificial mechanism that lay at the root of human culture. Ironically, this fiction-proof perspective was far more forgiving and hospitable to poets than Plato. It did not require their expulsion from the city.

2

BEYOND ARISTOTLE

1. The Questionable Influence of Aristotle's *Poetics*

> Until some rational answer to the objections urged against poetry
> in antiquity and in the Middle Ages was forthcoming, literary
> criticism in any true sense was fundamentally impossible; and that
> answer came only with the discovery of Aristotle's *Poetics*. . . . It
> was in Aristotle's *Poetics* that the Renaissance was to find, if not
> a complete, at least a rational justification of poetry, and an an-
> swer to every one of the Platonic and medieval objections to
> imaginative literature. (Spingarn, 15 and 18)

Spingarn's opinion typifies the nineteenth-century Romantic myth concerning what happened with poetry during the Renaissance. Put in a nutshell, it is something like this: for the most part poetry lay in shackles
throughout the Middle Ages, "disregarded or contemned, or . . . valued

if at all for virtues that least belong to it [i.e., 'as the handmaid of philosophy, and most of all as the vassal of theology']. The Renaissance was thus confronted with the necessity of justifying its appreciation of the vast body of literature which the Revival of learning had recovered for the modern world; and the function of Renaissance criticism was to reëstablish the aesthetic foundation of literature, to reaffirm the eternal lesson of Hellenic culture, and to restore once and for all the element of beauty to its rightful place in human life and in the world of art" (3–4).

In this restoration and reaffirmation, according to Spingarn and countless others after him, Aristotle's *Poetics* played a central role, by providing the first modern critics with the basic arguments in the rational defense of poetry. These Romantic admirers of the *Poetics* never stopped to consider the historical irony of the situation, as they saw it: Aristotle, the inspiration, the venerated authority figure of medieval Scholasticism, now becoming the rallying banner of the anti-Scholastic, antimedieval modern spirit! It is not my intention to enter into a detailed analysis of this Romantic myth and its internal contradictions. But we must dispel the idea that the fundamental concerns of Renaissance theoreticians coincided with those of Aristotle in the *Poetics*. I intend to show that this is not so.

To begin with, let me state the obvious: Aristotle's *Poetics* is not an answer "to every one of the Platonic and medieval objections to imaginative literature." In fact, it is not an answer to any of them. It is simply not intended to answer those objections, at least not directly. After expelling the poets from the ideal republic, Socrates remarks to Glaucon:

> Notwithstanding this, let us assure our sweet friend and the sister arts of imitation that if she will prove her title to exist in a well-ordered State we shall be delighted to receive her—we are very conscious of her charms; but we may not on that account betray the truth. I dare say, Glaucon, that you are as much charmed by her as I am, especially when she appears in Homer?
>
> Yes, indeed, I am greatly charmed.
>
> Shall I propose then that she be allowed to return from exile, but

upon this condition only—that she make a defense of herself in lyrical or some other meter?

Certainly.

And we may further grant to those of her defenders who are lovers of poetry and yet not poets the permission to speak in prose on her behalf: let them show not only that she is pleasant but also useful to States and to human life, and we will listen in a kindly spirit . . . but so long as she is unable to make good her defense, this argument of ours shall be a charm to us, which we will repeat to ourselves as we listen to her strains; that we may not fall away into the childish love of her which captivates the many. (*Republic*, X, 607c–d)

Aristotle did not provide such a defense. It is even doubtful that Socrates would have recognized anywhere in the *Poetics* the charming creature of which he was afraid. The poetry that was expelled from the ideal republic did not return with Aristotle. Aristotle's little treatise is a purely technical and analytical description that does not touch Plato's troubled concern.

The two Aristotelian pillars that Spingarn saw as the foundation of the Renaissance justification of poetry and the basis for the development of modern critical theory, are (1) the famous statement about poetry being more universal than history; and (2) the equally famous catharsis, which Spingarn simply understands as the capacity of poetry to purge the passions. The first statement reads as follows in the *Poetics:*

It is not the business of the poet to tell what has happened, but what might happen and what is possible according to probability or necessity. . . . Hence poetry is more philosophical and more serious than history, for poetry deals more with things in a universal way, but history with each thing for itself. To deal with them universally is to say that according to probability or necessity it happens that a certain sort of man does or says certain things, and poetry aims at this, when it gives names to the characters. (51a36)

This is not the place or the occasion to expand on what Aristotle means by "universal" or "universally." But I believe it is perfectly clear that such meaning has nothing to do with the Romantic conception of universality.

To read Aristotle's words in the context of nineteenth-century philosophical idealism will only distort them beyond recognition. He is not referring to any metaphysical and transcendental level of reality. It is a purely logical matter, a question of probability and/or logical necessity. And that is precisely how it was generally understood in the Renaissance. In Castelvetro, for example: "[The] term [universal] designates an incident known in summary form which may be said to possess the property of universality in so far as it may occur to many persons. . . . Aristotle . . . clearly intends it to be taken in exactly the same sense as 'the possible' and 'what may happen,' all three of which terms designate the thing that constitutes the subject matter of poetry" (94). In Trissino it is even clearer that "universal" simply means comprehensive, or even schematic, for it is said of the general outline of a plot: "It is necessary, therefore, for the poet to extend his words universally and then to insert the episodes therein. And to extend the words universally is nothing other than to write down the action that he wants to imitate as a whole, as it has been done in the *Sofonisba;* the action of which is that, there being a war between two republics, one of them made a pact with a king, and the other, in order to take that king [from its rival], gave him as wife the daughter of one of its captains, thereby taking him away. Later, those two republics, fighting together . . . [etc.](Weinberg, *Trattati,* 1:31)." I do not think these statements need any further comment.

The second theoretical pillar, the one about the famous catharsis, has been so little understood either in the Renaissance or ever since that it could not have served as a foundation for anything. Allan H. Gilbert translates the passage as follows: "Tragedy, then, is an imitation of an action that is serious and complete and has sufficient size, in language that is made sweet . . . presented by those who act and not by narrative, exciting pity and fear [*], bringing about the catharsis of such emotions. By language made sweet I mean language having rhythm and harmony and melody" (49b20). In a footnote Gilbert explains:

> Almost universally no comma is put at this point [i.e., at the point indicated by the asterisk] and the translation is substantially that of Butcher: "through pity and fear affecting the proper purgation of these emotions." The notion that pity and fear expel themselves seems to me unattractive . . . as it did to Vincentius Madius, *In Aristotelis librum de poetica* [Venice, 1550, p. 98]. At any rate there is so little agreement about the meaning of the passage as to

make the translation almost a matter of indifference. Fontanelle
wrote: "I never have understood the purgation of the passions by
means of the passions themselves." (*Réflexions sur la poétique* . . .
[Paris, 1766], 3:170–71)

This lack of agreement, however, does not mean that Renaissance
theoreticians paid little attention to Aristotle's treatise. On the contrary,
it aroused enormous interest, especially after Robortelli published his
critical edition in 1548, accompanied with a Latin translation and commentary. But it was not Aristotle who triggered the intense theoretical
interest in poetry in the sixteenth century. It was rather the other way
around. It was that intense interest, motivated by reasons that had nothing to do with Aristotle, that granted the *Poetics* an importance it had
never had. It seems that the treatise fell on deaf ears in antiquity and, for
the most part, in the Middle Ages as well. There are no clear references
to it in Cicero, Horace, or Quintilian, for example. In the words of Baxter
Hathaway, "one of the puzzling questions of all time has been why more
was not made of Aristotle's *Poetics* in classical times" (6). This question
becomes even more intriguing when this classical silence is compared
with the wide interest it stirred in sixteenth-century Italy: "If discovery
implies use, the sixteenth century Italians can be said to have invented
Aristotle's *Poetics*" (6).

But in terms of rational, convincing answers to the problems that poetry had always raised, the "discovery" of the *Poetics* was rather disap-
pointing. Nothing can be more instructive than to compare the efforts of
sixteenth-century theoreticians with what we find in Aristotle's book.
Those theoretical efforts were carried out in a spirit very different from
that of Aristotle. They are frequently motivated by a genuine, desacralized, spirit of inquiry, a struggling to find a scientific way to deal with
something extremely elusive and ambiguous. To the best of them Aristotle was just an excuse to engage in a fascinating theoretical investigation.

In reading the *Poetics*, on the other hand, one gets the distinct impression that there is nothing problematic about its subject. It is all matter-
of-fact description and classification. The "natural forms" of things are
just there, perfectly intelligible and accessible to the rational logic of the
observant philosopher. In reading the *Poetics* one wonders why Plato
was so apprehensive and so suspicious about poetry. In contrast with
that, the Renaissance theoretician found problems at every turn: imita-

tion, verisimilitude, selection of subject matter, the proper ends of poetry, the famous catharsis, and so many others.

Although not referring to the science of poetics in particular, the following passage by Bacon clearly illustrates this fundamental change in attitude from Aristotle to the Renaissance: "[In] my opinion both Empedocles and Democritus, who complain, the first madly enough, but the second very soberly, that all things are hidden away from us, that we know nothing . . . that truth is drowned in deep wells, that the true and the false are strangely joined and twisted together . . . are more to be approved than the school of Aristotle so confident and dogmatical" (*Essays*, 272). This passage is significant, not so much for what it reveals about pre-Socratic philosophy, but for what it reveals about the new spirit of inquiry.

The difference between the two attitudes stems, I believe, from their being rooted in two different ways of understanding what science or scientific inquiry is and what it is about. The extraordinary theoretical interest in the science of poetics during the sixteenth and seventeenth centuries cannot be separated from the new and developing spirit of scientific inquiry that gradually spread over the Western world. And this in spite of the fact that many of the formal arguments used, debated, and analyzed by those poetic theoreticians were anything but original. Most of them were taken from classical sources or even from Thomas Aquinas. The interest lay, not so much in the formal arguments and propositions themselves, but in the debates and the analyses. I maintain that that spirit of uninhibited scientific inquiry, which grew stronger in spite of occasional external hurdles, was inseparable from the process of desacralization of which we have been speaking.

Aristotle's science was something else entirely. As has been pointed out by historians of science, his rational naturalism was not an instrument of discovery or exploration of the world in a modern sense. In J. Mittelstrass's words Aristotle's concept of "empirical knowledge . . . has as its goal a stabilisation of everyday experience," which is why "in Aristotelian physics . . . propositions of everyday experience and propositions of physics never contradict each other." "*Phenomena* in Aristotle are not only (indeed, are seldom) empirical data, i.e. observed facts, but are also *endoxa* (common opinions on the subject) and *legomena* (a conceptual structure revealed by language)" (42–43).

It is also significant to note that, while empirical irregularities—observed phenomena that contradicted accepted theory—were taken into account in astronomy, and auxiliary theories devised "to save the appearances," nothing of the sort was admitted in Aristotelian physics; that is to say, closer to home, in the immediate human environment as perceived by empirical observation and/or received opinion. "According to the Aristotelian concept of experience, there are no irregularities, at least not 'under the moon'" (Bolgar, 50). Aristotle was not looking for trouble.

Aristotelian science is concerned above all with its internal logical coherence. Anything that appears to defy logic, to destabilize natural coherence, is simply left out. Louis Bourgey writes:

> Son idéal scientifique, herité de Platon, visait à atteindre les causes et les raisons. . . . Que la cause soit ou non ateinte directement à travers l'expérience sensible, la science demeure par nature toujours déductive, c'est une manière d'être demonstrative . . . son procédé propre est le syllogisme. A partir des principes nécessaires qu'appréhende la pensée intuitive, le *nous,* la conclusion est établie de maniére inéluctable excluant toute possibilité de réfutation. (101)

> (His scientific ideal, inherited from Plato, aimed at reaching causes and reasons. . . . Whether or not the cause was reached directly through sense experience, science remains by nature always deductive, it is a demonstrative way of being . . . its proper procedure is the syllogism. Beginning from necessary principles apprehended by intuitive thought, the *nous,* the conclusion is established inevitably, excluding all possibility of refutation.)

This is not science driven by a desire to explore the wonders of the universe, the order of creation, or the will of God written on the book of nature, as it will be much later. And it is certainly not the kind of science that was beginning to develop in the sixteenth century, an essentially risk-taking science. "Modern science differs from ancient science in its emphasis upon experimental testing. Instead of simply classifying phenomena as they exist in their 'natural' state, modern science creates new situations and circumstances in which the phenomena's new reactions may be studied" (Barnhart, 18).[1]

---

1. Galileo expresses the new notion of experiment, "in the sense of 'testing nature'" (Schmitt, 115), with the word *periculum.*

John Milbank has observed in Aristotle "a relative archaism as compared with Plato . . . , a reinvocation of *metis* or *phronesis,* as the ability to adapt cunningly to circumstances and to retain the upperhand . . . a self-government that retains stability and minimizes disturbances" (352). His view of prudence "both holds back an excessive action . . . and eschews a deficient one . . . , holding to the mean of magnificence . . . , just as in the city one ostracizes the excessively strong, and expels as a scapegoat *(pharmakos)* the excessively weak" (361).

Hans Blumenberg has also made a similar observation regarding Greek thought in general: "The light in which the landscape and things that surrounded the life of the Greeks stood gave to everything . . . clarity and unquestionable presence. . . . Internal homogeneity and external intensity of light allow the soul *and* its objects to belong to *one* world, in whose all-around appropriateness there cannot be such things as the too small and the too large, the hidden and the withheld, and in which existential fulfillment is guaranteed if what is planned to go together does come together" (243). Or, put somewhat differently, "the function of the idea of the cosmos is reassurance about the world and in the world" (140).

Aristotle is much closer to Epicurus's view of scientific knowledge than to any modern conception of science. And this is what Epicurus said in his letter to Pythocles: "We must assume [or know] that no other end is served by the study of celestial phenomena, whether considered by themselves or in some larger context, than mental composure and a sturdy self-reliance, just as in the case of the other disciplines. . . . [For] we have no use now for [vain opinions] and meaningless gueswork [but] to live the unperturbed life" (85–87; Epicurus, 158). In his doctoral dissertation on Democritus and Epicurus, Karl Marx had already seen this "therapeutic" function of science quite clearly: "What is abstractly possible, what can be conceived, constitutes for the thinking subject neither an obstacle nor a limit nor a stumbling block. Whether this possibility is also real is a matter of indifference, because we are not here interested in the object as object. Consequently Epicurus proceeded with a boundless nonchalance in explaining individual physical phenomena. . . . One can see that he is not at all interested in investigating the real causes of objects. He is merely interested in soothing the explaining subject" (quoted in Blumenberg, 158).

It is no surprise to hear how closely the foundation of Epicurus's system resembles that of Aristotle. In the words of F. M. Cornford: "We started from Epicurus' system to examine the common belief that this final expression of Ionian natural philosophy was pre-eminently scientific. We found out that it was not in fact anything of the kind, but a dogmatic structure based on *a priori* premises" (159)—which is exactly what we have heard about Aristotle.

2. The Old Science
and the "Howls of Hungry Acheron"

Reference to Epicurus is especially appropriate because in him we can clearly understand the kind of trouble that drove the philosopher to search for peace in science. Lucretius, Epicurus's admiring follower, will tell us about two hundred years after the philosopher's death, that his revered predecessor was the first to rise above the flaming ramparts of the world to step on the head of hideous *religio,* at a time "when human life lay for all to see upon the ground, crushed under the heavy weight of *religio,* which displayed her head from the regions of heaven, lowering over mortals with horrible aspect" (*De rerum natura,* I, 62–65). This religion is terror-filled, capable of generating such "murderous and impious deeds" as the sacrifice of Iphigenia (I, 83).

This hideous *religio* is why Epicurus wanted to keep the gods far away from the world of mortals, living in perfectly untroubled bliss, free from "weakness and fear and dependence on neighbours." To think of the gods otherwise "would contradict our notions of divine happiness and 'cause the greatest disturbance in our souls.' The last words [reveal] the fundamental objection" (Cornford, 20).

But Lucretius was wrong. Epicurus was by no means the first. Let us recall the words of Plato in the *Republic* about the need "to reject all the terrible and apalling names [with] which [the poets] describe the world below—Cocytus and Styx, ghosts under the earth, and sapless shades, and any similar words of which the very mention causes a shudder to pass through the inmost soul of him who hears them." Perhaps we should remind ourselves that the history of the sacred is to a large extent the history of the expulsion of the sacred, which is ultimately the sacred expulsion of the sacred victim, philosophically duplicated in the hiding of the victimary expulsion itself, as we have seen in Plato. Plato's philosophical project is a Herculean effort to place the sacred at a safe distance from the city, from the world of change, which is taken to be nothing but a world of fleeting shadows.

Only at such a distance could the old sacred shine in its good and only good brightness, indirectly revealing the world below as a dream. This is the quasi-mystical Plato of certain passages in the *Republic,* the *Phaedrus,* the *Symposium,* etc. But when we approach the sacrificial altar here below, as we do in the *Laws,* we are back amid the oldest fears of mankind: the sacred fears of the sacred; we are back in a world of taboos, where the sacred is also the untouchable, a frightening source of pollution.

Plato is the father of all such philosophical efforts. They are all in different ways attempts to "stabilise everyday experience," urgent appeals for a rational explanation, originating in a soul troubled by the "terror, the inexorable fate and the howls of hungry Acheron," as Virgil would say, almost paraphrasing his admired Lucretius:

> Felix, qui potuit rerum cognoscere causas,
> atque metus omnis et inexorabile fatum
> subiecit pedibus strepitumque Acherontis avari
> (*Georgics,* II, 490–92)

> (Blessed is he who has been able to win knowledge of the causes of things, and has cast beneath his feet all fear and unyielding fate, and the howls of hungry Acheron!)

Against this background we can easily understand an idea not uncommon in classical antiquity: rational thinking is akin to ritual practices, even those of an orgiastic character. Jeanmaire quotes the interesting testimony of Aristides Quintilian (2d century B.C.) in his *Dionysos: Histoire du Culte de Bacchus:* "C'est pourquoi, dit-on, les pratiques bacchiques et autres du même genre ont quelque chose à voir avec la raison, en ce qu'elles purgent (par *catharsis*) chez les personnes incultes l'angoise devant les traverses de la vie et de la fortune graces aux mélodies, aux danses et au jeu . . . qu'elles comportent" (321). (This is why it is said that Bacchic practices and others of the same kind have something in common with reason, in that they purge among the uncultivated their anguish before the obstacles of life and fortune, thanks to the melodies, the dances and the play . . . that they use.)

It is logical to assume that part of that anxiety in the face of life's unpredictable reverses included the "fear of inexorable fate and the howls of hungry Acheron." In other words, for those who have not been trained in the philosophical use of reason, sacred rituals will fulfill the same purging function—which says a lot about the cathartic function of philosophy and its intimate connection with the sacred. As Virgil writes: "fortunatus et ille, deos qui novit agrestis" (fortunate also is he who knows the rustic gods) (*Georgics*, II, 493).

Perhaps this idea may serve as the proper historical frame of reference for the following observation of F. M. Cornford in his seminal *Principium Sapientiae: The Origins of Greek Philosophic Thought:* "[The] wise man, whether called by his older title *sophistes* or by the more modest term 'lover of wisdom,' was still recognized in the fifth and fourth centuries as one of the differentiated types which had emerged from the complex prophet-poet-sage. . . . His affinities have been ignored by modern historians of philosophy whose minds have been obsessed by the nineteenth-century 'conflict of religion and science'" (107). There was a conflict, but certainly not the one imagined by the nineteenth century. As we saw in Chapter 1, philosophy wanted to do what religion had always done, only better.

Let us call this philosophical project salvation or escape through knowledge—escape, of course, from the unsettling terrors of Acheron. The ultimate aim of knowlege is always the same, peace of mind, the "stabilization of experience"; in sum, the discovery of an ideal reality, either in the stars (Plato) or in the intelligible forms of nature (Aristotle), that is stable, that is to say, clearly and reliably differentiated. This ideal reality is the deepest yearning of a sacrificial world strangled by the irreducible ambivalence of the victimary mechanism, a yearning that our blind and irresponsible Romanticism, always in search of titillating ambiguities, may never be able to understand fully.

In this conception of knowledge, to live in ignorance is not only to live in a world of changing shadows or in a dream; it is to live fundamentally exposed to a nightmare. In fact, that is how living in ignorance came to be described eventually in such texts as the Gnostic Gospels, to which we shall turn now, for they are exceptionally revealing, even retrospectively, with regard to the intellectual and existential context in which we should place the much earlier Aristotelian *Poetics.*[2]

2. The chronological gap between the fourth century B.C. and the Hellenistic period of the gnosis is not, in this case, significant. The Gnostics are the direct descendants of Plato, "qui peut

The Gospel of Truth, for example, speaks of the "terror and confusion and instability and doubt and division [and the] many illusions" experienced by those who lived in ignorance, before they woke up from their dreams into the reality of knowledge. According to the passage known to scholars as the "nightmare parable," they lived

> as if they were sunk in sleep and found themselves in disturbing dreams. Either (there is) a place to which they are fleeing, or, without strength, they come (from) having chased others, or they are involved in striking blows, or they are receiving blows themselves, or they have fallen from high places, or they take off into the air though they do not have wings. Again, sometimes (it is as) if people were murdering them, though there is no one even pursuing them, or they themselves are killing their neighbors, for they have been stained with their blood. When those who are going through all these things wake up, they see nothing, those who were in the midst of these disturbances, for they were nothing. Such is the way of those who have cast ignorance aside as sleep, leaving [its works] behind like a dream in the night. . . . This is the way everyone has acted, as though asleep at the time when he was ignorant. And this is the way he has come to knowledge, as if he had awakened. (Pagels, 125)

I do not think this passage is arbitrarily made up merely to make a point, to serve as an illustration. It is too central to the Gnostic text as well as too precise and elaborate to be the product of a random choice. I think it is meant to be a paradigmatic nightmare: the typical nightmare of those who live in ignorance, in other words, in fear, in the throes of anxiety; the type of nightmare that haunts their lives and keeps them chained to their fear. And this nightmare has a very clear "theme": the frightening symmetry of violent opposites: chasing and being chased, hitting and being hit, falling and rising, murdering and being murdered. Everything is violently imitated, reproduced, by a counteracting double.

This reproducing cannot be a random "theme." With ample anthropological backing Girard has shown how central the fear of the doubles is to the old sacred mentality. The primitive sacrificial mind is particularly

---

bien être dit le père de la philosophie religieuse hellénistique [who could well be called the father of Hellenistic religious philosophy]" (Festugière, *Le Dieu cosmique,* xii).

sensitive to phenomena of symmetry, because any such phenomenon is a reminder of the frightful, open-ended, equilibrium between enemy doubles; the violent internal equilibrium of an undifferentiating crisis that levels everything as it spreads. And it tends to spread with rising acceleration because it feeds upon itself through imitation; violence imitating, joining, violence.

The undifferentiating crisis of the doubles is the collective violence that Girard posits as the original sacrificial crisis that generates the unanimous killing of a random victim; a killing through which peace is at least temporarily restored. In other words, this is the crisis that *may* set in motion the victimizing mechanism on which the survival of the community rests (I say "may" because the crisis may also end in the complete destruction of the community). It must be in any case a horrifying violence, a hallucinating nightmare.

But my point is not to establish a perfect equivalence between the Gnostic nightmare and Girard's original sacrificial crisis. That is not necessary. I simply want to show that there are powerful indications that the nightmare is meant to have a prototypical or paradigmatic value, that it can be the typical nightmare of the primitive sacrificial mind.

What is truly revealing and what I emphasize at this point, is the function attributed to philosophical knowledge in the face of such a frightening nightmare: philosophical knowledge reveals that those fears were unfounded, that the nightmare was just that, a nightmare, a bad dream. The philosopher wakes up to realize that there really was no reason for the terror and the anxiety.[3] I fully agree that allaying of terror was the

---

3. Cf. Lucretius, once again, speaking of Epicurus:

> et genus humanum frustra plerumque probavit
> volvere curarum tristis in pectore fluctus.
> nam veluti pueri trepidant atque omnia caecis
> in tenebris metuunt, sic noc in luce timemus
> interdum nilo quae sunt metuenda magis quam
> quae pueri in tenebris pavitant finguntque futura.
> hunc igitur terrorem animi tenebrasque necessest
> non radii solis nec lucida tela diei
> discutiant, sed naturae species ratioque.
> (VI.34–41)

(and he proved that mankind had no reason for the most part to roll the sad waves of trouble within their breasts. For just as children tremble and fear all things in the blind darkness, so we in the light fear, at times, things that are no more to be feared than what children shiver at in the dark and imagine to be at hand. This terror of the mind, there-

function of philosophical knowledge. That function was already there at least from its Platonic beginning, from the moment Plato turned his eyes from the sacred victim and accused the mourning and wailing poets of blasphemy. All the Gnostic text does is to make explicit what had always been implied.

Of course, this book is grounded on the premise that there really was cause for concern, that the fear and the anxiety were fully justified, that there was a reason for the mourning and the wailing (even beyond the deceiving sacrificial reason, the "comedy of innocence"), that the victim was really victimized, etc. In other words, this book is grounded on the premise that the philosophical project was indeed a cover-up; or to be more precise, a cover-up of a previous cover-up, when this previous cover-up, woven by the poets, was wearing too thin.

To be sure, the Gnostic text does not know it is covering up anything. It simply follows the logic of the sacred expulsion of the sacred that structures all sacrificial texts. It is the rather naive product of a sacrificial mind that yearns, with a sort of mystical despair, for that liberation through wisdom which the philosophers had promised. In this sense it testifies to the failure of the philosophical project to calm the fears and silence the rumblings of Acheron. The Gnostic text shows the primitive, the mythopoetic, sacred seeping in through the widening cracks of the philosophical edifice.

It treats the crisis, the state of "Ignorance," in typically ambivalent fashion. On the one hand, it is the source of all error and illusion, on the other, even Wisdom would be powerless without it. It appears that in order for Wisdom, "the mother of all beings," to become creative, Ignorance must hide inside of it. Here is the Gnostic myth that tells us about it:

> [Valentinus] tells how the world originated when Wisdom, the mother of all beings, brought it forth out of her own suffering. The four elements that Greek philosophers said constituted the world . . . are concrete forms of her experiences:

> Thus earth arose from her confusion, water from her terror, air from the consolidation of her grief; while fire . . . was inherent in all three elements . . . as ignorance lay concealed in these three sufferings. (Pagels, 124)

---

fore, and this gloom must be dispelled, not by the sun's rays or the bright shafts of day, but by the aspect and law of nature.) (Smith trans.)

This is not a children's tale. The myth is referring to something of great importance. Indeed, had I tried to create a fictional allegory of what I have been saying about the philosophical cover-up, I could have hardly come up with a better one. "Ignorance," that is to say, the crisis, the nightmare, the terrors of Acheron, "lay concealed," hidden, covered up, inside the "Wisdom" of the philosopher. With Ignorance hiding in her bosom Wisdom suffered and, wanting to deliver herself of such suffering, she brought forth the basic elements of the world: earth, water, air, fire. In other words, she, being who she was, Wisdom, generated the world according to the philosophers. The order of the world that the Wisemen in their Wisdom discovered, owes its existence to the suffering of Wisdom, to the painful proddings of a hellish nightmare. That is what set Wisdom and, consequently, the Wisemen to work. Without terror-ridden Ignorance, who knows? Wisdom might have never appeared, philosophy might have never existed.

But the myth is a myth, because it is self-deceiving; it still hides the truth even as it reveals it. It is still playing the "comedy of innocence." Wisdom was not the innocent victim of sneaky Ignorance that the myth makes her out to be. It was not as if Ignorance secretly found her way into the bosom of unsuspecting Wisdom. It was Wisdom who covered her up and pretended that she was not there, which is why she named her Ignorance, and declared her to be nothing but a bad dream. She "created" all the elements of the world to cover up what she had named Ignorance. That is why Ignorance "lay concealed" in all these elements. The truth, therefore, is that Wisdom, the philosophers' wisdom, did not dispel ignorance. She just hid it everywhere.

From our point of view, the situation is not much different if we look at the Hermetic conception of science, which also developed during the Hellenistic period. Science itself becomes explicitly a form of religion, paying homage and adoration to its own object of study, to the divinity of the World or the Universe, that is to say, to the world as God. But in so doing, Hermetic literature did nothing but make manifest what was already implied in Plato and Aristotle. As noted by Erich Frank, "to the Greek philosophers, to Plato, Aristotle, and Plotinus . . . the world was animate, it was divine. Therefore, they did not have difficulty in ascribing soul or reason or thought to it, or in speaking of a world-soul, a world-*Nous*" (67). In the final analysis everything goes back to Plato:

A vrai dire, ni l'objet divin que l'*Epinomis* propose à l'adoration, ni les arguments qu'il emploie pour légitimer l'astrologie ne sont

originaux: divinité du Ciel et des astres, priorité de l'âme, régularité de mouvements célestes, tout cela se trouve déjà dans le *Phèdre,* le *Timée* et les *Lois.* Ce qui est neuf et original, c'est le
caractére religieux et proprement cultuel de l'ouvrage. L'auteur
parle tout ensemble en prophète et en législateur. Il annonce une
religion, et, parce qu'il est convaincu que cette religion est la seule
vraie, il a dessein de l'inscrire dans les lois. (Festugière, *Le Dieu
cosmique,* 2:210)

(In truth, neither the divine object that the *Epinomis* proposes
for worship nor the arguments it uses to legitimize astrology are
original: the divinity of the stars, the prior existence of the soul,
the regularity of celestial movements, all that is found already in
the *Phaedrus,* the *Timeus* and the *Laws.* What is new and original
is the religious and properly cultic character of the work. The
author speaks as a prophet and a legislator all together. He announces a religion, and, because he is convinced that this religion
is the only true one, he intends to inscribe it in the laws.)

This philosophico-scientific "cosmic piety" spreads far and wide.

[Elle] reparaît dans toute une serie d'ouvrages "hellénistiques,"
dans les *Tusculanes* et le *Songe de Scipion* de Cicéron, dans le
De Mundo, chez Philon, chez Sénèque, chez Epictète, chez Marc-
Aurèle, chez Plotin encore. Entre la religion populaire et la théosophie des gnostiques, elle est la forme particulière que revêt . . .
la religion de beaucoup d'hommes, on peut dire, d'une manière
générale, la religion des sages. (Festugière, *Le Dieu cosmique,*
2:55)

(It reappears in a whole series of "Hellenistic" works, in the *Tusculans* and *The Dream of Scipio* by Cicero, in the *De Mundo,*
in Philo, in Seneca, in Epictetus, in Marcus Aurelius, and still in
Plotinus. Between popular religion and the theosophy of the
Gnostics, it is the particular form that the religion of many took;
one could say that it is, in a general way, the religion of the sages.)

This situation can explain why eventually somebody like Kepler would
argue "against the Aristotelian as well as the Ptolemaic theory, on the

ground that they implied that the 'planets knew mathematics'" (quoted in Frank, 82 n. 39). But this philosophical religion was not restricted to astronomy and mathematics. We find a similar attitude in Galen, for instance, regarding his own field of human anatomy and physiology, to which he refers as "the sacred discourse which I am composing as a true hymn of praise to our Creator [i.e., the Platonic Demiurge, who always chooses the best among the different preexistent possibilities in a world matter that has no beginning]" (Book III, 10).

The philosophical "allergic" avoidance, expulsion, of the sacrificial expulsion is, inevitably, equally sacrificial. The sacred can only be covered up by the sacred.

3. The *Poetics* and the Sacred

We should now retrace our steps back to Aristotle. One of the striking differences between Plato and Aristotle is that in reading the latter, one would hardly guess that he lived in a cultural and social milieu where, as Thales had said, "everything is filled with gods." Reading the *Poetics* in particular, one would never know, for example, that tragedies were only performed in connection with sacrificial rituals, shortly after the killing of the victim, still under the awesome presence of the sacred—which, as we have seen, filled Plato with great anxiety. One would never know about the sacred prohibition against representing violent death visually on the stage, or about such a ritual phenomenon as the use of masks with which the tragic performers disguised their identity. For there is "no tragedy without masks. By preference the choruses of tragedy wear the masks of foreigners or women; if they represent Athenians, they can only be very old men . . . hardly ever the young citizens of Athens they really are" (Burkert, "Greek Tragedy," 114). Likewise, if we expect to find some social or historical elucidation regarding the origins of tragedy, we will be sorely disappointed. The philosophical explanation is as follows: "Tragedy, as well as comedy, was from the beginning an improvisation. From its early form tragedy was developed little by little as the authors added what presented itself to them. After going through many alterations, tragedy ceased to change, having come to its full natural form" (*Poetics*, 49a10).

The last sentence is especially significant. It is the philosophical statement par excellence on the general question of origins. It postulates a characteristically "white" origin, a timeless natural form, free of any violent associations. (Plato would call it an ideal form or an essence.) This natural form is there from the beginning. Although finding it is always a happy accident, an improvisation, even these improvisations are, in turn, guided by natural inclinations. For example, "Poetry is divided into two kinds according to the natures of the poets, for those who were of a graver sort imitated splendid deeds and the actions of great men, but those of a lower type imitated the doings of meaner men" (48b24).

The important thing is that, once the happy accident has happened, the natural form, which is there *in potentia*, teleologically guides the development of the poetic form until it fulfills itself *in actu*. This essence or intelligible form only needs time to develop, but time does not add or change anything essential. Historical development simply unfolds the logical conclusion that must follow necessarily from the timeless, natural, premise. As Aristotle says in the *Politics:* "[The] nature of a thing is its end. For what each thing is when fully developed, we call its nature" (1252b27). In Aristotle's concept of development there is no room for violent change, for the unpredictable, for structural ambivalence or ambiguity. None of those things would be "natural." They could only be understood as unnatural disturbances, radically alien, external, to the universal intelligibility of natural forms. And that means, among other things of great consequence in the history of science, that there is no place for the sacred in Aristotle's system.

From the point of view of the old conception of science that we have been describing, Aristotle's system is perhaps the "safest," the one that manages to keep the sacred and, therefore, the nightmare, most consistently out of the picture. In reading Aristotle, probably more than with any other classical philosopher, one could really get the impression that the entire business of the sacred was perfectly expendable, that it was nothing but a bad and stupid dream, something like what Marx would call "ideological garbage"—which must be why Marx felt such a deep admiration for Aristotle, as we shall see in a later chapter.

But to feel "safe" from the rumblings of Acheron is one thing and to be scientific in a modern sense is quite another. Speaking of logicoteleological thinking, Gregory Bateson remarked that "logic is a poor model of cause and effect," because "causality does not work backwards." "Logic can often be reversed, but the effect does not precede the cause. This generalization has been a stumbling block for the psychological and biological sciences since the times of Plato and Aristotle. The Greeks were inclined to believe in what were later called final causes. They believed that the pattern generated at the end of a sequence of events could be regarded as in some way causal of the pathway followed by that sequence" (66).

As we have just seen, it is not only in the psychological and biological sciences that this type of essentialist teleological thinking has held sway. Its extraordinary attraction and influence has been felt in every knowledge area. Not without reason has Derrida called it "the language of the West." This is the "cultural Platonism" of which Girard has also spoken: "By cultural Platonism we mean the unexamined conviction that human institutions have been and are what they are for all eternity, that they have little need to evolve and none whatsoever to be engendered. Human culture is an immutable idea that is immediately available to any human being who begins to think. To grasp it one has only to look within oneself where it resides, innate, or otherwise outside of oneself, where it can be found legibly inscribed in the heavens, as in Plato" (*Things,* 59). This essentialist thinking has nothing to do with the discovery or reconstruction of actual historical origins. When this "mythologie blanche" (Derrida, quoted in McKenna, 37) postulates a transparently intelligible, nonviolent origin, the only origin it is discovering is its own.

But not even Aristotle, the best concealer of the old sacred, could prevent a few cracks from appearing in his formal wall of logic. For our purpose the most conspicuous one is the famous and endlessly debated poetic *catharsis,* a part of his definition of tragedy. It forced some Renaissance commentators of the *Poetics* into bizarre mental acrobatics in their efforts to explain it, and it has remained strange and bothersome to succesive generations of critics. Let us recall the passage: "Tragedy is an imitation of an action that is serious and complete and has sufficient size, in language that is made sweet . . . presented by those who act and not by narrative, exciting pity and fear, bringing about the catharsis [purgation] of such emotions. By language made sweet I mean language having rhythm and harmony and melody."

Aristotle had mentioned the catharsis or purgation before, toward the end of the *Politics,* in his discussion of the different functions or benefits served by different kinds of music. One of these functions is "purgation," and he adds: "the word 'purgation' we use at present without explanation, but when hereafter we speak of poetry, we will treat the subject

with more precision" (1341b38). But in the *Poetics*, as it has come down
to us, no explanation is given.

At least some scholars in classical religion have had little difficulty in
seeing the ritual connections of the Aristotelian catharsis. Jeanmaire, for
example, writes,

> Que la *catharsis* aristotélicienne soit en rapport étroit avec des
> pratiques telles que celles qui relèvent du Corybantisme, c'est ce
> que Rhode avait aperçu d'une façon au moins générale. . . . De
> fait, la liaison du mode musical en question, c'est-à-dire du mode
> phrygien qui s'exécute normalement sur la flute . . . et des pra-
> tiques dionisiaques, est, pour Aristote, chose qui va de soi. (320)

> (That the Aristotelian catharsis is closely related to such practices
> as those which derive from Corybantism, is something that Rhode
> had perceived at least in a general way. . . . In fact, the association
> of the musical mode in question, that is to say, of the Phrygian
> mode normally executed on the flute . . . with Dionysiac practices
> is, for Aristotle, something that goes without saying.)

The most cursory reading of Aristotle's comments on music in the *Politics* will make the connection clear. Pity and fear, the "natural" feelings
of the tragic performance, together with "enthusiasm," in its etymologi-
cal sense of divine possession or inspiration, are the feelings or passions
aroused by purgative or cathartic melodies, usually played on the flute
in the Phrygian mode, because "the Phrygian inspires enthusiasm"
(1340b4):

> For feelings such as pity and fear, or, again, enthusiasm, exist very
> strongly in some souls, and have more or less influence over all.
> Some persons fall into a religious frenzy, whom we see as a result
> of the sacred melodies—when they have used the melodies that
> excite the soul to mystic frenzy—restored as though they had
> found healing and purgation. Those who are influenced by pity
> and fear, and every emotional nature, must have a like experience
> . . . and all are in a manner purged and their souls lightened and
> delighted. The purgative melodies likewise give an innocent plea-
> sure to mankind. Such are the modes and the melodies in which

those who perform music at the theater should be invited to compete. (1342a 6–18)

These are obviously the kinds of melodies to which scandalized Plato referred when he accused the poets of blasphemy, because he did not want such "mournful harmoniae" next to the sacrificial altar, the altar that is nowhere to be found in Aristotle. And yet it is interesting to notice that Aristotle appears to be even more conservative than Plato regarding the musical education of the young, from which he excludes the purgative modes, the Phrygian in particular, played on the flute; because "the flute is not an instrument which is expressive of moral character; it is too exciting" (1341a21). In fact, Aristotle reproaches the Socrates of the *Republic* (III, 399) for not eliminating the Phrygian mode from the education of children, especially as he had eliminated the flute, which seemed to Aristotle something of a contradiction:

> The Socrates of the *Republic* is wrong in retaining . . . the Phrygian mode . . . , and the more so because he rejects the flute; for the Phrygian is to the modes what the flute is to musical instruments—both of them are exciting and emotional. *Poetry proves this, for Bacchic frenzy and all similar emotions* are most suitably expressed by the flute, and are better set to the Phrygian than to any other mode. The dithyramb [the forerunner of tragedy], for example, is acknowledged to be Phrygian, a fact of which the connoisseurs of music offer many proofs, saying, among other things, that Philoxenus, having attempted to compose his *Mysians* as a dithyramb in the Dorian mode [which "produces a moderate and settled temper"], found it impossible, and fell back by the very nature of things into the more appropriate Phrygian. (1342b 1–14; italics mine)

Let this suffice to show the intimate connection of theatrical poetry with ritual religious practices, and not precisely of an intellectual and character-forming type.

There can be no doubt that the cathartic process that Aristotle contemplates as part of his definition of tragedy, belongs in the general category of Bacchic or religious cathartic frenzy induced by purgative melodies; melodies that purge or expel those very feelings or emotional states they have induced. So it is not exactly the case that pity and fear expel themselves. Put that way, the situation is a bit incomprehensible. It is rather that the tragic ritual, if we may call it so, brings forth a deeply ambivalent (pity and fear, attraction and rejection, sympathy and withdrawal) and obviously disturbing emotional state in order to expel it and thus calms the souls of those who will then feel "lightened and delighted."

One thing should be clear. If the pity and fear produced by the tragic ritual are purged, it must be because they need purging. And if those souls whose feelings are purged feel "lightened and delighted," that can only mean that unpurged pity and fear are an unpleasant or disturbing burden. Unfortunately Aristotle says nothing about this disturbance, which we must assume if the catharsis is going to make any sense at all. All he says is that "pity is felt for the undeserving man in his misfortune and fear for a man like ourselves" (53a5), which does not help at all to understand the cathartic or expelling process. His explanation is, in fact, misleading, because he gives us two different and separate causes, one for the fear and one for the pity, in characteristically analytical fashion. But there is only one man, one object of the pity and the fear. One man (Oedipus, Orestes, Thyestes, etc.), who, as a human being, is, of course, "like ourselves," but who is also, always, very much unlike ourselves. For he has typically committed, not an ordinary offense, but a horrible crime, parricide and/or incest, one of those crimes described by Plato as "hateful to the gods, and the most shameful of shameful things." Indeed, one of those crimes that are especially impure and polluting, not only to the perpetrator himself (regardless of whether he did it deliberately or in error), but to the entire community, which is under a sacred obligation to expel him. And the pity and the fear are not felt separately but together, so that it would have been more accurate to say that the person is torn between pity and fear, or greatly disturbed by the conjunction of the two.

I am happy to find out that I am not the only one to perceive this logical inconsistency in Aristotle. There is at least one seventeenth-century critic who saw it quite clearly:

[A. Mareschal, in his preface to *La Généreuse Allemande*] considers [Aristotle's catharsis] no less than an obstacle to an aesthetic experience of the theater. He mentions that the aim of a play is . . . pleasure; but Aristotle "en donne deux contraires [i.e. two contrary aims] qui sont la compassion et la crainte." Mareschal admits that these emotions should be present in tragedy, which always ends in disaster, but finds this "si voisin de l'horreur" that even the authors of antiquity, seeing "comme ils se contredissoient en leur fin propre, et que l'esprit pouvait s'effaroucher plustost que de se rendre à la peur ou à la compassion," reduced the catastrophe to a *récit*, thus shielding our eyes from bloodshed. (Phillips, 41)

The point is that Aristotle's definition of tragedy, abstracted as it is from its sacred environment, raises more questions than it can answer. His categorizing and classifying logic simply bypasses all the ambiguities inherent in the tragic performance.

And there is something else about Aristotle's inclusion of pity and fear and their purgation in the definition of tragedy that neither a purely formal or psychological approach can explain. It is strange that the effects should be included as part of the formal definition of the cause. Obviously pity and fear, and their catharsis are not parts of the formal structure of tragedy ("Every tragedy ... must have six parts ... plot, character, diction, thought, spectacle, and music" [*Poetics* 49b31].) We would be rather surprised today if we ever came across a definition of, say, science-fiction novels, or soap operas, in which the psychological effects of such genres in their audience or readers would be included in the definition of the genre on the same level as, for example, written in prose, of a certain length, dealing with this or that type of futuristic or personal situation, etc. First of all, it would be practically impossible to determine with analytical precision what those psychological effects would be, much less what they ought to be. Second, even if we managed to agree on some kind of psychological description, we could only say that the genre in question aims at producing those effects, or may produce them under appropriate circumstances.

Aristotle, however, appears to be much more definite. To begin with, there is not the slightest hesitation in identifying the emotions that tragedy ought to excite. They are repeated at different points in the *Poetics*, as they had been in the *Politics*, as a ready-made formula, as something that, in a sense, goes without saying, unquestioningly accepted by everybody; that is, on the same level of evidence as the fact that tragedy is presented by actors, or that it uses music, etc. In other words, it is presented as something that is not necessarily or only the result of personal observation and reflection.

Second, pity and fear and their purgation are not viewed as circumstantial to the tragic performance. Rather, they belong to the "natural" form of tragedy. A tragedy that does not in fact excite precisely these two emotions of pity and fear in the audience, or does not bring about the purgation of such emotions, cannot be properly called a mature or fully developed tragedy; at best, I suppose, we would have to call it a frustrated one. This does not seem to me the kind of formal definition of a literary genre that we would be willing to accept today. It looks much more like the definition of a rite or ritual performance, in which everything is geared to produce a definite, well-defined, effect: in a ritual performance the effect on the participating audience is the most important thing; if the proper effect is not produced the entire performance is frustrated.

Nonetheless, the fact that in the ritual performance the effect on the audience is crucial, does not mean that the rules that govern the performance itself are determined by the psychological reactions of the audience. The performance will continue to be what it ought to be (according to accepted tradition) regardless of whether or not the proper effects are produced at any given time. In other words, there is little or no feedback from audience reception to the performance of the ritual. The performance has a logic of its own that, in principle, is not supposed to react or adjust itself to the actual emotional response of the participants. The adjustment should work the other way. The emotional response ought to be that which is expected.

If we apply this logic to the situation of tragedy we realize that, even though its proper effects are pity and fear, these effects will not in any way influence the tragic development with its "natural" outcome, which in one way or another ought to present the downfall of the hero. The hero will never be saved through pity. If the "natural" tragic formula were sensitive to or dependent on its psychological effects, one would have to expect that sooner or later the perfect balance between pity and fear would tilt in favor of pity. (I am sure that such a Romantic soul as Spingarn's, for example, would have no objection to saving the hero once in a while.) In theory such a possibility could not be ignored. In fact, from a psychological point of view, it is extremely unrealistic, first, always to expect a perfect balance between pity and fear, and, second, to expect that neither pity nor fear would ever change the tragic outcome. And yet that change does not happen and it is not supposed to happen. It would be contrary to the "nature" of tragedy.

Aristotelian tragedy is not at the mercy of pity and fear as mere psychological processes. Obviously the pity and the fear demanded by the natural form of tragedy are not only supposed to be excited by that form but to be under its complete control as well. They are not just ordinary pity and fear, that is to say, pity and fear left to their own purely psychological tendencies. They are controlled, predetermined pity and fear, the kind expected for, and appropriate to, the ritual occasion.

In view of these considerations, I suggest that in order to fully understand Aristotle's definition of tragedy, one must take into account the ritual background, both empirical and semiological, against which tragedies were performed, a background Aristotle disregards for the most part, but cannot avoid completely. I am not saying that his definition is entirely that of a ritual performance, because he tells us that "tragedy can produce its effect without performance and without actors" (50b16). Nevertheless, such a tragedy would not achieve its "natural" form, and it would not produce the same cathartic effects, because it would be lacking, among other things, the proper Phrygian mode and the flute. It is in his conception of the "natural form" of tragedy where the echoes of the ritual performance can still be heard clearly.

I suspect that many modern readers may have heard these echoes without knowing what to do with them. After all, to say that tragedy originated in ritual performances is not saying much, compared with all that Aristotle said about it without even mentioning its ritual character or, at least, its ritual associations. Almost everybody would still turn to Aristotle, not to the ritual, for an explanation or an understanding of what tragedy is all about. Our unreflecting philosophical discourse, inherited from Plato and Aristotle, has succeeded in convincing most of us that the language of the sacred is essentially meaningless.

But the sacred has its own meaningful logic, and that logic is precisely that of the sacralizing expulsion, whereby the bad and threatening is turned into the good and protecting (which is not quite the same as to say that the good expels the bad; because the good sacred is generated out of the bad sacred). Everything turns on the expulsion itself, which is to say, on the object of the expulsion, the victim. It is in the victim where the good and the bad converge. It is the sacred victim who is the object of the pity and the fear. And it is the sacred expulsion of the sacred victim that turns disturbing pity and fear into reassuring, "innocent," pity and fear. For if catharsis, as Aristotle says, gives "an innocent [or harmless] pleasure to mankind," what pleasure could be more innocent than the pleasure of feeling innocent? In other words, if you take away the sacred, the proper catharsis of pity and fear required by the "natural" form of tragedy will make no sense.

Aristotle's rational description and explanation of poetry is believable and accurate up to the point where it has to come in contact with the sacred; at that moment everything he says will be mediated and determined by his fear of the victimizing sacred (his sacred allergy) and by the urgent philosophical need to skirt it and leave it out of the picture. At that point he will distort reality, perhaps without even knowing it. It will be much more important for him to maintain the internal coherence of his "secular" logic than to represent objective reality as accurately as possible.

4. The New Spirit of Science: Francis Bacon, the "Herald of the New Time"

The difference between Aristotle's attitude toward science—the basic historical and epistemological premises that conditioned his view of science—and that of the sixteenth- and seventeenth-century theoretician, cannot be properly understood without taking into account the fundamental difference between a science that exists as a buffer, as an insulating device or remedy, against the terrifying "rumblings of Acheron," and a new science driven by the liberating realization that it has nothing at all to hide or to fear. In the words of Thomas Browne, there is no scientific sanctum sanctorum, no forbidden knowledge; this new science knows that its only limitations are its own; in other words, a science that has been desacralized under the influence of the nonvictimizing Christian text.

At first glance it may seem strange to attribute the historical emergence of desacralized science to a text in which we also find, prominently displayed from the beginning, the story of the Fall of Man for having tasted the fruit of the Tree of Knowledge of Good and Evil. Basil Willey was right when he pointed out that that rejection of knowledge was the first objection Francis Bacon, the Christian herald of the new scientific spirit, had to address. Let us therefore hear what Bacon had to say in this regard:

I hear [it said] that Knowlege is of those things which are to be accepted of with great limitation and caution; that the aspiring to overmuch knowledge was the original temptation and sin whereupon ensued the fall of man; that Knowledge hath in it somewhat of the serpent. . . . To discover then the ignorance and error of this opinion . . . it may well appear these men do not observe or consider that it was not the pure knowlege of nature and universality, a knowledge by the light whereof man did give names unto other creatures in paradise, as they were brought before him, according unto their proprieties, which gave the occasion to the fall: but it was the proud knowlege of good and evil, with an intent in man to give law unto himself . . . , which was the form of the temptation. (*Advancement*, 4–5)

Bacon's observation regarding the clear difference that the Genesis story establishes between knowledge of nature and knowlege of good and evil, acquires special significance in the context of the theory of the sacred that serves as a basis for this book.

Indeed, what does it mean to say that man withdrew from the presence of God, was expelled from Paradise, as soon as he learned to distinguish between good and evil? What it means, I suggest, is that man's way to make such a fundamental distinction is not God's way. In other words, to the extent that man is governed by the way in which he distinguishes good from evil and by its consequences, he is on his own, that is, unsupported or unconfirmed by God. But I do not think the story has anything to do with man being a fuzzy thinker. If such were the case, man would have been expelled from Paradise for not knowing how to properly distinguish good from evil, which was not the case. The story should not be interpreted as a minilesson in moral theology. It simply says that the knowledge of good and evil, in anybody's hands other than God's, will bring death and suffering, that is, expulsion from Paradise. The fruit of the Tree of Knowledge of Good and Evil is poison to humanity. The prohibition was there, not to protect God, as the serpent said, but man from himself. Expulsion from Paradise was not so much a punishment as a logical consequence.

Now, our theory of the sacred says that it is precisely that separation of good and evil, above everything else, that human beings have always placed under the aegis of the sacred, seen in a sacred light; a sacred light that has served to blind them to the violent reality, all of their own making, through which they have managed to separate good from evil, the inside from the outside, what belongs from what does not, etc. In other words, they have made their own violence sacred in order not to see it as their own. Our theory says that human culture is grounded on a sacrificial, sacred-making, mechanism; a victimizing one that covers its own violence with a sacred veil.

Basically, therefore, what the Genesis story says is that God has nothing to do with that sacralizing process whereby human beings victimize one another and disclaim responsibility for it. What it says is that the God of Abraham, the God of Moses is not behind that man-made sacred veil. God did not give man the knowledge of good and evil. Man took it himself, after being deceived by the devil. What God did give man was, in Bacon's words, "the pure knowledge of nature and universality, a knowledge by the light whereof man did give names unto other creatures in paradise, as they were brought before him, according unto their properties." Therefore one should not get the two kinds of knowledge confused; while God supports one, he does not support the other.

Among many other things, this means that natural philosophy or science is not supposed to be an escape route from incriminating knowledge in the sacrificial sphere, where good and evil are violently separated. Such an activity would inevitably bend or twist natural knowledge toward an end that is not its own; it would restrict it and hold it hostage, as it were, to a foreign power. But that is precisely what happened in the case of Aristotle and Greek science in general. I do not want to deny Greek culture the uniqueness of its contribution to human civilization. Indeed, I do not see any other example of sacrificial escape into rational knowledge comparable to it either in depth or scope. The history of Western thought is simply inconceivable without the Greeks. But such an admirable rational accomplishment should not hide the fact that the Greek route was ultimately a dead end. The renewed interest in the Graeco-Roman classics during the sixteenth century and before is grounded on very different premises.

There is a profound and intimate connection between the gradual historical realization that man is entirely responsible for his own violence—that violence is not sacred—and the historical emergence and liberation of the scientific spirit of natural inquiry. Paradoxical though it may seem in the context of our usual mental parameters, man's sense of guilt in the face of God and his sense of liberation and confidence in the face of nature are inseparable phenomena. By the same token, if we understand this we may also understand the traditional Christian idea that the Fall of Man (his violent knowledge of good and evil) also corrupted nature (which I take to mean, not in itself, which would not make sense, but in regard to man) insofar as man is an integral part of nature and nature is, unavoidably, the immediate object of man's knowledge and perception.

Admittedly it will not always be easy to differentiate between a science ultimately driven by the need to quiet the noises of "hungry Acheron" and one that emerges because those noises have lost most of their power to frighten. After all, it is human reason in operation in both cases. At any given time the objective scientific results may be identical. And yet, in the end one will stagnate while the other will grow and diversify exponentially. In one case every scientific advance implies or hides either a sigh of relief at having successfully skirted the forbidden sacred truth or, as in the case of Lucretius, a cry of victory over "hideous religion." In the other case, truth appears precisely as that which has nothing to hide, as something that has already saved or redeemed humanity from the terrors of Acheron. Indeed, one finds in Bacon, that *buccinator novi temporis* (trumpeter of a new time) a profound conviction that, even though "natural philosophy" and "divinity" should not be confused, the two support each other: "[Any] one who properly considers the subject will find natural philosophy to be, after the Word of God, the surest remedy against [the fears of] superstition, and the most approved support of faith. She is, therefore, rightly bestowed upon religion as a most faithful attendant, for the one exhibits the will and the other the power of God" (*Novum Organum*, book 1, chap. 84).

I believe this confidence in the truth of natural philosophy is the fundamental difference between Aristotle's science and the spirit that moves scientific inquiry in sixteenth- and seventeenth-century Europe. This new scientific spirit, as one would expect, takes as its immediate and primary object the world of nature. Science—or philosophy—is understood to be, above all, natural science or natural philosophy. But, at the same time, the concept of nature becomes so encompassing that the only thing to stand beyond its scope will be the revealed word of God. Beyond natural science there is only the science of "divinity." The possibilities of study in each of these two sciences are without limit, although they must not be confused: "[Let] no man upon a weak conceit of sobriety or an ill-applied moderation think or maintain, that a man can search too far, or be too well studied in the book of God's word, or in the book of God's works [i.e. nature]; divinity or philosophy: but rather let men endeavour an endless progress or proficiency in both; only let men beware that they apply both to charity, and not to swelling . . . and again, that they do not unwisely mingle or confound these learnings together" (*Advancement,* book 1, chap. 3, p. 8).

Any truly scientific pursuit must be grounded directly or indirectly in "natural philosophy": "[Let] no one expect any great progress in the sciences . . . unless natural philosophy be applied to particular sciences, and particular sciences again referred back to natural philosophy. For want of this . . . [particular] sciences have no depth, but only glide over the surface and variety of things; because these sciences, when they have been once partitioned out and established, are no longer nourished by natural philosophy. . . . [We] can little wonder that the sciences grow not when separated from their roots." Even "moral and political philosophy, and the logical sciences" have their roots in natural philosophy (*Novum Organum,* book 1, chap. 80).

This is the historical context in which we should now place the extraordinary interest which the late Renaissance exhibited in the science of poetry.

5. Truth or Fiction: The New Dilemma of the Renaissance Theoretician

It is not difficult to see that poetry, by which it was generally understood poetic fiction, posed a monumental problem to the new theoreticians, a problem entirely absent from Aristotle's *Poetics.* The problem was fiction, which made the conception of poetry as a vehicle for truth extremely difficult. How could poetry be a proper, a natural, object of science, unless it was truthful even as any other natural object of science is truthful, an expression of God's creative power? A variety of answers were attempted, none of them conclusive.

We have already spoken of the problem that poetic fiction presented to the Renaissance moralist. We should note that the scientist also had a problem with poetic fiction, given the ethical dimension of what he considered to be the proper object of scientific investigation, the nature of things, that is to say, the natural, God-created, way in which things are truthfully what they are. The two problems, the moral and the scientific, are not specifically the same, but they are by no means unrelated.

That the poets do not always tell the truth was something everybody knew, at least since Hesiod. Poets were "licensed" to do such things. In their poetic activity they were permitted things not permitted elsewhere—much like things permitted in certain orgiastic rituals that would have been considered shameful outside the ritual framework. But such a license was far more difficult to deal with in the scientific context of Christian Europe. "*Poesy* is a part of learning in measure of words for the most part restrained, but in all other points extremely licensed, and doth truly refer to the imagination; which, being not tied to the laws of matter, may at pleasure join that which nature hath severed, and sever that which nature hath joined; and so make unlawful matches and divorces of things" (Bacon, *Advancement,* book 4, chap. 1, p. 82).

From the point of view of the scientific spirit of the new era (the spirit of natural philosophy), probably the only way in which poetic fiction (a semblance of the truth, but not the truth), could be thought of as a legitimate object of scientific inquiry was to link it to something nonfictional, that is, something having a natural existence, for example, history. Thus Bacon's: "*Poesy* . . . is nothing else but *feigned* history" (*Advancement,* book 4, chap. 1, p. 82).

In the end this new theoretical attempt to deal with poetry scientifically will fail, will not convince; not because poetry is above "natural philosophy" or science, as so many theoreticians from Tasso on will feel, but rather because poetry, as we will explain in a moment, deals with something prescientific, something no less real than science, but much more primitive and ambiguous, and, in this sense, below science. All that science, as such, could have done at that point was to explain why the human reality with which poetry dealt lacked the epistemological clarity, the definition required of any object to become a proper object of scientific investigation.

It was Castelvetro some years before Bacon, who had taken this perceived scientific need to connect poetry to something naturally true, to its logical consequences, in the following remarkable statement:

> If Aristotle or another had written a proper treatise on the art of history—and the art of history should logically have been treated before the art of poetry—poets and critics would have found the ideas in Aristotle's brief *Poetics* more useful . . . or they might even have dismissed them as superfluous. . . . Truth existed by nature before verisimilitude and the thing represented before representa-

tion. But since verisimilitude depends wholly upon truth and looks upon it as its model and precisely the same relationship exists between representation and the thing represented and since we cannot attain a right knowledge of dependent and reflecting things unless we first possess a knowledge of the things they depend upon and reflect, it necessarily follows that we cannot acquire the faculty of making right judgements about the adequacy and fidelity of representations and probabilities unless we first possess an accurate and exhaustive knowledge of the things represented and the truth. Then since history is the recital of memorable human actions that have happened and its distinguishing mark is truth, and poetry the recital of memorable human actions that may happen and its distinguishing mark is verisimilitude; and since, again, history is a thing represented and poetry . . . a representation, no art of poetry so far written can possibly offer a complete and accurate knowledge of poetry because we still lack a complete and distinct knowledge of history and future arts of poetry will continue to be less than serviceable as long as the art of history remains imperfectly known. . . . For poetry, as we have said, borrows all its light from history, whose light as yet burns dimly if at all, and unable to borrow it poetry must wander in great darkness. (3–4)

The statement is remarkable for its uncompromising simplicity. If we do not know yet how to deal with historical truth in a scientific way, how can we know how to deal scientifically with something that is only an imitation of that truth? We must know the truth properly, that is, scientifically, before we can imitate it properly. For that is what poetry is: not the truth but an imitation of the truth. In fact, if we knew precisely how to present the truth we would also know, *eo ipso,* how to create an imitation of the truth. Consistent with this view that poetry only offers a semblance of the truth but not the truth, Castelvetro also insisted that the end of poetry is not instruction, but only delight. For instruction can only be the end of those arts and sciences that deal with the truth. One cannot truly learn that which is not truly there.

Castelvetro did not stop to consider all the possible implications of his insight, some of which might turn against him. Nonetheless, somewhere along his line of thinking one might discover too perfect an imitation of the truth; that is, an imitation of the truth that would threaten the epistemological status of the truth itself, whose distinctness and clear difference from mere imitations stands as the basis of his argument. It is perhaps a testimony to his good faith or unshakable confidence in the inviolable character of the truth that he did not stop to consider such possible danger. In fact, so determined was he to raise poetics to the status of a real science that he ended up by turning poetics into a kind of Procrustean bed whereby he would either cut or stretch anything that did not fit properly. Truth being the only scientific criterion, the closer poetry resembles historical truth the more the science of poetics would deserve its name, and the better the intelligible essence of poetry would be understood and revealed. A perfect correspondence is assumed between poetry's intelligible essence (Aristotle's "natural form") and its adequacy as an object of scientific study.

Responding to this scientific need for poetry to reflect or resemble natural, historical, truth, Castelvetro will, for example, expand and distort Aristotle's statement about unity of action in tragedy to insist, for the first time, on the need for the famous three dramatic unities of action, time, and place. Thus "the magnitude of the plots that are apprehended by both sight and hearing should be equal to that of an actual event worthy of being recorded by history; for since the imaginary action from which the plot is formed represents words directly with words and things with things, it must of necessity fill as many hours on the stage as the imaginary action it represents would have filled or would fill in the world if it had actually occurred or were to occur there" (82). For the same reason, tragedy "must be set in a place no larger than the stage on which the actors perform" (243).

But since poetry is an imitation of natural truth and not natural truth itself, the subject matter of poetry should not be the same as that of history or of any of the other arts and sciences. "[He] expels from the ranks of the poets whole classes of writers whom many generations down to his own had unquestioningly honored as authentic poets. . . . Empedocles and Lucretius . . . Virgil and Hesiod as the authors of versified treatises on the art of agriculture; and Lucan, Silius Italicus, Fracastoro and unnamed others as the authors of versified histories" (xx).

Nevertheless, it should be pointed out that as Castelvetro looks back in history he realizes that not everything can be so clearly divided between historical reality and its fictitious look-alike: "[The] statement that as regards its matter poetry is not history but an imitation of history is to be interpreted with sobriety and moderation; for when the poet's story is one of kings and divine beings poetry and history are, to a certain point, identical, and then poetry is history and not an *imitation* of history" (20). "To a certain point" means, of course, that there must still be enough room for the poet to exercise his inventiveness. For this reason, as Tasso will specify later, this assimilation of poetry to history or vice versa within the context of the old sacred, does not extend to biblical history. Biblical subjects would not be the proper domain of the poets, because they could not exercise their inventiveness in such a field.

Observe the phrase, "kings and divine beings." In all likelihood Castelvetro is thinking of classical poetry and the epic in particular, where kings and divine beings usually go together. It is the contemplation of the old sacred, where the human and the divine mingle, that makes Castelvetro moderate his otherwise uncompromising separation between history and its imitation. Like most other sixteenth-century theoreticians, he is sensitive to the old association of poetry with the sacred. For that reason sacred oracles and sacred laws, even though they do not fall strictly within the definition of poetic matter, should be granted, in his opinion, the poetic privilege of verse or meter. Likewise, "metre is not to be denied to those maxims, sayings, and proverbs . . . like . . . the *Golden Verses* of Pythagoras [etc.] . . . for these sayings are of no less value than laws and seem in fact to be divine oracles rather than formulations of human wisdom" (21). Nevertheless, in spite of this "sobriety and moderation" in the face of the spirit of the old sacred, he will still deny poetry any inherent didactic intent: "The end of poetry is pleasure" (254).

But to come back to the separation of the true from the true-like, the verisimilar: if one insists that the proper subject of poetry is not the true, but only the verisimilar, then one is implying that the only proper subject of poetry is that which is not true. As Mazzoni, writing shortly after Castelvetro, remarks, "It would be very easy to fall into the view of those who maintain that poetry has no subject other than the fabulous or false, but is yet linked to the verisimilar" (70).

Nonetheless, Mazzoni tried to smooth things out, saying that even "Plato in the *Republic* and in the *Laws* . . . has demonstrated that he believes that truth is not repugnant to poetry" (71). He reaches two conclusions: "The first of them is that the false is not always necessarily the subject of poetry. The second is that since the subject of poetry is sometimes true and sometimes false, there is consequently a need to constitute a poetic subject that by itself can be sometimes true and sometimes false" (72). That poetic subject is the credible. And "since the poet has the credible as his subject, he ought therefore to oppose credible things to the true and the false, the possible and the impossible, by which I mean that he ought to give more importance to the credible than to any of the others. . . . Therefore, if it should happen that two things should appear before the poet, one of them false but credible and the other true but incredible or at least not very credible, then the poet must leave the true and follow the credible" (78).

Mazzoni will become even more specific. Since the credible, as he will discover, is also the proper subject of rhetoric, it will be necessary to specify that "the credible insofar as it is credible is the subject of rhetoric and the credible insofar as it is marvelous is the subject of poetry, for poetry must not only utter credible things but also marvelous things. And for this reason when it can do so credibly, it falsifies human and natural history and passes beyond them to impossible things" (85).

In pursuit of the credible marvelous the poet ought to speak "with such boldness as to profess to know all things by means of the Muses and Apollo." Mazzoni is happy to point out that Castelvetro agrees with him in this regard: "I was pleased to see the opinion of a well-read commentator on the *Poetics* who feels that it is not suitable to the poet in any way to use words or modes of speech which place in doubt the things he discusses, for professing the credible more than others, he ought to utter things with great assurance and boldness" (81).

Because of all this "the poet deserves the name of sophist." And here, again, Mazzoni tries to smooth things out. There are two kinds of sophistic, one "which misdirects the intellect with falsehood and the will with injustice" and another which does not. "This second species of sophistic . . . was never condemned by the ancients." But he knows he is standing on shaky grounds: "And if, even so, it should appear to someone that it deserves condemnation for misleading the intellect by some falsehood, I say that he should know that the ancient pagan philosophers (being at variance in this matter with the truth of sacred theology) have praised this misleading of the intellect in certain things, when it is directed to a legitimate end. And in this respect Plato preferred that the magistrate should be able to tell lies to his citizens for the sake of some public good" (83).

Tasso was not convinced:

> Mazzoni writes . . . that imitation is of two kinds, the one icastic, the other phantastic, here following Plato's doctrine in the *Soph-*

ist. He calls the kind that imitates things present or past icastic and the kind that imitates non-existent things phantastic. And this latter he chooses to call perfect poetry, which he places under the sophistic faculty, whose subject is the false and the non-existent. But to console the poets, and among them myself . . . he distinguishes two or three kinds of sophistic art, and places poetry under the first kind, which is the most ancient. Yet this, if I am not mistaken, is the very kind Socrates and Plato . . . argued against. (*Discourses,* 29)

Tasso's solution is revealing and, one might even say, prophetic. Pressed by the historical advance of "natural philosophy," he takes poetry out of the empirico-historical realm into the higher level of "divine philosophy, or theology as we may prefer to call it." The poet, we are told, is not a sophist; "rather we should say that he is a painter of images in the fashion of a speaking painter, and in that is like the divine theologian who forms images and commands them to be" (*Discourses,* 31). On the authority of Plato, Aristotle, and, especially, the Areopagite in his *Mystical Theology,* Tasso tells us of the two parts of the mind (other sources, including Arabic ones, like Avicenna, speak of the two faces of the soul), "which is composed of the divisible and the indivisible." The indivisible one is "intellect pure and simple," which contemplates the highest truth of the "most occult theology." It is the lower part of the mind that uses demonstration and is "much less noble than the indivisible." When Saint Thomas "assigned poetry to the lowest order of teaching . . . he meant that part of poetry which teaches by weak proofs, such as examples and comparisons" (*Discourses,* 32). But the poet can be like the mystical theologian; they both "lead to the contemplation of divine things and thus awaken the mind with images." Therefore,

[t]he poet as a maker of images is not a phantastic imitator, as Mazzoni held. . . . [W]hat shall we say exists, the intelligible or the visible? Surely the intelligible, in the opinion of Plato too, who put visible things in the genus of non-being and only the intelligible in the genus of being. Thus the images of the angels that Dionysius describes are of existences more real than all things human. So too the winged lion, the eagle, ox, and angel, which are the images of the evangelists, do not belong principally to phantasy . . . unless besides the phantasy which is a faculty of the

sensitive soul there were another which is a faculty of the intellective. . . . [Both] our theologians and the Platonic philosophers postulate this faculty, [which] Aristotle neither knew of nor admitted. . . . Perhaps this is what Dante was referring to when he said:

Here power failed the high phantasy

[A l'alta fantasia mancò qui possa]
(*Paradiso,* canto 33, line 142)
(*Discourses,* 33)

One may wonder if Tasso had already forgotten this passage when a little later in the *Discourses* he will tell us that a poet must have freedom to invent to deserve the name of poet; which is why he should avoid sacred subjects, "since with them discovery takes no effort and invention seems hardly permitted":

The argument of the epic poem should be drawn, then, from true history and a religion that is not false. But histories and other writings may be sacred or non-sacred, and among the sacred some have more and some have less authority. Ecclesiastical and spiritual writings command greater authority. . . . The others doubtless have less authority. The poet had better not touch histories of the first type; they may be left in their pure and simple truth, since with them discovery takes no effort and invention seems hardly permitted. And whoever does not invent or imitate . . . would be no poet but rather a historian. (39–40)

To be sure, Tasso is talking here about the subject of the epic poem, not about something like Dante's intellectual vision in *Paradiso.* But then he should tell us that when he is dealing with transcendental or mystical poetry, the rules that apply to earthly, historylike poetry, even of the highest type, like the epic, do not apply.[4] He should tell us that we are dealing with two very different sorts of things, which was not the case

4. He must have felt that way for he does not mention the *Divine Comedy* among his models for a Christian epic (see Kates, 41).

with Dante. Dante had no problem bringing the divine vision of his intellectual fantasy down to earth, to very concrete historical circumstances,
while Tasso would be facing an impossible task if he tried to reconcile his
own definition of down-to-earth, historylike, poetry with the poetry that
he sees in Dionysius the Areopagite or in Dante. In other words, the
appropriate reaction to Tasso's fine defense of the truth content of intellectual, mystical fantasy would be to tell him that that is not what either
he or Mazzoni were talking about.

The new scientific spirit of "natural philosophy"—which was spreading to the science of poetics thanks to critics like Castelvetro and Mazzoni—even with the best of intentions, threatened the high status and
nobility of poetry. And Tasso came to the rescue. In a sense, he went back
to the traditional defense of the poet-theologian. But he also was one of
the first to suggest a new line of defense: the truth of poetry as something
different from and superior to the truth of science. Ironically, it was not
Aristotle who provided the philosophical basis to rescue poetry from the
new rationalism of the age (which was proving to be no more hospitable
to it than the old Scholastic rationalism), but Plato. For now we see sacred poetry fleeing the desacralizing power of an increasingly desacralized natural philosophy, following the same philosophical route first
discovered by Plato to rescue the sacred from the sacrilegious proximity
of the poets. Now we see poetry joining Platonic philosophy in the metaphysical realm of ideal essences. Eventually, in some extreme Romantic
cases, as those of Matthew Arnold and others, we will actually see poetry
trying to displace philosophy as the guardian of the sacred, just as philosophy had once been invented to displace poetry from that same role
(we may remember Arnold's words, quoted above: "most of what now
passes for religion and philosophy will be replaced by poetry"). We may
take this as further proof that there was never much of a difference between the two.

So the situation comes down to this: if we consider poetry from the
perspective of science, of "natural philosophy," we must place it at the
bottom of the hierarchy of knowledge, given the paucity as well as the
ambiguity of its truth content. We may either accept this scientific verdict
or reject it. To my knowledge, there are only two ways in which this
rejection has been formulated: one leads to the separation of the truth of
science from the truth of poetry, keeping them on parallel and equal
tracks; the other goes a step further and, inverting the hierarchical structure, places the truth of poetry above the truth of science. But this inver-

sion, which does violence to all scientific rules of evidence, can only be maintained, by hiding such an irrational tour de force behind a sacred veil; that is to say, by conferring on poetry something that genuine science does not have or aspire to have: a sacred character.

Regarding the first possibility, I do not think that the distinction of the two truths on separate and equal tracks can be a very stable structure. It is not in the nature of either scientific inquiry or poetic feeling to live with each other without either questioning or suspecting each other. In other words, I do not think that such a solution is a real one, for it could only be maintained by an absolute and arbitrary prohibition on each of the two parties ever to look into the other—by placing, once again, some sort of sacred taboo between the two.

6. A Humble Way out of the Impasse

In the final analysis the only real question is whether or not poetry should be viewed as something of a sacred icon. If we do not want to sacralize poetry, we are faced with the need of having to accept poetry's status at the bottom of the hierarchy of knowledge; in other words, with having to accept what, to sacrificial eyes, is the marginal place of the outcast. So far, to my knowledge, nobody who ever thought that poetry had something important to say has ever been willing or able to accept such an outcast status for it. To put it differently, nobody has ever thought that the poetic outcast, as outcast, could reveal anything of value precisely to those who look upon her as an outcast.

Nobody wants to touch the outcast. They either want to throw her out or place her on the highest pedestal as a divine creature. And yet, what does this outcast do but imitate, mimic, stage, mirror all those who either want to throw her out or make her divine? The outcast is no stranger, she lives in the midst of those who do not want to touch her.

Let me explain this little allegory. If one holds to the idea that truth is an univocal concept, that there are not different truths, but only different degrees of proximity to or distance from the truth, in other words, different degrees of evidence, of clarity, in the separation of the true and the false, then the hierarchical model must be taken very seriously. At higher levels in the hierarchy, truth is clearer; the separation between the true and the false more stable. Therefore, as we go down the hierarchical ladder the possibility of error, of mistaking the false for the true, the unreal for the real, etc., increases. And it is there, at the bottom of the ladder, where we find poetry. Poetry, therefore, deals mostly with error, human error, the kind of error that springs from not being able to differentiate the true from the false. Thus, compared with all the other disciplines in the hierarchy of knowledge, poetry appears to be uniquely qualified to explore all kinds of human situations as sources of error.

Poetry ought to accept this ranking at the bottom of the ladder; that is, it ought to speak truthfully about itself, about its intimate relationship with the countless ways in which human beings can go astray, can err. This truthful discourse about itself will not remove poetic fiction from its position at the bottom of the epistemological hierarchy. Even at its best the fiction of poetry will still be fiction and, therefore, a rather ambiguous carrier of the truth. There will always be the possibility of taking it the wrong way, as it were, if one is so inclined or does not know better.

However, the lowest point in the hierarchy is still a part of the hierarchy; it *does* belong to it. The error and confusion that are the domain of poetry to a preeminent degree do not exist outside the structure but inside. The structure is by no means immune to them. In other words, poetry is not only located at the lowest point in the hierarchy, it *is* the lowest point of the hierarchy; of a hierarchy which is only such, insofar as the lowest can still communicate with the highest. Poetry, the lowest point, is the point at which the hierarchy itself becomes most vulnerable. In the final analysis, what the fiction of poetry enacts or represents is nothing short of the collapse and dissolution of the hierarchical structure—the crisis of degree, as the Ulysses of *Troilus and Cressida* might say, when all the arguments lose their objectivity and become purely ad hominem.

To accept poetry as the bottom of the shared hierarchy of knowledge is to look the crisis in the face: not just any crisis, but the crisis of difference itself, the undifferentiating spread of violence that is the totalizing crisis of the sacred; the very crisis that is at the root of the sacred. And it is to look it in the face from the position of the outcast, of the victim who is about to be expelled. Anything other than such terrifying acceptance is to participate in the sacralizing of poetic fiction, either by expelling the outcast or by raising it on a divine pedestal: the one implies the other; behind all such divine metamorphoses there is a sacralizing expulsion. Our Arnoldian worshipers of poetry are the predictable heirs to many generations of angry antipoetic moralists.

We could also approach the problem of the status of poetic fiction from a diachronic or historical perspective, as Tasso himself did in answer to Castelvetro, for having placed the art of poetry in a somewhat subservient or parasitic position to the art of history:

> I would make a fresh start in my treatment of the poet's art if I were not faced with an objection Castelvetro makes against Aristotle: that he ought not to have dealt with the poetic before the historic art, since just as history precedes poetry and truth verisimilitude, so the art of setting down the true should be given first. . . . Such an opinion strikes me as . . . false. . . . For poets are the most ancient of all writers, and historians began to write centuries later. . . . Moreover, if the historian's art allows a place to rhythm, ornament, and figures of speech, who does not know that these were virtually lent to the writer by the poet? Neither the orator nor others who write prose have anything that is not, so to speak, usurped. (*Discourses*, 18–19)

There was poetry before there was history-writing. Indeed, there was poetry, or rather myth (which looked very much like poetry), before there was almost anything else. Of all the arts and sciences that eventually constituted the hierarchical structure of knowledge, poetry appears to be the oldest. From Tasso's Platonic perspective this proximity to the origin conferred on poetry a very high degree of universality, for being close to the origin meant being close to the ideal exemplar. His view could be described as historical idealism.

However, from an empirical view of history as human experience things look rather different. First of all, it is questionable that what appears to Tasso, or to us, as poetry from a great historical distance (from the threshold of history), could in fact be conceived or function as what we now call poetry, since the structural relations that define poetry for us as something different from, say, history or philosophy did not yet exist. To say that there was poetry before there was history-writing, philosophy, theology, rhetoric, or any other well-defined field of knowledge is something of a contradiction, or a petitio principii.

And yet, it is most revealing that as we look back in history toward progressively earlier stages of increasing epistemological undifferentiation, everything seems to take on a somewhat poetic character. Obviously, there is something about poetry closely akin to such an undifferentiation. Indeed, we see that as history-writing, philosophy, and the other arts and sciences emerge from that state of undifferentiation and acquire specific epistemological contours they shed, as it were, their mythopoetic character.

Therefore, whether we consider the synchronic structure of the hierarchy of knowledge or its diachronic development in time, we see the same thing: whether vertically, from lower to higher, or horizontally, from earlier to later, the movement is always from undifferentiation to differentiation—which, as we have seen, is precisely the movement away from the sacred, the movement that tries to preserve everything from sacred contamination, that is, from the violence that lurks in the midst of cultural undifferentiation.

Everything emerges from the sacred and takes its distance from it, just as everything must take its distance from the mythopoetic in order to create and maintain its own cultural specificity. What is left is poetry, at the bottom of the hierarchy, the most visible remnant of and link with the primitive sacred. In nonsacrificial hands this old sacrificial tool is capable of revealing, through a sustained act of self-examination, the deepest secrets of mankind. Not because it is endowed with some God-given, privileged insight, but rather because of two basic reasons: (1) the hiding, the decoying, sacrificial function of poetic fiction has been wearing thin in our Western culture; (2) in spite of this thinning down and the predictable scandalized reaction it triggered to violently expel poetic fiction, the weakened condition of the expulsion mechanism itself suspended, as it were, the scandalized, Plato-like, expulsion of poetry and allowed for that sustained act of self-examination that can only be accomplished with a humble spirit. This thinning down is what I believe happened at the threshold of our modern era. And it is what made modern literary fiction possible.

It was something unprecedented. But I also insist that it was not only the thinning down of the sacrificial veil that made the unprecedented self-examination possible, but also that a human being could look through the thin veil and not be seized by intolerable anguish or fear-ridden despair. Virgil had already looked through the veil, but he could not sustain the vision.

3

BEYOND VIRGIL

Thou majestic in thy sadness at the doubtful
doom of human kind.
                        —Tennyson, "To Virgil"

1. Changing Views on the *Aeneid*

In the last several decades a change in perspective appears to have taken
place among critical readers of Virgil's *Aeneid*. W. R. Johnson writes:

> the studies of Virgil . . . which reaffirm both the unique greatness
> of his poem and his role as a maker of the myth of Europe evidence
> precision and vigor of imagination . . . so it is with real diffidence
> that I turn from the strengths of this school to its weaknesses.
> Those weaknesses can best be described by their being contrasted
> with the strengths of the somewhat pessimistic Harvard school.
> In this reading of the poem the superior virtues and the high ideals
> of Aeneas are sometimes grudgingly allowed him, but he is in the
> wrong poem. His being in the wrong poem furnishes him with a
> kind of tragic greatness that calls into question not only the hero-
> ism of Homer's poems but also Augustan heroism and indeed any
> heroism. (10)

One of those "Harvard school" critics, Adam Parry, said it this

This chapter is a modified and much expanded version of my article "Sacrificial Levels in Virgil's *Aeneid*," *Arethusa* 14 (1981): 217–39.

way: "The *Aeneid*, the supposed panegyric of Augustus and great propaganda piece of the new regime, has turned into something quite different. . . . Virgil continually insists on the public glory of the Roman achievement. . . . But he insists equally on the terrible price one must pay for this glory" (120). Another, Wendell Clausen, observed that "[the *Aeneid*'s] larger structure . . . enlists our sympathy on the side of loneliness, suffering, and defeat. For it is the paradox of the *Aeneid*, the surprise of its greatness, that a poem which celebrates the achievement of an exemplary hero and the founding of Rome itself should be a long history of defeat and loss" (82).

But this poses new questions. Why should such a "terrible price" be paid? Why do we have to find such "loneliness, suffering, and defeat" at the root of human civilization? Was it necessary for Virgil to accumulate so much violence and death as the human background from which the glory of Rome would emerge? As Mario A. Di Cesare has pointed out, "every book of the *Aeneid* . . . is sealed and, as it were, consecrated by death. Death is of course expected in an epic of journey and war. But the cumulative effect of death in the *Aeneid* is quite unlike what one expects in heroic song." And this is clearly no accident:

> Virgil has shaped this common material into complex symbolic rhythms—the death of fathers and leaders, and of sons; the death of quasi-sacrificial victims, like Orontes and Palinurus . . . each one marked as one dying for the many . . . the old man and the young [in Book VII] singled out as *primitiae*. The deaths of Mezentius and Camilla [which] prelude the death of Turnus. Mezentius was a stand-in for Turnus during his absence; as for Camilla . . . her protesting spirit flees with a moan to the world of shades: "vitaque cum gemitu fugit indignata sub umbras" (XI, 831) anticipating the last line of the poem (XII, 952). (215–16)

I think the answer can only lie in the direction pointed out, somewhat hesitatingly, by Di Cesare himself, that is, in the sacrificial direction. The sacrificial institution is the only cultural frame of reference in which death, violence, and suffering can find meaning for any given society. It is the only mechanism that can transform such a terrifying matter into social forms of human coexistence.

Nevertheless, this new and progressive realization of the enormous human cost that Virgil finds necessary for the founding of Rome, should not make us forget that the critical shift from the glory of Rome to the human cost underlying such glory is something relatively recent. In other words, the same poem that so starkly describes "tantos mortalibus esse labores" (such labors there are for mortals) has also, quite successfully, disguised the violence, gilded the pain, for many centuries. Thus, when reading the poem, we may be in the same position as Aeneas was as he contemplated his own tragedy, the destruction of Troy, painted on the temple of Juno in Carthage, when he saw "the tears of things" and "the mortal anguish that touches the mind." As A. Parry observed, "the whole poem is such a painting" (110). The undying fame conferred on such terrible human realities by either the art of the painter or of the poet brings a measure of consolation: "solve metus; feret haec aliquam tibi fama salutem" (dismiss thy fears [Priam]; this fame will bring thee some salvation) (II, 463).

One of the things I shall investigate in this chapter is the profound connection—the complicity, I would dare say—that exists between the sacrificial frame of reference in which violence and the suffering occurs and the so-called "aesthetic" or poetically crafted level.

2. Sacrificial Levels in Virgil's Poem

In order to investigate this connection, I observe that the sacrificial frame of reference itself is rather complex. At the very least there are two sacrificial levels in Virgil's poem. The first is explicit, the traditional form of sacrifice, recognized as such and carefully, ritually, regulated. Throughout the poem *pius* Aeneas offers numerous sacrifices to the gods, in the performance of which he shows his technical expertise in ritual matters, as H. J. Rose has pointed out, and of course his *pietas*.

But besides this institutional sacrificial presence, or sacrifice *stricto sensu,* which is always this or that ritual form specifically prescribed and regulated for the occasion at hand, there is another sacrificial level not formally defined as such, diffused throughout the poem, which becomes, as it were, the sacrificial texture of the text, and also something like an impulse that moves the poem along and guides its development. Aeneas's journey happens along this sacrificial level, which thus becomes the ground supporting all the other explicitly ritualized instances of sacrifice. But one can only speak of sacrifice if, in one way or another, there is a victim. And, in this regard, it must be pointed out immediately that at this background level the sacrificial victim is always human. Perhaps it would be better to call this second level the implicit or hidden one, because the sacrificial events that constitute it, are never presented explicitly, that is to say, ritually, as sacrifices in the technical sense of the word. On the contrary, with only one deliberately ambiguous exception, they appear as random events, purely accidental occurrences.

Although there is hardly any significant violent death in the *Aeneid* without sacrificial overtones, the quintessential sacrificial formulation, the one that expresses the fundamental sacrificial principle, *unum pro multis dabitur caput* (one head will be given up for the sake of many), rings with special distinctiveness in a few but crucial cases. Three such cases deserve our attention, because their deliberate strategic location along Aeneas's journey cannot be reasonably doubted. First is the death of Palinurus, where the wording of the formula—"unus erit tantum amissum . . . unum pro multis dabitur caput" (V, 814–15) (one only will be lost . . . one head will be given up for the sake of many)—is given full expression, but also the deaths of Creusa (Aeneas's Trojan wife) and that of Orontes. Like signposts along the Trojans' journey to Italy, they are a fitting sacrificial prelude to Aeneas's arrival in Italy and to the terrible, insane violence that awaits him on Italian soil.

His journey to Italy meanders up and down the eastern Mediterranean, but its overall pattern is anchored geographically and poetically at three points: Troy, Carthage, and Cumae on the Italian shore. As readers of the poem will remember, the "accidental" deaths to which I am referring occur as follows: Aeneas's wife, Creusa, is lost as he and his party are trying to find their way through dark and unfamiliar alleys out of the horrible confusion of burning Troy, and to reach the sacred mound of Ceres, the agreed-upon assembly point outside the city. Orontes and his ship are lost as the winds unleashed by Aeolus buffet the Trojan fleet fiercely against those hidden reefs in the middle of the sea that, appropriately, "are called aras," or Altars, by the Italians. After the storm abates, Aeneas and his men will reach the Libyan shore and Carthage. Palinurus, the helmsman, is lost in the dark of night, just before they reach the coast of Italy, while everybody is asleep and Sleep himself, in the form of Phorbas, causes Palinurus's senses to weaken as he is trying not to lose his course, looking at the stars, suspicious of the violent "monster" on whose crest the fleet is sailing.

As we said, it is in this last episode where the explicit formulation of the sacrificial principle occurs. Here the god Neptune demands (or announces) one human victim as a prerequisite for the salvation of all the others and their safe arrival in the promised land of Italy, as he tells Venus,

> tutus, quos optas, portus accedet Averni.
> *unus* erit tantum amissum quem gurgite quaeres;
> *unum pro multis dabitur caput.*
> (V, 813–15; italics added)

(Safe, as you wish, he will arrive at the harbour of Cumae—or Avernus. One only will be missed, lost in the sea; one head will be given up for the sake of many.)

But the formula echoes literally in the cases of Creusa and of Orontes as well. As they arrive at the sacred mound of Ceres after their escape, Aeneas realizes for the first time that all have finally gathered together except one, "one is missing":

> . . . hic demum *collectis omnibus una defuit*
> (II, 743; italics added)

In the Orontes case we have it in the words of Achates, when he and Aeneas discover to their amazement that all have actually been saved from the storm, all except one:

> *omnia tuta vides,* classem sociosque receptos.
> *una abest,* medio in fluctu quem vidimus ipsi
> summersum.
> (I, 583–85; italics added)

(You see, all is safe, our fleet and friends restored to us. One is missing, the one we saw drowned in the sea.)

Achates' words simply reiterate with increased clarity what had been said already during the storm:

> *unam, quae* Lycios fidumque *vehebat Oronten,*
> ipsius ante oculos ingens a vertice pontus
> in puppim ferit.
> (I, 113–15; italics mine)

(One, which bore the Lycians and loyal Orontes, before the eyes
of Aeneas a mighty toppling wave strikes astern.)

In case the meaning of that *unam* had been lost, Achates makes clear
now that it was the only one "hit by a huge wave"; all the others survived
the terrible storm. We have a clear pattern: at every crucial step forward
in the direction of their appointed destiny, the Trojans must "give up one
for the sake of many."

Before we proceed, however, we should reflect for a moment on the
internal logic of the sacrificial principle itself and its formidable implications, apart from any particular circumstances. To say that "one head
must be given up for many" and nothing else, is to say that it does not
make any difference which "one" it is. Strictly speaking, the principle
itself pays no attention to any individual or cultural differences, thereby
suggesting its liminal character, something that comes into view at the
limit, either prior to any system of meaningful differences or at the moment when all such differences have lost their meaning; that is, when
nothing makes any difference any longer.

The killing of the one makes a difference—the fundamental difference
between survival and utter annihilation, between meaning and nonmeaning—when nothing else does. For as long as meaningful cultural
differences remain, individuals in that culture cannot be assumed to be
perfectly interchangeable; therefore, one could not say that anyone chosen at random could actually and truthfully stand or substitute for any
and all others. The "one for the many" remedy is indeed very violent; it
only works, literally, in extremis. The violence that kills the saving victim
must have leveled everything; it must have turned the cultural landscape
into a flat wasteland. For the same reason, if true to itself, to its internal
logic taken to its ultimate consequences, the sacrificial formula can only
be posited as a universal and, in a sense, a transcendental one, since the
victim that must be given up, transcends, cannot be defined by, any established system of cultural differences. All that is required is that the victim
be one of those many who are to be saved through her demise, for the
formula promises that all will be saved minus one.

Let this brief reflection suffice to give us an indication of what it meant
for Virgil to conceive and develop the hidden or implicit sacrificial level
in his poem, in the light of the "one for the many" principle. Perhaps
now we can understand why the sacrificial events that structure Aeneas's
journey to Italy are conceived as accidental or random. For indeed in

rational, differentiated, terms the "choice" of the saving victim can only be described as utterly arbitrary and random. Perhaps we can also understand the logic that drives Virgil's thought from the accidental character of such victimizing "choices" to the contemplation of the maddening violence that will be unleashed on Italian soil in the second half of the poem.

Nothing decisive in the gradual unfolding of Aeneas's destiny happens without the intervention of some fatal accident, where one is lost before the action proceeds to another stage. It would be surprising if such a central event as Aeneas's descent to the underworld were not preceded or introduced by some such fatality. And, of course, it is. To the providentially accidental deaths of Creusa, Orontes, and Palinurus, a fourth one must be added: that of Misenus, the first dead on Italian soil, who became mad *(demens)* and was, by chance *(forte)*, sounding his hollow shell to the sea, when he was snatched by Triton, "si credere dignum est" (if the story deserves credit). Through this death another important step will become possible in the fulfillment of Aeneas's founding destiny.

Unknown to Aeneas, the death of Misenus happens while the hero is in the sacred cave of the Sibyl listening to her Phoebus-inspired instructions on how to find his way to Hades. But before he can proceed, she tells him, there is something he must do immediately: there lies an unburied corpse on the shore that is polluting the entire expedition and he must give it proper burial. This, of course, catches Aeneas completely by surprise, as it does the reader, who knew nothing about it either. And yet, this is presented by the Sibyl as an urgent duty that must be fulfilled *before* Aeneas can find the doors of Hades. It is no surprise, therefore, that Aeneas should find the golden bough, the key to Hades, while searching for the wood to build the funeral pyre for Misenus's corpse. Thus the "accidental" death of Misenus is linked directly to the climax of the first part of the poem, Aeneas's descent to the secrets of the underworld and the place where the future glory of Rome will be revealed to him. For such a revelation to take place one head, once again, must be given up. The death of Misenus serves no other purpose in the poem.

But simply to describe the death of Misenus as accidental, even surprising, does not do justice to everything connected with it. The way Virgil presents it, "accidental" does not only mean beyond anybody's control, unplanned, without deliberation or attention; it also means confusing, something that cannot be fully understood, and yet frightening.

Caught by surprise by the Sibyl's words, not knowing exactly what is happenning, as he leaves the cavern,

> Aeneas maesto defixus lumina voltu
> ingreditur, linquens antrum, caecosque volutat
> eventus animus secum.
>
> (VI, 156–58)

(Aeneas, with downcast eyes and a sorrowful face, walks away, leaving the cavern, and turns the dark issues within his own mind.)

This dark, confusing aspect of Misenus's death and its effects on Aeneas provides another link with the three other "accidental" deaths already mentioned, which also happen in the dark, both literally and figuratively—in the case of Palinurus, at the point when "dewy Night had reached almost its midgoal in the heavens" (V, 835). In the Creusa episode, also at night, *per umbram*. During the storm in which Orontes was lost,

> eripiunt subito nubes coelumque diemque
> Teucrorum ex oculis; ponto nox incubat astra.
>
> (I, 88–89)

(All of a sudden clouds take away the sky and the daylight from the eyes of the Trojans; gloomy night lies over the deep.)

The darkness is not only outside but especially inside, blunting the minds of the Trojans. When the fated accident happens, everybody appears to be in what might be called a state of diminished consciousness. This is true, not only in the episode of Palinurus, where everybody is asleep, except the helmsman, until Sleep itself catches up with him, but in the cases of Creusa (1) and Orontes (2):

> (1) Hic mihi nescio quod trepido male numen amicum
>   confusam eripuit mentem.
>
> (II, 735–36)

(At that point, in the commotion, I do not know what unfriendly spirit took away from me my confused mind.)

(2) extemplo Aeneae solvuntur frigore membra.
(I, 92)

(At once Aeneas's body weakens with a chill.)

In other words, Aeneas is terrified, enough of an indication as to his state of mind.

Contrary to what happens at the formally ritualized, explicit, sacrificial level, where the victim can only be the proper one, and everything is meticulously planned and executed; at the implicit or hidden level things happen in a random, accidental manner. At this second level people have no control over the course of the events in which they participate.

From the perspective of the hallowed ritual, approved by tradition and piously performed, what happens at this other level can only be described as unholy and meaningless, as well as terrifying, precisely because of its lack of recognizable meaning. And yet the two levels converge toward the same sacrificial principle, which demands that one head be given up for the sake of many. Behind the hallowed sacrifice one can hear the rumblings of the unholy one, which is muffled and kept from view through the careful avoidance of anything accidental, through the pushing aside of randomness and nonmeaning. The hallowed sacrificial level exists as a denial of the unholy, hidden one. To suggest any link between the two would amount to sacrilege.

It is of the essence for the sacrificial community to adhere strictly to its approved and well-regulated sacrificial practices, in other words, to prevent the disturbing sacrificial level from ever rising to the surface. However, this careful, ritualized, cover-up is as much a source of social stability as a result of it. When social stability is shaken for any reason (and reasons are never lacking completely; "accidents" can happen any time), then the disturbing random level can break through to the Apollonian surface, threatening the stability of the hallowed sacrificial rites. Bad sacrifices, strange ones that are not permitted in more peaceful times, appear on the scene to the scandalized horror of respectable citizens, who, in turn, blame such devious practices for what is happening.

We have it on the testimony of Livy, for example, when he tells us that "in the judgment of the most prudent and knowledgeable men in all kinds of divine and human laws, nothing dissolves religion as much as when people sacrifice according to foreign rites, not those of the fatherland" (39.16.9–10). He is talking here about the notorious Bacchanalian affair in the year 186 B.C., but there were many other such cases. *Lascivia*, that is, disorderly excitement, had broken out also in 213 B.C. to the point where "not only in a secret way and the privacy of the homes were Roman rites being abolished, but in public also, in the *forum* and the Capitol where a mob of women gathered, not sacrificing or praying to the gods in the [proper] manner of the fatherland" (quoted in Fowler, 324). And when this disorder happens, when the social order totters, the excited mobs are likely to clamor for the real thing: human victims, no more animal substitutes. Testimonies are plentiful throughout the history of Rome. As for the Greeks, Herodotus also found it hard to believe that Dionysiac rituals could "accord with the Hellenic temperament" (Gernet, 88).

To come back to the *Aeneid,* all those "accidentally" killed at the random, hidden sacrificial level are really unholy, a source of pollution, in precisely the same way and for the same reason that an abandoned, unburied corpse is unholy and polluting. Nothing is so symbolic of random violence as a corpse left unburied. The corpse of "accidentally" killed Misenus becomes the symbol of all the others; the symbol, therefore, of all that is going on at the nonritualized sacrificial level. Aeneas cannot possibly descend into the holy of holies without first hiding from view, burying, that most unholy symbol. The Sibyl's orders are unmistakable:

> sedibus hunc refer ante suis et conde sepulchro
> . . . .
> sic demum lucos Stygis et regna invia vivis
> aspicies.
> (VI, 152–55)

> (Take him first to his own place and hide him in a tomb . . . only so will you see the Stygian forests and the realms inaccessible to the living.)

The question of whether Misenus was in fact killed by a jealous god or not is left somewhat in doubt, with a "so the story goes"–type of comment; a fitting prelude to the incredible encounter with the ghost of Palinurus shortly after Aeneas enters Hades. He finds the ghost precisely among those who cannot be transported across the Stygian marsh because they have not received proper burial.

3. Palinurus's Deliberate Contradiction of Textual Evidence

It must sound strange to us—ignorant as we are of the logic that governs the old sacred need and duty to deny a truth that is lethal—to hear Palinurus in Hades saying: "Leader, son of Anchises, it was not a god that plunged me into the sea. For it was by accident [*forte*] that the helm was broken most violently, to which I was holding, as it was my charge, and steering the course" (VI, 348–50). Only a moment before we saw Venus pleading with Neptune to grant the Trojans safe passage to Italy and we heard Neptune himself accede to her request with one exception ("one head will be given up . . ."), and right away we saw Sleep take the shape of an old man and throw Palinurus overboard. We would not be surprised if Palinurus simply did not remember what happened to him, for the god Sleep shook over his temples "a bough dripping with Lethe's dew and steeped in the drowsy might of Styx" (V, 854–56). What is surprising is Palinurus's certainty that it was an accident, combined with his equally firm assurance that the gods have not forgotten Aeneas ("neither did Phoebus fail you, nor did a god throw me into the sea").

To all appearances there is an irreducible contradiction. And there is no question that the contradiction is deliberate. Aeneas's words are "quis te, Palinure, deorum / eripuit nobis medioque sub aequore mersit? (What god, Palinurus, tore you from us and plunged you underwater in the open sea?) (VI, 341–42). The words unmistakably refer us back to what we had read a moment before. So, it is definitely not that Virgil has forgotten what he wrote. There is no way around it; Palinurus's direct response to Aeneas's question is, at the literal level of the text, a clear denial of the way we were told things happened.

The only question, then, is, what is Virgil trying to do? What is the meaning of this deliberate contradiction? Was it an accident, a random occurrence that ended up in a totally unpredictable killing by a band of uncivilized savages who mistook Palinurus for prey, as his ghost says? Or was it something fated and Palinurus the victim required for the salvation of the many, as we were told? What makes it even more intriguing is that the ghost appears to be equally certain both of the fact that it was an accident and that the gods have not abandoned Aeneas: "neque te Phoebi cortina fefellit, / dux Anchisiade, nec me deus aequore mersit" (VI, 347–48). The explicit link between the two parts of this sentence leaves no room for doubt: "*neither* did Phoebus fail you, *nor* did a god throw me.*" How can these two things be linked to each other and still be both true?

I believe that this whole episode is a stunning confirmation of the underlying logic of the sacrificial principle, as I explained it before. First of all, we have to understand the question posed by this literal contradiction. The question is not whether any given god was literally involved in throwing Palinurus overboard, but whether Palinurus was the victim demanded by the most sacred of sacred principles, that is, the victim that must be sacrificed for the salvation of many. The fact that, in this case, the principle is stated explicitly by a god, Neptune, simply confirms the sacred character of the principle. It is not he, Neptune personally so to speak, who demands a victim in return for allowing the Trojans to proceed to their destiny. Neptune is only the voice of the sacred granting Venus her wish. She is happy with the god's words, "they soothe her heart." Now she knows that her request is in accordance with fate, that the Laurentine walls have been granted by the Fates—"dant ea moenia Parcae" (V, 798). That is the best that sacred fate can do: all except one are saved.

As we have already seen, the death of Palinurus serves the same function as those of Creusa, Orontes, or Misenus, namely, to allow Aeneas to proceed on his sacred path. All these deaths are to be seen as successive confirmations of his fated destiny, sacred stamps guaranteeing safe passage after paying the sacred toll. The fact that in the case of Palinurus a god literally appears and explicitly states the sacred reason for his demise, only confirms what was clearly implied in all the other cases. Now, if we overlook for a moment the fact that it is a ghost in Hell who tells Aeneas that "it was an accident"; if we step back from the poetic storyline and look at both episodes—Palinurus being marked as the sacrificial victim and Palinurus's ghost saying that it was an accident—simultaneously, that is, from Virgil's vantage point, we cannot escape the conclusion that Virgil is indeed saying that Palinurus's death signifies the death of the victim that will save the many *and also* that such a saving death is an accidental, an unpredictable, occurrence.

But if this is so, if the saving death is truly unpredictable, then Virgil is not only saying that it could have been anybody other than Palinurus, but also that, in principle, such saving death might not have occurred, that Rome might have never been. That was Virgil's extraordinary and terrifying discovery: Rome, human civilization, emerges out of a situation in which every member of the group is equally threatened with violent extinction, unless the death of one in the group deviates from that violent uniformity and becomes different from all the other deaths. But whether or not such a difference or deviation will occur and put an end to undifferentiating violence, is something radically uncertain. Fate can only be discovered a posteriori.

And yet that elusive, random, unpredictable difference is *the* sacred difference; all order and stability rest on it. Or rather, it becomes sacred as the foundation of all order and stability. Its becoming sacred is synonymous with the denial or the hiding of its random and unpredictable character. Virgil's vision, which simultaneously contemplates, on the one hand, the indifferent randomness in the choice of the victim and the unpredictability of its occurrence; and, on the other, its foundational character, is a vision utterly incompatible with the existing order and, therefore, unacceptable in the view of that inner sanctum, the guardian of the established order, which is Hades itself. No death that has not been cleansed, purged, of its randomness, can find admission to that sacred hall. Or, to put it in the graphic and ritual language of the sacred, all corpses must be properly buried. Hence the Sibyl's command to Aeneas, *conde sepulchro,* hide the unburied corpse, cover the polluting randomness and unpredictability of that death. Nothing could have been so meaningfully symbolic of what sacred Hades was all about as those words by the Sibyl, stating the prerequisite to finding the hidden entrance to the sacred underworld.

The ghost of Palinurus is not exactly lying, but he is not telling the whole truth either. His words are something of a symbolic riddle. It is true that his death was a violent accident. But as long as it remains merely that, it cannot become a meaningful sign, a cultural symbol of the saving victim. As long as it remains merely that, it cannot be properly said that a god, a sacred will, killed him. In order to become a proper, culturally acceptable sign of the one whose head must be given up for the sake of many—that is to say, a proper sign of the founding victim, as Virgil clearly intends—his death must be purged of its randomness; his corpse must be buried. Otherwise his death would remain fruitless; no civilized order could emerge from it. It would remain a body without a clear human identity destroyed by a band of barely human savages on a nameless beach.

It takes more than the arbitrary killing of one to save the many. It takes, in addition, an absolute denial of such arbitrariness, a process of sacralization that cleanses that death of its terrifying randomness and turns the victim into something unique; without this process the death of the one remains without issue. Hades is there to prevent the knowledge of the fundamental arbitrariness of the foundational killing from contaminating or disrupting the sacralizing process. Hades is there to bury a truth that nobody should ever discover.

I have said repeatedly that the death of Palinurus must be seen in the context of those other deaths (Creusa's, Orontes's, Misenus's), the random character of which is clearly emphasized by Virgil; and this, in spite of the fact that we see the god announcing the loss of one for the sake of many. The words of Palinurus's ghost confirm the correctness of our view. But at the same time we can look at those words as something like a correction addressed to Virgil by the voice of the underworld, a way of telling him: no, you cannot have it both ways. You cannot say that it is a random killing and also that such a killing is the one that will save the many. If you do that you are combating the most sacred. You are not simply discovering the foundations of Rome; you are destroying them. In other words, it was not just Aeneas who entered Hell, but Virgil himself to discover the secret that *must not* be told.

The *Aeneid* must hide as much as it reveals, it must conceal the truth it sees. This concealment is not arbitrary. The danger posed by the revelation of such a truth is not extraneous to the truth itself. We have understood nothing if we think that Virgil was free to reveal or not the terrifying truth he had discovered. First of all, such a truth could have only been an intolerable source of scandal. Chances are nobody would have believed him. But more immediately important to our purpose here, the *Aeneid* itself, the great Roman epic, would not have existed; the epic project in general would have disintegrated. Virgil's poem is a colossal, brilliant cover-up. Virgil's tragic pessimism is rooted in his knowing what is being covered. It seems that shortly before his death Virgil ordered his poem to be destroyed. Augustus, his friend and patron, prevented that order from being carried out. I do not know if there is sufficient historical evidence to support this belief. But the belief itself expresses a very profound truth about the character of the poem. Virgil's decision to destroy his poem could not have been unrelated to the profound pessimism that the poem conveys.

Perhaps all this can also help us understand the surprising way in which Virgil has Aeneas return to the world of the living.

4. The Shining and Deceiving Ivory Exit from Hell

At the end of Aeneas's journey through Hades, his father, Anchises, dismisses both him and the Sibyl through the "shining door of bright ivory [through which] the spirits send false dreams to the upper world," rather than through the other, the one made of horn, "which gives easy outlet to true shades."

> Sunt geminae Somni portae; quarum altera fertur
> cornea, qua veris facilis datur exitus umbris,
> altera candenti perfecta nitens elephanto,
> sed falsa ad caelum mittunt insomia Manes.
> his ubi tum natum Anchises unaque Sibyllam
> prosequitur dictis portaque emittit eburna.
>   (VI, 893–98)

(There are two gates of Sleep, of which one is said to be of horn, which gives easy outlet to true shades; the other shines with bright ivory, through which the spirits send false dreams to the upper world. That is where, with these words, Anchises takes his son and the Sibyl and sends them through the ivory gate.)

Each gate, of course, assimilates the nature of that to which it gives passage. Opaque horn gives passage to opaque, "shady" truths; bright, shining ivory, to bright visions which are, however, false. The contrast between "veris umbris" and "perfecta nitens . . . sed falsa . . . insomnia" is remarkable. But we must understand that Virgil is performing a double operation here. By opening the shining gate to Aeneas's vision he is also leaving the gate of horn closed to the "true shades." In other words, what he deliberately chooses not to do is as important as what he does.

I have never found an adequate explanation of this passage in modern classical scholarship. The traditional one was given by Granger at the turn of the century:

> Virgil here repeats the distinction with which we are now familiar. On the one hand are the genuine souls of the dead, which pass through the gate of horn; on the other the false dreams.
> What are these gates of sleep? *They are the eyes and the mouth respectively* [italics in original]. The eyeball furnishes the gate of horn; the teeth the gate of gleaming ivory. "The dreams," Homer says in the passage which Virgil is imitating, "the dreams that pass the polished ivory cheat with vain promises and bring unaccomplished words. But the dreams that pass through the smooth horn, bring sure things to pass when a mortal sees them." . . . [The] motive of the comparison is very widespread, cf. . . . Plautus *Truc.* ii. vi8 "pluris est oculatus testis unus quam auriti decem." Taubmann in his commentary on Plautus, gave the above interpretation quite clearly two centuries ago. . . . Hence when Virgil dismisses the travellers through the gates of ivory, he is reminding us that it is the poet's voice that has given them life. . . . The whole episode in fact, is like a vision interpolated in the course of the story of Aeneas. But, as the poet is careful to point out, it is not one of those visions which seem to bring their warrant with them. The poet does not, like Blake in his prophetic books, describe what has been revealed and told to him. He is throughout the self-conscious artist who uses the materials of legend as symbols of truth. (26)

I think there is some truth in this interpretation, beyond the fact that Virgil is obviously using "the materials of legend as symbols of truth." In a sense, Virgil, "the self-conscious artist," is making us aware of the poetic character of Aeneas's vision. He is telling us to read beyond the literal level; or what amounts to the same thing, he is warning us not to place our complete trust on "bright" and "shining" surfaces, because, somehow, they may be deceptive or misleading. As a general statement referring to the whole poem or to poetic activity at large, that is true, for there can be no doubt that Virgil is a very "self-conscious artist."

The problem is that in the particular case at hand that general proposition cannot be so easily applied. It is precisely at this point that the difference between the literal and the symbolic breaks down. This is literally what the poem says: "with these words," or, "having said these things," Anchises takes his son and the Sibyl to the gates of Sleep and sends them through the one made of ivory. But Anchises' words are those that have just explained to Aeneas the vision of the future history of Rome and have also warned him of the terrible wars that await him now in the upper world. These things cannot be taken as "the materials of legend" symbolic of something else. Whether or not Virgil is accurate as a historian, these things are meant literally, as factual history. The history of Rome seen by Anchises had, of course, already happened at the time Virgil was writing. He could not lie about it. And the announced terrible wars are supposed to have happened also. Anchises' words are not symbols of truth; they are literally true. So if these words are still to be taken as a deceptive shining surface, it cannot be because they point poetically beyond themselves to a deeper meaning; it can only be, perhaps, because they do *not* point in such a direction, because their truth is not the whole truth, because they hide something.

From our perspective it is not a question of the literal versus the symbolic, but rather a question of what literal historical reality itself hides or disguises in order to constitute itself as such, as meaningful historical reality. It is a question of the truth that cannot be spoken in order to be able to speak the sacred language of civilized history. As said before, what is important is that the gesture that opens the ivory door simultaneously closes the one made of horn.

Once again, the truth that cannot be revealed is that the violence that kills the one whose death will save the many, the sacred one, is a totally random and arbitrary violence; a violence that pays no attention to any individual or cultural differences, that seizes everybody equally, in the most horrendously indiscriminate manner. Such a state of violence is the breeding ground from which the dead one must emerge who will save the many—"si dant Parcae," if the Fates grant it. And it is by no means guaranteed that such will occur.

5. The "Inane Fury" Between People Destined to Live in "Eternal Peace"

The accidental deaths of Creusa, Orontes, Palinurus, Misenus, and in the final analysis all other deaths in the first six books of the poem are but the

prologue to the horrible and demented carnage that will be the subject of
the other six books—a carnage, by the way, the beginning of which, as
Juno herself points out, is also provided by accident, "quae fors prima
dedit" (VII, 554).

The violence that Allecto, the fiendish monster hated even by her father Pluto and her Tartarean sisters, instigates in the hearts of Latins
and Rutulians is sheer madness; what is more important, it is extremely
contagious. Once started it spreads with raging speed in every direction.
The textual passages are numerous, but it may be worthwhile to remember some of them. For example, the madness of Amata, which spreads
throughout the cities of Latium like a whirlwind, or to use Virgil's image,
like a spinning top, the sacred emblem of Bacchus:

> tum vero infelix ingentibus excita monstris
> immensam sine more furit lymphata per urbem.
> ceu quondam torto volitans sub verbere turbo,
> quem pueri magno in gyro vacua atria circum
> intenti ludo excercent . . .
> . . . non cursu segnior illo
> per medias urbes agitur populosque feroci.
>   (VII, 376–84)

(Then indeed the unfortunate [queen] excited by monstrous horrors rages without control, insane, throughout the city, just like
when a top goes spinning under the twisted las, which children
intent on their game drive in a large circle on an empty courtyard
. . . so [she] moves through cities and wild peoples.)

Then it is Turnus who becomes insanely furious:

> olli somnum ingens rumpit pavor, ossaque et artus
> perfundit toto proruptus corpore sudor.
> arma amens fremit, arma toro tectisque requirit:
> saevit amor ferri et scelerata insania belli,
> ira super.
>   (VII, 458–62)

(A monstrous terror broke his sleep, and the sweat, bursting forth
from his body, soaks his bones and limbs. Madly he yells for arms,

arms he seeks in couch and chamber: a desire for the sword rages in him, and the murderous insanity of war, and hatred.)

Virgil places special emphasis on the contagious character of this violence. A rumor, the sound of the horn, the clashing of weapons, the sight of the war flag, is enough to spread mass hysteria all around. For example:

> Ut belli signum Laurenti Turnus ab arce
> extulit et rauco strepuerunt cornua cantu,
> utque acris concussit equos utque impulit arma,
> extemplo turbati animi, simul omne tumultu
> coniurat trepido Latium seavitque iuventus
> effera.
>
> (VIII, 1–6)

(When Turnus raised the war flag from the Laurentine citadel and the horns rang with their hoarse song, when he lashed his fiery horses and clashed his arms, instantly souls were troubled, all at once all of Latium is leagued in tumultuous commotion and its youth rages madly.)

The frequent use of words such as *extemplo, simul, subitam*, etc. forcefully creates the impression of an instantaneous spreading of the spirit of violence. In such a state of hysterical violence all differences between the contending parties are quickly erased. Their mutual responses become symmetrical, exhibiting an almost perfect violent reciprocity, each one a mirror image of the other: "aequo dum Marte geruntur" (they wage even warfare) (VII, 540).

Perhaps nothing is so characteristic of the final books of the *Aeneid* as the deliberate multiplication of parallels between the enemy factions. Here is a telling example:

> Quis mihi nunc tot acerba deus, quis carmine caedes
> diversas obitumque ducum, quos aequore toto
> inque vicem nunc Turnus agit, nunc Troius heros,
> expediat? Tanton placuit concurrere motu,
> Iuppiter, aeterna gentis in pace futuras?
>
> (XII, 500–504)

(What god can now unfold for me so many horrors, who in song can tell such diverse deaths and the fall of captains inflicted, all over the battlefield, alternately, now by Turnus, now by the Trojan hero? Was it your will, Oh Jupiter, that in such a turmoil people should clash, who are destined to live in everlasting peace?)

In the perceptive words of Di Cesare:

The . . . passage portrays the alternating butchery of Aeneas and Turnus. The whole is epitomized in one line of the invocation:

inque vicem nunc Turnus agit, nunc Troius heros

—a line which is almost prosaic and flat ("now Turnus, now the Trojan hero takes his turn" at slaughter) and most effective for just that reason. Aeneas and Turnus are rhetorically juxtaposed, commingled, almost identified with each other. Vergil invites attention to the obviously balanced structure [in Book XII]: 505 *Aeneas,* 509 *Turnus,* 513 *ille* (Aeneas), 516 *hic* (Turnus), 529 *hic* (Aeneas), 535 *ille* (Turnus). The alternating movement gathers a stark inevitability; the two heroes pursue their work of butchery quite methodically, almost keeping time with each other. Gradually the view changes . . . to the victims, and the two heroes become anonymous agents of death as our attention is drawn to the recurring figure of the victim dying on alien ground. Finally the action broadens into large slaughter: *omnesque Latini, / omnes Dardanidae.* (219–20)

These are fraticidal wars, wars among equals, among people destined to live *in pace eterna.* As W. R. Johnson has argued, there are no good guys versus bad guys in the terrible wars of the *Aeneid* (115). William R. Nethercut is right when he points out that "it would be a mistake to insist that Aeneas is all duty and all order, while seeing Turnus as all chaos. *Furor* is not the special property of one sex or side; its figure throws a shadow over all the action of the epic, driving Trojans and Latins alike" (83). Even the gods cannot help feeling pity over such "iram inanem" (useless fury):

di Jovis in tectis iram miserantur inanem
amborum et tantos mortalibus esse labores.
(X, 758–59)

(The gods in Jove's halls pity the vain wrath of either host, and
grieve that mortals should endure such toils.)

The strength of that "amborum" (of both), reinforced by its position at
the beginning of the verse, leaves no room for doubt. The "useless fury"
belongs to both sides equally.

Another aspect of this "fearful symmetry" becomes apparent if we
consider the roles in which the contenders are cast. In this "second *Iliad*"
(Anderson) or "Iliadic *Aeneid*" (Otis, chap. 7), as the second part of the
poem has been called, the situation of the *Iliad* appears to be completely
reversed: the defeated Trojans have now consciously assumed the role of
their enemies, the Greeks. That is to say, Aeneas is now acting in the role
of Achilles. Or is it Turnus, the Rutulian hero, who should be cast in that
role? Turnus certainly thinks so, as he tells the huge Pandarus just before
he kills him: "Hic etiam inventum Priamo narrabis Achillem" (You will
tell Priam that you also found Achilles here) (IX, 742). The Sibyl had
also referred to Turnus as another Achilles (VI, 89). And of course so
thinks Amata, the Queen. After all, has Aeneas not come, like Trojan
Paris, to steal a bride away? It all depends on who has a proper right to
Lavinia; but that is precisely what is at stake in the fighting. As far as the
contenders are concerned, only the outcome of the war will reveal who
is a Paris and who is an Achilles.

Recent critics have often seen these parallels, and have at times taken
pains to demonstrate that, in spite of all the overwhelming symmetries,
Aeneas is still in the right and Turnus in the wrong. It is indeed very
difficult for us to imagine what the purpose could be of a perfectly even
battle, since such a battle would lead nowhere except to mutual annihilation. At some point, we rightly figure, there has to be an imbalance; the
violence of one of the contendants will overpower the violence of the
other. Thus the evenness of the battle as such is seen by us as meaningless
and purely provisional. We always read the battle retrospectively and
from the point of view of the victor. The victor, we automatically assume,
has to be the instrument of fate (for how can a defeated fate be fate at
all?), and the defeated party must of necessity appear as having been an
obstacle to the fulfillment of fate, an obstacle that simply had to be re-

moved. In other words, we should not attach too much importance to those Virgilian parallelisms.

The problem is that there are too many of them, either strikingly explicit or clearly implied. For example, if Aeneas is a second Achilles, then Turnus inevitably becomes the very image of Hector, the Trojan champion, whose mission as defender of the Trojan race has now been assumed by Aeneas himself. This reversal of roles is made abundantly clear in the battle between the two heroes with which the poem ends: Aeneas running in circles after Turnus just as Achilles ran in circles after Hector before the walls of Troy, which are now the walls of Laurentium. In other words, by deliberately creating a parallel between the end of his poem and the *Iliad,* Virgil is making clear that the roles are perfectly interchangeable. Aeneas is in fact fighting his own double, his enemy twin.

In the eyes of the combatants, the fighting reveals the irreconcilable character of their differences. In the eyes of Virgil, the more they fight the more alike they become. Something must happen to create an imbalance. But Virgil wants to show that such an imbalance must come after all reasons to stop the violence have failed, that it is an outcome in extremis.

Aeneas does not win because he is in the right, nor does Turnus lose because he is in the wrong. All ethical and purely rational differences between them have disappeared in the violent whirlwind. This is the founding moment, precisely because the entire future of Rome, or rather, the very possibility of there being a Rome at all, hangs in the balance, equally poised between being and not being. The decision to tip the scales one way or the other does not rest on any remaining arguable difference between the violent partners; this is why the decision is truly original in the most radical sense. This is the founding decision, because it will create the first difference, the decisive difference upon which all the others will come to rest.

The only remaining question at that moment is, Who will be the victim? The founding decision should not be interpreted as a determination of which of the contending parties is going to win, who is going to have the last word on violence, whose violence is going to prevail. Strictly speaking, nobody can have the last word on a violence that in order to reach the necessary founding intensity, must bring everybody down to the same level. In fact, the only one who can be said to have the last word on this violence is the victim. Jupiter does not nod in the direction of the winner, but only in the direction of the victim. At that crucial moment, in the eyes of Virgil, Aeneas is not "the winner," he is the sacrificer, the priest, who strikes the sacred blow that will kill the victim, who will become the cornerstone for the foundation of the city.

6. The End of the Poem and the Cry of the Victim

We must understand the profound meaning behind Jupiter's perfectly balanced scales of destiny, held up as the two contendants carry on their even fight, until the death of one of them breaks the balance by weighting one side of the scales (XII, 725–27). What gives meaning to the abrupt end of Virgil's poem is not so much Aeneas's victory but the sacrifice of Turnus. The poem ends, not with the outcry of the victor, but with the protesting moan of the dying victim: "vitaque cum gemitu fugit indignata sub umbras" (and life with a moan passed indignant to the Shades below). This is, once again, the founding moment; this is the last, or, if one prefers, the first word. Beyond that there is nothing more to say, or nothing has been said yet, nothing can be articulated. Sacrificially speaking, the victim is the alpha and the omega, the degree zero of human culture.

There is perhaps nothing in the entire poem so bluntly significant as that last line. And yet we have never known what to do with it. "It is no secret that there is general dissatisfaction or uneasiness with this famous closure" (W. R. Johnson, 115). We have always expected the victor, the poetic hero, to have the last word. We have always assumed that Rome, that human civilization, rested on the shoulders of its victorious heroes, not on those of its sacrificed victims. This emphasis on, this centrality of, the victim is profoundly disquieting to us. And there can be little doubt that Virgil knew of such disquiet; this is why his totally unexpected ending can only be interpreted as a blunt indication or revelation of the sacrificial logic that operates, half veiled, just below the traditional epic surface.

Not that Virgil's deliberate focusing of attention on the victim has passed unnoticed. W. R. Johnson is fully aware of it, and he asks some very pertinent questions: "Why does Vergil imagine his Turnus as a victim? Why does the victimization of Turnus become the central issue of the poem's climax?" (115). My answer can only be somewhat tautological, Virgil imagines his Turnus as a victim, because he is *the* victim, the sacrificial victim; and he makes this process of victimization the central issue of the poem's climax, because this is the founding moment, and the civilization to which this moment will give rise, emerges from the Italian victim, not from the Trojan victor. Their sacrificing function accomplished, "commixti corpore tantum / subsident Teucri" (the Trojans will sink down and merge into the [Ausonian or Italian] mass) (XII, 835–36).

There will no longer be a difference between Italians and Trojans. All will be blended together into a race of people from which the name and language of the Trojans will have disappeared:

> morem ritusque sacrorum
> adiciam faciamque omnis uno ore Latinos.
> hinc genus Ausonio mixtum quod sanguine surget
>
> (836–38)

(Their sacred laws and rites will I add and make them to be Latins of one tongue. Hence shall arise a race blended with Ausonian blood.)

Virgil's final vision of the origin of Rome is that of a blended, or, as it were, homogenized, equalized mass of people gathered together around the killing of the victim. But what an equalizing carnage it took, how many trials that failed to stop the violence, "et tantos mortalibus esse labores"!

The entire poem has been moving toward an increasing realization of the actual, unspeakable grounds in which such a strange formula as that which demands that one head, any head, be given up for the sake of many, can literally and historically make sense. The poem moves toward such a revelation beyond the purely mythical, that is, beyond the idea that the violence that requires one for the sake of many originates outside the community, as some sort of sacred toll to be paid in order to keep away the anger or jealousy of the gods. The only way in which the strange formula can make sense in a real situation is by postulating the collapse of all differences in the midst of a violence that is generated internally, a fratricidal violence, in which everybody sooner or later ends up participating equally. Once the violence is seen as immanent, as an internal breaking down of all established differences, then the arbitrary, the "accidental" character attached to the selection of the victim becomes inevitable; it becomes the only objective way to represent the crisis and to introduce a principle of differentiation, where all other attempts at creating a stable difference between the contenders, at keeping them apart, have failed. Toward the end of the poem, the situation is such that, even if we eliminate all divine creatures from the scene, either one, any one, stands in for everybody or the Trojans and the Italians will destroy each other.

And yet, if we eliminate Jupiter's decision, how is that tilting of the entire crisis in the direction of the *one* accomplished? How do things work out in the implied historical reality to which the poem alludes? Virgil does not say. There is nothing in the *Aeneid* to suggest an internal mechanism that would fulfill Jupiter's role in the real world. In other words, it appears that in Virgil's mind the *one*, the victim whose killing will serve as the cornerstone of civilized order, happens, as we already anticipated, in a totally haphazard and unpredictable way.

But still we have to ask why Virgil would imagine that things could happen like that at all. What kind of a reality model does he have in mind? Where do things ever happen that way? I believe we do not have to look very far to find the model that either inspired Virgil or acted as a confirmation of his poetic and sacrificial intuition: the Lucretian model.

7. The Lucretian Model

Virgil's admiration for Lucretius is well known. "From Gellius onward critics have remarked his indebtness to Lucretius" (Glover, 60). And as W. Y. Sellar said in reference to the *Georgics:* "The influence, direct and indirect, exercised by Lucretius on the thought, composition, and even the diction of the *Georgics* was perhaps stronger than that ever exercised, before or since, by one great poet on the work of another" (*Roman Poets of the Augustan Age,* 199) More recent critics have continued to acknowledge this extraordinary impact of the *De rerum natura* on Virgil. W. R. Johnson writes: "Virgil's reading of that poem was probably the most important thing in his life as a poet (to call that reading an event would be misleading since it is clear that the reading was habitual and unending)" (151).

But in the eyes of most critics, this Lucretian bent in Virgil's thought appears to be in clear contradiction with his epic project. One of the easiest ways to deal with this unresolved contradiction was that of T. R. Glover:

As [Virgil] grew older he became dissatisfied with Lucretius' philosophy, and tried to reconcile it somehow with other aspects of truth, which he had himself realized. . . . Virgil did not live to achieve the reconciliation which he felt to be necessary; and we find in him a man distracted with the spiritual necessity of holding opinions, which clearly conflict. . . . Dissastisfied with obvious antitheses as superficial, but unable to penetrate them and discover some fundamental unity underlying them, he seems at times to confuse rather than to reconcile, and eventually everything he does is apt to be affected by his habit. (63)

But as we shall see in a moment, the "distraction" and the "confusion" are only in the critic's mind.

A much more nuanced and sophisticated approach is W. R. Johnson's:

Why should a man who read *De rerum natura* so passionately and absorbed it so thoroughly undertake to write a poem that is not merely about what happens in history but is also about the vindication of the meaning of history in general and the meaning of the city in particular (in Epicurean terms, about how illusion is vindicated by illusion)? . . . These questions admit of no exact answer, but they invite speculation. Suppose Vergil's heart was divided. Suppose he read and reread his Lucretius as a religious atheist might peruse his Saint Paul—desperate, faithful in his disbelief, hoping, at some moment, for the illumination, because the fears that were so uncannily catalogued were, precisely, his own fears, and almost believing that he might discover the fears were, as the writer kept insisting, groundless? But suppose that, unpersuaded that the objects of his dread were unreal, he kept turning toward a belief in a divinely rational design wherein the small evils, though real, were part of a pattern, were christened by truth and justice, were gathered into the large goodness, invisible yet ineffably secure. If the stern freedoms of Epicurus could not save, then perhaps the rational cosmos and the renewed city, their microcosmos, might win what a single human being had not the strength to win—freedom from evil and fear, freedom for goodness and joy. (151)

Certainly Johnson's "speculation" deserves much more attention than we can give it here. But he almost turns Virgil into a Kierkegaardian or, perhaps, Unamunian Christian, which, of course, Virgil could never be. And I think that Johnson knows it. For he also says that

> the presence of the Stoic or the Epicurean sage on the Homeric battlefield creates a *concordia discors* that is clearly wrong for a celebration of *Roma aeterna* and evades any possible good resolution to the conflicts the poem mirrors. The historical and metaphysical stakes in this race between order and disorder are too high, and the hero, the order, and the disorder are all gathered up into, and at last devoured by, an implacable and unintelligible nihilism. (10–11)

But all of this is still a purely philosophical landscape. We really have not left the confines of intellectual history. And that is not quite the ground on which either Lucretius or Virgil operates. We should approach the problem from a different perspective.

In contrast to Aristotle, Lucretius is not primarily interested in developing a coherent theoretical construct, a philosophical grill, through which reality can be organized, classified, and made sense of. I think Michel Serres is right; he, Lucretius, and probably his revered master, Epicurus, too, are the first to be really interested in *things*, and more specifically, in how *things* are generated; *things*, not beliefs, or theories, or traditions; *things*, as opposed to people and their relationships. (Which does not mean that, in the final analysis, what moved them toward *things* was any different from what moved Plato or Aristotle toward philosophy). They believed, not without reason, that only the knowledge of *things* would be capable of calming the terrors of the mind. They sensed that the terrors of the mind were inextricably tied to the interindividual network of human relations, to the social, to the political, etc.

> Ecoutez maintenant les leçons de l'épicurisme. Elles se ramènent à ceci: réduisez au minimum le réseau des relations ou vous êtes plongés. Vivez au jardin, petit espace, avec quelques amis. Pas de famille, si possible, et pas de politique, en tout cas. Mais surtout, voici. Voici l'objet, les objets, le monde, la nature, la physique. Aphrodite plaisir naît du monde et des eaux. Mars est dans le forum et dans la foule en armes. Amenez vos relations à peu et

vos objets au monde, l'intersubjectif au minimum, et l'objectif au maximum. . . . Oubliez le sacré, cela signifie: oubliez la violence qui le fonde, et oubliez le religieux, qui relie les hommes entre eux. Considérez l'objet, les objets, la nature. Oui, celui qui a dit voici, *ecce, hoc est,* celui-là, Memmius, est un dieu, un dieu parmi les hommes. . . . Cependant, la peste revient. Elle détruit Athènes, ramène la violence et la mort. Pourquoi? *Revenons à l'objet.* Il n'y a que deux objets, constitutifs de toutes choses: les atomes, le vide. Le vide, *inane,* a pour racine le verbe grec . . . , *inein,* qui signifie purger, expulser, ou, au passif, être chassé par une purge. Le vide est partie du chaos, mais il est aussi une catharsis. Iphigénie sacrifiée, purge ou catharsis pour les roitelets grecs. . . . Passage à l'objet pour être libéré de Mars. Mais le premier objet c'est encore la purge, *ce n'est que le concept physique de la catharsis.* Deuxième objet, l'atome. La solution sacrée commence par une partition de l'espace, par un découpage. Le temple est un lieu dichotomisé, le mot même le dit. . . . *Le mot temple est bien de la même famille qu'atome.* Atome est le dernier ou le premier temple, et vide est la dernière ou la première purgation. . . . La nature est encore un substitut sacrificiel. La violence est encore, toujours, dans la physique. Alors les atome germes saccagent Athènes, les derniers survivants se surtuen entre eux. . . . Ce n'est pas la politique ou la sociologie qui est projetée dans la nature, c'est le sacré. En dessous du sacré, la violence. En dessous de l'objet, les relations réapparaissent. (Serres, 164–66)

(Now listen to the lessons of Epicureanism. They come down to this: reduce to the minimum the network of relationships in which you are immersed. Live in the garden, the small space, with a few friends. No family, if possible, and, in any case, no politics. But above all, there, look there, the object, the things, the world out there, nature, physics. Aphrodite-pleasure is born out of the world and the waters. Mars stands on the forum and amidst the crowd in arms. Bring your relationships to little and your objects to the world, the intersubjective to a minimum, and the objective to a maximum. . . . Forget the sacred, which means: forget the violence that grounds it, and forget religion, which ties up men with one another. Consider the object, all objects, nature. Yes, he who said, there! *ecce, hoc est,* that one over there, oh Memmius, he is a god, a god among men. . . .

And yet, the plague returns. It destroys Athens, it brings violence and death. Why? *Let's come back to the object.* There are only two objects, constitutive of all things: the atoms, the void. The root of the word void, *inane,* is the Greek verb *inein,* which means to purge, to expel, or, in the passive voice, to be chased away by a purge. The void is part of the chaos, but it is also a catharsis. Iphigenia sacrificed, a purge or catharsis for those Greek petty kings. . . . To pass to the object in order to be liberated from Mars. But the first object is still the purge, which is but the catharsis in terms of physics. Second objet, the atom. The sacred solution begins with a partition of the space, a cut out. The temple is a place dichotomised, as the word itself indicates. . . . The word temple is indeed of the same family as atom. The atom is the last or the first temple, and the void is the last or the first purgation. . . . Nature is still a sacrificial substitute. There is still, there is always, violence in physics. Then the atom germs devastate Athens, and the last survivors kill one another. . . . It is not politics or sociology that is projected into nature, but the sacred. Underneath the sacred, violence. Underneath the object, relationships reappear.) (my translation)

In other words, there is a perfect homology and a perfect parallelism between history and nature:

Ladite histoire humaine va se développer sur le même schéma que ladite histoire naturelle, mais en continuité avec elle. (221)

(The aforementioned human history is going to develop along the same scheme as the aforementioned natural history, but in continuity with it.)

In the final analysis, there is just one nature of things, one way of coming into being:

Il y a une nature des choses, un processus d'émergence, qui suffit. Sa fonction est universelle. Qu'il s'agisse des atomes, des espèces, et plus tard, de la société, le même schéma est toujours au travail.

Soit tout d'abord un équilibre et, ici, là, demain ou naguère, un écart. (218)

(There is one nature of things, one process of emergence, which is sufficient. Its function is universal. Whether it is atoms, species, and later, society, it is the same scheme that is always at work. That is, initially equilibrium, and then, here or there, tomorrow or only yesterday, a displacement.)

Even though a brilliant analysis like that of Michel Serres can reveal the internal logic of Lucretius's text, carry it to its ultimate consequences, and see through its implicit assumptions, it is by no means clear that such clarity of thought, such a transparent awareness, is a faithful reflection of Lucretius's own awareness. There is a lot that Michel Serres knows that Lucretius did not know.

When we get to Virgil, however, there can be little doubt. He knew. He saw the perfect homology, the striking parallelism, between "the nature—the nascence—of things" and that of the sacred. Order, that is to say, organization, structure, is generated out of disorder and randomness. Prior to this creative disorder, there is nothing but a situation of maximum entropy where energy is utterly and endlessly wasted through the void, where nothing stands out, nothing makes a difference, where the same repeats itself fruitlessly without end, a state of perfect equilibrium.

This dynamic equilibrium is described by Lucretius as an endless fall of the atoms through the void, each one carried by its own weight, but all traveling at exactly the same speed because the void offers no resistance at all to their fall. A deviation from symmetry must occur, a break in the equilibrium, a minimum of disorder, before anything can be born. This is, of course, Lucretius's famous *clinamen* (swerve):

> corpora cum deorsum rectum per inane feruntur
> ponderibus propriis, incerto tempore ferme
> incertisque locis spatio depellere paulum,
> tantum quod momen mutatum dicere possis.
> quod nisi declinare solerent, omnia deorsum,
> imbris uti guttae, caderent per inane profundum

nec foret offensus natus nec plaga creata
principiis: ita nil umquam natura creasset.

(2.217–24)

(When the atoms are being carried downwards by their own
weight in a straight line through the void, at a time totally unpredictable and in unpredictable places, they swerve just a little from
their course, just enough to be called a change of motion. For if
they were not apt to deviate, all would fall downwards like rain-
drops through the deep void, no collision would take place and
no blow would be caused among the first-beginnings: thus nature
would never have produced anything.)

And a little further he insists: "quare etiam atque etiam paulum inclinare
necessest / corpora, nec plus quam minimum" (2.243–44) (therefore
again and again I say, the atoms must incline a little, and not more than
just the minimum).

However, the same kind of disorder that creates everything, eventually—as the blows continue—returns everything to the original deadly
equilibrium from which it deviated, declined, emerged, was born. The
violence that created it will eventually destroy it. Thus the cause of death
and the precondition of life converge toward each other. As the living
structure approaches its doom it increasingly reveals the original equilibrium out of which it emerged by means of the smallest possible, random
and totally unpredictable, deviation from symmetry.

In view of this, all we have to do is substitute the human victim for the
original *clinamen* and we have the entire sacrificial logic that governs the
development of Virgil's *Aeneid*. Perhaps we can now understand how
literally Virgil must have meant the *inanity* of the violent fury that equal-
izes Trojans and Italians against each other, the *iram inanem* the gods
pity. For that is the precise Virgilian equivalent of Lucretius's *inane pro-
fundum,* through which the original particles endlessly fall in perfect
symmetry. When we reach that point in the poem we have reached the
founding moment, when either one death is made different or everything
will be death. But at that moment we must not forget all the accidental
deaths that have anticipated and prefigured the final (the original) death
of the founding victim.

It is important not to forget these deaths because the epic poem that
sings the great exploits of heroes and the glory of Rome, constitutes itself

as such, by hiding the underlying randomness of the one-for-the-many principle with a sacred veil, as already pointed out. In addition, as a carefully wrought work of art, the poem is guided from the beginning toward the final act of sacrificial victimization. Poetically speaking, that final act is anything but random. Everything the poem says points to, advances toward, the final victim—everything, precisely because the poem says absolutely nothing beyond that victim. Thus we have to turn the poem on its head. Everything emerges from the victim. Before the victim there is nothing but silence, the perfect symmetry of the atoms cascading into bottomless inanity. The "indignant moan" of the victim breaks the primeval silence. From then on there is language and meaning, and everything becomes possible. But everything will also bear the mark of the original random victimization.

There is much that one can learn, when reading the *Aeneid,* by keeping the Lucretian background in mind. And vice versa, Lucretius's text may become more revealing in the light of Virgil, for example, the strange and disturbing way in which Lucretius ends his poem, which is almost as strange and disturbing as that of the *Aeneid.*

The final vision of *De rerum natura* is a terrible one, the devastating effects of the plague in Athens. This final vision begins as a scientific description of how plagues occur and ends with a horrified presentation of how Athens's sacred institutions disintegrate and people start killing one another over the burial of their kindred. These are the poem's final verses:

> nec iam religio divom nec numina magni
> pendebantur enim: praesens dolor exsuperabat.
> nec mos ille sepulturae remanebat in urbe,
> quo prius hic populus semper consuerat humari;
> perturbatus enim totus trepidabat, et unus
> quisque suum pro re et pro tempore maestus humabat.
> multaque res subita et paupertas horrida suasit;
> namque suos consanguineos aliena rogorum
> insuper extructa ingenti clamore locabant
> subdebantque faces, multo cum sanguine saepe
> rixantes potius quam corpora desererentur.

(For indeed now neither the worship of the gods nor their power was much regarded: the present grief was too great. Nor did that custom of sepulture remain in the city, with which this nation in the past had been always accustomed to be buried; for the whole nation was in trepidation and dismay, and each one in his sorrow buried his own dead as time and circumstances allowed. Sudden need also and poverty persuaded [them] to many dreadful things: for they would lay their own kindred amidst loud lamentation upon [funeral] piles of wood not their own, and would set them on fire, often brawling with much shedding of blood rather than abandon the bodies.)

In the end, the physical horror of the plague merges with, becomes indistinguishable from, the sacred horror of all those corpses that must be given some kind of burial, taken from view. Clearly the pollution those abandoned bodies spread abroad is both physical and spiritual, that is, sacred. In the end, the terrors of the plague are no different from the terrors of hungry Acheron.

Lucretius has come full circle. Traveling along his scientific trajectory away from the sacred, in avoidance of the sacred, the very nature of things brings him back to the point of departure. It is no accident. In reality he had never left the sacred behind, cut himself loose from it. His scientific project was never meant to physically cure the plague, to avoid, to delay death. His physics never had any other purpose than to calm the sacred fears of the mind. It drew all of its vitality from it. Any weakness, any failure, would immediately bring the terrors of Acheron to the surface. Ideally Lucretian science ought to provide the citizens with the means to keep calm in the face of death, in the face of all those unburied corpses. But is that not precisely the function of the sacred as well? Was that not what the required burials of Misenus and Palinurus were all about? So it is not as if the effectiveness or the reality of the sacred were to be measured by scientific standards, but, rather, the opposite: the effectiveness of science would indeed be measured in sacred terms, in terms of how well it could keep the sacred under control, removed from the scene, that is to say, nonpolluting. Virgil probably knew all that already when he was writing the *Georgics*. Let us remember those famous lines again: "Felix, qui potuit rerum cognoscere causas . . . / . . . fortunatus et ille, deos qui novit agrestis."

But Virgil learned even further: Lucretius's materialist philosophy, his physics, was modeled on the inner logic of the old sacrificial principle of the one for the many. The physical clinamen that breaks the deadly undifferentiation of the atoms falling into endless inanity, echoes the victim required by the violent undifferentiation of the "even battle" waged by contending parties who look more and more like mirror images of each other. The final vision of *De rerum natura*, a terror-stricken population in which they are all hysterically killing one another, could easily become in Virgil's eyes the very image of the founding crisis, the violent grounds out of which either *one* is differentiated from the rest, made to bear responsibility for the entire crisis, or they will all perish. Of course, the violent elimination of this *one* is not going to save anybody from the real plague. But that is not ultimately the problem. Epicurean science will not save anybody from the plague either. The problem is, rather, how to maintain or to create some kind of order, both psychological and social, in the midst of a devastating violence—it does not matter at all whether natural or man-made—that nobody can control. And that ultimate possibility is inseparable, logically *and* physically inseparable, from the emergence of the sacred.

Lucretius the scientist was horrified by the utter arbitrariness of the victimizing process, which came to be typified in his mind by the cruel sacrificial killing of beautiful Iphigenia. Ironically, what Virgil the poet learned from Lucretius the scientist was that such arbitrariness was by no means accidental or capricious, but was in the final analysis required by the very nature, even the material nature, of things. What Lucretius unwittingly taught Virgil was not a way out of the sacred, but quite the opposite: the inevitability as well as the arbitrariness of the sacred.

Virgil's problem was not, as critics have so often said, that he could not bring together his interest in science, on the one hand, and his interest in history and the sacred, on the other. Quite the contrary, his problem was that he could see only too well the common sacred ground on which those two things stood mirroring each other, while simultaneously contradicting and opposing each other. But the contradiction was not in Virgil. It was in the object of his meditation, the sacred founding victim itself: history, civilization, spoke of a perfectly differentiated, unique victim; Lucretian science told him it could be anybody, in a totally random and unpredictable manner. The *Aeneid* constitutes itself by weaving a poetic veil of perfectly differentiated characters over a Lucretian base of random violence. But in doing that Virgil is following strictly the foundational logic of the sacred, without which the Lucretian base would not be able to generate civilized history. The *Aeneid* is a monumental trick, a sacred ruse, performed with open eyes and the sad realization that there is no other way.

"En dessous du sacré, la violence. En dessous de l'objet, les relations réapparaissent." (Underneath the sacred, violence; underneath the objet, [human] relationships reappear.) It is true, the violence underneath the sacred is human violence, violent human relationships. But human violence is not of itself sacred. It becomes sacred insofar as it extends or increases beyond human control. The transcendent character of the sacred refers, in its own way, to a real de facto situation. It is an attempt to take human violence away from human hands, because human beings are totally powerless to stop it. Thus it is at the same time a testimony to a human condition of helplessness and despair. The victimization process saves the situation in extremis, but it brings no sense of liberation whatsoever; it weighs very heavily on the consciousness of those who are saved by it.

Seen through the prism of the victimizing sacred, human beings caught in violent relationships are soon perceived as being possessed by forces or powers beyond their control—a vision that is far from fanciful. That is how Virgil describes the onslaught of the terror-stricken spirit of violence taking over a human being time and time again. We may bring to mind the case of Turnus once more, perhaps the most striking example in the entire poem:

> olli somnum ingens rumpit pavor, ossaque et artus
> perfundit toto proruptus corpore sudor.
> arma amens fremit arma toro tectisque requirit:
> saevit amor ferri et scelerata insania belli,
> ira super.
>   (VII, 458–62)

(A monstrous terror broke his sleep, and the sweat, bursting forth from his body, soaks his bones and limbs. Madly he yells for arms, arms he seeks in couch and chamber: a desire for the sword rages in him, and the murderous insanity of war, and hatred.)

We may completely ignore the mythical expression of this violent possession. It is not one of the furies from Hades who subdues the mind and body of the young warrior. It is a very real maddening violence filled with horrifying and uncontrollable terror—the violence of the founding crisis that is already in the air.

8. Beyond the Howls of Acheron

To put it mildly, this vision is not exactly of the sort that allows for an objective and detailed analysis of how those human relationships develop, which may eventually bring about a state of uncontrollable internecine violence. Before any such analysis becomes possible, one should be able to look simultaneously at the maddening vortex of the crisis and at specific human relationships, without being overcome by a sense of helplessness. One should be able to trace lines of responsibility. Terror must be subdued and hopeless despair broken before human beings can begin to experience a meaningful sense of rational, responsible guilt; before the realization may sink in that the founding maelstrom from which the victim emerges is of their own doing and can be avoided, the secret of it lying in the way human beings relate to one another.

All those who accuse Christianity of implanting a sense of guilt, an inner "conscience," in the human individual as such, as individual, are indeed right. But they do not have an inkling of what that "conscience" replaced. We are not used to thinking of guilt as a liberating experience. But it all depends on where you are coming from. It is a question of degree. Doom, hopelessness, and despair are far worse than responsible guilt. In fact, a rational and freely accepted sense of guilt may be a healthy antidote against despair. At any rate, this was certainly not the case with Virgil. The founding violence at which he is looking is long past the point where a sense of guilt can make any difference. He did not live that historical possibility. It was only in the Judeo-Christian tradition where a sense of guilt and of responsibility for the killing of the victim emerged and became fully developed, from the story of Cain and Abel to the Passion of Christ and his Resurrection (see Williams). It was only in this tradition that the terror and despair of the founding crisis was not disguised or bypassed, but looked straight in the eye, as it were, and broken. Because of this extraordinary victory over the terrifying rumblings of Acheron, the historical possibility arises to undertake a full, objective, and unafraid investigation of the way human relationships may develop into the kind of original situation that Virgil contemplated so somberly.

In my opinion, this bold investigation is what René Girard has done. Needless to say, he is fully aware that he owes the historical possibility of his research to the formidable power of the nonvictimizing spirit of the Judeo-Christian text. As is well known, at the basis of Girard's analysis of human relationships lies his theory of mimetic desire, a theory that can account for the two most typically Virgilian observations as the founding crisis rapidly develops: the almost instantaneous contagion of insane, consciousness-dissolving, human violence, and the deadly symmetry between the contending parties. The founding crisis is thoroughly mimetic:

RENE GIRARD: Only an arbitrary victim can resolve the crisis because acts of violence, as mimetic phenomena, are identical and distributed as such within the community. No one can assign an origin to the crisis or judge degrees of responsibility for it. Yet the *surrogate victim* will eventually appear and reconcile the community; the sheer escalation of the crisis, linked to progressively accumulating mimetic effects, will make the designation of such a victim automatic.

JEAN-MICHEL OUGHOURLIAN: I find this hard to follow. You assert that the mimetic crisis, an anarchy of conflict and violence in the community, not only can but must end with a certain type of arbitrary resolution. It would mean that the resolution is something like a natural mechanism. This seems to me a difficult point in your theory, one that requires clarification.

RENE GIRARD: It is necessary to think through the logic of mimetic conflict and its resulting violence. As rivalry becomes acute, the rivals are more apt to forget about whatever objects are, in principle, the cause of the rivalry and instead to become more fascinated with one another. In effect the rivalry is purified of any external stake and becomes a matter of pure rivalry and prestige. . . . At this point mimesis is stronger than ever but no longer exerts any force at the level of the object; the object has simply dropped from view. Only the antagonists remain; we designate them as doubles because from the point of view of the antagonism, nothing distinguishes them.

If the object is excluded there can no longer be any acquisitive mimesis. . . . There is no longer any support for mimesis but the antagonists themselves. What will occur at the heart of the crisis will therefore be the mimetic substitution of antagonists. If *acquisitive mimesis* divides by leading two or more individuals to converge on one and the same object with a view to appropriating it, conflictual mimesis will inevitably unify by leading two or more individuals to converge on one and the same adversary that all wish to strike down. Acquisitive mimesis is contagious, and if the number of individuals polarized around a single object increases, other members of the community, as yet not implicated, will tend to follow the example of those who are; conflictual mimesis necessarily follows the same course because the same force is involved. Once the object has disappeared and the mimetic frenzy has reached a high degree of intensity, one can expect conflictual mimesis to take over and snowball in its effects. Since the power of mimetic attraction multiplies with the number of those polarized, it is inevitable that at one moment the entire community will find itself unified against a single individual. Conflictual mimesis therefore creates a de facto allegiance against a common enemy, such that the conclusion of the crisis is nothing other than the reconciliation of the community.

Except in certain cases, there is no telling what insignificant reason will lead mimetic hostility to converge on one particular victim rather than on another; yet the victim will not appear to be any less absolutely unique and different, a result not only of the hate-filled idolatry to which the victim is subject, but also and especially of the effects of the reconciliation created by the unanimous polarization.

The community satisfies its rage against an arbitrary victim in the unshakable conviction that it has found the one and only source of its trouble. It then finds itself without adversaries, purged of all hostility against those for whom, a second before, it had shown the most extreme rage.

The return to a calmer state of affairs appears to confirm the responsibility of the victim for the mimetic discord that had troubled the community. The community thinks of itself as entirely passive *vis-à-vis* its own victim, whereas the latter appears, by contrast, to be the only active and responsible agent in the matter. Once it is understood that the inversion of the real relation between victim and community occurs in the resolution of the crisis, it is possible to see why the victim is believed to be *sacred*. The victim is held responsible for the renewed calm in the community and for the disorder that preceded this return. It is even believed to have brought about its own death. (*Things Hidden*, 25–27)

Clearly there is something here about which the traditional formulation of the sacrificial principle does not say anything. The principle says that one head will be given up for the sake of many. It says nothing about all those many murderously uniting against the one.

Like Girard, Virgil knows that "only an arbitrary victim can resolve the crisis." As he also knows that "no one can assign an origin to the crisis or judge degrees of responsibility for it." In other words, he knows that "the resolution [of the crisis] is something like a natural mechanism." He learned it from Lucretius. He even knows that in spite of such arbitrariness "the victim will not appear to be any less absolutely unique and different," precisely because it fulfills a sacred function. Indeed, he knows that this appearance must be preserved at all costs.

But knowing all that, what is the point of speaking at this juncture of mimetic desire, of rivals who "become more fascinated with one another," of "hate-filled idolatry," etc.? Such observations would appear to be scientifically pointless to Virgil, or, perhaps, the sort of thing in which young Ovid, for example, with his characteristic tongue-in-cheek attitude, might have been interested. When confronted with the terror-ridden maelstrom of the founding violence, what difference could it make to notice the way in which human beings become mimetically trapped in their relationships? The violence of the maelstrom itself would quickly make all such considerations irrelevant, not only in the reality of the crisis itself, but in Virgil's mind as well. In Virgil's mind, all those mimetic traps are already an aspect and an integral part of the crisis. They do not explain the crisis; they are explained by it. There is no getting around, no going behind the crisis except through the victim. The only uniqueness, the only individuality that survives the crisis is that of the victim.

To turn things around, to explain the crisis in terms of individual relationships, one must assume that the crisis and its sacred victim are not the final and definitive word about human beings and the way they may relate to one another; one must assume human beings capable of surviving without killing the founding victim. From a Virgilian perspective such an assumption would have been incomprehensible and, of course, totally unsupported by any scientific evidence.

And yet, on the basis of this scientifically unsupported assumption, one can explain scientifically what Lucretian science could not, namely, the way in which all the violence of the founding crisis gets tilted, "declined," and channeled toward one, and only one, individual. Even though the violence that kills the founding victim is not controlled by anybody, that does not mean that it is in itself utterly devoid of logic. Nobody controls the violence, but it seems that everybody is controlled by the violence in a rather predictable fashion. The victim can be anybody, but the victimizing mechanism is the same predictable one in every case.

What Girard has discovered is that the internal logic of the entire crisis, the logic that drives the uncontrollable violence, is exactly the same as that which keeps the violence alive between any two contenders. A big multitude of individuals fighting one another is essentially no different from the violent tit for tat that keeps two fighting individuals mimetically tied to each other. It is just a matter of degree. As soon as I strike my neighbor I am on my way to join the crowd that will sooner or later gather murderously around the body of the sacrificial founding victim, but now I know how I got there and what my participation has been.

To say that Girard has "discovered" this is something to be properly understood. He has only uncovered or rediscovered the scientific relevance of what was already there, either close to the surface or glaringly explicit, in the Christian text; the text that says that everything is at stake in the relationship between me and any other human being. My relationship with this other human being determines whether or not I join in the collective expulsion of the victim that inevitably sacralizes human violence. The way I relate to this other *is* the way I relate to the founding victim:

> Then the just will ask him: "Lord, when did we see you hungry and feed you or see you thirsty and give you drink? When did we welcome you away from home or clothe you in your nakedness? When did we visit you when you were ill or in prison?" The king will answer them: "I assure you, as often as you did it for one of my least brothers, you did it for me." (Matt. 25:37–40)

One cannot possibly exagerate the importance of this discovery. The sacred is the other! My neighbor! Or rather, the sacred is what stands between me and my neighbor, what protects both of us from each other, what has always mediated and shaped our relationship. I have never really seen my neighbor; I have always seen him through the eyes of the sacred, through the sacralized murder of the victim. But now it has become possible to see him face to face, so long as I recognize the murder of the founding victim for what it really is, murder, and refrain from participating in it. And vice versa, I refrain from participating in the founding murder, by refraining from killing my neighbor.

In the final analysis, the object of the process of desacralization is the other, my neighbor. This is why the maddening terror that accompanies the breakdown of the sacred and drives the uncontrollable violence that issues in the restoration of the sacred may adhere to *the other* in the new, the unprecedented, face-to-face encounter. Not without reason did Sartre say in *Huis Clos* that "L'Enfer, c'est les Autres" (hell is other people). Without the protection of the old, victimizing sacred, the other may become the very image of the frightening sacrificial crisis.

Long before modern existentialism the Epicureans had already heard the rumblings of Acheron at the very heart of social relationships. That is why they avoided them as much as possible and tried to live as far away from their neighbors as they would from the sacred itself. That is why they fixed their eyes on "the nature of things."

> *L'événement le plus révolutionnaire dans l'histoire des hommes, et, peut-être, l'évolution des hominiens, fut moins, je crois, l'accession à l'abstrait ou à la généralité, dans et par le langage, qu'un arrachement par rapport à l'ensemble des relations que nous entretenons dans la famille, le groupe, etc., et ne concernant qu'eux et nous, aboutissant à un accord, peut-être confus, mais, soudain, spécifique, au sujet d'une chose extérieure à cet ensemble. Avant cet événement, il n'existait que le réseau des relations, nous y étions plongés sans recours. Et tout-à-coup, une chose, quelque chose apparait hors le réseau. Les messages échangés ne disent plus: je, tu, il, nous, vous, etc., mais ceci, voici. Ecce. Voici la chose même. . . . L'hominisation consiste en ce message: voici du pain, qui que je sois, qui que tu sois. Hoc est, cela est, au neutre. Neutre, pour le genre, neutre, pour la guerre. . . . Ecoutez maintenant les leçons de l'épicurisme. (Serres, 163–64)*

(The most revolutionary event in human history and, perhaps, in the evolution of hominids, was not so much, I believe, the accession to abstract thinking or to generality by means of language, as it was rather a detachment, a pulling away, from the whole of relationships which we maintain within the family, the group, etc., which only concern them and us, and leading to an agreement, perhaps confused, but sudden, specific, with regard to a thing exterior to the whole of those relationships. Before this event there was nothing but the network of relationships; we were immersed in them unavoidably. And, all of a sudden, a thing, any thing, appears beyond the network. Messages exchanged no longer say: I, you, he, we, etc., but *this, this right there. Ecce.* The thing itself. . . . The process of hominization consists of this message: this is bread, no matter who I am, no matter who you are. *Hoc est,* this thing is, in the neuter. Neuter for gender, neuter for war. . . . Now listen to the lessons of Epicureanism. (my translation)

Nevertheless, we cannot forget that the first *thing* to stand out of the network of human relationships, out there, expelled from and by the violence of those relationships, the first thing about which there is an agreement that can be called human and yet a sign of something beyond the human, is the dead body of the collectively killed victim. All other *things* rest on that first one, piled up on top, burying it underneath. Nobody knows better than Michel Serres that human culture is a huge pyramid.

Epicureans run away from relationships, breathlessly taking refuge in "the nature of things." But in the end, inevitably, "en dessous de l'objet, les relations réapparaissent," underneath the *thing* relationships reappear, together with violence and the sacred. The breathless run from relationships to the *thing*, in order to avoid the sacred, will prove to be utterly futile. The *thing* thus found is still a sacred thing.

When the veil of the sacred is truly lifted the very first thing that comes into view is not a thing, it is your neighbor. You cannot run from your neighbor to a desacralized thing. You have to make peace with your neighbor first, refrain from killing him, before you can truly find that *thing*, "neuter for war," that is no longer a cover-up, because there is no longer anything to hide; that is the *thing* that will finally become a proper object of scientific investigation; an investigation that will only be truly scientific to the extent that it lets the thing rest in itself. We will find and save that *thing* in the process of finding and saving our neighbor, not the other way around. No-thing will save us from one another.

Virgil's somber pessimism is the most eloquent commentary on the Epicurean failure to break the stranglehold of the victimizing sacred. It was not the first attempt, as we already know, nor would it be the last, as we will see when we study Marx. In fact, we can already anticipate in what way the Epicurean attempt foreshadows that of Marx. For Marx will also try to avoid or bypass the violence of interindividual relationships in order to see the total violence of the "system," from which he would then return to explain the violence of those relationships as a function of the total violence of the system. In Marx, individuals never meet each other face to face, only through the "system." Human alienation is a systemic problem. The results were perfectly predictable: a return of the victimizing sacred even with a vengeance, a regression to the terrors of Acheron in secular and bureaucratic form but no less oppressive.

I do not mean to imply, however, that there is no difference between Lucretius and Marx. There are very significant differences. Lucretius lived close to the old, victimizing sacred and was deeply aware of its extraordinary power over human minds. His science of natural causes was meant as an individual's defense or antidote against sacred terror. But he never imagined that such terror would simply vanish entirely from the face of the earth. Marx, on the other hand, imagined just that. He knew (although he never knew why he knew) that the sacred was a cover-up for the violence of some men against others, of one part of society against the other. And he also knew that this situation was not the invention of anybody in particular but had come about in "the nature, the material nature, of things," so to speak. Then he made his great discovery: it was also in the nature of things to work themselves out in such a way as to eventually generate a clear and final culprit. Final, because there would be complete unanimity regarding the identity of the crisis-generated culprit. So, once this culprit was eliminated, the solution—he thought—had to be complete and total. In other words, the alienating and oppressive system, after going through a series of provisional or tentative expulsions that never quite managed to be clearly unanimous, would work itself out of existence upon finding the victim against which everybody would turn. And this is how Marx would get rid of the sacred!

Obviously, such a "solution" to free the world of the sacred cover-up of man's violence against man, could only be seen as such in a world that had already forgotten what the old sacred was all about and how it operated, in a world that was already largely liberated from that sacred.

Lucretius or Virgil would have never imagined that such a "solution" could be perceived as new.

It was not given to any of the traditional scientific disciplines, or to philosophy, to explore the labyrinthian genesis of specifically human violence in interindividual relationships, but to lowly poetry. When the sacred veil was lifted—when desacralization accelerated, issuing forth the modern era—two things happened: (1) the sacred function of poetry at its highest, the epic function, was hopelessly undermined; and (2) all those interpersonal relationships, that had always been the very stuff poetic fiction was made of, acquired unprecedented importance, moved center stage, were seen with new, wide open, eyes.

When the modern poet in sixteenth-century Europe tries to imitate Virgil in the creation of a new Christian epic, he sets for himself an impossible task: traditional epic violence can no longer hide, nor is it needed to hide, its human and nothing but human character, its origin in the hotbed of human relationships. His epic project will tend to be diverted time and time again into an exploration of those relationships, and the vagaries and ambiguities of human desire. The most symptomatic hero of this impossible epic task could very well be Orlando Furioso, forever lost in the intricate forests of desire, driven by love and maddening jealousy.

It fell primarily to the poet, and not the scientist, to investigate the reality and the newly discovered meaning of human alienation.

4

BEYOND THE EPIC MODEL

L'oeuvre héroique est celui qui donne le prix et le vrai titre de poète. Et il est donc d'une telle importance et d'un tel prestige qu'une langue ne peut passer pour célèbre pour les siècles si elle n'a pas traité le sujet héroique que sont les guerres. Nous dirons donc que les autres genres d'écrit sont les rivières et les ruisseaux, et l'héroique une mer, comme une forme et image d'univers: d'autant qu'il n'est matière, tant soit-elle ardue, précieuse, ou excellente en la nature des choses, qui ne s'y puisse apporter et qui n'y puisse entrer. (J. Peletier du Mans, Book 2, chap. 8)

(The heroic poem is the one that confers the prize and the true title of poet. It is of such importance and prestige that a language cannot be considered illustrious for the centuries if it has not treated the heroic subject, which is war. Therefore, we shall say that the other literary genres are the rivers and streams, and the heroic is the sea, as in the shape and image of a universe; so much so that there is no topic, no matter how difficult, precious, or excellent in the nature of things that cannot be brought in and entered into it.)

1. The Historical Failure of the Epic

If it were true that ideas make history, that is, that a transparent and unequivocal relationship exists between the history of ideas and the direction in which history may be developing at a given time, then the enormous interest, indeed fascination, with which men from the sixteenth to the eighteenth centuries viewed epic poetry, would have to be taken as evidence of its great historical relevance, especially when we see the large number of epic poems that were written in Europe during that time. But as we know now, that was certainly not the case. Underneath such an extraordinary showing of interest, what we actually see is the growing failure of the epic to meet that interest or to fulfill the great expectations placed in it.

The admiration, the reverence, with which the Homeric and Virgilian epics were contemplated can hardly be overemphasized. As E. M. W. Tillyard said, "every particle of all the motives that urged the men of the Renaissance to prize and to revere and imitate classical antiquity united in asserting the value, even the sacrosanctity, of the epic in its strict classical manifestation" (2). The epic was the representative of classical antiquity par excellence.

But the admiration itself was by no means confined to a view of the epic in such a representative role. When we read in Rymer's translation of René Rapin's *Réflexions sur La Poétique d'Aristote* (1674; repr. 1979) things like, "The Epick Poem is that which is the greatest and most noble in Poesie; it is the greatest work that humane wit is capable of" (72), the admiration is unbounded. There are no historical limitations placed on it.

The admiration continued unabated for almost two hundred years, which only made the epics of its own time pitifully inadequate by comparison. The expectations were such that practically every contemporary example was bound to fall short. As Rapin warns us, it may take whole ages to produce one true epic genius: "All the nobleness, and all the elevation of the most perfect genius, can hardly suffice to form one such as is requisite for an Heroick Poet. . . . [There] must be a judgment so solid, a discernment so exquisite, such perfect knowledge of the language, in which he writes; such obstinate study, profound meditation, vast capacity, that scarce whole ages can produce one genius fit for an Epick Poem" (72–73). It is no surprise that Rapin's feelings were shared by many: "Homer animates me, Virgil heats me, and all the rest freez me, so cold and flat they are" (70). Occasionally a few moderns are included in the "short File of Heroick Poets," as is the case with Davenant, who includes Tasso and Spenser, together with Homer, Virgil, Lucan, and Statius, in that "short File" of "Men, whose intellectuals were of so great a making . . . as perhaps they will in worthy memory outlast, even makers of Lawes, and Founders of Empires" (6). (This "short File," in spite of its shortness, does not speak too highly of Davenant's discriminating judgment.)

More often the explicit or implicit judgment on contemporaries was rather severe. In 1695, a little more than a century after Camoens's *Os Lusiadas* (1572) and Tasso's *Gerusalemme Liberata* (1581), even after Milton's *Paradise Lost* (1674, rev. ed.), Richard Blackmore could say without the slightest hesitation that "to write an epic poem is a work of that difficulty, that no one for near seventeen hundred years past has succeeded in it" (quoted in Hägin, 28). In other words, no one after Virgil has been able to write an epic poem worthy of its name. Certainly not for lack of trying, however; Blackmore himself apparently still had hopes. The passage just quoted appears in the preface to his *Prince Arthur*, a mere bibliographical curiosity today. But Blackmore's is only one among many other similar testimonies from the seventeenth century on, including, in addition to those already mentioned, the names of Boileau, Dryden, Voltaire, López de Sedano, Juan Pablo Forner, etc.

Speaking in particular about the eighteenth century, Stuart Curran remarks that "For nearly two centuries the vanity of eighteenth-century 'epic-ures' has been an accepted laughing-stock for otherwise tolerant literary historians, a safe arena in which to lavish pent-up temptations to ridicule." He advises understanding rather than scorn. For "it was, after all, the second age of Augustus, when civilization seemed to be consolidating into a limpid and cohesive structure. Unfortunately despite the numbers who vied for the role, there was no Virgil" (Le Bossu and Voltaire, introduction).

True, scorn will not help understanding. But we must realize two things: (1) the eighteenth century was only the lowest point of an irreversible decline already apparent in the sixteenth; and (2) to continue to think, or to imply that the cause of the decline was the unfortunate lack of poets with enough ability and epic genius, is to perpetuate the same misunderstanding that afflicted poetic theoreticians from the sixteenth century on. It was not an accident that there were no Homers or Virgils. The need for a more comprehensive and adequate explanation has been felt for some time: "It seems . . . that the failure of the epic can be explained very simply by the inadequate qualities of the writers and by certain social conditions. However, we must ask why, in view of the critical prestige of the epic, it did not attract the great writers and the great patrons. It is impossible to give a precise answer to this question, but it shows the need for a more general explanation" (Sayce, 253).

First of all, the failure of the epic cannot be properly understood as long as it is seen as the failure of one particular genre, which, to make the problem even more incomprehensible, happened to be the most prestigious one. We should listen carefully to those hyperbolic definitions of the epic we have been mentioning. The epic was much more than a branch of poetry; it was poetry itself at its highest, "that which is the greatest and most noble in Poesie," "the principal and most sublime part of all Poesie." Therefore, to say, as they did, that the epic of the new age had failed, was another way of saying that poetry itself had failed to fulfill their highest expectations, had failed to reach an epical level of significance. In other words, the problem with the epic was only the most visible symptom of what was happening to poetic fiction in general. And just as we tried to listen in Chapter 1 to the most radical antipoetic attacks and learn from them, we should do the same now and try to understand what the sixteenth- and seventeenth-century worshipers of classical epic poetry were seeing in it.

It could not be just a question of poetic craftsmanship. On purely poetic criteria, the best in the Renaissance could compete with Homer and Virgil. Actually in terms of stylistic subtlety, psychological depth, charm, realism, etc. there were many moments in the new epic superior to the old classics, as Voltaire and others frequently noticed (see Pierce, *Poesía épica*, 67–68, 79).

"The 'greatness' of literature," said T. S. Eliot, "cannot be determined solely by literary standards" ("Religion," 223). What the new admirers of the epic saw in Homer and Virgil went far beyond the literary. The "many great, extraordinary and almost miraculous effects" they saw attached to "the great performances of [their] extraordinary genius" (Le Bossu and Voltaire, translator's preface) could not possibly be explained by the poetic art or science alone.

It seems clear that they saw, if not the entire Graeco-Roman classical age, certainly the best or most memorable in it, through the prism of the Homeric and Virgilian epic; and then, as if taking, somehow, the visual medium for the cause, they took what they saw as deriving from, as an "almost miraculous" effect of their inimitable epic spirit. For example, it appeared that "even the refinedness of Athens was owing more to the poets, than to the philosophers' instructions." And the *Aeneid*

> seems to have had a strange and peculiar effect in the age, and upon the state [Virgil] lived under. For 'tis more than probable that the publishing of his *Aeneid* conduced very much to the set-tling Augustus on the imperial throne. We know what a strange aversion the Romans had to the very name of monarchy, and 'tis not likely they would so soon have exchanged their beloved de-mocracy for that which they so much hated, had they not been worked over to it by the instructions of Virgil: who informs them, "That when Heaven decrees to settle a State upon such or such foundation, 'tis atheism and irreligion to oppose its designs; and such an affront to the divine majesty and wisdom as should cer-tainly meet with speedy, and condign punishment." (Le Bossu and Voltaire, translator's preface)

There was no doubt a certain "optical illusion" involved in these exag-gerated historical perceptions. Nevertheless, there was a fundamental truthful core in them. Scholars sensed the perfect fit, as it were, of those epic poems in their historical environment, and were rightly amazed at their centrality and influence.

Apart from the rather naive and exaggerated manner in which the scholars of that time expressed their amazement, the scholar of today would agree with their basic intuition. Homer was indeed at the center of the Greek *paideia*. With regard to Virgil's *Aeneid,* let it suffice to quote an illustrious historian of the epic, C. M. Bowra: "More than any other book it dominated Roman education and literature. It became a 'set book' for centuries of schoolboys and was admired by almost every writer from Petronius to St. Augustine. Sevius composed his massive commentary on its interpretation, text, grammar, and mythology; Donatus expatiated on the moral lessons to be drawn from it; Macrobius devoted his *Saturnalia* to a discussion of its problems. It survived both the rise of Christianity and the fall of Rome" (33).

What was really admired in the "perfect genius," the "solid judgment," the "vast capacity" of the heroic poem was its mysterious and fascinating ability to generate unanimity, to elicit widespread, universal, agreement; that, somehow, it was capable of producing a meaning that nobody would question, and thus appeared to hold the key to the meaning of meaning. No wonder it could be called "the greatest work that humane wit is capable of" (Rapin, 72). Now, that is precisely the kind of greatness the epic, "the principal and most sublime part of all poesie," and, a fortiori, poetry in general had lost forever and no amount of poetic sensitivity and craftsmanship would restore.

They kept trying, though. In general they thought they could reproduce those wonderful effects by Christianizing the epic, by treating a subject "drawn from true history and a religion that is not false," to use Tasso's words, according to the rules of the poetic art. After all, if heroic subjects "sont les guerres," there were plenty of Christian wars and Christian warriors to choose from.

Among the best practitioners of the epic, including Tasso (a distinction should be made between Tasso the theoretician and Tasso the author of the *Liberata*), there is evidence of serious doubts about the possibility of such a Christianizing process. But these doubts, to the best of my knowledge, did not find theoretical expression. The closest thing to a theoretical formulation linking the demise of the amazingly civilizing effects of the epic to Christianity, appears in Sir William Davenant's preface to *Gondibert*. It is a rather unusual observation:

> After this contemplation, how acceptable the voice of Poesy hath been to God, we may (by descending from Heaven to Earth) consider how usefull it is to Men; and among Men, Divines are the cheef, because ordained to temper the rage of human power by spirituall menaces. . . . [Therefore] to Divines I first address my self; and presume to ask them, why, ever since their dominion was first allowed, at the great change of Religions, (though ours more than any inculcates obedience . . .) mankinde hath been more unruly then before? it being visible that Empire decrease with the

encrease of Christianity; and that one weake Prince did anciently suffice to governe many strong nations; but now one little Province is too hard for their own wise King; and a small Republique hath Seventy yeares maintained their revolt to the disquiet of many Monarchs. (28)

Davenant explicitly attributes this erosion of pagan civic order and cohesion, not directly to Christianity, but to the diminished role played by poetry in Christian society. Preaching Christian meekness and obedience has proved insufficient "in taming this wilde Monster the People":

> Thus unapt for obedience . . . the People have often been, since a long, and notorious power hath continued with Divines; whom though with reverence we accuse for mistaken lenity. . . . But our meaning is to shew how much their Christian meekness hath deceaved them in taming this wilde Monster the People; and a little to rebuke them for neglecting the assitance of poets; and for upbraiding the Ethnics, because the poets mannaged their religion . . . it being no less true that during the Dominion of Poesy, a willing and peacefull obedience to Superiors becalmed the World. . . . Such are the effets of Sacred Poesy, which charm's the People, with harmonious precepts. (30)

It is a mirage, of course. We have already seen in Virgil what lies just below the harmonious surface in the "Dominion of Poesy." But there is no denying the extraordinary hiding (and thus "becalming") power of that poetic surface. We should remember that until very recently almost nobody saw the insane violence that drives so much of the action in the *Aeneid*. Or rather, they must have seen it, but the vision does not seem to have made any meaningful difference; it did not even touch the perfect exemplary character of "pius Aeneas." And this, in spite of Virgil's being fully aware of what the poetic "ritual" ritualizes, makes reference to; his awareness is, in turn, an integral part of his poem. In the case of Homer, the sacred veil over the violence, especially Achilles' terrible violence, is even more effective.

The nostalgia for that serene, essentially unproblemtic, "Dominion of poesy" is still very much with us. The world of Homer still beckoned to the romantic Hegelianism of Georg Lukács in *The Theory of the Novel:*

Happy are those ages when the starry sky is the map of all possible paths—ages whose paths are illuminated by the light of the stars. Everything in such ages is new and yet familiar, full of adventure and yet their own. The world is wide and yet is like a home, for the fire that burns in the soul is of the same essential nature as the stars; the world and the self, the light and the fire, are sharply distinct, yet they never become permanent strangers to one another, for fire is the soul of all light and all fire clothes itself in light. . . . There is not yet any interiority, for there is not yet any exterior, any "otherness" for the soul. The soul goes out to seek adventures . . . but it does not know the real torment of seeking and the real danger of finding . . . it does not yet know that it can lose itself, it never thinks of having to look for itself. Such an age is the age of the epic. (29–30)

By "the age of the epic" Lukács means Homer's, "for, strictly speaking, his works alone are epic." He does not care much for Virgil: "Virgil's heroes lead a cool and measured shadow-existence, nourished by the blood of a splendid ardour that has sacrificed itself in order to conjure up what has vanished forever" (49). And with good reason: what "Virgil's heroes conjure up" is what lies beneath the "splendid ardour," what *must* be sacrificed in order to maintain that perfect, sacred, correspondence between immanence and transcendance, between the self and the world, that forms the surface of Homeric epic. As C. S. Lewis writes: "[But] an inch beneath the bright surface of Homer we find not melancholy [as in Virgil] but despair. 'Hell' was the word Goethe used of it. It is all the more terrible because the poet takes it all for granted, makes no complaint. It comes out casually, in similes" (30).

Lukács knew that it was the Christian Logos, "The new spirit of destiny [that] would indeed seem 'a folly to the Greeks'" (36), that had opened an irreparable crack on that bright Homeric surface. He did not know why or how, because he never looked through the crack to see what lay hidden inside. All he knew is that in a world abandoned by the old gods and alienated from the sacred, the traditional epic form is an empty and essentially meaningless shell.

Lukács is right, "strictly speaking," only Homer's works are fully and unambiguously epic. Virgil is already a significant step in the direction of the Christian undermining of the epic model. But it has not been sufficiently understood in this particular context that Virgil is not simply imitating Homer; he is interpreting him. The *Aeneid* is Virgil's response to Homer; it is his view and understanding of the *Iliad*. I do not think it would be an overstatement to say that what we see in the *Aeneid* is what Virgil saw in the *Iliad*. As C. S. Lewis wrote: "[Virgil's poem] is 'great' in a sense in which no poem of the same type as the *Iliad* can ever be great. The real question is whether any epic development beyond Virgil is possible. But one thing is certain. If we are to have another epic it must go on from Virgil; it is the only further development left" (39).

Whether or not one sees Virgil as an *anima naturaliter Christiana* (a naturally Christian soul)—and I agree with T. S. Eliot "that he just falls short" (*On Poetry*, 130)—one can see the *Aeneid* as the poem of fallen man, man as the sacrificial founder of his own *civitas terrena* (earthly city), thereby caught in the vicious circle of his own violence, struggling to separate good from evil; in other words, the poem of fallen man *without the promise of redemption*. In this sense, there is only one successor to Virgil in Christian Europe: Milton.

When Milton, after "long choosing, and beginning late," decided not "to indite / wars, hitherto the only argument / heroic deemed" (*Paradise Lost*, book 9, lines 26–29), and gave up his previous plans to resurrect King Arthur or any other of the traditional Christian heroes as a subject for his poem; when he, instead, chose the universal Christian "epic" of the Fall of man and the historical journey of his redemption, he was probably choosing the only way to go beyond Virgil: anything less would be either out of place or already contained in Virgil.

However, even though Milton's subject is undoubtedly "epic"—if by "epic," we understand of a large enough scope and central to universal human concerns—it suffers from an insurmountable internal contradiction between its subject and the traditional epic form in which it is molded. Because "fallen man," understood in the sense in which the Judeo-Christian text means it, cannot be a hero. It is certainly not for a hero that the Christian promise of redemption is meant. And needless to say, the Judeo-Christian God, or Christ, cannot simply substitute for Jupiter or any other inhabitant of Olympus. C. S. Lewis was right again: "Milton has failed to disentangle himself from the bad tradition (seen at its worst in Vida's *Christiad* and at its best in the *Gerusalemme Liberata*) of trying to make Heaven look too like Olympus" (131). This contradiction between subject matter and form created problems from the beginning, and it is still open to debate whether *Paradise Lost* is a genuine epic or who its hero might be (see Moore and Hagin).

2. A "Burning Issue": The Mixture of Christian and Pagan Elements in the Epic

Milton's poem, being the best, simply magnifies the inevitable contradiction of all Renaissance attempts to emulate and Christianize Virgil's achievement. A "burning issue" throughout that period, as it has been rightly described, was the poetic mixture of Christian and pagan elements; a mixture decried and lamented by most critics, and much more symptomatic of the underlying impasse facing the epic than it has been credited for by critics who can provide no clues to the "continuing enigma [of] the disparity between [epic] theory and practice" in the Neoclassical era (Le Bossu and Voltaire, introduction, v). This issue, the allergic reaction to the mixture of pagan and Christian elements, is only another manifestation of the underlying allergy to the mixing of "the human and the divine," of which we have been speaking.

The issue was still "burning" for Voltaire, whose testimony should have special significance; he was not only the most perceptive, but also the most independent-minded of all the theoreticians who, up to his time, had written on the modern epic. He was also the most tolerant and open to poetic innovations. He thought that each poem should be judged, not according to an inherited set of fixed rules, but on its individual merits, with no critical guide other than common sense, which "belongs to all the Nations of the World." For "'tis not enough to be acquainted with Virgil, and Homer [only]. As in regard to Tragedy, a man who has only perus'd Sophocles and Euripides, could not have an entire notion of the stage. We should be their admirers, not their slaves. We do not speak the same language. Our religion (the great basis of epic poetry) is the very reverse of their mythology" (Le Bossu and Voltaire, 45).

But it was here, on the "burning issue" of the religious underpinnings of the epic that his tolerance finds its limit. The old sense of scandal still burns in him. For example, about Camoens's poem: "There is another kind of Machinery continued throughout all the poem, which nothing can excuse, in any country whatever; 'tis an unjudicious mixture of the heathen gods with our religion. Gama in a storm addresses his prayers to Christ, but 'tis Venus who comes to his relief; the heroes are Christian, and the poet heathen. The main design which the Portuguese are supposed to have (next to the promoting of their trade) is to propagate Christianity; yet Jupiter, Bacchus and Venus have in their hands, all the management of the voyage" (75).[1]

And about Tasso's *Liberata:* "[It] is unaccountable how men of sense can approve of the Christian magicians, who help Rinaldo out of hands of the Mahometan wizards. It is singular to see in Tasso lewdness, mass, confession, the litanies of the saints, and pieces of witchcraft heaped to-

---

1. See Swedenberg, chap. 11, "Machines," which includes fifty-nine passages from various critics of the epic from Cowley (1650) to Ogilvie (1801), regarding the controversy on whether "machines" should be used or not, what kind, their allegorical interpretation, etc. "In general there was agreement that pagan and Christian machines should not be used in the same work" (270). With special reference to Camoens's "machinery," see Frank Pierce, "Place of Mythology." Pierce rightly points out that the Inquisition was more tolerant than Voltaire of the use of classical mythology in a Christian epic, and he quotes "the well-known statement of Frei Bertholameu [*sic*] Ferreira, censor of the Holy Office, approving the first edition [of the Lusiads in] 1572:

> nao achey . . . cousa algua escandalosa, nem contraria a fe & bos costumes, somente me pareceo que era necessario advertir os Lectores que o Autor pera encarecer a difficultade da navegaçao & entrada dos Portugueses na India, usa de hua fiçao dos Deoses dos Gentios. . . . Toda via como isto he Poesia & fingimento, & o Autor como poeta, nao pretenda mais que ornar o estilo Poetico, nao tivemos per inconveniente y esta fabula dos Deuses na obra canhecendo a por tal, & fincando sempre salva a verdade de nossa sancta fe, que todos os Deoses dos Gentios sam Demonios.

> (I did not find .. anything scandalous or contrary to the faith and morals. Only it seemed to me it was necessary to warn the readers that the author, in order to highlight the difficulties of navigation and the arrival of the Portuguese in India, uses a fiction of Gentile Gods. . . . Nevertheless since this is poetry and fiction, and the author as a poet only wants to adorn his poetic style, we did not object to the inclusion of this fable of the Gods in the poem, recognizing it as such a fable, and always safeguarding the truth of our holy faith that says that all the Gods of the Gentiles are Devils.)

But these words of the censor hardly express the casual confidence implied by the critic when he says that "Here, within a few lines of a common legal formula, is expressed what to Camoes and his contemporaries was a perfectly ordinary and accepted idea concerning the use of pagan myths in Christian poetry." (98) On the contrary, what we see is a qualified approval immediately followed by an uneasy warning that such pagan "machinery" is acceptable only as a poetic ornament and as long as it is understood that it is only fiction, safeguarding "a verdade de nossa sancta fe." Apparently the same censor changed his mind a few years later in the approval of a 1584 edition, and made "extensive excisions of every reference to 'gods' and 'goddesses'" (99). Nevertheless, it is true that between the end of the sixteenth century and Voltaire the mixing of pagan and Christian machines had become increasingly unacceptable, although the feeling changed also from one of apprehension about possible danger to the faith to one of embarrassment as an offense to common sense and good taste.

gether" (86). He returns a moment later to the same point and to make a fundamental observation: "He [Tasso] is guilty of indulging the inaccurate custom of calling the evil spirits by the names of Pluto, Alecto, and of mingling often pagan ideas with Christian mythology. 'Tis strange that none of the modern poets are free from that fault. It seems that our devils and our Christian Hell have something in them low and mean, and must be raised by the Hell of the pagans, which owes its dignity to its antiquity. *Certain it is that the Hell of the Gospel is not so fitted for poetry as that of Homer and Virgil*" (92).

This last observation expresses the entire problem in a nutshell. Christian mythology is basically unfit for poetic fiction, especially for poetic fiction of the highest kind, epic poetry; because it is inspired by a logos or spirit that undermines the setting up of a human being on a pedestal, because it has discovered that such a pedestal is the altar on which the sacrificial victim is immolated. In other words, the literal, explicit mingling of Christ with Bacchus or Venus, or the presence of Pluto or Alecto in a deeply Christian environment, whether viewed as scandalous, embarrassing, or just plain silly, is ultimately no different from what Milton does, solemnly, in *Paradise Lost*. The universal relevance, the sublime character, of the theme is not enough to rescue the traditional epic form from its downward slide into irrelevance. It is in this sense that I say that Milton's poem magnifies the common problem faced by other Renaissance epics.

Of course, in reference to the problem concerning the historical possibility of actualizing the traditional epic, of Christianizing Virgil, as it were, these other Renaissance epics faced another, even bigger problem. They did not have the proper subject matter. There were certainly Christian wars and conquests to rival or surpass any ancient war or conquest. But no matter how big or politically, commercially, or ideologically important, no Christian war or violent conquest could have what *any* ancient war or conquest could in the hands of a Homer or a Virgil: the potential to become the historical expression of the sacred foundation of the city, that is to say, of the possibility of living in organized society. No Christian war could have that kind of universal meaning. In this sense, all wars had become of local significance only.

Tasso was perhaps the poet who most clearly tried to Christianize the Virgilian epic. He paid special attention to the selection of the proper subject. But when he formally describes that subject, his description sounds very much like a definition of poetic marginality. We have already

seen that he excluded sacred subjects of "great authority" from the argument of the epic, although he insisted that "the argument of the epic
poem should be drawn . . . from true history and a religion that is not
false." But there are still further distinctions to be made, for example,
what kind of historical subject should it be? The answer is worth quoting
at length:

> Another distinction can be made among these stories in terms of
> whether they relate events of our own or of remote times, or
> things neither very recent nor very ancient. On some grounds the
> story of an extremely remote century or nation seems a subject
> highly appropriate to the heroic poem, because, since such things
> are so nearly buried in antiquity that the feeblest, dimmest mem-
> ory of them scarcely remains, the poet can change them over and
> over again and narrate them as he pleases. But with this advantage
> may go a disadvantage, and that no slight one, that the poem must
> introduce archaic customs along with the olden times. And the
> . . . habits of a remote era sometimes strike people as tedious and
> disagreeable. . . .
>
> Modern stories offer a great advantage and convenience in this
> matter of customs and usage, but almost entirely remove the free-
> dom to invent and imitate, which is esential to poets, particularly
> epic poets. . . . [The] present or the recent past should not be the
> subject of a heroic poem. . . . We may add to these arguments the
> word of Aristotle in the *Problems,* and the reason he adduces for
> our preferring narratives of things neither too new nor too old.
> (*Discourses,* 39–41)

A little further Tasso comes back to the same idea, but from a geographi-
cal perspective:

> The poet should then avoid fictitious arguments, especially about
> occurrences in a nearby familiar land or a friendly nation. We can
> easily invent many fictions about faraway people and unfamiliar
> lands without costing the fable its credibility. And hence we must
> take the matter for such poems from Gothland, Norway, Sweden,
> Iceland, the East Indies, or countries recently discovered in the
> vast ocean beyond the Pillars of Hercules. (50)

One could hardly ask for a more explicit definition of marginality. First of all, the epic poem should keep away from that sacred center, from which, as we saw, Plato also wanted to exclude the poets. It must also avoid the historical present or the immediate past, where any manipulation of well-known events would be either dangerous or ridiculous. It should be close enough to be of interest to contemporary society, but not so close as to interfere with the handling of any serious business. Tasso even delineates geographically what were for him the outer margins of historical relevance, at which poetic freedom begins. Beyond those margins the poet could invent almost anything. The formula is quite clear: true enough to have some relevance, fictitious enough to be poetic. The ideal epic poem *ought to* exist in a sort of historical and epistemological twilight, where truth and fiction can easily merge into each other.

Tasso's theoretical honesty and candor is only equaled by his blindness, as seen now in retrospect. So convinced is he of the historical relevance and fundamental truth of the epic, that he is not in the least afraid to stretch such relevance and truth to its limits. So confident is he, that he walks on the very edge of the precipice over which the epic will fall, without suspecting anything.

Yet Tasso is no fool. He knows that the epic can no longer exist at the center. He is trying to define a safe place for it, a place where, he thinks, it can survive and retain its splendor. And he defines that place with perfect and candid accuracy. What he could not know was that he was in fact defining the twilight of the epic itself. For such a delicate and ambiguous combination of truth and fiction was inherently unstable, the quicksand in which the epic poem had lost its historical relevance, after having lost its sacred function.

This marginality became an accepted formal feature of the epic, even by those who thought that poetry could still produce the wonderful social and political effects it had once produced during the "Dominion of Poesy," as we find in Davenant's preface:

> When I consider'd the actions which I ment to describe . . . I was againe persuaded rather to chuse those of a former age, then the present; and in a Century so farr removed, as might preserve me from their improper examinations who know not the requisites of a Poem, nor how much pleasure they lose . . . who take away the liberty of a Poet, and fetter his feet in the shackles of a Historian. . . . As in the choice of time, so of place . . . (10–11)

But if the theoreticians were still defending their faith in the epic, even if they had to go searching for subject matter in the margins, the *best* practitioners of the traditional epic, the Camoens of *Os Lusiadas* and the Tasso of the *Liberata*—in other words, those who were explicitly setting themselves as rivals to Virgil—had serious doubts about the compatibility of the epic enterprise with Christianity and, therefore, about the significance of the epic to ultimate or universal human concerns.

3. The Hesitation of the Best Epic Poets

Tasso begins his poem by asking forgiveness from the Christian Muse for mixing fictions with the truth and including delightful ornaments of a non-Christian nature:

> O Muse, that do not wreathe your brow on Helicon with fading bays, but among the blessed choirs in Heaven above possess a golden crown of deathless stars: breathe into my breast celestial ardors, illuminate my song, and grant me pardon if with the truth I interweave embroiderings [*s'intesso fregi al ver*], if partly with pleasures other than yours I ornament my pages. (canto 1, 2)

The hesitations and religious scruples of Tasso, both in his life and as reflected in his most famous poem, have been noticed by modern critics. In the words of Joseph Tusiani, "The *Jerusalem Delivered* is a Christian epic written by a poet who believed that no perfect Christian epos was ever possible on this earth" (Tasso, *Jerusalem Delivered*, trans. Tusiani, 17).

But it is in Camoens where we find the most elaborately explicit questioning of the epic enterprise at the center of the poem. Here is part of the well-known, striking speech by the old man of Belem in *The Lusiads,* just as the Portuguese fleet is about to raise anchor on its epic journey around the Cape of Good Hope and the Indies:

> Oh, the folly of it, this craving for power, this thirsting after the vanity we call fame, this fraudulent pleasure known as honour that thrives on popular esteem! . . . Men call it illustrious, and noble, when it merits instead the obloquy of infamy; they call it

fame, and sovereign glory, mere names with which the common people delude themselves in their ignorance. . . .

Now your fickle fancy has become infatuated with this folly that describes as enterprise and valour what is but the cruel ferocity of the brute creation, and boasts of its contempt for life, which should always be held dear if only because he who gives it was so loath to lose his own. (canto 4, pp. 119–20)

Perhaps doubt is not the word in the case of Camoens. The elaborate vigor and eloquence of the old man's speech makes it abundantly clear that the fame and recognition, which are the specific goal of the epic poem to confer on its subject and its characters, are not Christian in spirit. Such fame and recognition emulate and replicate classical pagan values. In fact, they become explicitly allegorized in the long, sensuously detailed, and titillating episode of the Island of Venus with all its bathing or fleeing nymphs "more cunning than swift, little by little and with many a smile and cry [allowing] the hounds to overtake them," where the Portuguese can satisfy every one of their fleshly desires:

For Tethys, the so lovely ocean-nymphs, the magic island with its rich colourings, all are but symbols of the honours, delightful in themselves, that can make life sublime. The thrilling exaltation to the heights, the triumphs, the brow garlanded with palm and laurel, the glory and the wonder of it all, these are the island's joys. (canto 9, p. 216)

The honors "delightful in themselves," the "thrilling exaltation to the heights," the "palm and laurel"—these are precisely the things rejected by the old man of Belem as illusory, vain, fraudulent, infamous, etc., in other words, clearly anti-Christian. Indeed, as if to leave no room for doubt, the immediately following verses will identify such "thrilling exaltation to the heights" as the very stuff the Olympian gods and heroes are made of:

The ancients loved greatness, and were wont in imagination to endow with immortality, on the peaks of starry Olympus, the hero who had mounted aloft on the soaring wings of fame. . . . Jupiter, Mercury, Apollo, Mars, Aeneas, Romulus, Bacchus, Hercules . . . all in their origin were but frail humanity. It was fame, trumpeting their exploits abroad, who gave them these strange titles of gods, semi-gods, immortals, tutelary deities, heroes and supermen. (canto 9, p. 216)

Camoens's poem, therefore, does not promise its heroes a Christian reward. It offers them only poetic fame and tells them that that is exactly what all the ancient heroes got, no more no less.

Now, what is especially interesting is Camoens's symbolic identification of this pagan poetic fame with the pleasures of the flesh and, in particular, erotic desire. Because that identification is not either Homeric or Virgilian. In spite of his explicit reference to the passionate love for Aeneas that Venus instills in Dido, nothing can be more revealing than to see how differently Virgil and Camoens conceive their respective episodes. The most fundamental difference is that, in Virgil, Aeneas's love affair with Dido is not conceived in any way as a reward for the Trojan's heroic exploits (he has not done much yet, when it happens), as it is in Camoens. Not only is it not a reward to anybody, it is a tragic event, a crafty, treacherous scheme prepared by Venus to protect her son from possible and likely harm by the Carthagenians; after all, they are the devotees of her archrival, Juno: "In truth, she fears the uncertain house and double-tongued Tyrians; Juno's hate chafes her, and at nightfall her care rushes back" (I, 661–62). When Dido's maddening love for Aeneas is no longer useful and, instead, becomes an obstacle on the hero's fated path, she is simply left behind to face her tragic end, one more victim made necessary by the advancement of the Trojans' destiny. There is not the slightest suggestion that Aeneas's immortal fame, derived from the fulfillment of his destiny, is in any way akin to his passionate affair with Dido; in fact, the opposite is the case.

The association of poetic fame and triumph with human desire and the yearnings of the flesh is something that Camoens finds, not in his classical models, but in the Christian tradition from Saint Augustine on. It is not difficult to see Camoens in this regard as an immediate precursor of Tasso. For in Tasso, too, there is an intimate connection between the classical epic ideal and the enticements of desire. They are both temptations besetting the Christian crusaders and luring them away from their path. This has been clearly observed by Judith A. Kates: "The direct imitation of classical culture [in the *Liberata*] tends to occur in [an] ambivalent or negative context. Classical allusions, images derived from Graeco-Roman mythology . . . are almost exclusively confined to situ-

ations that involve pagan characters or demons. Tasso constantly associ-
ates such imagery with Armida, for instance" (68; see also 82–83). And
Armida's garden, Tasso's version of the island of Venus, is, of course, the
erotic trap from which the hero, Rinaldo, must be rescued. The difference
between Camoens and Tasso is that, while the former clearly separates
the classical model from the Christian one, the latter goes a step further,
telling us that one must renounce the classical to follow the Christian.

And yet, all of this is being said, in both cases, in and by a poem that
is still trying to rival Virgil's. It was a hopeless task. What Camoens and
Tasso demonstrate is that all that the Renaissance epic at its best could
do was tell the story of its own impossibility. What has survived in those
poems is not their imitation of Virgil but their anticipation of the novel;
in Tasso much more clearly so than in Camoens. In the end Tasso could
not save the classical epic model from the unabashed deterioration it had
suffered at the hands of Ariosto in the *Orlando furioso*.

Virgil had no successor. The epic was replaced by the novel. Ariosto,
Camoens, and Tasso are simply the signposts of the transition between
the two, each pointing in its own way from one to the other. After Virgil,
Cervantes. The *Quijote* must be seen not only in reference to chivalric
romances, but in the much wider context of the epic in general. It is clear
that Don Quixote would have been even more of a madman if, instead
of trying to be a second Amadís, he had tried to be a second Achilles or
a second Aeneas.

But the prestige of the epic was such that even Cervantes believed in
the possibility of actualizing and Christianizing the traditional epic form.
It could be done in prose, he thought: as we read in the conversation
betweeen the judicious Canon of Toledo and the priest, as long as it followed "good sense [and] the [poetic] art," such a work could make its
author as famous in prose "as the two princes of poetry, Greek and Latin,
are in verse" (Part 1, chap. 48).

The Canon says that he has written "more than a hundred pages" of
such a modern epic, but decided to give up the project, "because it
seemed to me a task unfitting to my profession," and also because he
did not think it would be appreciated by the multitude of the ignorant.
Cervantes did not write such a work either, although he may have
thought he was doing just that with the *Persiles*. The fact is that Don
Quixote's fictional failure to resurrect knight-errantry parallels the real
historical impossibility of resurrecting the epic model. It is both ironic
and revealing to find that belief in the possibility of a Christian epic cap-

able of competing with the old one, in a book destined to become the very symbol of the hopelessness of such a task.

Cherished dreams are hard to give up. Even today many critics feel that it is important to demonstrate that being a Christian does not mean having to give up such things as epic or tragedy. The amount of critical energy, even of the highest caliber, spent in demonstrating that this or that modern work deserves the honor of being called a tragedy or an epic is enormous. There is still something sacred about those labels, even though they can no longer be anything but labels.

4. Reviewing a Critical Commentary on the *Orlando Furioso*

In my view, one of the most perceptive and articulate expositions of the differences between Renaissance Christian epic and its classical models, Virgil in particular, is that of Andrew Fichter in his *Poets Historical: Dynastic Epic in the Renaissance*. Fichter believes that even Ariosto's *Orlando furioso* is fundamentally a Christian epic:

> Critics have protested that the *Furioso* cannot qualify as genuine epic because it contains no real heroic agon, no confronting of human will and *virtus* with their limitations. Struggles are decided by external forces, chance or Providence, and not by an individual functioning within the limits of his character. Ruggiero's conversion brings such objections into focus since it establishes him as a hero by virtue of his reception of Christian faith and not through any exercise of personal prowess. It will be God's glory, one feels, and not Ruggiero's own that any subsequent trial will affirm. Now in the long run one may wish to exclude the *Furioso* from the category of epic poetry, but one should be conscious of denying the possibility of Christian epic altogether in doing so. And before doing so one should weigh the Christian poet's claim that his religion can indeed accomodate epic, however unlike Virgil it may be. (101)

If I understand these words correctly, it seems to me that the critic is too ready to concede his opponents' objections to the epic character of Ariosto's poem. If the poem is not a "genuine epic," it is certainly not for the reasons they adduce. So, before I comment directly on the implications of the Christian character of the poem as seen by Fichter, something should be said about the objections to which he refers, because they are the standard objections, repeated in a very uncritical fashion, not only against the notion of a Christian epic but also against that of a Christian tragedy.

Let us assume it is true (my intention is not to analyze Ariosto's poem) that the *Furioso* "contains no real heroic agon, no confronting of human will and *virtus* with their limitations. [Because] struggles are decided by external forces . . . and not by an individual functioning within the limits of his character." How could that be an objection against the epic quality of anything, if we accept Homer and Virgil as the deciding criterion? Does that mean that the course of events in the *Iliad*, the *Odyssey*, or the *Aeneid* is not governed by external forces, chance, or fate? Do Achilles, or Ulysses, or Aeneas confront the problem of the human will and *virtus* facing its own limitations, as individuals functioning within the limits of their character? What about all those gods constantly intervening in the action, sending messages and dreams, stirring thoughts and feelings in the hearts of unsuspecting heroes, tilting the balance one way or another in the field of battle?

One must wonder why those critics do not perceive such "external forces" in the Homeric and Virgilian epics, while they immediately detect the external character of their sixteenth-century imitations. They accuse Ariosto of doing what his models did all the time. But, of course, the problem is that Ariosto could not do with impunity what they did without a thought, as the most natural thing in the world.

What the critics should ask is why those "external forces" blend with and fit so well in their classical habitat, while they appear so "external" and arbitrary in the historical context of the Renaissance. And they should direct the question to themselves, for the answer is already assumed in the form of their question. Only by assuming a situation in which the human will must face itself and take ultimate responsibility for its own acts, can the problem arise of an encounter of the will with its own limitations. And only against the background of such a situation can the external forces stand revealed as such and perceived as fundamentally arbitrary. That background does not exist in Homer or Virgil,

and the critics mistake the nonexistence of the problem for a perfect solution.

A genuine problem can only arise to the extent that, at least in principle, it admits to a solution. The problem of the human will having to
deal with its own inadequacy can only make sense on the assumption
that somehow it is possible to conceive the human will as being other
than inadequate, other than hopelessly limited. Classical heroes never
assumed such a possibility. They simply could not conceive of the human
will as anything other than limited, bound on all sides by forces with a
will of their own, which they could not control. But such a limitation
was just a fact, full of consequences to be sure, but in itself totally unproblematic. The hero may well be aware of it, but in a sense no different
from his awareness of the impossibility to jump over a mountain in a
single bound. He may regret it deeply, but there is nothing he can do
about it, except through the help of some "external force" acting, not on
his will to make it adequate to the task, but as a physical agent doing for
him what he cannot do on his own.

The problem is that while the old epic environment could hide the
external and arbitrary character of those forces perfectly, it cannot do
the same with the "heroic" conversion of Ruggiero. It rejects it immediately, and with good reason, as something unconvincing. And if the conversion is taken seriously, then the epic character of the hero ceases to
convince. The two things are "external" to each other.

I assume that Fichter is right when he says that "[the] subject of the
Furioso becomes not so much a coming into Italy as a coming into being.
The Virgilian theme of founding an empire is superseded by the Augustinian theme of self-discovery. . . . Empire is forged with the resolution of
all the dualisms Bradamante and Ruggiero embody, love and arms, passion and reason, charity and justice. Here, then, is Ariosto's most fundamental transformation of the Aeneid, in that the quest for empire entails
not, as it seems for Aeneas, a choice between these apparent opposites
but the discovery of their interdependence, their oneness. This is empire
defined in Augustinian terms, not an objective for which human love and
selfhood must be suppressed but one in which they are fulfilled" (90–91).

But this is precisely where the problem lies not only for the epic, but
for poetic fiction in general, from a Christian perspective. If coming into
being reveals that all incompatibilities are only apparent, that all obstacles to self-fulfillment, although psychologically real, are ultimately arbitrary, a misdirection or disorientation of the will, an artificial, man-made

obstacle, then what can be the ethical status of a poetic creation whose very condition of possibility rests on such obstacles, a poetic creation that cannot exist without inventing them? The Christian coming into being will inevitably reveal the poetic creation itself as the clearest sign and symptom of the problem; it will expose its cultivated need and desire for the arbitrary obstacle, its willful re-creation of the difficulties and problems that the will throws on its own path to self-fulfillment. In other words, the poetic creation cannot be a truthful representation of the Christian quest for Being without questioning itself ethically in a most fundamental way. And that is the questioning that undermines the epic search for adventure.

There was, indeed, a time when the overriding concern was the foundation of the city, not of the individual; a time when the willful re-creation or representation of the troubles that beset the human members of the city was a necessity; it was the only way, the only ritual, to get rid of those troubles that were piled up on a hero's shoulders; a hero who was different from everybody else and who either eliminated those troubles or was himself eliminated, amid great lamentations, at the end.

But such a sacred way to get rid of one's troubles was not working very well in the Renaissance, because it was becoming increasingly and unavoidably obvious that those troubles were of one's own making. It was then that poetic fiction was revealed, on the one hand, as nothing but fiction, and on the other, as an activity linked to pagan, anti-Christian practices. And while all this was happening, the best poets were discovering in amazement all the intricate ways in which human beings get themselves into troubles of their own making. Thus, said Calderón, in *El mayor monstruo del mundo:*

> El ser uno desdichado
> todos han dicho que es fácil,
> mas yo digo que es difícil,
> que es tan industrioso arte
> que aunque le platiquen todos
> no le ha penetrado nadie.
>
> (act 1)

(Everybody believes it is easy for a man to be wretched, but I say it is difficult; because it is such an intricate art that, even though everybody practices it, nobody has been able to penetrate it.)

5. From Tasso to Cervantes

In the *Quijote* Cervantes took up the problem of the epic where Tasso had left it and carried it much further. Tasso knew that the vagaries of desire diverted the Christian warriors from their epic task, even as they were diverted from themselves. Their true self and their epic task coincided. Tasso internalizes the epic. The fulfillment of the epic task now becomes self-fulfillment; thus a new inner dimension is added to the old epic, and this new dimension is clearly a Christian one. But the individual is never in doubt concerning the true identity of his epic goal and, therefore, of his true self. He is never at a loss regarding his epic duty and what he has to do in order to fulfill it, thus fulfilling himself. It is enough for a warrior like Rinaldo, for example, to see himself in the mirror of his own polished shield in order to wake up from the slumber of desire where cunning and beautiful Armida had kept him away from the Christian army, and quickly return to his heroic task:

> As a man by deep and heavy sleep oppressed returns to himself after long delirious raving, so he returned by gazing upon himself; but truly he cannot bear to look at himself . . . he is possessed by shame. . . .
>
> But after shame gave place to anger—anger, fierce warrior of the reason—and to the blushing of his face succeeded a new flame that blazes stronger and boils more, he ripped off his idle trims, and those unworthy gauds, the wretched insignia of slavery;
>
> and hastened his departure and issued forth from the tortuous confusion of the labyrinth. (XVI, 31–35)

This epic certainty, this clear distinction between reality and the fictitious projections of desire, becomes somewhat shaken and greatly problematized in Cervantes's novelistic intuition. Human desire can not only take the individual away from himself and his true goal; it can in fact veil the goal, substitute a look-alike simulacrum for the real thing, so that the individual may be deceived even in perfectly good faith. Cervantes tells us that human desire may transform even the most beautiful and noble into an alienating trap, an object of destructive idolatry. It has been said of Shakespeare that in *Othello* he conveys "one of the essential moral experiences, the painful discovery that human impulses for good can by a mysterious process turn into something evil and destructive" (Brower, 28). It could be said equally well of Cervantes, at least from the *Quijote* on.

This insight is given quasi-allegorical expression in Cervantes's last novel, *Persiles y Sigismunda,* through the character of its beautiful and pure protagonist, Sigismunda. Throughout the novel she and her beloved Persiles have been pretending to be brother and sister under the names of Periandro and Auristela, a fictional device that has allowed them to overcome heroically all kinds of difficult adventures in pursuit of their goal of reaching Rome, where they will be instructed in the Christian faith, reveal their true identities and get married.

But once they are in Rome, at the end of their travails, not the least of which was to behave toward each other as brother and sister, their successful struggle, the victory of their virtue itself threatens to become an even more formidable obstacle when Sigismunda, all of a sudden, is seized by a desire for both of them to continue in their roles as brother and sister. Let me quote from what I said years ago on this passage of the novel: "All of these dangers and adventures in which Sigismunda, in her feigned role as Auristela, has been involved, once they have been overcome, are in danger of turning into a fascinating novel. The transcendent meaning of those dangers and adventures risks being absorbed by the very literary form which gives them expression. . . . Sigismunda is suddenly attracted by her own heroic role as Auristela and thinks, why not continue in that role, even though it is no longer necessary to pretend, even though all the obstacles have already disappeared?" (*Mímesis conflictiva,* 127). In other words, when the obstacles are no longer there, the lack of obstacles, accepting reality pure and simple, turns out to be the greatest obstacle.

The very beauty of triumphant virtue, the exemplary subject of the novel that "dared to compete with Heliodorus," becomes a fictional substitute for virtue itself. It is at this point that the narrator pauses to reflect: "It seems that good and evil are so close to each other as to be like two converging lines, which, though having separate and different beginnings, end up in one point" (book 4, chap. 12). In the end the situation with the two lovers will be resolved. But for a moment their relationship is in shambles. Persiles runs away in despair, accusing Sigismunda of criminal and cruel behavior. Sigismunda is so confused that she does not know for sure who she is.

The realization that evil can put on the appearance of good, that even the most sincere and honest intention may be deceived by good appearances, is constant in Cervantes. It is essential to a proper understanding of the *Quijote*. It is not only implicit in his parodic conception of the protagonist, Don Quixote, a good and honest man, Alonso Quijano *el Bueno*, who so often wrongs himself and others, while thinking he is doing the right thing, but it actually becomes explicit in open reflection at certain moments in the novel: for example, in the sonnet that lovelorn Cardenio, betrayed by his best friend with his own unwitting complicity, sings in Sierra Morena:

> Santa amistad, que con ligeras alas,
> tu apariencia quedándose en el suelo,
> entre benditas almas, en el cielo,
> subiste alegre a las impíreas salas,
>
> desde allá, cuando quieres, nos señalas
> la justa paz cubierta con un velo,
> por quien a veces se trasluce el celo
> de buenas obras que a la fin son malas.
>
> Deja el cielo, oh amistad!, o no permitas
> que el engaño se vista tu librea,
> con que destruye a la intención sincera;
>
> que si tus apariencias no le quitas,
> presto ha de verse el mundo en la pelea
> de la discorde confusión primera.
> (Part 1, chap. 27)

> (O holy friendship that with nimble wing,
> Thy phantom leaving here on earth below,
> With blessed souls in heaven communing,
> Up through the empyrean halls dost go.
>
> Thence, at thy pleasure, for us you point
> Towards just peace covered with a veil,
> Through which, at times, we see the zeal
> Of good works which, in the end, are bad.
>
> Leave heaven, friendship, or do not permit
> Foul fraud thus openly thy robes to wear
> And so the honest purpose to defeat.

For if you leave him in your semblance fair
Dark chaos will soon engulf the world
And all to primal anarchy be hurled.)[2]

The idea is clear, "holy friendship" is a transcendent reality. Gone to "heaven," what is left below, in the immanent world of human relationships, is only its *apariencia*. Because of it "just peace," the goal or aim toward which "holy friendship" points, is "covered with a veil"; it cannot be seen clearly, it becomes something ambiguous, "through which"—in the pursuit of which—"honest purpose," *la intención sincera*, becomes distorted and turns out to be bad.[3]

Even though the sonnet is an integral part of the story of Cardenio, Luscinda, and Don Fernando, Cervantes gives it a much larger scope. Its central idea could be applied to a number of other stories in the novel and, as I said, to Don Quixote himself. The end of the sonnet is rather apocalyptic: if good cannot be clearly separated from evil, the world of civil society can easily revert to a primeval state of violent confusion. The veil that covers "just peace" is the blurring of the clear distinction between good and evil. It is the point where the two "converging lines" meet.

Furthermore, quite frequently in Cervantes the false appearance that blurs the peace, by blurring the distinction between good and its evil counterfeit, is a poetic appearance. Thus poetic fiction, driven by desire, is presented as something capable of fictionalizing the truth or draining the real of its reality, which is something very different from the purely formal notion that poetic fiction is a mimetic representation of reality Aristotelian style.

It must also be pointed out that this fictionalization of the truth always takes place within the context of an interpersonal relationship. It can be said that, in the novelistic world of Cervantes, it takes at least two to get into trouble. Human problems are never the problems of the individual in isolation, or even the individual in face of the world at large. The problems of the individual are always the result of interpersonal relations gone wrong, relations that have been fictionalized, driven off target in the deflecting crisscrossing of human desires.

2. I have used J. M. Cohen's translation of the novel (Penguin Classics) but have modified the second stanza substantially to make it conform much more closely to Cervantes's original.
3. For an analysis of the sonnet within the context of Cardenio's story, see my *Mímesis conflictiva*, chap. 4, "La locura de Cardenio y la penitencia de don Quijote."

At first glance, this does not seem to fit the quixotic image very well. Don Quixote appears as a unique individual. The strange madness that isolates him and sets him apart from everybody else does not appear to be linked to any preexisting personal relationship. We are told that he went mad because his brain dried up from reading so many books of chivalry. Nevertheless, regardless of what Cervantes may have thought concerning the scientific merit of such drying of the brain, within the context of the novel this explanation is of no consequence whatsoever. What is of central significance is the fact that Don Quixote's fictionalized individuality, modeled on the fictional uniqueness of Amadís, isolates him from his social environment and sets him at odds with everybody else. To cure him of his madness is not to find some remedy for the dryness of his brain, but to bring him home in every sense of the word, to return him to himself, to restore his relationship with others.

But we must be careful lest we fall into some sort of romantic trap here, as happened to Unamuno. The Cervantine choice is not between an individuality set against all others and no individuality at all, but between genuine individuality, which respects others and does not interfere with them, and fictionalized or fiction-driven individuality, which asserts itself by challenging others. The Cervantine choice is between the real and the unreal, the authentic and the counterfeit, which is also a choice between peace and violence. In principle a very clear choice, in practice a very difficult one.

Don Quixote's uniqueness is as fictitious as that of Amadís, his revered model. But just as there is a windmill behind every giant, there is a real human being behind every Amadís, and a real uniqueness behind the fictitious one. Cervantes's profound interest lies in the exploration of how the real one is lost or given up for the sake of the fictitious one. Another way of expressing it might be to say that behind every quixotic hero there is a real one who is wasted away. Or, in the larger historical context of the demise of the epic, there is a kind of human nobility and singularity that can no longer be expressed adequately by the poetic image of the epic warrior.

It is precisely this human reality, genuinely singular and noble, that is placed at stake and at risk in every human relationship; that is to say, every time that this singular and noble individual meets her equal. But obviously this cannot mean that the noble individual has every reason to become paranoid in the presence of another. It is not the behavior of the other, not anything that the other can do or say, that sets this noble singularity at risk; it is rather the opposite, the behavior of the individual toward the other that will decide the fate of her own singularity. For how could such nobility and singularity truly deserve their name if they were at the mercy of another? Such is the meaning of that other pervasive Cervantine idea, the freedom of the human individual, a freedom inseparable from her nobility and singularity. It cannot be bought, sold, or destroyed in any way by another, as the end of one of the *Exemplary Novels, El amante liberal,* makes explicitly clear. But it can be lost or forfeited by the free subject itself; and in fact so it is, time and time again, in the pursuit of something that looks just like it but is not.

In Cervantes the loss of genuine individual freedom is always, in one way or another, a form of seduction. The individual is lured out of herself by a desire for something that is not real, but is made to look real by another desire necessarily situated beyond the seduced individual. The individual's desire is always drawn out by another desire, that is to say, by somebody else's desire, which may, in turn, be seduced by the very desire it has itself seduced, thereby creating a vicious circle, or rather a feedback situation where each desire feeds on the other, and all sense of reality, or of the difference between reality and fiction, disappears. In this process of de-realization or fictionalization of reality, poetic fiction usually plays a prominent role. Such is the case, for example, in the story of Marcela and Crisóstomo, as well as that of Cardenio and Luscinda in the *Quijote.*

Don Quixote parades his poetic madness through a series of so-called interpolated love stories, which are all different manifestations of the mimetic character of human desire. The difference between these stories and that of Don Quixote is that, while the latter transforms windmills into giants and road inns into castles, at the fascinating suggestion of chivalric fiction, the characters in those other stories transform other human beings into divine Amadises or Dianas, and, therefore, condemn themselves to inevitable frustration. Turning windmills into giants is comical, transforming a human being into a nonexistent god or goddess at whose feet the individual lays her freedom, can have rather tragic consequences. Thus Don Quixote's funny metamorphoses become the parodic symbol of something that Cervantes knows perfectly well is not funny at all.

There is only one interpolated story, which happens in the midst of all the others in Part 1, and stands in sharp contrast with them. Full of real autobiographical details, it is the story of the escaped Christian captive and the beautiful moorish girl Zoraida. It is not a story of destructive mimetic desire, not a typical love story, but one of Christian conversion and marriage. And yet, it fits there at a moment when all the other characters of all the other typical love stories, having lost their way in the labyrinth of mimetic desire, and being stranded from one another, have just been or are about to be "providentially" reunited. There can be little doubt that all these themes, providential finding and reunion, freedom from non-Christian captivity, and Christian conversion, have a common denominator in Cervantes's mind: their Christian significance. And "Christian significance" means to Cervantes that the ambiguities and contradictions of mimetic desire, through which essentially free individuals surrender their freedom and those who are meant to live together are set at odds, have much more than a psychological or, say, "clinical," interest. He is deeply disturbed by what his extraordinary power of observation and analysis discovers in the intricate maze of human relationships; more specifically it is his Christian conscience that is so deeply disturbed.

What he sees strikes him as un-Christian as well as violently primitive, something akin to "primal anarchy" ("la pelea de la discorde confusión primera"). Perhaps this is one point in which Cervantes differs somewhat from the other great observer and analyzer of mimetic desire: Shakespeare. The incredible precision, the relentless pursuing of the meandering logic of desire by the English master, has been fully disclosed by Girard in his recent *A Theater of Envy*. But there is in much of Shakespeare a cool, analytical detachment, which can indeed sharpen the outline of his analysis, but can also give the impression of a certain unconcern, a certain lack of compassion for those human characters lost and locked in a web of conflicting desires.

Cervantes's analysis can follow the inner logic of mimetic desire down to its last and bitter consequences, which can be either insanity (Cardenio), or eternal damnation (Crisóstomo). And yet, he still has faith in the inner dignity of the human being and continues to hope that this lost individual may find rescue, be redeemed, in the end. This is why he is so critical of artificial or "magic" solutions, like those found in the magic potions of the Good Witch Felicia in Montemayor's *Diana,* which he criticizes in chapter 6 of the *Quijote*. In Cervantes's eyes the fundamental difference between Felicia's magic solution and the somewhat unrealistic accumulation of coincidences at Juan Palomeque's inn in the *Quijote,* is the difference between primitive magic and the Christian promise of redemption, a gratuitous promise, purely out of love, and, from a strictly rational point of view, totally unexpected. But while primitive magic is an illusory solution, which attempts to substitute an external power for the power of the human will, Cervantes's providential solution is not imposed on the individual, it does not dull or overpower his will, it does not replace it; on the contrary, as the situation at the inn makes abundantly clear, it is only an appeal to the will, a renewed pleading, the giving of a second chance. In other words, the improbable accumulation of coincidences at the inn, explicitly labeled by Cervantes as providential, is charged with a symbolic meaning that inevitably excludes the magic solution.[4]

If we take Cervantes's testimony as historically representative, we can say that the human subject that replaces the waning epic hero, is this Cervantine individual that is both fallen and redeemable. The intense interest in the exploration of the countless subtle ways in which this individual may become alienated (the "intricate art that everybody practices but nobody has penetrated"), as well as the enormously tragic consequences (including the placing of human civilization at risk) that are seen as inherent to such an alienation, must not be taken exclusively as a sign of dark pessimism. The alienation of the human individual would not be given such a universal significance, if the inherent value of the individual, which is forfeited through the alienation, were not also given universal significance. Furthermore, beyond the possibility of alienation, that inherent value manifests itself in the revealed faith in human redemption. Everything holds together in one package, as it were, the positive with the negative. It is also important to point out that, since alienation is always, by definition, a matter of human relationships, in the final analysis everything, absolutely everything, is potentially at stake in the way in which that human individual meets, enters into a relationship with, another human individual.

6. The Existential Problematic of Calderonian Honor

It was Calderón who dramatized like nobody else the universal, even cosmic, dimension of the Fall of man, seen through the aspect of the loss

---

4. I am aware that this is not exactly the explanation I gave of these episodes in *Mímesis conflictiva*. I am taking this opportunity to correct my thinking on this subject.

of inalienable singularity, the alienating fall into radical intersubjective immanence. We already saw in Chapter 1 that the fallen condition of the human being is carried inwardly by every individual like a shameful secret, a Clarín-like void which the individual struggles anxiously to hide not only from others but from himself too. This hidden void is the reason why the individual always, automatically "gives credit to," that is, believes in the truth of, his own misfortune; an existential prerational reaction the logic of which may be questioned occasionally by the Calderonian character, as does the Tetrarca in *El mayor monstruo del mundo:* "why is it that in our phantasy, a prediction of good fortune is a lie, while one of misfortune is true?" (67). The idea is widespread in Calderón's drama, and it is central to *La vida es sueño.* "¿Quién no da crédito al daño?" (Who doesn't believe in his own misfortune), asks Basilio rhetorically. Or as Astolfo says of *el hado* (fate) in the same play, "what a good astrologer it would be, if it would always make cruel predictions, for undoubtedly they would always turn out to be true!" (*Obras,* 1:382). As soon as it is perceived by the individual, a bad omen becomes a self-fulfilling prophecy. The human individual chains himself to whatever threatens him. This is also why misfortunes rarely come alone, but "in chains" ("encadenadas las unas a las otras"), each one calling for another. And the force that strings them up or draws them on is the unfortunate individual himself. To say that Calderón's best drama is a profound meditation on the fallen condition of humanity is not enough. What is really at the heart of his dramatic intuition is the observation that the individual is actually attracted to, drawn toward, the unhappy consequences, the misfortunes, of his fallen condition.

This secret connivance, this shameful complicity that chains him to his radical existential weakness, is what the Calderonian individual anxiously tries not to see or hear. He lashes out violently against any threat to his freedom, not so much to defend it, but to prove to himself and others that he is not what his secret voice tells him he is, an accomplice to his own slavery; he becomes violent to prove to himself and others that he does not deserve what that secret voice tells him he does. His violence is not primarily a response to the objective reality of the outside threat, but rather to the inner threat; a response that inevitably acknowledges the weakness by acknowledging the threat, and thus places the individual into an agonising double-bind.

But all this is much more than a psychological reality to Calderón. At the birth of that famous Calderonian individual, the Segismundo of *La vida es sueño,* a cataclysm of cosmic proportions occurs, in particular,

El mayor, el más horrendo
eclipse que ha padecido
el sol, después que con sangre
lloró la muerte de Cristo
(lines 688–91)

(The biggest, the most horrendous eclipse which the sun has suffered since it wept with blood at the death of Christ)

Whatever one may think about this kind of typically baroque imagery,
Calderón clearly intends to establish a connection between the birth, the
existence, of rebellious and radically insecure Segismundo, and the Christian meaning of Christ's historical existence and death. To say that the
eclipse at the birth of Segismundo is something of a replica of the one
that occurred at the death of Christ, is to make Segismundo's condition
the very symbol of the fallen human condition that gave purpose to the
coming of Christ and his Passion.

Fallen man is an alienated man; that is to say, an individual human
being fallen from his individual dignity and deprived of his, in principle,
inalienable singularity, a shameful individual who connives with everything that threatens such singularity. But in Calderón this alienation has
a special name: dishonor.

"Honor cases," said Lope de Vega, move theater audiences more than
any others. And among honor cases those of Calderón are, by far, the
most striking and famous. The phrase, "honor calderoniano" (Calderonian honor) is almost as much a part of standard educated Spanish as
the adjective "quijotesco" (quixotic). But there are two kinds of Calderonian honor: the one exemplified by Pedro Crespo, the mayor in *El alcalde de Zalamea,* who defined honor in the famous lines,

Al rey, la hacienda y la vida
se ha de dar, pero el honor
es patrimonio del alma
y el alma sólo es de Dios.
(*Obras,* 1:862)

(To the King, riches and life are due, but honor belongs to the
soul, and the soul belongs only to God)

and the honor of those insanely jealous husbands in *El médico de su honra, A secreto agravio secreta venganza,* and *El pintor de su deshonra,* for example, who can, to restore their honor, murder a completely inno-cent wife in premeditated cold blood on the mere suspicion of infidelity.

These two kinds of honor are diametrically opposite. In fact, the one defined by Pedro Crespo as belonging to the soul, God's gift, requires a renunciation of the other. This other kind is repeatedly defined in all those dramas as placing, not only the public worth of the individual, but his own self-esteem, the image that the individual has of himself, entirely in the hands of another. Says Don Juan, the dishonored husband in *El pintor:*

> ¿El honor que nace mío,
> esclavo de otro? Eso no!
> Y que me condene yo
> por el ajeno albedrío!
> ¿Cómo bárbaro consiente
> el mundo este infame rito?
> (*Obras,* 1:995)

(The honor which is born mine, the slave of another? No! And I, condemned because of somebody else's choice? How can the world be so barbaric as to accept such an infamous rite?)

These questions are indeed a most literal and radical definition of the very concept of alienation. In spite of his denunciation of such a "bar-baric and infamous rite," the protesting individual will in fact place, not just his work, or his body, or even his public image at the mercy of an-other, but his most intimate and personal sense of worth.

The extent of this individual's enslavement to the other is measured indirectly, but rather graphically, by the extent of Pedro Crespo's willing renunciation as he begs and pleads on his knees with the proud captain who has raped his totally innocent daughter, to restore his daughter's honor by marrying her. Pedro Crespo offers everything; not only every-thing he owns, but himself and his own son to be branded as slaves and put entirely at the mercy of his disdainful enemy, if he would only do the honorable thing and rescue his daughter from shame.

But Pedro Crespo's generous and willing renunciation of everything that can be externally perceived, saves his inner worth, his gift from God,

from enslavement to the other, while the murderous husbands manage
to preserve a rather precarious appearance at the expense of their inner
loss of freedom.

When Don Gutierre, the husband who will kill his innocent wife in *El
médico,* wonders in distress how there can be a law "that condemns the
innocent to die, to suffer," he is thinking of himself, who would be dishonored because of something his wife, not he, supposedly did. But in
the end it will be another innocent victim, who will take his place and
actually die for something she never did. The law of honor demands a
victim, and the husband has no choice; he must either take the place of
the victim himself, as Pedro Crespo is willing to do for the sake of his
daughter, and be utterly ostracized and subject to public scorn, or he
must find a substitute victim on whose shoulders he will place the burden
of his own dishonor. For undoubtedly the wife is not killed as a punishment for what she did or was thought to have done, but only as a carrier
of her husband's dishonor. In Calderón, as opposed to Lope de Vega, it
becomes shockingly clear that the question of the actual guilt or innocence of the wife is completely secondary, a needed excuse to cover up
the internal sacrificial logic at work in the victimizing process. Everything
appears to turn around the question of whether the wife did or did not
actually engage in some kind of adulterous behavior. But it is only an
appearance. The victimizing "honor" mechanism can be triggered by
anything, no matter how insignificant. As Don Gutierre tells the King in
answer to the King's question, "What did you see?"

> Nada: que hombres como yo
> no ven; basta que imaginen,
> que sospechen, que prevengan,
> que recelen, que adivinen,
> que . . . no sé cómo lo diga;
> que no hay voz que signifique
> una cosa, que no sea
> un átomo indivisible.
> *(Obras,* 1:650)

(Nothing: men such as I do not have to see; it is enough for them
to imagine, to suspect, to anticipate, to be apprehensive, to guess,
to . . . I do not know how to express it; there is no word to signify
something, which is not even an indivisible atom.)

Indeed, the purer, the more exquisite the sense of honor the less it takes to dishonor it, and the greater the likelihood that the victimizing mechanism will be triggered. According to the murderous logic of this law of honor, the more insignificant the evidence of the wife's guilt, the brighter the honor that kills her. Taken to its logical limit, the perfect case of honor requires an innocent victim killed on the slightest possible suspicion. Only then could it be said that the victim has been killed just for the sake of honor. Some of Calderón's plays, in particular *El médico de su honra*, approach that truly revolting limit, and Calderón knows it.

That limit is never approached in Lope, Calderón's immediate predecessor and the creator of the modern national Spanish theater. In Lope's "honor cases" the wives or daughters are properly guilty, if not of outright adultery (which might have been too shocking to stage), at the very least of willfully reckless behavior. In other words, in Lope the objective signs of guilt are much more solid than in Calderón; they never reach that rarefied, almost ethereal thinness that they may have in the latter's famous honor plays.

Calderón purposely deemphasizes anything that may lie outside the inner logic of the law of honor itself, which is a collective mechanism whereby the individual submits to the sacrificial, victimizing, demands of the group. Submission to such victimizing demands is what it takes to be accepted as a full, that is, honorable, member of the group. At the end of the famous Calderonian cases the King himself, the head and symbol of society, accepts the killing as properly motivated and justified. In the Italian setting of *El pintor de su deshonra*, where there is no King, the noble parents of the victims themselves (innocent wife and would-be lover) justify the killing and let the husband, caught in flagrante delicto, go free.

In a primitive society such a sacrificial demand poses no problem to the individual as such, because individuality itself is group-given: the individual recognizes himself as such and as a member of the group in the same act of self-awareness. But this is no longer the case in Calderón's world. Calderón's individuals know that the sacrificial demand is a cruel demand imposed on them by the group, or more precisely by the full, honorable, members of the group. They know they are surrendering their power of free choice (*libre albedrío*) and individual responsibility to something alien (*ajeno*), imposed on them from the outside. They all bitterly and anguishedly question such an imposition, and yet, they submit to it. At this point it is important to emphasize this questioning of the law and its arbitrariness on the part of the individual who will, nevertheless, submit to it. Because this questioning clearly indicates that the collective law of honor is not working quite so smoothly as it may have in the past; for now it takes the willing, though wrenching, complicity of the individual to be put into effect.

And, of course, one questioning individual leads easily to another, and yet another, and so on and so forth. For what is the difference between the murdering husbands, Don Gutierre, Don Juan Roca, Don Lope, and any of the other noble dramatis personae? So what is really at issue in the problematic working of the law of honor is its collective character; the old unanimity around the victim is cracking everywhere. In Calderón's victimizing law of honor what we have is no longer the old unhesitating group, which knows its victim and does the job in perfectly good conscience, but a bunch of accomplices playing a role and sworn to secrecy. The collective sacrificial ritual has become a theatrical performance, a comedy of innocence played not in fear of a sacred power, but in fear of the other; for every playing accomplice knows what the others know, and pretends not to know. "The play's the thing," when the old violence has lost its sacred status. But if the play could help Hamlet "to catch the conscience of the king," it could just as well serve to hide it.

The honor-case Calderonian protagonist is indeed a man "to double business bound." He must cleanse his stained honor with the blood of the victim, but the blood of the victim has lost most of its sacred cleansing power. It is too weak to wipe away the dishonoring stain completely. In fact, in its weakened status, the blood of the honor victim becomes a piece of incriminating evidence of the dishonor that made it necessary. Therefore, the killing must be done and, at the same time, it must be covered up. This is the explicit theme of one of the famous honor plays, *A secreto agravio secreta venganza* (A secret vengeance for a secret offense). And yet, it cannot be covered up completely: if nobody knows about it the killing is utterly useless, since it is done to restore one's image before the others. So it must be done but, if at all possible, in such a way as to provide for the possibility of a verisimilar, though false, explanation of why and how it happened; an explanation that everybody can plausibly pretend to believe.

Anthropologists tell of a Siberian tribe, the Tungus, who hunt the bear for a living. When they kill the animal, they leave it on the spot and walk away. Hours later they return and pretend to find the dead animal as if by chance. Look, a dead bear! Who may have killed it? They blame either the Russians or the English for the killing. Obviously they must believe that if they do not follow strictly this kind of ritual behavior, they will put themselves in danger from some kind of sacred power. Our Calderonian honor player places the other in the role of that sacred power. But with a difference: in all likelihood the relationship between the Tungus and the sacred is far more stable than the one between the Calderonian subject and his pretending accomplices.

> To my sick soul, as sin's true nature is,
> Each toy seems prologue to some great amiss:
> So full of artless jealousy is guilt,
> It spills itself in fearing to be spilt.
>
> (act 4, scene 5)

Thus speaks Hamlet's mother, the Queen. Her words express in a nutshell the complex existential problematic that grips the typical Calderonian subject. This subject suffers, not from an accidental but an original sickness of the soul, and as such, his soul is full of fear: anything, no matter how trifling, "seems a prologue to some great amiss," or in Calderón's own words,

> en tan confuso abismo,
> es todo el cielo un presagio
> y es todo el mundo un prodigio.
> (La vida es sueño, lines
> 983–85)

(In so confusing an abyss, all of heaven is an omen, all the world is a portent.)

This sick and fearful, this guilty soul is the perfect breeding ground, the original cradle, of jealousy. Guilt is full of jealousy. It is its jealous character that takes guilt out of itself, its hiding place in the dark, for which it has an original affinity; jealous guilt cannot hide itself. But when it comes out prompted by "artless jealousy," it speaks with double tongue; it shows itself through its fear of showing itself.

A detailed analysis of any of Calderón's wife-murder honor plays would provide ample evidence of the truth of Shakespeare's profound intuition. These honor-obsessed husbands are insanely jealous. And this jealousy terrifies them; they make efforts to conceal it, they do not want to face it, but cannot help themselves; it comes out uncontrollably, in spurts.

"Mintió quien dijo que calló con celos" (He lied who said he was jealous and kept quiet), says Don Gutierre, as he stealthily, "with the steps of a thief," finds his way at night into his own house to spy on his wife, Mencía:

> En el mudo silencio
> de la noche, que adoro y reverencio,
> por sombra aborrecida,
> como sepulcro de la humana vida,
> de secreto he venido
> hasta mi casa.
> (*El médico,* in *Obras,* 1:647).

(In the mute silence of the night, which I adore and reverence, through a darkness abhorred as the tomb of human life, in secret I have come to my own house.)

His words have a clear allegorical value. The jealous man seeks in reverence an abhorrent darkness, which is the very symbol of death, which is normally in Calderón the symbol of original sin, since death was the immediate consequence of sin. Jealous man is spiritually dead, a "living corpse," to use one of Calderón's favorite images. And that means he has forfeited his original dignity and freedom. Such a man regresses to a lower animal status. He becomes, like violent Segismundo, "a man among wild beasts and a wild beast among men."

A moment later Don Gutierre speaks in riddles using double meanings with his wife. She does not quite understand the import of his words:

DOÑA MENCÍA: Parece que celoso
            hablas en dos sentidos.

DON GUTIERRE: ¿Celoso? ¿Sabes tú lo que son celos?
            Que yo no sé qué son, ¡viven los cielos!;
            porque si lo supiera,
            y celos . . .
            . . . llegar pudiera
            a tener . . . ¿Qué son celos?

átomos, ilusiones, y desvelos; . . .
no más que de una esclava, una criada,
por sombra imaginada,
con hechos inhumanos,
a pedazos sacara con mis manos
el corazón, y luego
envuelto en sangre, desatado en fuego,
el corazón comiera
a bocados, la sangre me bebiera,
el alma le sacara,
y el alma, ¡vive Dios!, despedazara,
si capaz de dolor el alma fuera.
¿Pero cómo hablo yo desta manera?

DOÑA MENCÍA: Temor al alma ofreces.

DON GUTIERRE: ¡Jesús, Jesús mil veces!
¡Mi bien, mi esposa, cielo, gloria mía!
. . . .
Perdona, por tus ojos,
esta descompostura, estos enojos;
. . . .
y vete, por tu vida; que prometo
que te miro con miedo y con respeto,
corrido deste exceso.
¡Jesús! No estuve en mí, no tuve seso.
(*Obras*, 1:649)

(DOÑA MENCÍA: It seems that, like a jealous man, you speak with two
meanings.

DON GUTIERRE: Jealous? Do you know what jealousy is? Because, heavens! I don't know what it is. If I knew . . . if I could ever become
jealous . . . —what is jealousy? an atom, an illusion, a disquiet
. . . —of no more than a slave, a servant, by a purely imagined
shadow, with acts inhuman I would rip out her heart with my
bare hands, and then, soaked in blood and breathing fire, I would
eat up the heart and gulp its blood; I would take out her soul and,
by God!, I would tear it to pieces, if only the soul were capable of
feeling pain. But how can I be talking this way?

DOÑA MENCÍA: You frighten my soul.

DON GUTIERRE: My God, my God, a thousand times! Dear wife, my
solace, my heaven, my glory! For the light of your eyes, forgive
this disorder, this anger. . . . And please go, for your life; because
I assure you I look at you with fear and reverence, ashamed of
this excess. My God! I was not myself, I lost my reason.)

Don Gutierre is the man who, in spite of his anguished questioning of
the "unjust law of honor that condemns the innocent to die, to suffer,"
will submit to it and keep such a law alive. Now we know why: he is
jealous; and we know what jealousy means.

He is not exactly submitting to any "law." He is desperately and violently trying to hide an unshakable sense of guilt from the sight of the
other, for it is in the sight of the other where he finds himself guilty. He
does not submit to a "law," he submits to the other, his neighbor, his
equal. He surrenders his dignity and his freedom eagerly, and yet in bitter
resentment, at the feet of the other. He kills out of jealousy, but with
"double meaning": trying to hide the fact that he kills out of jealousy.
He "spills" his jealousy "in fear of being spilt." For it is his jealousy that
testifies against him in the presence of the other.

It is not his wife's (supposed) behavior that dishonors him, but the
jealousy it instills in his heart. This jealousy dishonors him, because it
reveals his fallen condition, his original and inescapable guilt, not in the
sight of God, but in the sight of another human being, who ipso facto
turns from offender to accuser. And this is what makes the guilt unbearable and terrifying, because the human idol (the human made into an
idol) has no power to forgive; it offers no respite or redemption. The
human idol only accuses. It derives its idolatrous power over the accused
from the accusation itself. The more it is idolized the stronger the evidence against the accused, and vice versa. There is no way out of it. Left
to its own logic, this intersubjective situation can only end in suicide or
murder, or both.

Such is the basic human drama that Calderón discovers behind the veil
of a collective law of honor that had already worn rather thin. The law
of honor adds the collective dimension to the basic drama. It ranges the
honorable members of the group on the side of the accuser. As Calderón
sees through the law of honor, he discovers it has no power of its own.
It derives all its power from the basic human drama that jealousy exposes. And yet this empty shell serves a purpose at the bidding of jealousy

itself: it hides, or attempts to hide, what the jealous individual finds unbearable; namely, his own inescapable guilt, which is the "poison" that
jealousy forces out of the individual and then turns against him on a
rebound, as it were, from the other. The law of honor collectivizes the
other, dilutes or softens the interindividual encounter, draws a veil over
the hatefully accusing eyes of the other. But there can be no doubt about
it; it is jealousy that triggers the "law of honor" as a "cure" or an antidote against its own self-poisonous nature. This becomes as explicit as
can be in *El médico*. Here is Don Gutierre again, as he plans his stealthy
entry into his own house:

> Esta noche iré a mi casa
> de secreto, entraré en ella,
> por ver qué malicia tiene
> el mal; y hasta apurar ésta,
> disimularé, si puedo,
> esta desdicha, esta pena,
> este rigor, este agravio,
> este dolor, esta ofensa,
> este asombro, este delirio,
> este cuidado, esta afrenta
> estos celos . . . ¿Celos dije?
> ¡Qué mal hice! Vuelva, vuelva
> al pecho la voz; mas no,
> que si es ponzoña que engendra
> mi pecho, si no me dio
> la muerte, ¡ay de mí!, al verterla,
> al volverla a mí podrá
>
> .   .   .   .
>
> ¿Celos dije? Celos dije;
> pues basta; que cuando llega
> un marido a saber que hay
> celos, faltará la ciencia;
> y es la cura postrera
> que el médico de honor hacer intenta.
> (*Obras*, 1:645)

(Tonight I'll go to and enter my house in secret to see how much
malice there is in my misfortune. Until I find out, I will pretend

and hide, if I can, this misfortune, this sorrow, this rigor, this insult, this pain, this offense, this wonder, this delirium, this care, this affront, this jealousy. . . . Did I say jealousy? How wrong was I in saying it! Let the voice, let it come back inside; but no, it's a poison engendered in my chest, if it did not kill me, woe is me! as it came out, it probably will on coming back. . . . Did I say jealousy? I did say jealousy. Then that's enough, because when a husband gets to know that there is jealousy involved, there will not be enough science to cure it, and I intend to apply the last cure as a surgeon of honor.)

There is a most revealing ambiguity, even contradiction, in these last words by Don Gutierre: "Did I say jealousy?" He thinks, then, that he has said enough. Because if it is jealousy, there is no science in the world that will cure it, and Don Gutierre intends to use the last, the final, cure that honor provides or indicates. Which really means that if this honor cure is going to work, he has to stop talking about jealousy. Honor can only cure jealousy to the extent that it can hide from everybody, including himself, the surgeon of his honor, that it is jealousy it is curing. Honor is only allowed to say that it cures itself.

I do not know what else Calderón would have to do to disabuse generation after generation of critics who are still talking about these wife murders as being motivated by some peculiar notion of the "concept" of honor, not by jealousy. They all believe Don Gutierre, they do not believe Calderón. Take but jealousy away, and the Calderonian subject will find the strength to resist the "unjust law that condemns the innocent to die, to suffer," even to a heroic degree, as we saw in the case of Pedro Crespo, the mayor of Zalamea. Pedro Crespo is as deeply hurt as any loving father would be to see his daughter violently taken from his home, raped, and publicly humiliated, but he is not jealous. Therefore, even though his public honor is as clearly at stake as in the case of the jealous husbands, he will not give in to the public demand for vengeance.

On the other hand, take the "law of honor" away, but leave jealousy in, and the result will be similar to the cases of wives murdered supposedly for the sake of honor: witness *El mayor monstruo del mundo*. In reference to vengeance and murder, it is not the "law of honor" that makes the decisive difference, but the presence or absence of jealousy. Jealousy is the active ingredient, the triggering mechanism.

Now, could it be that in Calderón "jealousy" is restricted to a sex triangle, husband-wife-lover? Are we perhaps comparing apples and oranges when we bring together the wife-murder cases on the one hand, and *El alcalde de Zalamea,* on the other? Not at all. Calderón's answer is already contained in the most famous wife-murder case, *El médico de su honra.*

The rivalry between Don Gutierre and the King's brother, Don Enrique, unfolds against the background of the actual historical rivalry between King Pedro I of Castile and his brother Enrique of Trastamara in the fourteenth century. The historical civil war between the two brothers ended with Pedro's death at the hands of Enrique. In the play, the King's reaction to the latent threat from the rival brother is a clear echo of Doña Mencía's reaction to the threat from her husband, or Don Gutierre's own reaction to the one from Don Enrique. All of them, victims and murderers alike, experience a world full of signs of their misfortune. They anticipate either death or dishonor in the same guilty manner, whether or not they are actually guilty of any wrongdoing against the other. Don Enrique's rivalry with the husband, Don Gutierre, is paralleled by the latent one between him and his brother the King. In fact, this is presented by Calderón in a rather dramatic fashion: as the King, with a stern warning, gives back to his brother the dagger the latter had unknowingly left in Doña Mencía's room, Don Enrique, greatly distressed and anguished by what he is hearing, accidentally cuts the King's hand. The King is horrified; he immediately sees this as a clear sign of his own death:

REY: ¿Qué hiciste?

D. ENRIQUE: ¿Yo?

REY: . . . .
       ¿Tú la daga que te di,
       hoy contra mi pecho esgrimes?
       ¿Tú me quieres dar la muerte?

D. ENRIQUE: Mira, señor, lo que dices;
             que yo turbado . . .

REY: . . . .
       ¡Enrique, Enrique!
       Detén el puñal, ya muero.

Don Enrique leaves and the King begins to recover his senses:

¡Válgame el cielo! ¿qué es esto?
¡Oh, qué aprensión insufrible!
Bañado me vi en mi sangre,
muerto estuve. ¿Qué infelice
imaginación me cerca,
que con espantos horribles
y con helados temores
el pecho y el alma oprime?
Ruego a Dios que estos principios
no lleguen a tales fines,
que con diluvios de sangre
el mundo se escandalice.

(KING: What did you do?

DON ENRIQUE: I?

KING: The dagger I just gave you,
you turn against my heart?
You want to kill me?

DON ENRIQUE: Milord, look what you're saying;
I was disturbed . . .

KING: Enrique! Enrique!
Stop your dagger, I'm dying.

Heavens! What is this?
What an unbearable apprehension!
I saw myself soaked in my own blood;
I was dead. What an unhappy
imagination lays siege on me
and oppresses my heart and my soul
with horrible fright
and icy fears?
I pray to God that these beginnings
may not reach such end
as to scandalize the world
with a deluge of blood.)

The King leaves. Don Gutierre, who has secretly been listening to everything, enters and picks up the dagger that is lying on the floor:

Muera Mencía . . .
y pues aqueste puñal
hoy segunda vez me rinde
el Infante, con él muera.
(*Obras,* 1:651–52)

(Let Mencía die . . .
and since this dagger
is given back to me
by the Infante for a second time today
let her die with it.)

The same dagger that symbolically kills Mencía (she will actually be
bled to death by a surgeon under threat of death from Don Gutierre),
will also kill the King and flood the kingdom "with a deluge of blood"
(see Parker, 17). This can only mean that Calderón's attention is not
directed primarily to the object of the rivalry, whether wife or kingdom,
but to the human problematic of the rivalry itself, the way the rivals
relate to one another, and its violent and cruel consequences. Whether
one or a thousand are killed, what ultimately kills them is the same violent intersubjective process.

Should we not, then, speak of rivalry rather than jealousy as the triggering mechanism of the "honor" case? We certainly could. But we
would have to add that, in Calderón, jealousy is a fundamental ingredient
of violent rivalry, regardless of the object of the rivalry. Jealousy expresses the mediating or modeling role automatically granted by the jealous subject to the rival; it expresses the subject's submission, the hate-
filled idolatry with which he views the rival. He hates the rival for wanting what he wants and, at the same time, the rival's desire fascinates him:
he wants what the rival wants, he follows the rival's desire, exchanges
places with him, becomes the rival's secret accomplice against himself.

This exchangeable character, this unspeakable complicity, is suggested
either subtly or spectacularly by Calderón in all his famous wife-murder
cases. In *El médico,* for example: we just saw Don Gutierre stealthily
entering his own house "in the mute silence of the night," "with the steps
of a thief," to surprise Doña Mencía who has fallen asleep in the garden.
But this scene is a clear reminder of the way in which, a little before, the
rival, Don Enrique, had entered the house, also in the dark, with "feet
hardly touching the ground," in silence, because he is afraid even "of

the winds listening," to surprise Doña Mencía who has fallen asleep in the garden.

In *A secreto agravio secreta venganza* the husband will kill the rival as he is literally ferrying him toward the place where the wife is waiting. The unsuspecting rival cannot believe his "good luck": "¡Que me viniese a servir / de tercero su marido!" (Incredible, her husband serving as a procurer for me!) (*Obras* 1:616).

In *El pintor de su deshonra* the suggestion of existential complicity is even more spectacular: it is carnival time in Barcelona, where husband, wife, and friends are attending a masque. All of a sudden fire spreads in the house where the married couple is; the husband picks up his fainted wife and runs with her out of the house looking for somebody in whose care to leave her, while he returns to the burning site to provide further assistance; but, behold! he delivers her, still unconscious, into the hands of the masked rival, who takes advantage of the opportunity to abduct her to Italy. The "dishonored" husband will follow in pursuit, track them down, and kill both.

An earlier critic had noticed the many textual parallels between the husband, Don Juan Roca, and the rival, Don Alvaro: "There are series of correspondences between what happens to Don Alvaro, what he says and does, and what happens to Don Juan Roca, what he says and does. At times, even, they use the same or very similar words on similar occasions. . . . Such parallels cannot be accidental. Calderón used them to show that there were strong links to bind together the lives of these two men" (Wilson, 73–74). The critic, however, does not suspect how existentially strong those "links" really are.

It is also in *El pintor* where jealousy's role is the most literally spectacular. Don Juan, the husband and painter, will actually paint a mythological allegory of his own dishonor (as the title indicates). The subject of the painting is jealous Hercules pursuing the Centaur who has abducted Deyanira. So realistic is the figure of Hercules—we are told—that "nobody can see it without saying that the man is jealous." Hercules "seems to be coming out of the panel; and he would come out if he would see that the Centaur he is after, were also out" (*Obras*, 1:996). It is the Centaur he is after, Deyanira has become secondary. It is not out of love that he pursues, but out of jealousy. The jealous husband is wherever the rival is; a proposition that must be seen in its full existential implications. This is, once again, why jealousy is so fundamentally dishonoring, why it calls for honor to cover its insufferable appearance. There is no "law of honor"; there is only jealousy anxiously pleading for cover, an unspeakable truth searching for a lie. The "law of honor" is that lie; it is not what it says it is, but a collective, sacrificial, victimizing fiction that does not restore honor, but covers up the dishonor, though, in fact, no longer very efficiently.

If Shakespeare's theater is "a theater of envy," Calderón's is a theater of jealousy. In Calderón jealousy is not just a particular existential condition among many, one sin among others; it is at the root of sin, a cipher and a symptom of human sinfulness or fallen condition. Indeed, the very title of one of his plays, *El mayor monstruo del mundo,* declares it "the world's biggest monster"; and the innocent wife and victim in the play, Mariene, calls it "the most cruel, horrible and strong."

I would like to finish these reflections on Calderón's theater with some comments on this play, in which jealousy is the explicit theme. Like most of Calderón's plays, *El mayor monstruo* is very complex. But if one wanted to reduce this complexity to one final message, one moral of the story, so to speak, it could be, among other possibilities, the following: there is no amount of riches, power, or worldly success enough to fill the existential vacuum at the heart of jealous man.

The play is an extremely free adaptation of the story of Herod, tetrarch and king of the Jews, and his strangely obsessive love for his wife Mariamne, as told by Flavius Josephus, both in *The Jewish War* and, in much greater detail, in *The Antiquities of the Jews,* where we read that

[Herod's] love to [his wife] was not of a calm nature, nor such as we usually meet with among other husbands, for at its commencement it was of the enthusiastic kind, nor was it by their long cohabitation and free conversation together, brought under his power to manage; but at this time [after he had her killed] his love to Mariamne seemed to seize him in such a peculiar manner, as looked like divine vengeance upon him, for the taking away her life. . . . [He] therefore laid aside the administration of public affairs, and was so far conquered by his passion, that he would order his servants to call for Mariamne, as if she were still alive. . . . And when he was in this way, there arose a pestilential disease, and carried off the greatest part of the multitude, and of his best and most esteemed friends, and made all men suspect that this distemper was brought upon them by the anger of God, for the injustice that had been done to Mariamne. (Book 15, chap. 7, 7)

The story was well known. In Italy it had already inspired Lodovico Dolce's *Marianna* (Venice, 1565) and, in France, Alexandre Hardy and Tristan L'Hermite, whose *La Mariane* was published in 1636, precisely the year in which the first version of Calderón's play was also published.

Calderón's Herod is a very ambitious man. Being the ruler of Palestine and king of the Jews is not enough for him. He wants nothing less than to enter Rome in triumph and become the sole ruler of the entire Roman Empire, which is saying that he wants everything; he wants to be the most powerful man in the world. To that objective he is trying to take advantage of the war between Anthony and Octavian. As he sees the latter getting the upper hand, he secretly sends help to Anthony in Egypt, not enough to make him win, but just to even out the forces. He wants the two rivals to destroy each other, and thus clear the way to Rome for him. His plan fails; Octavian destroys the combined forces of Anthony and Herod. When the news of the disaster reach him, the Tetrarch becomes dejected; disconsolate, he sighs and weeps. Filipo, his counsellor, reproaches him for such a show of weakness, and tries to instill some courage in him:

FILIPO: Señor . . .

    . . . . .

    Ensancha el pecho, verás
    que en él tus desdichas caben,
    sin que a la voz ni a los ojos
    se asomen.

TETRARCA: ¡Ay, que no sabes,
    Filipo, cuál es mi pena,
    pues quieres darla esa cárcel!

(FILIPO: Sir . . .

    . . . .

    Broaden your heart, you'll see that all of your misfortunes can be held within it, without your voice or your eyes betraying them.

TETRARCH: Ah! Filipo, you don't know the nature of my pain, for you want me to lock it in such a prison.

FILIPO *(surprised):* Of course, I know, since I know that you have lost your fleet.)

The dialogue continues:

TETRARCA: No es su pérdida la mía.

FILIPO: Serálo el mirar triunfante
a Octaviano, con la duda
de que penetre o alcance
ser su enemigo.

TETRARCA: No tengo
miedo a las adversidades.

FILIPO: De Aristóbolo, tu hermano,
ni de Marco Antonio sabes.

TETRARCA: Cuando sepa que murieron,
tendré envidia a bien tan grande.

FILIPO: Los presagios del puñal,
premisas son bien notables.

TETRARCA: Al magnánimo varon,
no hay prodigio que le espante.

FILIPO: Pues si prodigios, fortunas,
pérdidas, adversidades
no te afligen, ¿Qué te aflige?

TETRARCA: ¡Ay, Filipo, no te canses
en adivinarlo, puesto
que mientras no adivinares
que es amor de Mariene,
todo es discurrir en balde!
Todos mis anhelos fueron
coronarla y coronarme
en Roma, porque no tenga
que envidiar mi esposa a nadie.
¿Por qué ha de gozar belleza,
que no hay otra que la iguale
. . . . un hombre
que hay otro que le aventaje?
. . . .
Piérdase la armada; muera
Antonio, mi parcial; falte
Aristóbolo; Octaviano

sepa o no mi intento; mande
vuelva el prodigioso acero
a mi poder; que a postrarme
nada basta, nada importa,
sino que el medio se atrase
de hacer reina a Mariene
del mundo. Ya en esta parte
dirás, y lo dirán todos,
que es locura. No te espante,
que cuando amor no es locura,
no es amor; y el mío es tan grande,
que pienso—atiende Filipo—
que pasando los umbrales
de la muerte, ha de quedar
a las futuras edades
grabado con letras de oro
en láminas de diamante.
                              (Austral, 75–77)

(TETRARCH: Its loss is not mine.

FILIPO: Then it must be to see Octavian triumph, and to
wonder whether he'll find out you were his
enemy.

TETRARCH: I do not fear adversity.

FILIPO: You have no news of your brother, Aristobolus,
or of Marc Anthony.

TETRARCH: Even if I find out they died, I will envy them
their good fortune.

FILIPO: The predictions about the dagger are rather
ominous. [It has been predicted Herod will kill
what he loves most].

TETRARCH: Omens do not frighten a magnanimous man.

FILIPO: Then, if neither omens, bad fortune, losses, or
adversity are the cause of your affliction, what
is it?

TETRARCH: Ah, Filipo, do not waste your time guessing,
for unless you guess it is my love for Mariene,
all your effort is in vain.
My whole desire was to crown her and me in Rome,
so that my wife would have to envy nobody. For
why should a beauty that has no equal, be
enjoyed by a man . . . who is bettered by another?

. . . .

Let the fleet perish; let Anthony, my ally, die;
let Aristobolus be gone; let Octavian find out
or not about my intentions; let the dagger
prodigiously come back to me; nothing is enough
to break me, nothing matters, except that I must
delay making Mariene queen of the world. At
this point, you must think, everybody must
think, that this is madness. Don't be startled,
if love is not madness, it is not love; and mine
is so intense that I think—listen, Filipo—that
it will go beyond the threshold of death and
remain inscribed with golden letters on diamond
sheets for future ages to see.)

It is indeed a mad and strange love, for it has nothing to do with generosity. Herod does not want to conquer the world simply to put it at Mariene's feet for her undisturbed enjoyment. He wants to conquer the world in the hope that he can convince himself that he deserves Mariene. The whole world is not really the measure of Mariene's worth, but of the depth of his own self-perceived lack of merit, as he lifts his eyes toward the inaccessible pedestal on which he has placed her. He must be the greatest, the most powerful man on earth, so that his wife "will not have to envy anybody." Which means that, at least for the moment, Herod must live in a state of great anxiety in the face of the ever-present possibility that anything or anybody may trigger his wife's envy, may in any way attract his wife's desire. No wonder that his "passion" will be defined by himself later in the play as "an offspring of love and a mother of hatred" (Austral, 164). Nor is it any wonder that in such an existential predicament, he, the anguished subject, would see rivals and obstacles everywhere, tortured by a passion that feeds on insubstantial shadows, extremely sensitive to the slightest changes in his human environment: "For if I had to define jealousy, / I would portray it as a chameleon / which feeds on nothing but air / and changes color with every change of light" (164).

The thought of Mariene belonging to somebody else becomes utterly unbearable. Not because of his love for her, but because of his hatred of the rival, the inevitable, real or imagined rival, generated by the agonizing experience of his guilt, that is, of his fundamental inadequacy. Or rather, because he cannot possibly separate one from the other, so that, in the final analysis, the love and the hatred commingle and so must their respective objects. He will kill her if he cannot kill the rival. Having been taken prisoner by Octavian in Egypt, and expecting his rival to take possession of Mariene once he sees her in Jerusalem, the Tetrarch orders Filipo to have Mariene killed as soon as the news of his own execution reach them.

Let us assume for a moment that the pathologically jealous Tetrarch could have gotten his way and, entering Rome in triumph, could have crowned Mariene queen of the world. Would he have been satisfied? Could that have cured his jealousy? Of course not. He would have spied upon Mariene's every movement, every change in mood; at the slightest sign of unhappiness, he would have blamed himself for it, felt the stinging suggestion of the implicit rival, the voice of his existential emptiness, just as he does at the very beginning of the play.

Mariene comes on the stage weeping, which upsets him, because he does not know why. He inquires anxiously: "What do you wish, or want, / or envy? What are you lacking? Are you not, / my dear wife, queen in Jerusalem?. . . / Are you not adored by me / and worshiped by my people? . . .

> Let not so much splendor
> yield so easily to a mere accident;
> let your gladness, generous, give back
> its light to the dawn, its brightness to the day
> . . . .
> and my life to me; for in the midst of grave fears
> your worries drive me to jealousy . . .
> What else can I say, I already said jealousy . . .

Herod's perception of what happens to his wife is also a good description of his state of mind. For he is indeed a prime candidate "to let so much splendor yield so easily to a mere accident." Quite appropriately and prophetically, what in the midst of such a splendor clouds Mariene's (and, therefore, Herod's) happiness is "the world's biggest monster"— which will turn out to be, not surprisingly, her husband's jealousy.

Thus Herod is caught in a vicious circle. His jealousy drives him to conquer the world, but it is also his jealousy that will forever undermine such conquest and defeat its purpose. Hence the double prediction: she will be killed by "the world's biggest monster" and he will kill "what he loves most."

Herod is his own worst enemy. He will forever want what he will forever prevent himself from getting. He will always mistrust his own happiness. In what was probably the original version of the play, published in 1636, we find this idea expressed quite explicitly and dramatically: in the third act, after Mariene has pleaded successfully with Octavian for her husband's life (while knowing already that he had arranged for her to be killed), she shuts herself in her chambers, after forbidding her husband to follow her or ever go inside. Herod is stunned. He did not know she knew about his secret plan to have her killed. But in a devious way he is glad she has locked herself up of her own accord. In fact, he will lock the door on the outside as well, just as she has done on the inside,

> and I myself will not go in,
> for I am not sure I would not make myself jealous.
> In fact, I think I would.
> For if I saw myself in her arms
> and felt so happy,
> I would immediately not recognize myself
> and would imagine to be somebody else.
>
> (*Obras,* 473)

In a later revision this action and words were dropped in favor of the image of the jealous husband trying to sneak into his wife's chambers, "furtively," like a thief "trying to steal his own treasure," a favorite image of Calderón, which we already saw in the case of that other jealous husband, Don Gutierre.

The two versions are equally Calderonian, and, existentially speaking, equally accurate. They both express the doubling of the subject against himself. The second or later version, however, gives more relief to the visual, scenographic parallel between the jealous subject and the rival, in this case Octavian, who also approaches the object of the jealousy furtively and in the dark.

The contrasting symmetry between the two rivals, so typical of Calderón, is most striking and revealing in this play. Each one has what the other wants. Octavian has the rule of the world, which is what Herod wants, but he does not have Mariene; as a result, in spite of all his power and glory, he is an unhappy man, his triumph has become hollow. His "hopeless passion" (he has fallen in love with Mariene's portrait, not knowing whose portrait it is, but believing the woman is dead) is also described as

> madness, and so obsessive
> that neither triumphs, applause,
> laurels or emblems
> can help it, since in no way
> can they relieve me from such a
> stubbornly senseless
> apprehension.
>
> (Austral, 102)

Of course, this parallelism between the two rivals does not mean that they complement each other, being the two perfectly fitting parts of a complete whole. Such a whole is utterly illusory, forever precluded by the rivalry itself. They are rather like mirror images of each other, but with a very interesting difference. As they mirror each other, each one reveals something about the other that would not have been so clear otherwise.

I would like to point out one of these mirroring effects in particular. We have just seen the parallel character of the two rival passions; they are equally mad and obsessive, and, of course, they share the same object; enough of a suggestion of their basic identity. Yet, in other respects, they appear to be entirely different. In particular, Herod appears to be in love with the real Mariene, and Octavian with only an image. Furthermore, the text clearly links the agonizing obsessive character of Octavian's passion to the utter lack of reality of its object.

When Aristobolus, Mariene's brother, tells Octavian that the beautiful woman represented in the portrait is dead, so that he would forget about her, his words have exactly the opposite effect. It is precisely the hopelessness of his passion that keeps Octavian chained to it. But in Calderón such a passion is not only "mad," it is also the very definition of idolatry, the worship of a false god, a lifeless image, a fiction. Octavian swears by her, as by a deity: "¡Vive ella!" (By her!) he cries, instead of "¡Vive Dios!" (By God!),

> for I can offer her this homage,
> as to a deity I adore.
> (Austral, 108)

I suggest that this idolatrous behavior is also a revealing mirror image of Herod's own behavior toward Mariene. His "passion" has in fact transformed her into a deity. From the bottomless depth of his jealous despair, he has created a fascinating idol, at whose feet he is ready to sacrifice everything. In other words, the Mariene that Herod adores is no more real, or any less of an idol, than the object of Octavian's adoration.

It should perhaps be remembered at this point that in Calderón's likely source for his play, Josephus's *Antiquities*, Herod is portrayed as an avid imitator of many pagan customs, especially those of his Roman mentors, "by which means we became guilty of great wickedness," writes Josephus. But it was, above all, the public display of "trophies," that is to say, sculptured images commemorating the military conquests of the Romans, that most deeply disturbed the piety of the Jewish nation:

> Above all the rest, the trophies gave most distaste to the Jews, for as they imagined them to be images, included within the armour that hung round about them, they were sorely displeased at them, because it was not the custom of their country to pay honours to such images. (Book 15, chap. 7, 1)

In other words, in the text that transmits the story of Herod that will be used by dramatists like Tristan L'Hermite or Calderón, the Tetrarch is already portrayed, if not as an outright idolater, certainly as one who did not take seriously the biblical injunction against any form of idolatry. It is only logical to think that when Calderón's Herod describes Octavian as "twice a gentile" because "he makes idols of a sun without light and a deity without soul" (121), referring to Mariene's portrait and its copy, the old image of the quasi-pagan Tetrarch must have crossed his mind, as one more element in the violent symmetry that structures their relationship.

Seen through the mirror of his rival, Herod's behavior toward his wife appears as a form of idolatry. But the full import of this Calderonian insight will only be grasped if we realize that this is not only an existential insight but a historical one as well: idolatry does not only describe a particularly agonizing experience of intersubjectivity; it is also a socio-historical institution. If behind every divinized Mariene in Herodian eyes, there is a fabricated "deity without soul," a publicly worshiped idol, then the converse must also be true: behind the very institution of pagan idolatry, what Calderón sees is the radical immanence of an intersubjective situation in which a human being becomes a fascinating and hateful god in the eyes of another human being; pagan idolatry hides a world of rampant intersubjective alienation, as already anticipated in Chapter 1.

The link between these two levels or aspects of idolatry, the existential and the public or institutional, is sacrifice: more specifically, human sacrifice. The idol is not simply a nonexistent god; it is a diabolical creation. In this respect, Calderón is of one mind with most contemporary moralists. The idol demands a human victim, any victim; if it be innocent and pure so much the better. Idolatry is much more than a mistaken belief; it is the very embodiment of the anti-Christian, the Antichrist. In a way, it is Christianity upside down: instead of an innocent God who dies in place of a guilty human being, idolatry offers a bloodthirsty god who demands the killing of an innocent human being. To put it in the words of beautiful Guacolda, a virgin priestess of the Inca sun-god in Calderón's *La aurora en Copacabana,* who has been chosen to be sacrificed to the god, but senses with her "natural light" that there is something basically unjust about it,

> I don't know
> if I will be able to accept
> to die as a sacrifice
> . . . .
> for some kind of natural
> light in me finds it infinitely repugnant
> that, without my being guilty of any crime,
> there should be a god
> thirsting for human blood
> in such an inhuman and cruel manner,

as to force one of the faithful
to kill another one, without any hatred existing
between them. Tell me, is it a just law
that a god who does not die for me
demand that I die for him?

(*Obras,* 1:1371)

According to Calderón, Christianity does two things simultaneously: it breaks the cruel grip of the bloodthirsty public idol, and it reveals the true human source of the fictitious idol's power, the intersubjective breeding ground from which idols emerge, public idols whose sacred character hides their purely human etiology. In other words, Christianity does these two things simultaneously, because public, institutionalized idolatry is a cover-up for the other, the existential idolatry, the hate-filled fascination that keeps the two rivals locked into each other. Once the cover is blown, the underlying intersubjective spectacle is revealed.

Perhaps we can now see the connection between Calderón's understanding of the public institution of idolatry in general, and the notion of honor that, in a different historical context, is claimed by those other jealous husbands as a justification for their murder. The two serve the same diversionary, hiding function. They both provide a public cover-up as well as a barrier between the two rivals, which affords each of them some respite from the agonizingly ambivalent encounter with the other. The public honor to which those jealous husbands refer is indeed a displaced form of idolatry in a society where public, institutional idolatry, idolatry *stricto sensu,* is no longer possible. Calderón discovers exactly the same intersubjective sacrificial mechanism underneath both of them. They are equally deceptive and equally anti-Christian.

Finally, it may be worth reflecting for a moment on the similarities and differences between Cervantes and Calderón, as paradigmatic examples of what literary fiction was left to say beyond the decline of the epic model. As the human individual is left to face the inevitable other human individual without any of the traditional and sacred safeguards, the first, the most immediate discovery, will be that of dependency. The individual reveals her dependence on the other individual. She mimics the other, models her desire on the other, even sets the other up as a divine substitute. This is the Cervantine moment. The potential for violent disaster and rivalry inherent in this mimetic situation does not by any means escape Cervantes's attention. The story of Marcela and Chrysostom, for example, followed first by that of Cardenio, Luscinda, and Don Fernando, and then by "The tale of foolish curiosity," in Part 1 of the *Quijote,* are unmistakable proof of Cervantes's profound awareness of the problem. But all along this intersubjective road to either insanity or deadly rivalry, the primary focus of his attention remains the mimetic phenomenon as such, the process whereby an individual can reach the point where he only sees meaning in things and find them desirable through the eyes and desires of another individual.

Calderón, on the other hand, concentrates on a more advanced stage of what might be called the pathology of the mimetic disease. His attention is drawn to the point where the model has already become an obstacle, a deadly rival. We no longer see the fascinating divinity of the model directly, but rather, for the most part, implicitly reflected in the bottomless emptiness of the agonizing subject; the subject who chains himself to his "misfortune," who "gives credit" to any obstacle thrown in his path, who is his own worst enemy, a secret collaborator and imitator of whatever rival may bump into him. Calderón begins, as it were, at the end of the process, but fully intuiting the mimetic etiology that is implied in such a deadly outcome. This is why he insists on the symmetry between the two rivals, frequently suggesting their exchangeable character, as they proceed with equal steps toward their common object of desire. And this is also why he deemphasizes and undermines any external or objective reasons for the rivalry, which constantly feeds upon itself.

In the transition from Cervantes to Calderón we witness that aggravation of the "metaphysical desire" of which Girard speaks in *Deceit, Desire, and the Novel,* as he examines the trajectory of the modern novel from Cervantes to Proust and Dostoyevsky. As the mimetic relationship becomes increasingly pathological, what both Cervantes and Calderón perceive is an accelerated regression to a primitive, pre-Christian situation of radical intersubjective immanence presided over by a fictitious or makeshift transcendance, an idol, a simulacrum. In other words, as they peel off all the sacrificial layers, they get to what may be called, literally, the *crucial* moment, the moment of the cross, of the victim, in which, from their Christian perspective, the choice is between the victim-demanding idol and Christ.

5

HISTORICAL SIGNPOSTS

1. The Christian Threshold of the Modern Era

Most attempts at penetrating the historical mystery of the birth of modern Europe have looked for a grand portal bearing the emblem of the human spirit in its heroic march through history. Whether or not such spirit has been abandoned by the gods, or even by God, in no way diminishes its heroic quality; quite the contrary, its Romantic isolation clearly adds to its heroic stature. Therefore the suggestion that the human spirit only crosses the threshold of the modern era as it drops all claims to heroic status and is forced to confront itself through an unavoidable sense of individualized guilt and responsibility, must still sound strange to many, even though scholarly perceptions of this phenomenon are changing.[1]

Within the logic of the theory of the sacred that grounds our approach to the Renaissance, such an event as occurred in Europe between the

---

1. See Marcel Gauchet: "L'apparition du sujet moderne, c'est, du point de vue religieux, son *inculpation* [author's emphasis]—et pas qu'au figuré. L'extrémité du péché: voilà l'étalon de la subjectivité comme liberté. . . . Aussi ne suffit-il pas d'attribuer la culpabilisation massive des

fifteenth and the seventeenth centuries became possible, in principle, with the advent of Christianity, insofar as the sacrificial killing of Christ—the historical event to which Christianity became the witness—shatters the sacred cover-up of the collective victimizing mechanism and forces each and every one of the persecutors to discover him or herself as such, as violent persecutor. This is precisely what transfers the responsibility for the historical here and now from the hands of God to the hands of man, not as crushing burden—it must be noted at this point—but as a foundation for hope and relief (*Non enim misit Deus Filium suum in mundum, sed ut salvetur mundus per ipsum.* Io. 3, 17 [God did not send His Son to the world in order to judge the world, but in order to save it through Him]). This is also what does away with all the sacred taboos that protected the fearsome truth from being revealed, and that had also prompted a "scientific" endeavor designed to calm the fear of such a revelation.

The fact that it took fifteen hundred years, a relatively long time, for the Christian seed to bear the fruit of the modern era, is also perfectly consistent with our theory of the sacred. If the victimizing mechanism can account for the very existence of human society, as long as it can be sacralized, it stands to reason that human society can only take the desacralizing power of the Christian revelation very gradually, in small doses, so to speak. If what is at stake in the desacralizing process is something that evolved, in all likelihood, over hundreds of thousands of years, the fact that it took fifteen hundred years to erode it to the point where something like the modern era could emerge, does not seem unreasonable.

---

fidèles développée dans le sillage des deux Réformes à la contrainte arbitraire d'une pastorale dévoyée. Il faut mesurer à quel point elle participe du tournant fondateur de la modernité" (241). (From the point of view of religion, the modern subject appears through its incrimination, and not just in a figurative sense. The extremity of sin: that is the measure of subjectivity as freedom. . . . Likewise it is not enough to attribute the massive development of a guilt culture in the wake of the two Reformations to the arbitrary constraint of a mistaken pastoral action on the faithful. One has to measure the extent to which such a development is part of the founding turning point of modernity.) Gauchet is here referring to Jean Delumeau's *Le peché et la peur: La culpabilisation en Occident (XIII–XVIII siècles)* (see Delumeau, *Sin and Fear*). I think Gauchet is right. Delumeau's extensive historical description of the "culpabilisation" of Western society in the transition from the Middle Ages to the Modern Era fails to properly make the connection between such a widespread and deeply felt sense of guilt, on the one hand, and the emergence of modernity, on the other. (See also Charles Taylor's *Sources of the Self: The Making of the Modern Identity.*) Taylor's notion of the "affirmation of ordinary life" as an important development in the birth of modern Europe has obvious points of contact with my

The very success of the desacralizing process has made us blind to the extraordinary power and durability of the sacred; for the same reason we fail to see the formidable desacralizing power of Christianity. We stand in awe when, occasionally, we catch a glimpse of it:

> [To] a contemporary "scientific" historian the rise of the world empires in the Near East from the 8th to the 6th centuries B.C. would have seemed the only historical reality. He could not have imagined that 2000 years later all this drama of world history would only be remembered in so far as it affected the spiritual fortunes of one of the smallest and least materially civilized of the subject peoples. And in the same way, what contemporary observer could have imagined that the execution of an obscure Jewish religious leader in the first century of the Roman Empire would affect the life and thought of millions who never heard the names of the great statemens and generals of the age? (Dawson, 257)

Clearly this is not only a story about the "contemporary" historian who could not predict the future. This is also a story about the modern historian writing those words. He knows how things have developed, but he still does not know why. We could tell the same story about the spread of Islam, and we would not know why either.[2]

---

view of the abandonment of the heroic model. In other crucial respects his work is very different from mine.

2. Of course, we have always known that the sacred is there and that it has power to influence the course of history (we just do not know, or not until now, why this should be so). Witness, for example, Max Weber and his theory about the influence of Calvinism on the development of a capitalist mentality in the West, in his *Protestant Ethic*. See also Winthrop S. Hudson, "The Weber Thesis Reexamined." More recently the idea of the influence of the sacred on secular events has been developed within a larger anthropological framework by Louis Dumont; see his *Essays on Individualism*. The idea is also central to the work of Pierre Chaunu, who writes in *Le Temps des Réformes* (39): "Mais, au vrai, nous ne visons à rien d'autre: montrer que l'histoire religieuse constitue un point départ favorable pour tenter d'atteindre au coeur un système de civilisation" (But, in truth, we aim at nothing other than to show that religious history constitutes a favorable point of departure to reach the heart of a system of civilization). The following statement by Chaunu (*Le Temps des Réformes*, 14) underscores, in its own way, the futility of any struggle to expel the sacred: "Le secteur religieux occupe plus ou moins de place. On ne peut le supprimer. Il est possible de le faire régresser. Il n'y a a de dépassement du christianisme, mais un nombre infini de régressions dialectiques possibles. Le religieux est a peu près aussi indissociable de la vie consciente que le cycle de l'oxigène et de l'azote l'est de la vie terrestre. La volonté consciente de supprimer le religieux aboutit a des phénomènes de refoulement et de résurgence, sous des formes dégradées" (The religious space may be large or small.

Not surprisingly, philosophy, in particular, has been traditionally impervious to the historical phenomenology of the sacred. Tobin Siebers has recently remarked in his "Violence and Philosophy" that the phenomenon of violence is "the other" of philosophy, that which philosophy "represses" in order to constitute itself as philosophy: "[Philosophy] represents violence not as a phenomenon but as an idea . . . the phenomenon

---

It cannot be eliminated. It is possible to make it regress. One cannot leave Christianism behind, but there are an infinite number of possible dialectical regressions. The religious is almost as inseparable from conscious life as the cycle of oxygen and nitrogen is to earth life. The conscious will to eliminate the religious results in phenomena of repression and resurgence in degraded forms). The desacralizing potential of Christianity has also been a frequent topic of discussion among Protestant theologians in the last several decades. Thus, for example, Jacques Ellul: "[It] is indeed true that the revelation of the living God is desacralizing. When God enters the picture he destroys man's sacred. It is true that he secularizes (and, to be sure, that he opens the door to man's action on a secularized nature), but one forgets that it is the word of God which secularizes, and not philosophy, science, or technology—that this word of God is independent of our analysis, and that it is given in the Bible and in the incarnation or it is just our imagination. . . . Here . . . we encounter Harvey Cox's childishness, when he sings the praises of scientific exorcism: 'Exorcism is that process by which the stubborn deposits of town and tribal pasts are scraped from the social consciousness of man and he is free to face his world matter of factly' [Cox, *The Secular City*, 134]. And science of course, is the great handmaid of exorcism— as though he had never heard of the house which was swept and garnished. Scientific exorcism, like psychoanalysis, is in fact the very remarkable operation whereby one sweeps the heart and mind of man, airs it out, and cleanses it. Then, when the house is empty and open, seven other demons come in to take the place of the one. Consequent upon this scientific operation, modern man is much more religious, much more dependent, much more sacralized than ever before, and more insidiously so" (*The New Demons*, 212–13). There is indeed much truth in this. But Ellul's understanding of desacralization is far from clear. If the passage just quoted is correct, how can he also say the following: "[Man] constantly and everywhere in the same way, has tried to establish an order, which implies something sacred. But the latter has frequently been called into question. . . . Historically in the West we have known two attempts: Christianity, which called in question and desacralized the pagan sacred, and the Reformation, which called in question and desacralized the medieval sacred" (58). In what way, then, is God's "destruction of man's sacred" different from man's destruction, or "calling in question," of man's sacred? Likewise, is Christianity's "calling in question" of the pagan sacred any different from any other of the "frequent" attempts at doing the same, including—it would seem—pagan attempts? Obviously Ellul's notion of desacralization is only vaguely related to the one we are using in this study. His "desacralization" looks too much like the sacred expulsion of the sacred of which we have been speaking, and which indeed has been frequent both in the pagan world and in historical Christianity. Witness the sacred expulsion of the sacred accomplished by the Reformation, which is clearly the model for his understanding of the desacralizing power in "the revelation of the living God." The desacralization of which we speak, is not a revolt against, or an expulsion of, the sacred but quite simply the revelation of the violent truth that the sacrificial—sacred-making—mechanism inevitably hides. This revelation is not accomplished by expelling the sacred but, on the contrary, by letting it run its course; not by accusing the sacred from outside, but by letting it bear witness against itself. The accuser is not God, but man himself.

of violence has remained virtually untouched as a philosophical subject."[3] If this is so (and I think it is), it must come as no surprise to learn
that philosophy has likewise "repressed" the sacred as a historical phenomenon; for as we should know by now, violence and the sacred have
always been intimately connected. We already saw that in Plato and Aristotle, the two pillars of Western philosophical discourse.

2. A Commentary on the Notion of "Self-Assertion" in Hans Blumenberg's *The Legitimacy of the Modern Era*

Keeping this in mind, let me briefly summarize the latest significant attempt—that of Hans Blumenberg—to explain the legitimacy of the modern era from a philosophical viewpoint. It is something like this, in
outline: while it is true in a fundamental way that "the modern age is
unthinkable without Christianity" (30), that does not mean that the
modern age is a secularized version of Christianity. On the contrary, the
modern age constitutes itself as an act of "self-assertion" in the context
of, but also against, late medieval Christianity. What must be investigated is the inner logic of the philosophical movement that led to such
moment of "self-assertion."
    It all began when the reassuring, soul-soothing, cosmos of Greek phi-
losphy started to disintegrate. At that moment, the Gnostic moment, philosophy must deal with the problem of the existence of evil, or
imperfection, in the world. The tendency in Gnostic philosophy will be
to postulate two divine agents (a supreme God and a demiurge). The
demiurge would be the one responsible for the imperfection of the world,
that is, for the presence of evil. But then comes Saint Augustine with the
theological Christian answer: not any demiurge, but man himself is the
one responsible for the presence of evil in the world. "The answer that
Augustine gave to this question was to have the most important consequences of all the decisions that he made for the Middle Ages. With a
gesture just as stirring as it was fateful, he took for man and upon man

---

3. "Violence and Philosophy," a paper read at the annual meeting of the Society for Phenomenology and Existential Philosophy, Boston, 1992, unpublished at the time of this writing.

the responsibility for the burden oppressing the world" (Blumenberg, 133; all page references in this section, unless otherwise indicated, are to Blumenberg).

Augustine's answer, however, does not eliminate completely the Gnostic dualism. The latter "lived on in the bosom of mankind and its history as the absolute separation of the elect from the rejected." Medieval theological speculation will relive and aggravate this partial failure. "The Gnosticism that had not been overcome but only transposed returns in the form of the 'hidden God' and His inconceivable absolute sovereignty. It was with this that the self-assertion of reason had to deal" (135).

The situation will reach a climax with the crisis of medieval Scholasticism and the emergence of the radical voluntarism of nominalist philosophy. Nominalism postulates a God whose creation ex nihilo is not subject to any kind of rationality accessible to human beings. The created world rests ultimately on the absolute omnipotence of God's will. Everything is the way it is *quia voluit,* because he wanted it so, and his will is totally beyond the possibility of human comprehension. Therefore, man cannot aspire to find his way to salvation through a rational apprehension and understanding of the created world-universe.

There is a revealing analogy between this absolute voluntarism and Epicurean atomism, which Leibniz would later perceive: "La volonté sans raison seroit le hazard des Epicuriens" (Will without reason would be the chance of the Epicureans) (150). But this analogy only serves to bring out the fact that

> Recourse to intraworldly composure of the mind, to . . . Epicurean ataraxia, is . . . blocked. The method of neutralizing the phenomena and the problems of nature would have been found to have lost its efficacy, if anyone had tried to apply it once more, because [now] its presupposition of the finite and hence completely describable possibilities of natural processes had become untenable against the background of the infinitude of divine power. The dependence of ataraxia on physics could not be reestablished. (154–55)

"Truth has become the result of a renunciation for the modern age . . . , a renunciation that lies in the separation between cognitive achievement and the production of happiness" (404), or perhaps as we have been saying, in the separation of "the human and the divine."

Thus we end up with a situation in which, on the one hand, God withdraws to his unreachable and unrecognizable omnipotence, and on the other, man is left alone laden with guilt. But it is precisely through this guilt that man inherits the world, for he has been made responsible for all the imperfection of this world. It is, of course, an enormous responsibility. "Can man bear the burden of being responsible for the cosmos, that is, for seeing to it that God's design for His work does not miscarry?" (134). If man could simply free himself from this guilt-ridden burden by "the unconditional capitulation of the act of faith" (150), no doubt he would do it. But the initiative for such an act of faith has also been taken away from him. Faith is a totally gratuitous gift of divine grace. Those who receive it will be saved; those who do not, will be rejected, and human rationality cannot hope to penetrate the ultimate criterion for the selection. There is no way to shake the guilt, to find reassurance; neither the old soothing cosmos nor the nominalist God can come to the rescue. And yet this guilt-ridden man has also been told that he was made in God's image and, as a consequence, that his "cognitive capacity was adequate to nature." So, alone and unable to shake his guilt, but also aware of his "cognitive" relationship with an imperfect natural world, in a gesture of self-preservation, man will take the only alternative left to him, "self-assertion," which carries with it taking possession of the world and using it to assert himself over it. "[The] disintegration of the Middle Ages pulled self-preservation out of its biologically determined normality, where it went unnoticed, and turned it into the 'theme' of human self-comprehension. . . . Man keeps in view the deficiency of nature as the motive of his activity as a whole" (139).

We must reflect on this for a moment. Something is missing here. As we contemplate the spectacle of this human being unable to escape his guilt, whether he turns his gaze toward God or the world, how can we avoid thinking, Is this not precisely the moment when the Son of God is supposed to come to the rescue? Where is Christ?

Indeed, "Christian theology . . . contains in the form of the God Who became man, a potential for human assurance, to realize which . . . would have been its noblest endeavor" (177). But, alas! medieval Scholasticism was unable

> to combine systematically the biblical premises of its anthropology and its Christology. Scholasticism always feared the consequences of ascribing to man's maker an obligation for the

salvation of what he created. . . . Avoidance of the premise that
God had irrevocably obliged Himself to the only creature He
made in his own image . . . led finally to the speculative attempt
to eliminate altogether the motivational connection between the
creation and the Incarnation. . . . In spite of the unambiguous formula of the Nicene creed, that God became man for the sake of
man (*propter nos homines . . . homo factus est*), there emerges
Duns Scotus's peculiar doctrine of the absolute predestination of
Christ, which turns the *propter nos homines* into a *propter se ipsum* [for His own sake]. (174)

What a pity that Duns Scotus and the rest of them could not manage
to produce a coherent theologico-philosophical system that, we assume,
could have spared guilt-ridden man a lot of anguish. For "the crisis-laden
self-dissolution of the Middle Ages can be linked to the systematic relations in the metaphysical triangle: man, God, world" (484). Systematic
relations, the "consistency [of which was] insufficient; [it was rather a]
superficially harmonized heterogeneity" (484).

What a pity that just at the moment when all that was really needed
was a philosophically well-integrated Incarnation, Christian theo-philosophical discourse failed to deliver. *Felix* failure, of course: out of it
emerged the spirit of the modern era. Nevertheless, it was clearly a failure
to deliver something that had been promised from the moment man was
told that he had been made in God's image:

A religion that, beyond the expectation of salvation and confidence in justification . . . could deduce from the fundamental notion of creation and the principle that man was made in God's
image the conclusion that man's cognitive capacity was adequate
to nature; but that finally, in its medieval pursuit of the logic of
its concern for the infinite power and absolute freedom of God,
itself destroyed the conditions that it had asserted to hold for
man's relation to the world—such a religion, as a consequence of
its contradictory turning away from its presuppositions, inevitably ends up owing to man a restitution of what belongs to
him. . . . A concept of history that resulted from appreciation of
tradition has committed us to seeing obligations above all in the
relation of each age to what went before it and the sources of the

values handed down to it. In the process the ability to see the debt
that history owes to succeeding ages has been weakened. (115–16)

In other words, the notion of the Incarnation should have been the
logical point of entry into the modern world, if only it could have been
properly integrated with the rest of the theo-philosophical system. It was
there, at that crucial moment when man felt the full impact of his unique
responsibility for everything that had ever gone wrong in the world, that
Christ must have indeed showed up. But, once again, he had not been
properly integrated into the theo-philosophical system: "The basic conflict that was never admitted, perhaps was never perceived, but was latent
in the Middle Ages was unsparingly articulated by Ludwig Feuerbach as
the antinomy between theology and Christology" (177).

Nicholas of Cusa in the fifteenth century represents the last attempt,
we are told, to integrate the Incarnation into the system. He fell short.
He did not cross "the epochal threshold." About a century later Giordano Bruno, the Nolan, had just crossed it. But in order to understand
that "threshold" one has to compare the two. "[Both] are distinguished
by their relation to the epochal threshold. That threshold is compre-
hended not with them or in them but by interpolation between them"
(478–79). But we should be more specific: Where exactly is the culminat-
ing point of difference between the Cusan and the Nolan? If we can pin-
point that pivotal difference we will understand what it was that the
Cusan fell short of and the Nolan crossed over:

> For the Cusan, the moment of the Incarnation of the Son of God
> . . . [was] the culminating point of metaphysical speculation, with
> its all-dominating effort to "overtake" the transcendence of the
> Divinity by means of the communicating transcendence of man
> and to draw the universe, in its representation by man, by an indi-
> vidual man, into the reflection process of the Divinity. Precisely
> this basic figure of the Christian self-conception—God's entry
> into the singularity of man in the universe—becomes the funda-
> mental scandal, the offense that could not be suppressed by any
> threat, to which Giordano Bruno of Nola testified on February
> 17, 1600 at the stake in the Roman Campo di Fiore by averting
> his face from the crucifix that was held before him. (549)

So now we know for sure, in case we had any lingering doubts, what constituted that "epochal threshold." Nevertheless we may still wonder about the novelty, the newness, of Giordano Bruno's gesture. We had always known that the Incarnation was a scandal to the Greeks, that is, to philosophy. Indeed, apart from the "epochal" significance attributed to his gesture, there is little else that is new or modern in Bruno's system, a system, we are told, that presents "many problems of consistency" (552). In fact, his cyclical notion of time is clearly a regression to a pagan past. "The modern age was to repeat, purely formally, in its self-understanding the Christian conception of a unique turning point and epochal new beginning of history. . . . Just this is not possible for the Nolan because with his rejection of the singular historical act of the Incarnation, he had deprived himself of even the point of reference for a counterconception" (553). Definitely Giordano Bruno "has not yet found the fundamental formulas of the modern age." Thus "[he] remains standing in the entryway to the historical self-consciousness of the modern age—in fact precisely because he is unable, on account of his negation of the Christian understanding of history, to accept the formal structure of the change of epoch itself as it had been developed by the Middle Ages. Thus he is forced back to a concept of history whose implications put in question the pathos of the new beginning and its rationality" (553).

And yet he is still supposed to be on this side, our side, of "the epochal threshold." How can that be? In what way is his scandalized aversion to the Cross any different from the old pagan one? There can only be one answer to that: his aversion is different from the old one, because he comes historically *after* the failed promise, *after* the historical failure of the promise. That is to say, the very fact that he existed, that he averted his face from the crucifix, publicly, at the moment of his execution, becomes, in Blumenberg's eyes, the proof that the Incarnation, the Cross, had failed. Having lived *after* the failure of the Cross, he is already, automatically, on the side of "self-assertion," the self-assertion that could not exist prior to the historical failure of the Cross. The "self-assertion" that inaugurates and constitutes the modern age, was instigated by, was a direct result of, the failure of the Incarnation at the waning of the Middle Ages.

All of which inevitably implies that, as the Middle Ages drew to a close, everything conspired or cooperated to grant the issue of the Incarnation and the Cross center stage; everything was going to pivot historically on that particular point. I could not agree more.

But it should be clear by now that the failure Blumenberg describes is not the failure of the Cross, it is the failure of philosophy to deal with the Cross. Blumenberg cannot see that because in his eyes the Cross, all by itself, is utterly meaningless. In fact, he never talks about the Cross; he only talks about the "idea" of the Incarnation. And the touchstone against which such an idea must prove itself is philosphy. In his view, if the idea cannot be integrated into a fully coherent philosophical system, the idea has failed the test and should be discarded as irrelevant. This is Aristotle all over again. The facts are quite different. The anthropological and historical context from which the Cross derives its meaning and upon which it impacts with devastating and liberating force is prior to and far more universal than philosophy. The Cross owes absolutely nothing to philosophy; nor, for the same reason, does it owe anything at all to Western culture, to the "language of the West," whereas Western culture would not exist without it. In the final analysis, it is not the Cross that must account for itself before the tribunal of philosophy, but the other way around.

In spite of his repeated assertion that the modern era is not a continuation, after a long hiatus, of Hellenism, Blumenberg's complete inability to deal with the historical phenomenology of the sacred bears all the marks of its Hellenic predecessors. He has no credible explanation for the ancient fears that drove the Greeks to the philosophical construction of their reassuring cosmos, because he does not understand the terrifying "rumblings of hungry Acheron," or "all the terrible and apalling names [with] which [the poets]—as we saw in Plato's *Republic*—describe the world below . . . of which the very mention causes a shudder to pass through the inmost soul of him who hears them." His passing comment on "the human uneasiness caused by natural phenomena" is woefully inadequate. For the same reason, he fails to make the obvious connection between the profound Christian sense of guilt and responsibility for what goes on in the world, of which he speaks, and the killing of Christ on the Cross. Indeed, in total disregard of the obvious, we are told that "the guide to [the] solution of the problem of the bad (*unde malum?*) had already been given to Augustine by the linguistic fact that ancient philosophy had not distinguished in its language between the wickedness that man perpetrates and the bad things that he encounters. That these bad things are the world's reflex to his own wickedness was thus already implicit in the formulation of the question" (133). One wonders, What is the difference, then, between Augustine's Christian answer to the problem of the origin of evil and the most primitive and superstitious kind of animism or magic? But there is no wonder at all that Blumenberg will find the idea of the Incarnation wanting, when it was supposed to come to the rescue of a human subject burdened with the responsibility of an imperfect world, at the end of the Middle Ages.

I have no intention of or interest in undertaking a critique of Blumenberg's philosophical account of how the modern era came to be; nor do I want to pass judgment on the accuracy or the fairness of his analysis of classical, Hellenistic, or medieval philosophy. I leave that to the philosophers. As far as I am concerned, I take his words at face value, because I find them extraordinarily revealing. They are probably the closest that a strictly philosophical approach can come to what I am trying to say, given the fact that such an approach does not have the benefit of the anthropological theory of the sacred on which I base my argument.

All the pieces in this latest philosophical puzzle are there except, of course, the centerpiece, the victim, that is to say, the Cross. It is precisely there, in the space left vacant by the absence of the Cross, that he tries to fit the "self-assertion" that constitutes the soul of modern man. But this "self-assertion" is rather suspect. To begin with, it looks too much like a mere echo, a reflex, of the absolute "self-assertion" of Blumenberg's nominalist God, a kind of tit for tat between God and man, which is not exactly an indication of its radical break with the past, its independence and self-sustaining identity. Second, it is far from clear that "self-assertion," the "self-preserving" embracing of one's own guilt and responsibility for all that is wrong in the world, was the only way left open to the human subject. This subject must have been deeply frustrated, perhaps terrified, as God withdraws from rational visibility and goes into willful hiding, especially because, as God does that, human guilt and responsibility is brought to the foreground and the human subject is forced to confront it. Why couldn't this subject repeat the self-preservation gesture of its Greek predecessors, when they were confronted with the menacing and terrifying rumblings of Acheron; that is, why couldn't this subject also build a reassuring, soul-soothing cosmos? It would have been the logical thing to do, especially because, as God goes into hiding and human guilt comes to the fore, apparently a voice is also heard that says: "Look at this imperfect world, it is all your fault; take it and do with it as your reason dictates." It was the perfect setup for the building of a reassuring cosmos! And yet, that is not at all what happened. Why? Why was it easier to embrace one's guilt and face the real world without flinching, than it was for the Hellenic predecessors to hear the noises of

Acheron? What gave man such an unprecedented strength? The answer lies, not in the history of philosophy, but in that which philosophy expels in order to constitute itself as such. The "self-assertion" of the rational subject of philosophy rests on such an expulsion, or, more exactly, on the possibility of hiding such an expulsion; as soon as the expulsion is revealed, the rational consistency of the "self-assertion" begins to unravel.

Blumenberg could have learned a thing or two from Cervantes, Shakespeare, or Calderón. Just as Lucretius could have learned from Virgil. It is most interesting to see Blumenberg refer time and again to the "instructive value of . . . a comparison between Epicurus's teachings and the late medieval conception of God's sovereign freedom to do what He pleases" (148), and to the "structural connection between nominalism as a late-medieval phenomenon and atomism" (151). For "the nominalistic God is [as] superfluous" as the gods of Epicurus and Lucretius. But we may remember here what we said about Virgil and his admired Lucretius. It was precisely at that original moment of the *"uncaused divergence of atoms"* (151), the utterly unpredictable deviation from symmetry, where Lucretius saw the final triumph of his godlike master Epicurus over "hideous religion," that Virgil the poet saw the sacrificial founding moment, the utterly random choice of the victim, the "one head that must be given up for the sake of many." It seems that history repeats itself.

3. The Increasing Centrality of the Crucifixion in the Late Medieval Experience of the Sacred

The desacralizing potential of Christianity is not a doctrinal or philosophical matter. It does not rest on any particular exegesis of the entire corpus of Christian doctrine; it rests specifically on the historical account of the life of Christ leading to the Crucifixion and the Resurrection. Without that there would be no clear and explicit unmasking of the sacrificial mechanism and therefore no especially powerful desacralizing potential. If this is so, one would expect that the process of desacralization would be intimately associated with those central Christian events and would bring them to historical prominence in the religious life of the period, that is to say, in the way in which the Christian text is historically experienced. And, indeed, quite apart from theological and philosophical disputes, as we look at the historical evolution of religious life in the Middle Ages, a movement in the direction of what might be called the spirituality of the Cross can be clearly perceived.

Here I can do no better than quote at length from Gustaf Aulén's by now classic study on the history of the main types of the idea of atonement. The later Middle Ages are characterized by a shift in emphasis from the classic idea of atonement, which prevailed in early Christianity, where the central notion is the victory of Christ over death, sin, and the devil, thus liberating man from bondage; to a more personal relationship with the event of the Crucifixion, where individual attention is drawn specifically to Christ's Passion, to the suffering humanity of Christ. Aulén describes the Middle Ages in general as "an age which was laying ever greater stress on the death [of Christ], both in theology and in devotional practice" (97). The most important factor in this change of emphasis

> was the influence of the religious phenomenon of the *Devotion to the Passion,* or Passion mysticism; indeed it would be hard to exaggerate the importance of this, either in the Middle Ages or in the subsequent period, both in Roman and Protestant Christendom. Unfortunately, this chapter in the history of the Christian religion has never yet received a thorough investigation. . . . It can truly be said that the appeal of the passion, the martyrdom of Christ, has never been so deeply felt as in medieval religion: "The whole life of Christ was a cross and a martyrdom," says à Kempis in the *Imitatio Christi.* . . . What was lost was the note of triumph, which is as much absent in the contemplation of the Sacred Wounds as in the theory of satisfaction of God's justice. This is reflected very significantly in later mediaeval art. The triumph-crucifix of an earlier period is now ousted by the crucifix which depicts the human Sufferer. (97)

Of course, this does not mean that the classic idea was completely forgotten: "Yet it would be wrong to infer that the classic idea of the Atonement had been wholly lost. It was far too deep-rooted and powerful to disappear altogether" (98).

In the second half of the fourteenth century, Catherine of Siena's spirituality was indicative of what would soon spread in the next century throughout Europe with the *devotio moderna.* As Francis Rapp characterizes the saint from Siena: "Pour la *Mantellata* siennoise, le Sacrifice du Calvaire, plutôt que la satisfaction offerte par le Fils pour réparer l'offense faite au Père, est le chef-d'oeuvre qui accomplit une éducation" (232). (For the *Mantellata* of Siena, the Sacrifice of Calvary, rather than the satisfaction offered by the Son to atone for the offense done to the Father, is the masterpiece of an accomplished education.)

There, in a nutshell, is the difference between the earlier and the later medieval interpretations of the Crucifixion. The earlier one is fundamentally legalistic and typical of a feudal society. An offense has been committed: man has sinned against God; given the infinite dignity of the offended person, an infinite reparation is necessary. But man, a finite and sinful creature, cannot provide such a reparation. Only God's own Son, equal in dignity to the Father, can repair the offense.[4] The emphasis here is on God the Father and his divine Son. Christ's humanity is somewhat secondary. Indeed in some cases it was presented as a disguise, a way to trick the devil.

In this earlier interpretation God is above all the source and the upholder of the law, the *pantokrator,* the universal ruler, so often represented on the tympanum of Romanesque cathedrals. Jaroslav Pelikan writes: "So close was the identification of law and gospel that the statement of the apostle Paul, 'Christ is the end of the law,' was taken to mean that 'those who are without the law come to be without Christ'"(25). Romanesque crucifixes sculpt the majesty, not the suffering, of Christ. He is "the teacher," "the lawgiver." The new law was revealed in the Sermon on the Mount: "In the Old Testament the revelation of the will of God had come through Moses on Mount Sinai; so likewise in the New Testament it was on a mountain that the new and complete revelation had been given. Therefore Christ the teacher, like Moses the teacher, could be called "the lawgiver'" (148). The relationship between God and man could be conceived on a legal basis as a pact: "One of the most striking ways of speaking about baptism [during the eighth and ninth centuries] was the description of it as a 'compact (pactum)' made with God. A compact, according to commonly accepted etymology, was an agreement of 'peace (pax)' between two parties" (31).

Of course a more evangelical and less legalistic understanding of the gospel had never been totally absent, and it begins to gain ground from

---

4. A logical consequence of the "legal" necessity of sacrifice was the conception of monastic life as primarily a state penance. "Traditionally the monastic life had been primarily thought of for its penitential value, as providing vicarious penance for all the faithful" (M. D. Chenu, O.P., 229).

the twelfth century on. But it is not until we reach the fourteenth and fifteenth centuries, the end of the Middle Ages, that the emphasis clearly shifts toward the human sacrifice at the Cross and the suffering humanity of Christ. The change becomes apparent in the evolution of religious sculpture and painting. The hieratic majesty of Christ on the Cross will give way to a more realistic, even naturalistic, representation. The Passion of Christ ceases to be experienced as a divinely ordered requirement for salvation, and becomes instead an extraordinary act of sheer generosity out of pure love for an undeserving humanity: an act of love that begs to be imitated, that invites and challenges the individual to do the same, to bear his cross willingly, even joyfully. This is perhaps the central theme of the most influential book of the period, the *Imitation of Christ*.

4. The *devotio moderna* and the Non-Heroic Individual Before the World

This is the time of the *devotio moderna* and its extraordinary impact on the spiritual life of the period. Chaunu writes:

> Entre 1420 et 1440, le milieu des Frères de la Vie commune— Thomas à Kempis (1380–1471) presque surement—aura produit ce chef-d'oeuvre de la basse latinité, le livre le plus diffusé après la Bible, l'incomparable *Imitation*. La religion de l'*Imitation,* en un mot la *devotio moderna,* fait tache d'huile, a partir des Pays-Bas néerlandophones dans les secteurs les plus peuplés de la vieille Chrétienté nombreuse. . . . Il serait évidemment injuste "d'accuser les moines du Moyen Age d'avoir fait de l'*Opus Dei* un simple formalisme." La filiation est évidente entre la devotio moderna et certains aspects de la spiritualité de saint Bernard. Et pourtant, moins collective, moins sensible au sacré, moins panique, la devotio moderna correspond a une dissociation du religieux, elle est bien contemporaine de la rupture du lignage et du renforcement dans la structure familiale de la cellule matrimoniale la plus étroite.
>
> Mais surtout elle est *imitatio Christi.* Elle est proche du Christ de douleur; elle vit la *pieta.* Son Christ est homme; il est descendu du vitrail. Dans le mystère de l'Incarnation, elle est du coté

de la sainte humanité, de l'homme Dieu et non du Dieu fait homme. (259)

(Between 1420 and 1440, the Brothers of the Common Life— almost certainly Thomas à Kempis (1380–1471)—produced this masterpiece of late medieval latinity, the most widely distributed book after the Bible, the incomparable *Imitation*. The religion of the *Imitation*, in one word, the *devotio moderna*, spreads like an oil spill from the Netherlands into the most populated sectors of the old numerous Christendom. . . . It would obviously be unjust "to accuse the monks of the Middle Ages of having turned the *Opus Dei* into a mere formalism." There is an obvious filiation between the *devotio moderna* and certain aspects of Saint Bernard's spirituality. Nevertheless, being less collective, less sensitive to the sacred, less Pan-like pagan, the *devotio moderna* corresponds to a dissociation of the religious; it is very contemporary to the break of the extended family lineage and the reinforcement of the narrower matrimonial nucleus within the family structure. But above all it is *imitatio Christi*. It is close to the Christ of sorrow; it lives the *pietà*. Its Christ is human; he has come down from the stained church windows. In the mystery of the Incarnation, it is on the side of holy humanity, of the man God rather than the God made man).

As a source or an influence, the *devotio moderna* has been connected to the most varied intellectual and religious developments in the life of sixteenth-century Europe, from somewhat marginal phenomena like the Anabaptist movement to the influential humanism of Erasmus, for example, and of course the Protestant Reformation itself. The historical resurgence of mysticism, especially in Spain, would be hard to understand without this background and influence, as would Saint Ignatius's *Spiritual Exercises*. One of the best known (it is in every anthology of Golden Age Spanish verse) and most beautiful poems written in sixteenth-century Spain is the anonymous sonnet "To Christ Crucified," which expresses the very essence of the new spirituality.

No me mueve, mi Dios, para quererte,
el cielo que me tienes prometido,
ni me mueve el infierno tan temido
para dejar por eso de ofenderte.

Tú me mueves, Señor; muéveme el verte
clavado en esa cruz y escarnecido;
muéveme el ver tu rostro tan herido,
muévenme tus afrentas y tu muerte.

Muéveme, al fin, tu amor, y en tal manera,
que aunque no hubiera cielo yo te amara,
y aunque no hubiera infierno te temiera.

No me tienes que dar porque te quiera;
pues aunque lo que espero no esperara,
lo mismo que te quiero te quisiera.

(It is not the heaven that You have promised me, my God, that moves me to love you, nor is it the hell I so fear that moves me to cease sinning against You.

You move me, Lord; it moves me to see You nailed to the cross and despised; it moves me to see Your body so wounded; the insults you suffered and Your death move me.

Finally, Your love moves me, and so much that even if there were no heaven, I should love You; and even if there were no hell, I should fear You.

You have not to give me anything to make me love You; for even if I did not hope for what I do hope for, I should love You just as I do.) (Trans. J. M. Cohen, 163).

    This radical interiorization of the human drama of the Crucifixion also frees the outside world of its sacred attachments. The subject acquires the realization that it is she, as a human being, who is responsible for the sacrifice of the innocent victim. It is not anything out there, not even the law, that requires or demands that sacrifice. It is a human-made affair. The sacrificial reasons are human reasons, "my" reasons; a realization that demands a thorough self-analysis, and a withdrawal from the world. But this withdrawal is very different from previous withdrawals, Christian and otherwise, especially the Stoic one. The subject withdraws from the world, not because the world is wicked but because that is not where the problem is. The problem lies inside; the sacrificial guilt is "my" guilt, and any transfer of this guilt onto something or somebody else is wrong, an attempt to escape the truth. There is nothing morbid or masochistic about this. In recognizing and experiencing his sacrificial guilt, the subject also experiences the liberating power of Christ's love. One thing does not go without the other.

This withdrawal from the world actually returns the subject to a liberated world:

> If you were good and pure inwardly in your soul, you would be able to see and understand all things without impediment and understand them aright.
>
> A pure heart penetrates both Heaven and Hell.
>
> As a man is inwardly in his heart, so he judges outwardly.
>
> If there is true joy in the world, surely a man of a pure heart possesses it.
>
> And if there is any tribulation and anguish, an evil conscience knows it best. (*Imitation of Christ*, book 2, chap. 4, sect. 2)

This is not the same thing as the scientific outlook on the world that the modern era will develop, but it is its historical precondition. This attitude is the opposite of the Epicurean-Lucretian formula, or the Gnostic one. That formula said that if you know the rational causes of things in the world, you will calm the fears and anxieties of your soul. Knowledge was the way to achieve inward peace. Now instead, inward peace, for which the individual alone is responsible, becomes the way to a clear and unobstructed view of the world. The fears and the anxieties do not assault the mind from a world resounding with the noises of Acheron. They are the fears and the anxieties of an impure heart; the world has nothing to do with that. To a mind at peace with itself corresponds a world liberated from its sacrificial attachments.

Now, the outcome of this evolution of medieval spirituality at the threshold of the modern era should not make us forget earlier stages, even the Romanesque, the Anselmian one, from which the new spirituality differs so much. For at the heart of such a legalistic view of the atonement stands a very important development; namely, the understanding that the Incarnation and the Passion were made necessary by human behavior. It was a debt man owed to God because man had offended him. This emphasis on the guilt of man was not present in the original, the "classic" view of the atonement, as Aulén has pointed out.

In other words, it is possible to see the *devotio moderna* as the final stage of a graduated progression. The first, and perhaps the most important, stage in the Christian experience of Christ's sacrifice sees it as an extraordinarily liberating event. Humanity was in shackles and ridden with fear, enslaved to Sin, Death, and the Devil. Christ's sacrifice broke the shackles and dispelled the fear. In the words of Ireneus, "[the] passion of Christ brought us courage and power. . . . The Lord through His passion destroyed death, brought error to an end, abolished corruption, banished ignorance, manifested life, declared truth, and bestowed incorruption" (quoted in Aulén, 32). Sin, Death, and the devil are intimately tied together: "By the side of Sin and Death Ireneus ranges the devil. But the phrase 'by the side of' scarcely does justice to his thought; it is rather that, like later Eastern theologians, he passes insensibly from the one to the other" (Aulén, 25). In all of this, it is the objective reality of evil that is emphasized. Christ's passion and Resurrection are above all the victory of God over the Devil, "the lord of sin and death," the deceiver of humanity.

5. The Emergence of the Non-Systemic and the "Open Society"

How are we to understand the diabolical character of that which kept humanity in bondage? I find the words of Colin E. Gunton, a modern historian of religion, particularly appropriate:

> If we are neither to give a purely psychological account [of the demonic or diabolical], with the attendant danger of failing to do justice to the objective reality of evil; nor to understand the demonic of the Bible in such tendentious terms that it appears ridiculously primitive; then we must come to terms with the fact that in this area of discourse we meet an attempt to express the objectivity and irrationality of evil in the only way in which it can adequately be expressed: as a reality generating its own momentum and sweeping up human beings into its power. Human life is lived in interrelationships with other human beings and with the world, leaving on one side for a moment the so-called "vertical" relationship with God. We are what we are partly by virtue of that net-

work of relationships. When it goes badly awry, the person or society is rightly described as enslaved, another familiar metaphor in this connection. . . . The language of possession by demonic forces, then, is used to express the helplessness of human agents in the face of psychological, social, and cosmic forces in various combinations. Theologically, we must see the origins of the bondage in the idolatrous worship of that which is not God. (69–70)

I do not know what Gunton means by "cosmic forces." But I think he is fundamentally correct in interpreting the "diabolical" as something that transcends the power of any single individual and involves "the network of interrelationships with other human beings . . . when it goes badly awry." In fact, I believe we could go a little further than that and view the objectivity of the "diabolical," not only "as a reality generating its own momentum and sweeping up human beings into its power"; that could also be said of "sin" or "death," insofar as "death" is the result of "sin." I believe the "diabolical" expresses further a powerful intuition into the *systemic* character of the transindividual reality of evil. Even though evil may destroy rationality, it is not itself irrational. It has a logic of its own, it manifests itself systematically. Evil does not simply overpower the individual; it forces the individual to function in accordance with its power, which is the power of death itself.

In other words, to say that the sacrifice of Christ breaks the power of the devil amounts to saying that it breaks the power of the system of death, the power that systematizes death, that derives its strength from the systematic use of death—or, to put it in the context of our theory of the sacred, the power of the victimizing or sacralizing system.

It stands to reason that the first, the "classic" view of the atonement should be one of joyful victory and triumph over the "diabolical" power of death intimately associated with lying and deception. But the emphasis will soon change toward the realization that ultimately it was all a consequence of human sinfulness. In the early Middle Ages this sinfulness is seen primarily in reference to God the Father, who must then send his Son to restore justice to the world. But as we approach the end of the Middle Ages and the *devotio moderna,* human sinfulness is seen in direct reference to Christ crucified. It is above all the sacrifice of the Cross that reveals man as sacrificer, speaking directly to the individual. This appears to be the momentous shift that set the stage for the advent of the modern era.

This historical progression from the breakup of the sacrificial idolatrous system toward a deepening sense of individual responsibility and,
therefore, freedom, in the face of the crucified describes the trajectory
that, in a certain sense, is traveled in reverse by the existential intuition
of the great poets, both dramatic and narrative, who would become the
classics of modern literature. As we have seen in Cervantes and Calderón, they begin with the plight of the individual who, in one way or another, shows herself unable to sustain the burden of her individual, nontransferable, responsibility and freedom, and will end up with the vision
of a primitive and violent system of intersubjective relationships in which
the individual loses her freedom completely and/or innocent victims are
sacrificed to keep the system in place. What I have been trying to say is
that this poetic intuition, which is probably the most profound and the
most decisive in the genesis of modern literature, would not have been
possible without that historical progression in the Christian consciousness and experience of the system-breaking event of the Crucifixion.

I have also said from the beginning that the breakup of the sacrificial
system under the impact of the Christian event and its text, could not
mean that, historically speaking, the sacrificial system simply vanishes
from history. Perhaps I should put it somewhat differently now. It was
never a question of the sacrificial system's being replaced by a Christian
system. I do not think there is such a thing as a "Christian system." Insofar as human beings cannot avoid living in some kind of system, such a
system qua system, will always be ultimately a version of the sacrificial
system, no matter how modified or influenced by Christianity that version may be.

Thus the breakup of the sacrificial system—of the *system*, for short—
can only mean the arrival into it of a nonsystemic element, an element
that cannot be assimilated by the system qua system. This is the element
that keeps the system from ever closing itself completely. This is the expulsion that cannot be expelled, that is to say, justified, glossed over,
hidden. It is also the element that opens the system to an authentic future,
a future that is unpredictable from within the system itself.

In conclusion, I must bring these two things together: (1) the development of an unprecedented type of individuality, responsibility and freedom, for which the catalytic agent, so to speak, was the vision of Christ
crucified; and (2) the radically nonsystemic, nonsacrificial character of
such a vision. The result is the historical advent of a human individuality
that recognizes itself as such by reference to something that transcends

and resists the system qua system; an individuality that recognizes itself as nonsystemic in a most fundamental sense. In other words, the kind of individuality destined to live, for good and for bad, in "the open society."

All of which also implies that any attempt to preserve this modern individuality from alienating dangers, by purely systemic means, by closing the nonsystemic opening, will fail. It will either fail to close the system, or it will destroy the individuality it is trying to preserve. Any such attempt can only be a sacrificial regression. The case of Karl Marx is of paradigmatic value in this regard. Contrary to what Marx thought, the system that, unknowingly, he discovered, was much better suited to a pre-Christian or otherwise primitive society than to the one that emerged from the Christian Middle Ages, as recent history has amply proven. For the only system that can be generated out of the collapse or disintegration of the nonsystemic modern individuality is the one envisioned and analyzed by the great modern poets: the old sacrificial system. It does not make any sense to read Cervantes or Calderón in the light of Marx; one has to do exactly the opposite.

A MARXIAN EPILOGUE

Preliminary Remarks: Karl Popper's View of the Problem

This book . . . sketches some of the difficulties faced by our civilization—a civilization which might be perhaps described as aiming at humaneness and reasonableness, at equality and freedom; a civilization which is still in its infancy, as it were, and which continues to grow in spite of the fact that it has been so often betrayed by so many of the intellectual leaders of mankind. It attempts to show that this civilization has not yet fully recovered from the shock of its birth—the transition from the tribal or "closed society," with its submission to magical forces, to the "open society" which sets free the critical powers of man. It attempts to show that the shock of this transition is one of the factors that have made possible the rise of those reactionary movements which have tried, and still try, to overthrow civilization and to return to tribalism. And it suggests that what we call nowadays totalitarianism belongs to a tradition which is just as old or just as young as our civilization itself. (Popper, *Open Society*, 3)

An extraordinary intuition sustains Karl Popper's famous *Open Society*. Modern totalitarianism—anthropologically speaking—is the latest attempt to go back to the old security of the tribe, the apparent safety of the "closed society." It is a biological attempt, perhaps as biological as the self-preservation instinct. In other words, the passage from the closed to the open society is anything but "natural."[1] It is, on the contrary, a shocking and traumatic experience: "[The] transition from the closed to the open society can be described as one of the deepest revolutions through which mankind has passed. Owing to what we have called the biological character of the closed society, this transition must be felt deeply indeed" (171).

Not enough attention has been paid to Popper's idea. Perhaps the reason is that it remains for the most part in the background, as a frame of reference to his more specific critique of "historicism," which he had defined earlier as "the belief that it is the task of the social sciences to lay bare the *law of evolution of society* in order to foretell its future" (*Selections*, 298).

It was probably the totalitarian aspect of those historicist doctrines that led to World War II and its aftermath, that gave Popper a clearer insight into the regressive, primitive character of "historicism." "[The final] decision to write [*The Open Society*] was made in March 1938, on the day I received the news of the invasion of Austria . . . it was an attempt to understand those events and their background . . . [the] expectation that Marxism would become a major problem was the reason for treating it at some length" (preface to the revised edition of 1950).

The historicist attempt to "lay bare the law of evolution of society" betrays a fundamental, primitive fear of the open society:

> Historicism . . . is born of fear, for it shrinks from realizing that we bear the ultimate responsibility even for the standards we choose. But such an attempt seems to me to represent precisely what is usually described as superstition. For it assumes that we can reap where we have not sown; it tries to persuade us that if we merely try to fall into step with history everything will and must go right . . . it tries to shift our responsibility on to history, and thereby on to the play of demoniac powers beyond our-

1. This is also the fundamental idea in Henri Bergson's *The Two Sources of Morality and Religion* (see especially chap. 4, "Mechanics and Mysticism"), from which Popper developed his own idea.

selves. . . . It is a debased hope and a debased faith, an attempt to replace the hope and the faith that springs from our moral enthusiasm and the contempt for success by a certainty that springs from a pseudo-science; a pseudo-science of the stars, or of "human nature," or of historical destiny.

Historicism, I assert, is not only rationally untenable, it is also in conflict with any religion that teaches the importance of conscience. For such a religion must agree with the rationalist attitude towards history in its emphasis on our supreme responsibility for our actions. . . . True, we need hope; to act, to live without hope goes beyond our strength. But we do *not* need more. . . . We do not need certainty. . . . The historicist element in religion is an element of idolatry, of superstition. (*The Open Society,* 462)

I fully agree. The only thing Popper lacks is an articulate theory of the sacred capable of explaining the social mechanism that keeps idolatry and superstition in place. How do idolatry and superstition work? How do they protect the group? How do they build a wall around it? Fear of the open must be channeled through some kind of social structure in order to be socially effective. In our theory of the sacred, that is precisely the function of the sacrificial mechanism, the closing of the community as a result of the expulsion of the victim. Amazingly, there are moments in Popper when his powerful intuition comes very close to the sacrificial scenario we have been dealing with.

In "Prediction and Prophecy in the Social Sciences," for example, he discards "two naive theories of society." The first maintains that the object of study of the social sciences is

the behaviour of social wholes, such as groups, nations, classes, societies, civilizations, etc. . . . conceived as empirical objects which the social sciences study in the same way in which biology studies animals or plants. This view . . . completely overlooks the fact that these so-called social wholes are very largely postulates of popular social theories rather than empirical objects. . . . Accordingly, the belief in the empirical existence of social wholes . . . has to be replaced by the demand that social phenomena, including collectives, should be analyzed in terms of individuals and their actions and relations.

No sooner does he discard the "social wholes" theory than he realizes that "another mistaken view" must be discarded as well:

> It may be described as the *conspiracy theory of society*. It is the view that whatever happens in society—including things which people as a rule dislike, such as war, unemployment, poverty, shortages—are the results of direct design by some powerful individuals or groups. This view is very widespread, although it is, I have no doubt, a somewhat primitive kind of superstition. It is older than historicism (which may even be said to be a derivative of the conspiracy theory) . . . it is the typical result of the secularization of religious superstitions. The belief in the Homeric gods whose conspiracies were responsible for the vicissitudes of the Trojan war is gone. But the place of the gods on Homer's Olympus is now taken by the Learned Elders of Zion, or the monopolists, or the capitalists, or the imperialists. (281)

Popper does not make an explicit connection between these "two naive theories of society," except, of course, the purely negative one that they are both misleading and unscientific. But there is some intimation that the "social wholes" theory, which he has just rejected, may reappear in the more primitive form of the "conspiracy theory" as a subversion or distortion of what he has just recommended; namely, that "social phenomena be analyzed in terms of individuals and their actions and relations." This impression is reinforced by his parenthetical remark that historicism "may even be said to be a derivative of the conspiracy theory." For historicist theories are, by definition, "social wholes" theories. Popper is indeed very close to establishing a historical, genetic, connection between the primitive, "superstitious," "conspiracy theory" and much modern social theory, which is based to a large extent on the analysis of social wholes.

But the "conspiracy theory" is *the* sacrificial theory par excellence. It gives the most naive theoretical expression to the sacrificial spirit in search of a victim. Behind the collective hysteria of every lynching mob there is always some form or other of "conspiracy theory." It is the expulsion of the evil, "conspiratorial" victim that creates the communal inside, the most basic "social whole." The "conspiracy theory" as well as its pseudoscientific descendant, the "social wholes theory," are therefore characteristic of the closed society. They both ignore the rich social problematic of intersubjective phenomena, the close-knit network of interdependent individual relations through which social life necessarily runs. And, of course, they ignore it for a very good reason: the interdependence of individual relations must greatly complicate the application of the sacrificial principle; a principle that can only work effectively as long as the identity of the victim (individual or group) can be clearly recognized.

All these considerations apply equally to the historicist totalitarian systems of the right and of the left. Their historical results are the same: regressive, tribalistic. And yet these two systems are irreconcilable enemy twins. Furthermore, their radical hatred of each other is rooted precisely in their apparently incompatible positions with regard to the sacred: in one case, a violent attempt to resacralize society and the fatherland, to stop what is perceived as a historical decomposition of the old values; in the other case, just the opposite, an equally violent attempt to leave the sacred behind once and for all, to achieve a complete and final removal of the sacred mist that, we are told, has always clouded human vision and prevented man from seeing things the way they really are. Can the struggle against the sacred be just another attempt to return to the old sacred?

One can only regret that Popper never addressed such a question. If Marxist historicism, like all historicisms, is ultimately driven by a yearning for the tribal past, shouldn't one respond to Marx's claim that the march of history is precisely in the opposite direction, away from the sacred toward full human responsibility?

Let what follows be a modest contribution to Popper's defense of the open society, without which probably I would never have paid much attention to Marx. I could not find a more fitting introduction to my own study of Marx than Popper's profound vision of the historically regressive character of modern totalitarianism. My specific goal is to show that Marx's regression is governed through and through by the logic of the sacrificial expulsion of the sacred, and that, therefore, it runs directly counter to the vision of humanity that inspires and sustains the great literary classics of the modern era. In this sense, Marx provides the perfect illustration *a contrario*.

262   A Marxian Epilogue

1. The Parallel Between Religious and Economic Alienation

"As, in religion, man is governed by the products of his own brain, so in capitalistic production, he is governed by the products of his own hand" (Marx, *Capital*, 1909 ed., 681). The functional parallelism between religious and economic alienation does not belong exclusively to the historical stage of "capitalistic production"; it has always been there in one way or another since the time of the most primitive division of labor. Man, as presented by Marx, has never mastered the social system of production in which he has lived and worked at any given stage of historical development; he has always been governed by something that, even though created by him, has been alien to him. In fact, religious alienation is nothing but a "reflex" of this real, economic alienation. The former would not exist without the latter, of which it is but a mythical (i.e., illusory) interpretation.

"The religious reflex of the real world can . . . only then finally vanish, when the practical relations of everyday life offer to man none but perfectly intelligible and reasonable relations with regard to his fellowmen and to nature" (*Capital*, 1909 ed., 1:91–92). Actually it will take more than mere knowledge to eliminate this mythical reflex, as Engels points out in his *Anti-Dühring*:

> [Religion] can continue to exist . . . so long as men remain under the control of [alien natural and social] forces. However, we have seen repeatedly that in existing bourgeois society men are dominated by the economic conditions created by themselves, by the means of production which they themselves have produced, as if by an alien force. . . . And although bourgeois political economy has given a certain insight into the causal connection of this alien domination, this makes no essential difference. . . . Mere knowledge . . . is not enough. . . . What is above all necessary . . . is a social act. And when this act has been accomplished, when society, by taking possession of all means of production and using them on a planned basis, has freed itself and all its members from the bondage in which they are now held by these means of production . . . only then will the last alien force which is still reflected in religion vanish. (Marx and Engels, *On Religion*, 148–49)

Clearly, once the real (i.e., economic) cause of human alienation is fully understood, it will be just a matter of time before the appropriate "social act" is accomplished that will put an end to it and, therefore, to religious alienation as well.

The religious "reflex," Marx tells us, is a mirage. The difference between religious beliefs and the socioeconomic mode of production is the difference between illusion and reality, ignorance and knowledge, and, in the final analysis, the difference between the possibility of having or not having rational, "perfectly intelligible" control over one's own destiny. The difference could not be any sharper or clearer in principle.

Historically, however, things have never been that clear. And we must remember that in Marx history is everything; man himself, human consciousness, is history-bound and determined in the most radical sense. To begin with, the realization that the mode of production is the key to everything and that once you master it you can control and predict human destiny, is something very recent. It has been brought about, made historically possible, by the latest stage in the evolution of the modes of production, namely, the capitalist stage. Before human consciousness reached this latest stage, nothing, therefore, could have existed that was not, inevitably, a combination of ignorance and knowledge, of control and lack of control, of illusion and reality, inextricably linked together. If human consciousness and deliberation is a factor in man-made history (and I do not see how Marx could deny that without contradicting himself) then ignorance is as much of a history-making tool as knowledge. To be sure, the results will be very different in each case, but all of them will be equally historical and real. The idea that one can clearly separate the material mode of production from social religious practices and beliefs throughout the course of human history is—within the logic of Marx's own system—nothing but an illusory projection of a present historical possibility into the past. It is in fact the result of a certain type of teleological thinking, dear to Marx, with which I shall deal briefly in a moment.

We can also look at the problem in the following way: the difference between lack of control of the material mode of production and complete control defines, according to Marx, the very movement of human history. Human history moves inexorably in the direction of complete control (and therefore toward the disappearance of all kinds of human alienation). But complete control rests on the historical possibility of the economic sphere emerging as something with a specific cultural and material identity clearly recognizable as such. To postulate the economic sphere, even the materiality of the material mode of production, as something possessing a transhistorical identity, a realm of reality subsisting on its own, unaffected in its essence by changes in other spheres of human activity, is to turn that material and economic sphere into a metaphysical entity, an unmoved mover—which is not what one should find in a system designed to do away with all sorts of metaphysical and religious entities.

Religion is supposed to be nothing but a reflex of what is actually happening in the material, economic system. This means that religious phenomena can only make sense or be properly explained in terms of economic factors. But any careful reader of Marx will be surprised by the frequency with which he turns to religious analogies, symbols, or events, in order to throw light on, or unveil, the specific nature, the underlying character, of an economic phenomenon. Phrases like, "as, in religion," "just as in religion," and many other similar ones can be found throughout Marx's text. And this includes revealing parallelisms between the histories of religious and economic thought. Adam Smith, for example, is "the Luther of Political Economy" (*1844*, 94). Time and again Marx's powerful analysis shows itself at its best and most perceptive when he discovers an example of religious logic working underneath some sort of economic phenomenon, a religious logic that nobody had suspected before, or would have been scandalized by.

2. The "Metaphysical Subtleties and Theological Niceties" of Commodities

The striking case in point is, of course, Marx's analysis of commodities and the form of value, that is to say, the beginning and, perhaps, the very foundation of his analysis of the capitalist system: "A commodity appears, at first sight, a very trivial thing, and easily understood. Its analysis shows that it is, in reality, a very queer thing, abounding in metaphysical subtleties and theological niceties" (*Capital*, 1909 ed., 1:81).

The first and most important characteristic of commodities qua commodities, is that their existence has "absolutely no connection with their physical properties and with the material relations arising therefrom" (83). They are entirely social entities. So much so, in fact, that the value relations among them act as a substitute for real human relations. By means of the exchange of commodities human relations assume, in men's eyes, "the fantastic form of a relation between things." This is why a commodity is "a mysterious thing." In order to find a similar phenomenon, that is to say, a social process whereby men endow what they have created with the power to substitute for their creators, one "must have recourse to the mist-enveloped regions of the religious world. In that world the productions of the human brain appear as independent beings endowed with life, and entering into relations both with one another and the human race. So it is in the world of commodities with the products of men's hands" (*Capital*, 1909 ed., 1:83). We should look more closely into this analogy.

A commodity is never the inert object it may appear to be. In their exchange, therefore, even at the most elementary level of barter in which quantity *a* of commodity *A* is exchanged for quantity *b* of commodity *B*, much more is at stake than meets the eye. As Michel Aglietta and André Orléan have pointed out in their analysis of Marx's "Elementary Form of Value," "le troc symétrique et stable, cher aux économistes, n'existe pas" (38) (the stable and symmetrical exchange [of merchandise], dear to economists, does not exist).

In every exchange of commodities a fundamental and irreducible antagonism is expressed, the antagonism between use value and exchange value; or, the antagonism between the relative form of value and the equivalent form, "the two poles of the expression of value," or of the value equation: "*x* commodity *A* = *y* commodity *B*, or *x* commodity *A* is worth *y* commodity *B*. 20 yards of linen = 1 coat, or 20 yards of linen are worth 1 coat" (*Capital*, 1909 ed., 1:56). And as Marx said,

> The whole mystery of the form of value lies hidden in this elementary form. Its analysis, therefore, is our real difficulty.
>
> Here two different kinds of commodities . . . evidently play two different parts. The linen expresses its value in the coat; the coat serves as the material in which that value is expressed. The former plays an active, the latter a passive, part. The value of the linen is represented as relative value, or appears in relative form. The coat officiates as equivalent, or appears in equivalent form.
>
> The relative form and the equivalent form are two intimately connected, mutually dependent and inseparable elements of the expression of value; but, at the same time, are mutually exclusive,

antagonistic extremes. . . . It is not possible to express the value of the linen in linen. 20 yards of linen = 20 yards of linen is no expression of value. . . . The value of the linen can be expressed only relatively—*i.e.*, in some other commodity . . . under the form of an equivalent. On the other hand, the commodity that figures as the equivalent cannot at the same time assume the relative form. That second commodity is not the one whose value is expressed. A single commodity cannot, therefore, simultaneously assume, in the same expression of value, both forms. The very polarity of these forms makes them mutually exclusive. (*Capital*, 1909 ed., 1:56–57)

As Marx becomes increasingly aware of the "mystery" surrounding this elemental form of commodity exchange, he derides the blind self-complacency of the bourgeois political economist, who does not really understand what he is dealing with. Only a few pages later:

Since the relative form of value of a commodity—the linen, for example—expresses the value of that commodity, as being something wholly different from its substance and properties, as being, for instance, coat-like, we see that this expression itself indicates that some social relation lies at the bottom of it. With the equivalent form it is just the contrary. The very essence of this form is that the material commodity itself—the coat—just as it is, expresses value, and is endowed with the form of value by Nature itself. Of course this holds good only so long as the value relation exists, in which the coat stands in the position of equivalent to the linen. Since, however, the properties of a thing are not the result of its relations to other things, but only manifest themselves in such relations, the coat seems to be endowed with its equivalent form, its property of being directly exchangeable, just as much by nature as it is endowed with the property of being heavy, or the capacity to keep us warm. Hence the enigmatical character of the equivalent form which escapes the notice of the bourgeois political economist, until this form, completely developed, confronts him in the shape of money. He then tries to explain away the mystical character of gold and silver, by substituting for them less dazzling commodities, and by reciting, with ever renewed satisfaction, the catalogue of all possible commodities which at one time or another have played the part of equivalent. He has not the least suspicion that the most simple expression of value, such as 20 yards of linen = 1 coat, already propounds the riddle of the equivalent form for our solution. (*Capital*, 1909 ed., 1:66)

Now, we know that behind this relationship between commodities lies a very real and very human relationship between individuals in all their concrete, "material," and practical complexity, and not simply as producers of those commodities; for they do not only *produce* them, they also *possess* them.

What Marx's analysis of the elementary form of value reveals to us is that this relationship is far from being the peaceful and unproblematic one that bourgeois economists had imagined. It is more like an adversarial relationship between individual *A* and individual *B*. Each one wants what the other has but neither will abandon what it has because its possession is made valuable by the other's desire, thus becoming a measure of value for the other, the only one. Value is always in the hands of the other and only insofar as it is in the hands of the other. If either of the two individuals, or both of them, were to abandon their individual possession as soon as they faced each other, they might live very happily together in some earthly paradise but no economic form of value would have ever been generated.

3. The Adversarial Relationship of the Elementary Form of Value

The elementary form of value, as defined by Marx, is not, therefore, an expression of the harmonious coincidence or complementary reciprocity of two human desires, where the self-interest of each necessarily works to the benefit of the other, but rather a formula that at least temporarily bypasses—in extremis, so to speak—the ever-present possibility of a violent encounter between two individuals, each trying to capture what the other has. Aglietta and Orléan write:

Pour comprendre la logique de l'échange élémentaire, il ne faut pas en faire le simulacre d'une prédisposition préalable. Il faut, au contraire, partir d'une séparation radicale qui est apparemment l'opposé du libre contrat, à savoir la capture. La capture est le rapport le plus général et le plus essentiel du monde vivant parce qu'il désigne l'incomplétude de tout organisme vivant. Elle est la modalité première de l'ouverture sur l'extérieur de toute unité biologique. (37)

(In order to understand the logic of the elementary exchange, one does not have to pretend that there is a prior predisposition. On the contrary, one must begin from a radical separation that is apparently the opposite of a free contract, namely capture. Capture is the most general and the most essential relation of the living world, because it indicates the incompleteness of every living organism. It is the primary mode of openness toward the outside of every biological unit.)

Marx himself was somewhat aware of the violent possibilities inherent even in the most elemental form of exchange, as we can infer from the following passage in the *Grundrisse*:

This mutual dependence ["the interdependence of the producers"] is expressed in the constant need for exchange, value being the universal intermediary. The economists express it like this: each person has his private interest in mind, and nothing else; as a consequence he serves everyone's private interest, i.e. the general interest, without wishing to or knowing that he is. The irony of this is not that the totality of private interests . . . can be attained by the individual following his own interest. *Rather it could be inferred from this abstract phrase that everyone hinders the satisfaction of everyone else's interest, that instead of a general affirmation, the result of this war of all against all is rather a general negation.* (McLellan, 65; italics mine)

But the elementary form of value is too isolated, too accidental, to be capable of generating the universal equivalent form—money—all by itself ("In the first form, 20 yards of linen = 1 coat, it might for ought that otherwise appears be pure accident, that these two commodities are exchangeable in definite quantities" [73]). The elementary form has to be expanded, has to multiply itself. And this expansion can be formulated as follows: "20 yards of linen = 1 coat or = 10 lb tea or = 40 lb coffee or = 1 quarter corn or = 2 ounces gold or = ½ ton iron or = &c" (*Capital,* 1909 ed., 1:72). This, however, only generalizes the inherent instability, the adversarial relationship, of the elementary form. In the language of commodities, we simply end up with "a many-coloured mosaic of disparate and independent expressions of value." And "since the bodily form of each single commodity is one particular equivalent form amongst numberless others, we have, on the whole, nothing but fragmentary equivalent forms, each excluding the others" (1:74). Or in the words, once again, of Aglietta and Orléan, "la forme F_{ii} est une forme de crise parce que la concurrence des sujets rivaux concerne l'impossibilité de s'accorder sur la base d'évaluation des objets que leurs possesseurs désirent voir devenir des valeurs d'usage" (1:40). (Form F_{ii} is a form of crisis because the competition among rival subjects concerns the impossibility of reaching an agreement on the basis of the evaluation of objects possessed by people who want to see them become use values.)

And yet, at this chaotic moment when every thing competes with everything else as an embodiment of value, at this moment of maximum instability throughout the exchange system, we are in fact closest to the moment when the entire system is going to turn around and find its final stabilizing formula. For if 20 yards of linen are worth 1 coat or 10 lbs. of tea or 40 lbs. of coffee, etc., we can turn the formula around and measure the value of the coat, the tea, the coffee, and everything else in terms of so many yards of linen. Now we are just one step from achieving unprecedented stability in the system. All we have to do is to expel the linen from the community of commodities and, thus, make this particular commodity different from all the rest.

4. The "Exclusion" of One Commodity "from the Rest of All Other Commodities"

This is the birth moment of the "Money form":

> The universal equivalent form is a form of value in general. It can, therefore, be assumed by any commodity. On the other hand, *if a commodity be found to have assumed the universal equivalent*

*form . . . this is only because and in so far as it has been excluded
from the rest of all other commodities as their equivalent, and
that by their own act. And from the moment that this exclusion
becomes finally restricted to one particular commodity, from that
moment only,* the general form of *the relative value of the world of
commodities obtains real consistence and general social validity.*
(*Capital,* 1909 ed., 1:80; italics mine)

To sum up, first we contemplate the elementary or essential form of an
adversarial relationship, a conflict of interests (the inherent contradiction
in every commodity between use value and exchange value) between two
partners; second, we move to a situation in which this core conflict is
"expanded," becomes generalized; and finally, the solution is found and
order (even a higher level of order) is restored through the expulsion of
one among the many competing material embodiments of value.

Needless to say, Marx could not have fully known how closely the
logic of the market economy he was so brilliantly analyzing reflected
the logic of what actually happens "in the mist-enveloped regions of the
religious world." He knew nothing or very little explicitly about the intimate connection between human violence and the sacred, or about what
Girard has called the sacrificial crisis, in the midst of which "one head
must be given up for the sake of many." And yet one cannot but feel that
his extraordinary intuition must have suspected everything.[2]

Nevertheless, had he fully understood the victimizing logic of the old
sacred, he would have also understood the extraordinary significance of
substituting things, commodities, for people. Or, in Marx's own words,
the fact that "a definite social relation between men . . . assumes, in their
eyes, the fantastic form of a relation between things." This "fantastic
form" has a very practical function; by means of such a substitution a
violence that would have threatened the very existence of a primitive
community is, not only averted, but turned, in fact, into a source of order

---

2. There is no doubt that Marx was aware that in the exchange of commodities "personal
power" was also at stake: "In exchange value, the social relations of individuals have become
transformed into the social connections of material things; personal power has changed into
material power. The less social power the means of exchange possess and the closer they are
still connected with the nature of the direct product of labour and the immediate needs of those
exchanging, the greater must be the power of the community to bind the individuals together. . . . If the object is deprived of its social power then this power must be exercised by
people over people" (McLellan, 66–67).

and prosperity.[3] As we follow Marx's own analysis, we see the violent logic of the sacred unfolding, and yet not a drop of blood will be shed: instead, things will be given up, exchangeable things that are indeed exchangeable because they bear the imprint of the sacred; that is, the collective or social act of expulsion that creates the point of reference for meaning and value:

> A particular commodity cannot become the universal equivalent except by a social act. The social action . . . of all other commodities, [which] sets apart the particular commodity in which they all represent their values. . . . To be the universal equivalent becomes, by this social process, the specific function of the commodity thus excluded by the rest. Thus it becomes—money. "Illi unum consilium habent et virtutem et potestatem suam bestiae tradunt. Et ne quis possit emere aut vendere, nisi qui habet characterem aut nomem bestiae, aut numerum nominis ejus." Apocalypse.[4] (Capital, 1909 ed., 1:98–99)

The analogy with what happens in the world of the sacred has become much more than an analogy. The internal logic of the operations that take place in the real world with very real and material consequences is the same as the logic that operates with sacred categories. The process of socialization that turns very material things into exchangeable com-

3. "La dialectique des formes de la valeur, que l'on pourrait aussi bien appeler dialectique des formes de la violence, est le déploiement de cette contradiction [sujet-rival, valeur d'usage-valeur d'échange] lorsqu'elle est acquisitive, c'est-à-dire lorsqu'un objet s'interpose entre le sujet et le rival. Cette position de l'objet donne la signification sociale première de la valeur d'usage qui est de détourner et de canaliser la violence. En effet, en l'absence de l'objet, le face à face du sujet et de son rival est dominé par le désir de s'emparer directement de la personne de l'autre. . . . Le paroxysme d'un désir qui ne trouve pas d'objet sur lequel se fixer est nécessairement un désir de meurtre et de vengeance. . . . A contrario, le processus historique qui a autonomisé les rapports économiques a été décisif dans le devenir des sociétés humaines. Une société capable de detourner le désir sur l'accaparement des objets, de maintenir une distance entre la valeur d'usage que l'on convoite et la personne du rival qui la possède, peut supporter une violence beaucoup plus grande qu'une société dans laquelle les objets sont les symboles représentatifs des personnes vivantes ou mortes. Il en est ainsi parce que, dans les sociétés 'économiques,' le court-circuit mortel du désir cherchant à s'emparer de l'autre peut être plus aisément conjuré" (Aglietta and Orléan, 35).
4. "For they have but a single purpose among them and will confer their power and authority upon the beast. And no one was allowed to buy or sell unless he bore the beast's mark, either name or number." Marx has actually combined two different passages in one: Revelation 17:13 and 13:16–18 (New English Bible).

modities—a process that cannot fail to have profound effects on the material forces of production—is also a process of sacralization. And, as one would expect, this process of sacralization leads to ambivalent results. On the one hand it is, clearly, a process of undifferentiation, for it rests on the equalization of very different things: "Whether 20 yards of linen = 1 coat or = 20 coats or = x coats . . . every such statement implies that the linen and coats, as magnitudes of value, are expressions of the same unit, things of the same kind. Linen = coat is the basis of the equation" (1:58). This equalization is why "every qualitative difference between commodities is extinguished in money, [and] money, on its side, like the radical leveller that it is, does away with all distinctions"; and it is also why "the ancients . . . denounced money as subversive of the economical and moral order of things. [While] modern society, which soon after its birth, pulled Plutus by the hair of his head from the bowels of the earth, greets gold as its Holy Grail, as the glittering incarnation of the very principle of its own life" (1:148–49). Money, or gold as money, the "common whore of mankind," is the result and the very embodiment of this undifferentiating process.

On the other hand, this "common whore" is but one side—the unholy, prostituted, side—of that which is, according to Marx, the very substance of all truly social value, human labor. For "we [must] bear in mind that the value of commodities has a purely social reality, and that they acquire this reality only in so far as they are expressions or embodiments of one identical social substance, viz., human labour" (1:55). Indeed, "money is the measure of value inasmuch as it is the socially recognised incarnation of human labour" (1:110). Like any other sacred *pharmakos,* this one also is both a remedy and a poison.

Marx's unwitting intuition into the workings of the sacred is so perceptive as to be aware of the need for the sacred expulsion to erase its own tracks. In his own terms:

What appears to happen is, not that gold becomes money, in consequence of all other commodities expressing their values in it [by excluding it from their company], but, on the contrary, that all other commodities universally express their value in gold, because it is money. The intermediate steps of the process vanish in the results and leave no trace behind. . . . Hence the magic of money. (1:105)

This erasure is also what happens if we turn commodity relations back into people's relations. As Girard has explained, those who expel the victim do so in the belief that the victim is sacred; they do not know (and would not believe) that it is the other way around, that it is the expulsion itself that sacralizes the victim.

Marx's intuition is too penetrating for its own good. What we are actually seeing is much more than a formal analogy between the realm of the sacred and that of commodities; it is a real substitution of the latter for the former, and this substitution itself is a sacred ruse, a sacred stratagem. Therefore what Marx is, in reality, showing us is a historical example of a lack of difference between those two realms.[5]

But even as the ground shakes underneath the very foundation of his supposedly uncontaminated materialism, Marx remains undisturbed, apparently unaware of the danger. Obviously he feels that once he has discovered the internal logic, the rationality, that governs the exchange of commodities from its embryonic form to its full development with the appearance of money, he stands on solid ground. The analogy with what happens in the "mist-enveloped regions of the religious world" simply becomes a way of saying that, till now, nobody has understood rationally, coherently, what was going on in that realm of commodity exchange. Marx never stopped to ponder the astonishing implications of what his own analysis had just discovered by piercing through the "fetishism of commodities": namely, that the material production of society can be as much of a "reflex" of what happens in the world of religion as religion can be a "reflex" of the world of material production. The parallelism between the two, a source of fascination for Marx, constantly attracting his attention, actually *works both ways*, and the dividing line between the two is somewhat illusory.

5. Roberto Calasso is absolutely right when he summarizes Marx's discovery as follows: "La découverte de Marx se rapport à ceci: au passage de la valeur d'échange de puissance périphérique et marginale à puissance primaire et centrale dans le monde moderne, à son passage a la puissance capitale. Toutes les formes de la vie sont à présent marquées par l'accomplissement de ce processus. . . . Toute réflexion sur les structures et les superstructures est pur *blabla* (mot inventé par Céline), bon pour l'Encyclopédie soviétique, une fois que sont acquises les implications de ce passage: il n'est nul besoin d'une superstructure qui corresponde à une quelconque structure conditionnante. Il suffit de dire que l'on vit sous le *signe* de la valeur d'échange et que la valeur d'échange est le *nom* économique d'une puissance que se manifeste autrement dans la substitution, dans la convention, dans le représenter en général, dans toutes ses formes" (307–8). And, of course, the original "power which manifests itself in substitution," is the power of the sacred. If we live "under the sign of the exchange value" it is no surprise at all that Marx would find what happens in our capitalist world so similar to what goes on "in the mist-

It is, of course, no accident that Marx was so persistently drawn to the dangerous borderline between those two worlds. Such an attraction lies at the very heart of his revolutionary project, for which it is essential to keep religion and material production clearly separate, or rather to keep the sociohistorical laws of material production free from, uncontaminated by, religious non-sense or illusion. He knows that "criticism of religion is the premise of all criticism" (*Karl Marx: A Reader*, 301). And yet, to the extent that he knows or sees himself in possession of a truth that had never been clearly apprehended before—for it is only now, in the fullness of time, so to speak, that "the prehistory of human society [comes] to a close" (188) and true communism announces itself as "the riddle of history solved" (*1844*, 103)—he should have contemplated the obvious possibility that, as we said before, history-making may have been the result of an unclear, though very real, combination of the religious and material realms. In other words, he should have contemplated the possibility that religious representations may have been adequate to deal with something as truly historical as, for example . . . commodities.

Instead, in order to keep material truth, reality, totally free from religious intrusion, Marx would prefer to believe in the possibility of a human history being made by men as mere instruments of historical forces of which they were totally unaware. He would not hesitate to sacrifice human will and deliberation in order to keep religion away from the materiality of the truth, the truth of the truth.

5. The Logic of Marx's Admiration for "the Brilliancy of Aristotle's Genius"

Thus, in spite of his avowed intention to maintain at all times a historical approach, he never really inquires into the historical emergence, the genesis, of the socioeconomic system, or, put differently, the emergence of the historical conditions of possibility of socioeconomic reality as a culturally meaningful system. For example, the basic forms of commodity exchange, we are told, appear all by themselves and without any particular cultural warning or anticipation of their coming; they just appear as the

---

enveloped regions of the religious world." For the same reason the difference between the economic structure and the ideological superstructure is pure "blabla."

most natural thing in the world. Like Athena, they spring forth, fully armed, from a social matrix that has apparently gone through no period of gestation. In the beginning was the fact itself, the fully formed fact ready to claim its place in history: "[Our] commodity-owners think like Faust: 'Im Anfang war die Tat.' They therefore acted and transacted before they thought. Instinctively they conform to the laws imposed by the nature of commodities" (*Capital*, 1909 ed., 1:98)

Once the fact is in existence it will necessarily evolve according to its own internal logic, until in the end one particular commodity will be expelled from the company of the rest and converted into money:

> *Money is a crystal formed of necessity* in the course of exchanges, whereby different products of labour are practically equated to one another and thus by practice converted into commodities. *The historical progress* and extension of exchanges *develops the contrast, latent in commodities,* between use-value and [exchange] value. The *necessity* for giving an external expression to this contrast . . . *urges on the establishment of an independent form of value, and finds no rest until it is once for all satisfied* by the differentiation of commodities into commodities and money. (1:00; italics mine)

This is clearly reminiscent of a certain teleological Aristotelianism. And we must remember what was said about that in the case of Aristotle and the origin of tragedy. In the beginning was something so natural and so much in accord with the fundamental needs of man in society, that it needs no further explanation. And once it is there, as Aristotle would say, its development is little by little by constantly improving on what was already there according to the natural logic of the thing.

Marx's admiration for Aristotle (he calls him "the great thinker," "a giant thinker"; he speaks of "the brilliancy of Aristotle's genius," etc.) is profound and revealing. Here is not the place for an analysis of this most interesting intellectual affinity; but it must be mentioned in order, not only to help characterize Marx's thought, but also to throw light on what I regarded in Chapter 2 as an unstated, yet fundamental, aim of Aristotle's philosophico-scientific enterprise: namely, to keep the sacred at bay, to develop a discourse as free from sacred ambivalence and ambiguity as possible; a discourse that, far from being opposed to Plato, would

actually fulfill the master's most fervent desire, indeed, the desire—and
the fear—to which philosophy owes its very existence.

That desire, that aim, which, in Aristotle, would have been a scandalous blasphemy to utter, becomes an avowed goal and purpose in Marx.
In spite of all differences, Marx remains an Aristotelian at heart. Neither
wants to have his eyes averted from the *thing*, the natural, empirical fact.
Both can indeed say, "Im Anfang war die Tat," which is much more than
a simple statement of fact, and must be understood also as an injunction:
take only the fact, specially at the beginning. The fact itself will account
for its own origin and development. The end is already contained in the
beginning; what's more, the beginning can only be properly understood
by reference to the end. Let us compare the following two passages, the
first from Aristotle's *Politics* (1252b, 27), the second from the introduction to the *Grundrisse*:

> When several villages are united in a single complete community,
> large enough to be nearly or quite self-sufficing, the state comes
> into existence, originating in the bare needs of life, and continuing
> in existence for the sake of a good life. And therefore, if the earlier
> forms of society are natural, so is the state, for it is the end of
> them, and *the nature of a thing is its end. For what each thing is
> when fully developed, we call its nature*, whether we are speaking
> of a man, a horse, or a family. *Besides, the final cause and end of
> a thing is the best*, and to be self-sufficing is the end and the best.

> Bourgeois society is the most highly developed and most highly
> differentiated historical organization of production. The cate-
> gories which serve as the expressions of its conditions and the
> comprehension of its own organization enable it at the same time
> to gain an insight into the organization and the relationships of
> production which have prevailed under all the past forms of soci-
> ety. . . . The anatomy of the human being is the key to the anat-
> omy of the ape. But the intimations of a higher animal in lower
> ones can be understood only if the animal of the higher order is
> already known. The bourgeois economy furnishes a key to ancient
> economy, etc. (*Karl Marx: A Reader*, 14–15; italics mine)

The teleological Aristotelianism of Marx's passage needs no demonstration. It would probably take us too far afield to examine with enough

precision the ways in which such statements contain an element of truth, and to separate such truth from misleading fallacies. But it is clear enough that this type of thinking ignores the radical uncertainty into which every living organism, group, or autonomous organization is born. The internal logic of any "material" fact is always confronted by the ever-present possibility of being diverted from its path, driven into an impasse, or being permanently interrupted by either its own genetic quirks or other environmental forces. That is the fundamental difference between a syllogism and a space/time-bound reality.

When Marx says that "we must begin by stating the first premise of all human existence and, therefore, of all history, the premise, namely, that men must be in a position to live in order to be able to 'make history'" (Marx and Engels, *The German Ideology*, 48), apparently he forgets that in order to "be in a position to live" men not only need "eating and drinking, a habitation, clothing and many other things"; they also must have some kind of protection against being killed, especially against being killed by those in their immediate vicinity. For no matter how well fed and clothed, a man is in no position to make much history himself if he is dead.

"Morality, religion, metaphysics, all the rest of ideology and their corresponding forms of consciousness [have no] independence . . . no history, no development [of their own]; but men developing their material production and their material intercourse, alter, along with this their real existence, their thinking and the products of their thinking" (*The German Ideology*, 47). Let us assume for a moment that this is so. That still does not tell us whether "ideology" has any real function to fulfill or is a totally useless appendix, a forever gratuitous obstacle to the discovery of the real, material, truth.What Marx does not see is that "ideology" has always been the realm where human beings have moved in search of devices to protect themselves from their own violence, mostly, as we have seen already, by hiding it from their view, by searching for increasingly effective ways to claim innocence.

Marx's failure to recognize, on the one hand, the unpredictable effects of human violence on any system of "material production," due to the unpredictable (i.e., open-ended) character of human violence itself, and, on the other hand, his failure to see any reality, any practico-historical significance, in the sacred (the "ideological" product par excellence) are one and the same, the two sides of the same failure or blindness.

The fact of the matter is that the fundamental structure of the sacred,

the sacrificial structure, has remained basically unchanged since time immemorial across all kinds of forms of "material production and material
intercourse." That sacrificial structure has operated at all levels of hunting, nomadic, or agricultural societies, for example; in rural or urban
communities. Marcel Gauchet has noted that "un changement aussi capital dans les moyens de production et de subsistance que la 'revolution
néolithique,' l'une des deux grandes transformations de la base matérielle
des societés, a pu survenir sans du tout systématiquement entraîner de
mutation culturelle et religieuse" (14). (A change so capital in the means
of production and subsistence as the "neolithic revolution," one of the
two great transformations of the material base of societies, could come
about without in the least causing a systematic cultural and religious
mutation.) Marx himself could have suspected this extraordinary resil-
ience and longevity of sacral forms when he discovered them in operation
in the history of commodities and money. However, by expelling "ideology" to a basically meaningless margin of human history, Marx is not
exactly expelling human violence, but rather its unpredictability and open-endedness, the violence of violence, so to speak. Indeed, human violence is very much needed by Marx as the very soul, or rather the engine,
or the fuel, of history. But it must be a rationally controlled violence. Let
us consider the following famous passage from the 1859 preface to *A
Contribution to the Critique of Political Economy*, which I quote at some
length because of its crucial importance:

> In the social production of their life, men enter into definite
> relations that are indispensable and independent of their will,
> relations of production which correspond to a definite stage of
> development of their material productive forces. . . . At a certain
> stage of their development, the material productive forces of soci-
> ety come in conflict with the existing [social] relations of produc-
> tion. . . . From forms of development of the productive forces
> these relations turn into their fetters. Then begins an epoch of
> social revolution. With the change of the economic foundations
> the entire immense superstructure is more or less rapidly trans-
> formed. In considering such transformations a distinction should
> always be made between the material transformation of the eco-
> nomic conditions of production, which can be determined with
> the precision of natural science, and the legal, political, religious,
> aesthetic, or philosophic—in short, ideological forms in which

men become conscious of this conflict and fight it out. Just as our opinion of an individual is not based on what he thinks of himself, so can we not judge of such a period of transformation by its own consciousness. . . . *No social order ever perishes before all the productive forces for which there is room in it have developed; and new higher relations of production never appear before the material conditions of their existence have matured in the womb of the old society itself. Therefore mankind always sets itself such tasks as it can solve; since, looking at the matter more closely, it will always be found that the task itself arises only when the material conditions for its solution already exist or are at least in the process of formation.* (in *Karl Marx: A Reader*, 187–88; italics mine)

So the "material productive forces of society" function as a powerful self-regulating machine that, though in need of the fuel of human violence to advance and evolve, never consumes more fuel than it needs; marvelously efficient, it never takes more than it can handle.

Marx in effect tells us that we should not pay too much attention to the "ideological" level "where men become conscious of this conflict and fight it out"; all such violence is purely instrumental, a tool in the hands of something more real and powerful that does not make mistakes, and that will ultimately control it and keep it within bounds. That is to say, no amount of human violence can alter certain fundamental facts, which men cannot do without. But this is also, unavoidably, a way of saying that human violence is perfectly predictable and controllable, that human beings do not fight unless they have to, and that they do not carry their violence any further than is needed in order to achieve material objectives, of which they may not be aware but which can be determined with scientific precision and clarity. Any other evidence to the contrary must be considered pure "ideological" rubbish. Men may think that they are fighting for all kinds of metaphysical reasons. But how can that be? It would amount to fighting for nothing, a ridiculous notion—or a terrifying one. A real reason must be found; a reason that will make sense of the fight and, thereby, subject it to rational control. Thus, we get Marx's discovery and analysis of the all-powerful material forces of production, the "indispensable" human relations of production they generate, and the link between the two.

In the final analysis, the problem that Marx wants to solve is not the technical one posed by the interplay of the material productive forces, but the human one posed by the violence of man against man. What Marx really wants to discover is not the economic law of material production for its own sake, but rather the law or laws that govern human violence. He wants to succeed where philosophy, religion, morality, etc. have failed. For, in his eyes, they have failed; he sees them not as a bulwark against violence but as so many justifications of the violence of some (the winners) against others (the losers) in the economic game. Marx wants to do better, and in order to do better he will look for a better way to take human violence out of human hands and root it (tie it, hide it) in totally objective material conditions that can be analyzed, understood and, therefore, controlled in a perfectly rational manner. In order to give man his freedom Marx will take away from him everything that threatens that freedom and put it someplace else called material productive forces. If we scratch the surface of these forces, we soon discover that the stuff they are made of is nothing but domesticated, predictable, rationalized human violence.

Occasionally Marx becomes somewhat aware that human violence may be more uncontrollable than anticipated by his theory and, thus, poses a problem to his interpretation of history:

> This whole interpretation of history appears to be contradicted by the fact of conquest. Up till now violence, war, pillage, murder and robbery, etc. have been accepted as the driving force of history. Here we must limit ourselves to the chief points and take, therefore, only the most striking example—the destruction of an old civilisation by a barbarous people and the resulting formation of an entirely new organisation of society. (Rome and the barbarians; feudalism and Gaul; the Byzantine Empire and the Turks.) (Marx and Engels, *The German Ideology*, 89)

But he will immediately show us that all that "violence, war, pillage, murder and robbery" does not destroy anything of real consequence; it does not touch the pillars of his theory. For example, we learn that nothing fundamental was destroyed—or even changed, for that matter—in the *taking* of Rome by the barbarians. Because such

> taking is . . . determined by the object taken. A banker's fortune, consisting of paper, cannot be taken at all, without the taker's

submitting to the conditions of production and intercourse of the
country taken. . . . [Besides] everywhere there is very soon an end
to taking, and when there is nothing more to take, you have to set
about producing. From this necessity of producing . . . it follows
that the form of community adopted by the settling conquerors
must correspond to the stage of development of the productive
forces they find in existence. By this, too, is explained the fact . . .
that the conquerors very soon took over language, culture and
manners from the conquered.

In other words, no amount of human violence will ultimately change the
way things really are. The true material reality of things and facts will in
the end tame that violence and bend it to the laws of its inherent logic.

Of course this rational confidence can only be postulated a posteriori.
In the midst of "violence, war, pillage, murder," things look far more
unpredictable. Long after violence ceases and everything that was destroyed or changed because of it is no longer visible, it will always be
possible to find a rational explanation for the way things happened to
finally settle down. The way Marx disposes of the problem of human
violence, by simply draining it of its unpredictable and destructive character, is another example of his teleological Aristotelianism.

But, as we have said, he cannot do without human violence altogether.
The interlocking system of productive forces and productive relations
needs human violence in order to work properly, that is to say, in order
to make history, to grow and evolve. And human violence, as Marx knew
so well and we have said repeatedly, is, above all, the violence of man
against man. Therefore, such a system cannot possibly function without
human victims. In order to work properly it must work for some at the
expense of others. In summary form we find this "law" of history clearly
expressed in the *Communist Manifesto*: "The history of all past society
has consisted in the development of class antagonisms, antagonisms that
assumed different forms at different epochs. But whatever form they may
have taken, one fact is common to all past ages, viz., *the exploitation of
one part of society by the other*" (*1844*, 229; italics mine). This is the
best that the self-regulating movement governing the "transformation of
the economic conditions of production, which can be determined with
the precision of natural science," has been able to do for the human race
till now. This automatic mechanism will not work for all, only for some;

the others will be consumed by this mechanical monster in order to keep it going at a healthy pace.

Quite frankly, as a way of managing human violence the old sacred one sounded more promising, more efficient than the scientific one constructed by Marx. The old monster only needed one victim. Only one had to be sacrificed for the sake of all the others. After all, if the system cannot possibly do without human violence, then the old sacred formula is absolutely its most economical expression: good for all except one; wherein lies a lesson to be learned. For it now appears that, in spite of all his efforts to outsmart the old sacred and leave it behind once and for all, the old monster is still ahead of Marx—which is not surprising, because, unbeknownst to him, he has been playing the old sacred game all along.

Marx thought he had left the sacred hanging dry as a mere self-deluding and illusory "reflex" of the laws of material production. But it turns out that in doing that he was still following the inner logic of the old sacred—which does not mean that the old sacred proves him wrong. The amazing thing is that he can be right in what he says about the sacred and still be fooled by the sacred, because what he says is still said from within the logic of the old sacred. For the moment, however, in terms of violent efficiency or efficient violence, the old sacred appears to be ahead of the game. But Marx is a fast and profound learner. He is going to catch up very soon.

6. Human Consciousness and "the First Form of Ideologists, Priests"

First, however, I would like to bring up a passage in *The German Ideology*, where one can see with special clarity what might be described as Marx and Engels's discovery of something approaching the status of original sin, that is to say, the historical appearance of social conflict linked to the emergence of human consciousness itself, linked to the moment when human consciousness dares to stand on its own and dream the "ideological" dream of its own freedom:

> Consciousness is at first, of course, merely consciousness concerning the immediate sensuous environment and consciousness of the

limited connections with other persons and things. . . . At the same time it is consciousness of nature, which first appears to men as a completely alien, all-powerful and unassailable force, with which men's relations are purely animal and by which they are overawed like beasts. . . . On the other hand, man's consciousness of the necessity of associating with the individuals around him is the beginning of the consciousness that he is living in society at all. . . . It is mere herd-consciousness . . . [which] receives its further development and extension through increased productivity . . . and, what is fundamental . . . , the increase of population. With these there develops the division of labour, which was originally nothing but the division of labour in the sexual act, then that division of labour which develops spontaneously . . . by virtue of natural predisposition . . . needs, accidents, etc. etc. *Division of labour only becomes truly such from the moment when a division of material and mental labour appears. (The first form of ideologists, priests , is concurrent.)* [This parenthetical remark appears in the original manuscript as a marginal note in Marx's own handwriting: "Erste Form der Ideologen, *Pfaffen*, fällt zusammen."] *From this moment onwards consciousness can really flatter itself that it is something other than consciousness of existing practice, that it really represents something without representing something real; from now on consciousness is in a position to emancipate itself from the world and to proceed to the formation of "pure" theory, theology, philosophy, ethics, etc. . . . [It] is quite immaterial what consciousness starts to do on its own: out of all such muck we get only one inference that these three moments, the forces of production, the state of society, and consciousness, can and must come into contradiction with one another, because the division of labour implies the possibility, nay the fact that intellectual and material activity . . . devolve on different individuals, and that the only possibility of their not coming into contradiction lies in the negation in its turn of the division of labour.* (51–52; italics mine)

The sentence "these three moments, the forces of production, the state of society, and consciousness, can and must come into contradiction" may be misleading. In good Marxist theory conflict arises when the material forces of production outpace, or no longer coincide with, the structure of social relations those forces of production generated to begin with. At some point the forces of production and the social relations get out of step with each other; the original coincidence is broken. Something, therefore, must happen in the midst of those social relations, which, according to Marx, are based on and are an expression of the division of labor; something that introduces an element of indeterminacy, of arbitrariness, in those relations and thus breaks an otherwise "natural," material, spontaneous link between forces of production and social relations. And the only possible conduit for such an original indeterminacy to come in is consciousness, human consciousness. Thus, to say that "it is quite immaterial what consciousness starts to do on its own" is simply not true. What we get "out of all such muck" is not exactly that the "three moments . . . must come into contradiction with one another," but rather that two "moments," forces of production and social relations ("the state of society"), must come into contradiction with each other *because of* the development of the third one, *human consciousness.*

However, human consciousness itself emerges out of the development of the social division of labor. And it emerges as something with a distinct identity precisely as (at) the moment "when a division of material and mental labour appears." This is the real birth of a consciousness that can truly be called human, as distinct from "purely animal consciousness of nature" as well as from "mere herd-consciousness." "From this moment onwards consciousness *can* really flatter itself that it is something other than consciousness of existing practice." That is to say, it "can flatter itself" by believing that it is something more than a mere natural, material, extension of purely natural, material, forces of production. Clearly it is at this moment, and not before, that an arbitrary, "ideological," deviation from the perfectly ascertainable laws of material production can occur. But, note! This birth of human consciousness, is also the birth of the sacred! For, as Marx wrote on the margin of his manuscript, as something like an afterthought, "the first form of ideologists, *priests,* is concurrent." Quite an appropriate thought to occur precisely at this juncture, in spite of its marginal status (which is in itself extremely significant). Marx has just presented the birth of human consciousness as a form of self-flattery, the emergence of the self-deluding notion of spiritual independence and freedom from material production; clearly a form of pride that breaks some original and necessary harmony, an illusory attempt at controlling one's own destiny before the time had come when "the riddle of history [would be] solved"—which is just as good a definition of original sin as any theologian could provide.

What a quaint manner of saying it, "the first form of ideologists, *priests*, is concurrent." "Concurrent" with what? Obviously with that moment when "the division of labour becomes truly such"; that is to say "when a division of material and mental labour appears." "Concurrent" therefore with the very birth of self-consciousness, with the transition from "purely animal consciousness" or "mere herd-consciousness" to distinctly human consciousness.

But Marx does not really want to say what he is already saying. He does not want to say that the emergence of human consciousness coincides, "is concurrent," with the emergence of the sacred. That would explicitly grant the sacred—all that ideological "muck"—a most annoying and disgusting centrality even as an agent of delusion. The only proper way of dealing with the sacred is to push it aside, expel it, isolate it, send it—most literally—to the margin: there, on the margin, it will bear the mark of the outcast, the sign of its isolation; it will be called not by its sacred name, but by the name of its despised embodiments: "ideologists," "priests."

Thus, the role of the sacred in the historical emergence and development of human consciousness is alluded to in the very act of pushing it aside. What we are told explicitly is not that, at a certain moment, human consciousness detaches itself from its moorings in material production and, for the first time, becomes aware of itself as consciousness of something sacred; that is, taboo, something to be dealt with in a totally unprecedented way. Instead, what we hear is that at a certain moment, the first "ideologists, *priests*" appear, with the implication that they are the ones to blame for creating the first separation of mental from material labor, thereby introducing a totally arbitrary element in social relations, that will be the source of all conflicts with the material sources of production and, therefore, the source of all social conflicts as well.

But the expulsion is too obvious, the cover-up too transparent. If the first "mental labour" was an affair of the priests, where was the rest of humanity? Were humans other than priests still at the level of "purely animal consciousness" or "herd-consciousness"? How could such a "division of labour" occur, which would imply a fundamental difference in mental development between individuals within the same social organization? I do not think that Marx would have liked to suggest that there were individuals naturally closer to an animalistic level of consciousness than others, individuals born to be led and fooled by others, as his admired Aristotle might say about individuals naturally born to be slaves.

The German Ideology was a rather early work and also one with an explicit polemical intent; there is a certain hurried, unmeditated quality about it. But it is also, in its first part, the first full exposé of the principles of the new philosophy of dialectical materialism. And it is there, from the beginning, where we can see clearly that religion, as Marx understood it, that is, the old sacred, was not just one form of "ideology" among others, it is the root and origin of all "ideological" constructs, *the* ideology par excellence.

Marx's expulsion of the sacred in the guise of "ideology" is essentially no different from even the most primitive forms of sacred expulsion. What is expelled in one way or another is always the same thing: the indeterminate character, the unpredictability of human conflict, the frightening arbitrariness that lurks at the bottomless bottom of human violence, no matter what the reasons—justifiable or not, real or imaginary—that trigger it.

Regardless of the many valid and truly revealing insights that one can find in Marx, his intellectual project is ultimately a very elaborate device to prevent that violent arbitrariness from running out of control. Marx wants to break every barrier, every control ever established by human society between one human being and another, but he wants to do it in a totally controlled and predictable manner. He fears and hates unpredictability. This is probably why, as Calasso has pointed out, he spent so much time and so much bitter sarcasm against somebody like Max Stirner:

> Il reconnut en Stirner le héraut de cette troupe empoisonnée [les *Lumpen* . . . les fascistes . . . innombrables et proliférants, qui l'épouvantaient et lui apparaissaient non maîtrisables, comme une migration de méduses] . . . la rupture du schéma des classes, l'irruption chaotique qui venait gâcher . . . la Représentation Sacrée de l'histoire. C'était là le péché impardonnable par excellence—et ceci suffit à justifier la furie de l'attaque contre Stirner. (329)

> (He recognized in Stirner the herald of this poisoned crowd [the *Lumpen* . . . the fascists . . . innumerable and multiplying, who frightened him and appeared to him as beyond control, like a migration of Medusa] . . . the breakdown of the scheme of [social]

classes, a chaotic irruption that came to mess up . . . the Sacred Representation of history. That was the unpardonable sin par excellence—and this was enough to justify the fury of his attack against Stirner.)

7. From Theory to Practice:
The Theoretical Demonstration ad hominem and the
"Gripping of the Masses"

But in the final analysis, we must remember, all this intellectual expulsion is but a prologue to action. For while "the philosophers have only interpreted the world, in various ways; the point is to change it" (*Karl Marx: A Reader*, 23). Everything that has been said must acquire its real meaning in the light of revolutionary practice. There has to be a correspondence between the radicalism of theory and that of practice. In other words, "theory [must be] capable of gripping the masses," and it will do so "as soon as it demonstrates *ad hominem*" (Marx and Engels, *On Religion*, 50). In fact, theory cannot become radical enough to "grip the masses" unless "it demonstrates *ad hominem.*" However, there is another way of proving the radicalism of theory, without which theory would be ineffective; that is, it would not grip the masses. This way, according to Marx, is evident in the case of German theory: "The evident proof of the radicalism of German theory, and hence of its practical energy, is that it proceeds from a resolute *positive* abolition of religion" (*On Religion*, 50). It is all, really, the same thing, the demonstration ad hominem that grips the masses and the "abolition of religion" (*On Religion*, 50). This is indeed the point where "theory" joins the "practice" of the ages since time immemorial, the constantly renewed expulsion of the sacred. It is indeed there that the difference between the most "radical" theory and the oldest practice disappears. (It is both ironic and enormously instructive that the "*radical* revolution" that gripped the German masses, turned out to be, not exactly what Marx had anticipated but a massive, overwhelming regression to the most primitive form of sacred scapegoating, National Socialism).

Marx understands the internal logic of revolutionary practice perfectly.

Of course until the "*radical* revolution . . . the *general human* emancipation" arrives, all revolutions must be considered "partial" or "*merely* political." We must ask, therefore, "on what is a partial, a merely political revolution based?" (*On Religion*, 53). And the answer is, "on a definite class, proceeding from its *particular* situation, undertaking the general emancipation of society." In order to play that role a "class of civil society [must arouse] a moment of enthusiasm in itself and in the masses, a moment in which it fraternizes and merges with society in general, becomes confused with it and is perceived and acknowledged as its *general representative*." However,

> [for] the storming of this emancipatory position . . . revolutionary energy and spiritual self-feeling alone are not sufficient. For the *revolution of a nation* and the *emancipation of a particular class* of civil society to coincide, for one estate to be acknowledged as the estate of the whole society, *all the defects of society must conversely be concentrated in another class, a particular estate must be the estate of the general stumbling-block . . . a particular social sphere must be recognized as the notorious crime of the whole of society, so that liberation from that sphere appears as general self-liberation For one estate to be par excellence the state of liberation, another estate must conversely be the obvious estate of oppression.* (*On Religion*, 54)

This was clearly the case of the French Revolution, in which "the negative . . . significance of the French nobility and the French clergy determined the positive . . . significance of the . . . *bourgeoisie*" (*On Religion*, 54).

But this "partial or merely political revolution" is only a somewhat artificial rehearsal for the real, the "radical," one. It is partial because the deprivation of the class that rises up against the oppressor is only partial and relative, as is the oppression itself. The revolutionary class or estate is still a class or estate that belongs within the structure of the existing civil society. Even though it appears, in the midst of revolutionary enthusiasm, to embody the whole of society, in reality, it does not. Its "storming of [the] emancipatory position" is in fact a "political exploitation of all sections of society in the interests of its own section." In other words, it only appears to be the real thing, but in point of fact, it is not.

The truly radical revolution can only take place when the deprivation, on one hand, and the oppression, on the other, have reached such an extent that it is no longer possible to speak of the deprived and the oppressors as belonging together in the same structured social whole; when the evil is such that it has dissolved all social bonds. The possibility of such a radical revolution and emancipation lies,

> in the formation of a class with radical chains, a class of civil society which is not a class of civil society, an estate which is the dissolution of all estates, a sphere which has a universal character by its universal suffering and claims no particular right because no *particular wrong* but *wrong generally* is perpetrated against it; which can invoke no *historical* but only its *human* title . . . ; a sphere . . . which, in a word, is the *complete loss* of man and hence can win itself only through the *complete re-winning of man.* This dissolution of society as a particular estate is the *proletariat.* . . . By heralding the *dissolution of the hereto existing world order* the proletariat merely proclaims the *secret of its own existence*, for it is the *factual* dissolution of that world order. (*On Religion*, 56–57)

All previous, "partial," revolutions merely borrowed the logic of the real, final, one. They were only rehearsals of the ultimate crisis. Nevertheless, the internal logic is the same in every case. Only the historical circumstances have changed, so that the same sacrificial mechanism, the same logic, will produce very different results.

This historical change in circumstances has been brought about by capitalism, or rather by the class that has benefited most from the capitalist system, the bourgeoisie. For the bourgeoisie "historically, has played a most revolutionary part," as Marx and Engels declare in the *Communist Manifesto*:

> The bourgeoisie . . . has put an end to all feudal, patriarchal, idyllic relations. It has pitilessly torn asunder the motley feudal ties that bound man to his "natural superiors," and has left remaining no other nexus between man and man than naked self-interest. . . . It has drowned the most heavenly ecstasies of religious fervor, of chivalrous enthusiasm, of Philistine sentimentalism in the icy water of egotistical calculation. . . . The bourgeoisie can-

not exist without constantly revolutionizing the instruments of production, and thereby the relations of production, and with them the whole relations of society. . . . Constant revolutionizing of production, uninterrupted disturbance of all social conditions, everlasting uncertainty and agitation distinguish the bourgeois epoch from earlier ones. . . . All that is solid melts into air, all that is holy profaned, and man is at last compelled to face with sober senses his real conditions of life and his relations with his kind.

. . . But the bourgeoisie [has] forged the weapons that bring death to itself; [and] it has called into existence the men who are to wield those weapons . . . the proletarians. (*1844*, 211–15)

So the historical stage is set for the final showdown. For "our epoch . . . has simplified the class antagonisms. Society as a whole is more and more splitting up into two great hostile camps, into two great classes directly facing each other: bourgeoisie and proletariat" (*1844*, 210).

The logic that leads to this final confrontation is relentless, unavoidable; it is inscribed from the beginning in the very structure of organized human society. It is "in no way based on ideas or principles that have been invented, or discovered, by this or that would-be universal reformer" (*1844*, 223). We should, therefore, pay close attention to the way in which the end of the capitalist bourgeoisie is played out on the universal stage, that is to say, for all human beings everywhere to see and learn. What is at stake is not the fate of this or that society or civilization, but the fate of humanity.

Capitalism has an insatiable appetite. No sacred barriers will stop it. Totally indifferent to the quality of human relations, it will spread social undifferentiation as it advances: "Never, in any earlier period, have the productive forces taken on a form so indifferent to the intercourse of individuals *as* individuals" (Marx and Engels, *The German Ideology*, 92). Its only criterion is to outdo itself, production for the sake of production. In other words, the only soul of this soulless monster is unbridled competition:

By universal competition it forced all individuals to strain their energies to the utmost. It destroyed as far as possible ideology, religion, morality, etc. . . . It produced world history for the first time . . . destroying the former natural exclusiveness of separate nations . . . took from the division of labour the last semblance of its natural character. . . . [It] makes for the worker not only the relation to the capitalist, but labour itself, unbearable. (*The German Ideology*, 78)[6]

Needless to say, the inevitable historical tendency of capital is toward increasing accumulation and concentration of the means of production and, ultimately, toward centralization. Driven by fierce competition, capitalists not only increase their capital at the expense of the workers, but also at the expense of other capitalists who fall victim to this competitive madness and thus join the ranks of the dispossesed, the proletarians. It is indeed a bloody history: according to Augier, "If money 'comes into the world with a congenital blood-stain on one cheek,' capital comes dripping from head to foot, from every pore, with blood and dirt" (*Capital*, 1909 ed., 1:834).

Capitalism begins with the

annihilation . . . of the individualised and scattered means of production into socially concentrated ones, of the pigmy property of the many into the huge property of the few . . . [which] was accomplished with merciless Vandalism, and under the stimulus of passions the most infamous, the most sordid, the pettiest, the most meanly odious. . . . As soon as this process . . . has sufficiently decomposed the old society from top to bottom, as soon as the labourers are turned into proletarians . . . then the further socialisation of labour and further transformation of the . . . means of production . . . takes a new form. That which is now to be expropriated is no longer the labourer . . . but the capitalist exploiting many labourers. This expropriation is accomplished by the action of the immanent laws of capitalistic production itself, by the centralisation of capital. One capitalist always kills many. (*Capital*, 1909 ed., 1:835–36)

But the accumulation and centralization of capital, in and by them-

6. Compare Engels's comment on Darwin, in *Dialectics of Nature*: "Darwin did not know what a bitter satire he wrote on mankind, and especially on his countrymen, when he showed that free competition, the struggle for existence, which the economists celebrate as the highest historical achievement, is the normal state of the *animal kingdom*. Only conscious organization of social production, in which production and distribution are carried on in a planned way, can lift mankind above the rest of the animal world as regards the social aspect" (*On Religion*, 169).

selves, would not necessarily bring about the collapse of the capitalist
system if it were not tied to the corresponding "law of increasing misery,"
as Popper calls it. This is how Marx explains what at one point he calls
"the absolute general law of capitalist accumulation":

> Within the capitalist system all methods for raising the social
> productiveness of labour are brought about at the cost of the in-
> dividual labourer; all means for the development of production
> transform themselves into means of domination over, and exploi-
> tation of, the producers; they mutilate the labourer into a frag-
> ment of a man . . . degrade him . . . destroy every remnant of
> charm in his work . . . transform his life-time into working-time,
> and drag his wife and child beneath the wheels of the Juggernaut
> of capital. But all methods for the production of surplus value are
> at the same time methods of accumulation. . . . It follows there-
> fore that in proportion as capital accumulates, the lot of the la-
> bourer . . . must grow worse. The law, finally, that always
> equilibrates the relative surplus-population . . . to the extent and
> energy of accumulation ["the relative mass of the industrial re-
> serve-army increases with the potential energy of wealth. But the
> greater this reserve-army . . . the greater is the mass of a consoli-
> dated surplus-population, whose misery is in inverse ratio to its
> torment of labour"] . . . establishes an accumulation of misery,
> corresponding with accumulation of capital. Accumulation of
> wealth at one pole is, therefore, at the same time accumulation of
> misery, agony of toil, slavery, ignorance, brutality, mental degra-
> dation, at the opposite pole. (*Capital,* 1909 ed., 1:708–9)

It is important to realize that this "accumulation of misery" must be
understood, not only in qualitative terms but quantitatively as well. For

> along with the constantly diminishing number of the magnates of
> capital . . . grows the mass of misery . . . but with this too grows
> the revolt of the working class, a class always increasing in num-
> bers, and disciplined, united, organised by the very mechanism of
> the process of capitalist production itself. . . . Centralisation of
> the means of production and socialisation of labour at last reach
> a point where they become incompatible with their capitalist in-

tegument. This integument is burst asunder. The knell of capitalist
private property sounds. (*Capital,* 1909 ed., 1:836–37)

The dawn of Communist society appears on the horizon.

Even at the time when Popper was writing *The Open Society* it had
become perfectly clear that the close connection that Marx establishes
between the law of capitalist accumulation and that of increasing misery
was not only scientifically suspect but had also been proven wrong by
history:

> Marx's terrible picture of the economy of his time is only too true.
> But his law that misery must increase together with accumulation
> does not hold. Means of production have accumulated and the
> productivity of labour has increased since his day to an extent
> which even he would hardly have thought possible. But child la-
> bour, working hours, the agony of toil, and the precariousness of
> the worker's existence, have not increased; they have de-
> clined. . . . [The] actual situation is briefly and fairly summed up
> by Parkes in one sentence: "Low wages, long hours, and child
> labour have been characteristic of capitalism not, as Marx pre-
> dicted, in its old age, but in its infancy." (186)

Today there is no longer any need to demonstrate that Marx's predictions regarding the Communist solution to "the riddle of history," were
wrong; the Communist solution is no solution. But that is not what concerns us here. What is important to realize is that the logic that governs
Marx's predictions is not the dispassionate logic of scientific investigation, but the logic that has always driven the collective operation of the
sacrificial mechanism. From within this logic, Marx clearly understood
that the new Communist society was not supposed to come about by
reforming capitalism. *The new society had to emerge from the dead body
of capitalism itself and in no other way.* Capitalism was at once the only
real enemy of Communism and the only soil on which it could grow.
The solution was already contained in the unprecedented character of
capitalist society, in its extraordinary creativity, which far surpasses the
potential of any other human society. But the solution, the new society,
was contained in capitalism as in a prison from which it had to be liberated. Peel the capitalist cover away and the new society will rise from the
throbbing carcass of the freshly sacrificed victim.

[The] ancient conception, in which man always appears (in however narrowly national, religious or political a definition) as the
aim of production, seems very much more exalted than the modern world, in which production is the aim of man and wealth the
aim of production. In fact, however, *when the narrow bourgeois
form has been peeled away, what is wealth, if not the universality
of needs, capacities, enjoyments, productive powers, etc., of individuals, produced in universal exchange?* (Marx, *Pre-Capitalist
Economic Formations*, 84; italics mine)

Capitalism had to be sacrificed so that evil could be turned to good,
the poison into the remedy. But first the poisonous crisis had to reach a
maximum of intensity. During this crisis undifferentiation spreads rapidly in every direction; all sacred barriers are destroyed, all taboos broken. But this process of undifferentiation is also a way of defining with
ever-increasing clarity the identity of the culprit, the victim that, in the
end, will have to be sacrificed. In fact, in the ideal sacrificial process the
identity of the culprit would be so clearly revealed, and its isolation from
the fast-growing mass of undifferentiated sacrificers so great, that, in the
end, it would practically destroy itself, thus relieving everybody from
apprehensive fears of criminal contamination. That is precisely Marx's
vision of the end of capitalism. In his last scenario, capitalism would be
destroyed with a minimum of effort, surrounded by huge masses of people, all made equal in their deprivation, fraternally united in their hatred
of the monster; they would prod the beast on all sides and would see it
collapse under its own weight. In the end, the situation would be practically that of all against one, or very nearly so. This is why the "final
struggle" for socialism could not possibly end in any way except in victory. Probably Popper did not fully understand the extraordinary extent
to which he was indeed right when he saw Marxism and other forms of
totalitarianism as a return to a tribal origin.

But this does not mean that Marx was simply imagining things. Quite
the contrary, Marx really saw the sacrificial logic at work in the development of human history, without actually knowing it. What he knew was
that he had touched something very profound and very real, something
that truly was in the nature of things, so to speak; the internal logic of
"the riddle of history." This is why Marx was so confident that his theory
was fully capable of "gripping the masses." And he was not mistaken.
He was a false prophet but he was believed by countless millions in all

walks of life, not just proletarians, everywhere in the world. What philosopher, or economist, or historian, or intellectual theoretician in general has ever been able to claim that much? Only religious prophets, founders of religion, have been able to "grip the masses" in such a way. Marx was one such prophet. The strength of his persuasion did not rest on the soundness of his scientific method, but on the oldest, most primitive, method of social action operating in human history: the sacrificial one.

He not only discovered the violence that lurked behind the old sacred; he also saw that the final hour of that sacrificial cover-up had sounded. But he badly misjudged the power and the cunning of what he was dealing with; or what amounts to the same thing, he was blinded by intellectual pride. He thought that once the sacred veil was rent and all ideological "nonsense" dissipated, the old mechanism could be manipulated at will and made to work for man, rather than the other way around. In other words, he thought he could beat the old monster at its own game. It did not work, of course. The only way to undermine the old sacrificial mechanism is to avoid it as much as possible.

Today probably nothing remains of Marx's prophecies except his concern for the victims of the social system that he analyzed. And that is not a theoretical concern but a moral one. Furthermore, such a concern is fundamentally alien to any version of the closed society, whether modern or primitive. What remains is precisely that aspect of his approach to history which is fundamentally antisacrificial. Of course, it was not he who discovered that. Christianity had done so for him.

8. Comparing Marx, Virgil, and the Great Modern Poets

Now it is time to ask the question to which our analysis of Marx has been leading: In what way can the failure of Marx's sacrificial operation help our understanding of the historical role of literature in the modern world; that is to say, the world that produced the Renaissance, in which the demise of the old sacred (of its capacity to be truly effective) accelerated to an unprecedented degree?

Let us begin by comparing Marx's operation with that of Virgil as examined in Chapter 3. Both of them share something fundamental from a sacrificial viewpoint. Just as in Virgil the horrible, leveling, violence in which the two sides of the conflict are equally trapped, is but a necessary prelude to the emergence of the victim—or, if you will, the "revelation" of the identity of the victim, whose sacrifice becomes the foundation of a new order—so in Marx, the dehumanizing horrors, the culturally undifferentiating power of capitalism that does away with all sacred barriers, provides the sine qua non historical conditions that finally reveal capitalism itself as the victim whose death becomes the foundation of a new and humane universal order. Both Virgil and Marx know that the foundational sacrifice, in order to be truly foundational, can only happen at (as) the end of a violent process of cultural undifferentiation, by which "all that is solid melts into air, all that is holy profaned."

According to Marx, this is the moment when "man is at last compelled to face with sober senses his real conditions of life and his relations with his kind." Virgil would surely agree. But when they both look at the situation "with sober senses," Virgil, the poet, sees more clearly. Like Marx, he sees that, at that moment, either a victim is found or all will perish. But he also realizes something to which Marx remains completely blind: at the crucial, sacrificial, moment it *no longer* makes any difference who the victim might be. All that is required is one head on which to transfer the responsibility for the entire, undifferentiating, crisis. How could it be otherwise, since the violence of the crisis itself has made all natural and cultural differences among men meaningless? Needless to say, Virgil also knew, as we saw, that this arbitrariness in the selection of the victim cannot be openly revealed if the victimization process is to work properly and effectively.

At the crucial moment, totally unaware that he is treading along an immemorial sacrificial path, Marx, the proud intellectual, "discovers" who the culprit really is: not any single individual or group of individuals as such, qua individuals, but the *system*, which he calls "capitalism." And if we ask how he has been able to identify the culprit with such reassuring clarity, he will tell us that it is not a question of his identifying anything by intellectual means; rather, capitalism is the historical stage itself in which we live; all we have to do is look around and see the real conditions in which we live, brutal competition, dehumanization, increasing agony and suffering etc., in order to understand what capitalism truly is. For that is really *all* that we or the masses, that is to say the real protagonists and agents of history, have to see clearly in order to understand capitalism as a historical reality and not a mere analytical construct. We do not even have to read *Das Kapital*. In other words, "capitalism" is the crisis itself with its own violent, self-feeding, internal logic.

And yet the theoretical representation that gives a name to the crisis and confirms at the level of theory that the crisis is indeed violent, self-feeding, dehumanizing, etc., is a fundamental sacrificial act; it is what Girard has called a persecutory representation: that is, the representation of the crisis in the eyes of the victimizers, a theoretical representation, generated by the crisis itself, whose function it is to provide both a target or aim, and a channel for everybody's violence, so that it can be thrown off everybody's shoulders, literally, explained away.

We should not be misled, however, by the apparent scientific character of such a theoretical operation. The victim, the creature blamed for the crisis, had always been an embodiment of the crisis itself. Its expulsion was always instrumental, a roundabout way to get rid of the crisis. This is why, in purely objective terms (which is never the way convinced victimizers see things), it did not make any difference who the victim was, as long as it could take the heavy burden of the crisis away from everybody. The theoretical construct called the "capitalist system" fulfills exactly the same sacrificial function in Marx. No amount of "scientific" evidence can change that. And because of this sacrificial character, all of Marx's analytical brilliance and critical sophistication is doomed from the start; historically speaking it will remain sterile, linked to a sacrificial mechanism that is no longer going anywhere except in circles.

At the very moment when Marx tells us that "man is at last compelled to face with sober senses his real conditions of life and his relations with his kind," he, Marx, does not do as he says; he blinks, so to speak. He did what all the sacrificers had always done when confronted with that kind of situation: he raises a barrier between man and "his kind," that is, between each man and his neighbor; or what amounts to the same thing, he tries to divert each man's hate-filled eyes away from his equal toward this intervening or mediating barrier called the "system." That is, he "scientifically" diverts all accusations from their immediate target, the neighbor, onto the "system," which thus becomes both the culprit and the savior. Needless to say, in revolutionay praxis, in order "to grip the masses" the theory "must demonstrate *ad hominem*"; because the violent blows will not really fall on such a bloodless entity as the "system," but on something far more sacrificially satisfying, the real flesh-

and-blood "representatives of the system," in other words, the neighbor, whose murder it is the function of the "system" to cover up and to justify.

At such a crucial, victimizing moment there is no difference between what Marx does and what Virgil did. However, Marx, the social, "systemic" philosopher, is fooled by his own sacrificial operation in a way Virgil was not. Virgil knew that in the end, underlying all the social and natural differences on which the crisis eagerly feeds and grows, there is nothing but the "inane fury" of neighbor killing neighbor. In terms of its capacity for objective understanding of the role of human violence in the foundation and maintenance of social institutions, Marx's text is a sacrificial regression compared with Virgil's.

And yet, even though Marx's sacrificial elimination of the "capitalist system" is as regressive and primitive as can be, no primitive sacrificer was ever able to perform his sacrifice with such a spirit of hopeful confidence in its outcome and, therefore, in the future. Of course, if he had fully understood what he was doing, his optimism would have vanished, as happened in the case of Virgil. Nevertheless, this lack of understanding, this blindness, cannot adequately account for such an unprecedented hope and confidence. The primitive sacrificer did not really know what he was doing either, but his ignorance did not shield him from acute apprehension and foreboding. Marx placed, or rather *misplaced*, more confidence and hope in the sacrificial mechanism than any primitive sacrificer; he felt much more protected against the frightening truth of human violence without sacrificial protection, its undifferentiating, spiraling, open-endedness.

The question is, Whence came this excess of hope and confidence, this extra protection against the frightening truth that made Marx's self-delusion all the more complete and tight? Clearly it could not come from the "capitalist system," which was fundamentally evil and exclusively concerned with perpetuating itself. It could only come from that which Marx suspected the least. Paradoxically, what gave the sacrificial hiding of the truth such a convincing and truthful appearance was its historical association with the nonsacrificial truth itself. What Marx saw in human history was not revealed to him by the merciless and destructive action of "capitalism," but by the Christian word in its nonsacrificial efficacy. It was not, as he thought, "capitalism" that had gradually undermined and rendered insignificant all previous barriers between human beings, compelling them "to face with sober senses [their] real conditions of life and [their] relations with [one another]," but the nonsacrificial dimension of Christianity.

Virgil saw the frightening truth and had to keep it from view because he had no other protection against it. Marx was too well protected against it and, as a result, did not see it (he misinterpreted what he saw). In this sense, it can be said that Virgil and Marx stand in complementary distribution to each other; each one may illuminate or give meaning to the other. Nevertheless, behind the panic of the one and the blindness of the other lies the same resistance, the same incapacity to contemplate the violent collapse of all differential (and differing) barriers between human antagonists, without becoming scandalized and looking for a victim through which to build new sacred barriers once again.

And yet, that vision that neither Virgil nor Marx could sustain, is the one that was given as a historical possibility to modern literature; a vision capable of going beyond Virgil's fear and Marx's blindness; capable of being both clear-sighted and hopeful. Such a possibility only existed within the nonsacrificial spirit of Christianity. Christians, too, are supposed to see one another *in* Christ. But contrary to what happens sacrificially in the case of the "system," Christ's mediating, intervening, sacrifice is perfectly transparent, not a stonewall, or rather, not a stumbling block; it is not meant to hide anything about the crisis. Quite the contrary, it is meant to reveal the arbitrariness of a crisis, the responsibility for which rests entirely on the shoulders of each and every one of its violent participants. It allows them to see through all the barriers that they have set up among themselves—in a futile attempt to stop the crisis—and to look at themselves, so to speak, in the nude. Thus, while allowing everybody to see what is actually going on *strictly among themselves*, it prevents them from accusing one another.

Christ diverts all accusations onto himself, but in full knowledge of what he is doing and why; a knowledge that is allowed to stand in the light precisely because he does not resist it; he does not rebel against the role in which the sacrificial mechanism casts him. On the other hand, he does not cooperate with the mechanism either; he does not shift the accusation onto somebody or something else, nor does he perpetuate the crisis (and the hiding of the truth from the eyes of the victimizers), by turning the accusation back against the accusers. He unmasks the crisis as the violence of neighbor against neighbor, by avoiding any kind of sacrificial manipulation. This lifting of opaque, defensive barriers between man and man, this nonsacrificial discovery of man's nakedness in his own eyes, did more than anything, I submit, to make modern literature possible and give it an unprecedented historical opportunity.

This is not to say that pre-Christian literature, in particular the best of it, Greek tragedy and the epic of Homer and Virgil, was incapable of revealing the naked violence of man against man as such. Few poets have ever revealed the undifferentiating symmetry between contending human parties so clearly as Virgil. And who can forget the famous Homeric objectivity, equidistant from each of the warring factions; or the ritual standing aside of the tragic chorus, anticipating and mourning the terrible outcome? In fact, it is probably true that no modern poet could match that kind of equilibrium in the representation of human violence; an equilibrium that, as we have seen in Virgil, stands dangerously posed on the verge of revealing too much for the good of the sacrificial system.

This should not be surprising. A sacrificial mind still uninhibited by any nonsacrificial scruples, exclusively concerned with making the sacrificial process work, may actually be more keenly aware than a historically Christian one of the kind of situation that makes the sacrifice of the victim urgently needed. But this sacrificial representation of evenly reciprocal violence, this perfect balance between enemy twins, is there only as a prelude to, or a ritual preparation for, the eagerly anticipated sacrifice of the victim that will put an end to it. The perfect equilibrium between the enemy twins has been deliberately staged for sacrificial purposes and it has a purely provisional status. (Of course, somebody like Virgil could see much more than sacrificial piety allowed through that provisional window onto the truth).

What distinguishes the vision of the great modern classics from that of their predecessors is that at the crucial moment when all the eyes turn in search of the one culprit, the ultimate source of all the trouble, they are seen to be searching in vain, and yet the situation does not become hopeless, it does not lead to utter despair. The great modern poet now has the possibility of letting the spectacle stand of those human eyes looking into each other. He now has the possibility of exploring at length and in detail the infinite ways in which human beings relate to one another for good and for bad, even beyond the point where his predecessors would become scandalized and the victimizing mechanism would be triggered.

This, I believe, is what made the modern novel and the modern theater historically possible. They did not just sprout spontaneously on the soil of a world "abandoned by the gods." A world abandoned by the gods can only be a world in crisis looking for a victim to reconstitute itself all over again, unless the entire sacrificial mentality is turned upside down, reversed, and hope is found precisely in what had always been a terrifying prospect: renouncing the search for the victim altogether. This is the hope that sustained the freedom of the modern poet.

Going beyond Virgil, this modern poet became witness to a truth that neither Marx nor any other "systemic" sacrificer in our modern world has ever been able to contemplate without becoming scandalized, that is to say, without closing his eyes and stopping his ears.

However, it was hope, not certainty—to use Popper's words—that sustained the great modern poet. For what the poet held in view was far from reassuring, and it concerned him precisely in his role as poet. The purely immanent interacting of violently undifferentiated human beings was something like a quicksand on which he stood, not only as a human being, but also, specifically, as a poet, for such a quicksand is precisely the soil on which poetry prospers, the stuff it is made of. The human truth he discovered was also the ground in which truth can sink or become hopelessly distorted. This is why his discovery tended to make him humble, even profoundly apprehensive, about his own poetic task. Humble, I insist, not panic-stricken, not scandalized.

SELECT BIBLIOGRAPHY

Aglietta, Michel and André Orléan. *La violence de la monnaie*. Paris: PUF, 1982.

Anselm of Canterbury. *Why God Became Man and the Virgin Conception and Original Sin*. Translated by Joseph M. Colleran. Albany, N.Y.: Magi Books, 1969.

Arias, Ricardo. *The Spanish Sacramental Plays*. Boston: Twayne, 1980.

Aristotle. *The Basic Works of Aristotle*. Edited by Richard McKeon. New York: Random House, 1941.

———. "The Poetics." In *Literary Criticism: Plato to Dryden*, edited by Allan H. Gilbert, 63–124. Detroit: Wayne State University Press, 1982.

Arnold, Matthew. "The Study of Poetry." In *Essays: English and American*, edited by Charles W. Eliot, 65–90. Harvard Classics. New York: P.F. Collier and Son, 1938.

Arróniz, Othón. *Teatros y escenarios del Siglo de Oro*. Madrid: Gredos, 1977.

Auerbach, Erich. *Literary Language and Its Public in Late Latin Antiquity and in the Middle Ages*. Translated by Ralph Manheim. London: Routledge and Kegan Paul, 1965.

Aulén, Gustaf. *Christus Victor: An Historical Study of the Three Main Types of the Idea of Atonement*. New York: Macmillan, 1951.

Bacon, Francis. *The Advancement of Learning and the New Atlantis*. Introduction by Thomas Case. World's Classics 93. London: Oxford University Press, 1906. Reprint, 1974.

———. *The Essays*. Edited by John Pitcher. Harmondsworth, Middlesex: Penguin, 1985.

———. *The Physical and Metaphysical Works of Lord Bacon*. Edited by Joseph Dewey. London, 1891.

Bandera, Cesáreo. *Mímesis conflictiva: Ficción literaria y violencia en Cervantes y Calderón*. Madrid: Gredos, 1975.

———. "La muerte de Clarín y apuntes sobre la tragedia calderoniana." *Barroco* 4 (1972): 57–75.

Barish, Jonas. *The Antitheatrical Prejudice*. Berkeley and Los Angeles: University of California Press, 1981.

Barnhardt, J. E. *The Study of Religion and Its Meaning: New Explorations in Light of Karl Popper and Emile Durkheim*. The Hague: Mouton, 1977.

Barras, M. *The Stage Controversy in France from Corneille to Rousseau*. New York: Institute of French Studies, 1933.

Bateson, Gregory. *Mind and Nature: A Necessary Unity*. New York: Bantam, 1980.

Bergson, Henri. *The Two Sources of Morality and Religion*. Translated by R. Ashley Audra and Cloudesley Brereton, with the assistance of W. Horsfall Carter. New York: H. Holt, 1935. Reprint. Garden City, N.Y.: Doubleday, 1954.

Blumenberg, Hans. *The Legitimacy of the Modern Age*. Cambridge: MIT Press, 1983.

Boileau, Nicholas. *Satires et Epitres*. Paris: Larousse, 1941.

Bolgar, R. R., ed. *Classical Influences on Western Thought, A.D. 1650–1870*. Cambridge: Cambridge University Press, 1979.

Bourgey, Louis. *Observation et Expérience chez Aristote*. Paris: Vrin, 1955.

Bowra, C. M. *From Virgil to Milton*. London: MacMillan, 1948.

Brand, C. P. *Torquato Tasso*. Cambridge: Cambridge University Press, 1965.

Brower, Reuben A. *Hero and Saint: Shakespeare and the Graeco-Roman Heroic Tradition*. New York: Oxford University Press, 1971.

Browne, Sir Thomas. *Religio Medici, Hydriotaphia, and the Garden of Cyrus*. Edited by R. H. A. Robbins. Oxford: Clarendon Press, 1972.

Buckley, Vincent. *Poetry and Morality: Studies on the Criticism of Matthew Arnold, T. S. Eliot and F. R. Leavis*. London: Chatto and Windus, 1959.

———. *Poetry and the Sacred*. London: Chatto and Windus, 1968.

Burkert, Walter. *Greek Religion*. Translated by John Raffan. Cambridge: Harvard University Press, 1985.

———. "Greek Tragedy and Sacrificial Ritual." *Greek, Roman, and Byzantine Studies* 7 (1966): 87–121.

———. *Structure and History in Greek Mythology and Ritual*. Sather Classical Lectures 47. Berkeley and Los Angeles: University of California Press, 1979.

Calasso, Roberto. *La Ruine de Kasch*. Paris: Gallimard, 1987.

Calderón de la Barca, Pedro. *La vida es sueño*. Edited by Ciriaco Morón Arroyo. Madrid: Cátedra, 1990.

———. *El mayor monstruo del mundo*. Edited by Jose María Ruano de la Haza. Colección Austral 81. Madrid: Espasa-Calpe, 1989.

———. *Obras Completas*. Edited by Angel Valbuena Briones. 2 vols. Vol. 1, *Dramas*. Vol. 2, *Comedias*. Madrid: Aguilar, 1959 (vol. 1) and 1973 (vol. 2).

Camoens, Luís Vaz de. *The Lusiads*. Translated by William C. Atkinson. Harmondsworth, Middlesex: Penguin, 1987.

———. *The Lusiads of Luiz de Camoens*. Translated by Leonard Bacon. New York: Hispanic Society of America, 1950.

Castelvetro, Lodovico. *Castelvetro on the Art of Poetry: An Abridged Translation of Lodovico Castelvetro's Poetica d'Aristotele Vulgarizzata et Sposta*. Translated by Andrew Bongiorno. Medieval and Renaissance Texts and Studies 29. Binghamton, N.Y.: Center for Medieval and Early Renaissance Studies, State University of New York at Binghamton, 1984.

Cervantes, Miguel de. *The Adventures of Don Quixote*. Translated by J. M. Cohen. Harmondsworth, Middlesex: Penguin, 1950.

————. *Don Quijote de la Mancha*. 2 vols. Edited by John Jay Allen. Madrid: Cáte-dra, 1989.

————. *Obras completas*. Vol. 2. Edited by A. Valbuena Prat. Madrid: Aguilar, 1970.

Chaunu, Pierre. *Le Temps des Réformes: Histoire religieuse et système de civilisation*. Paris: Fayard, 1975.

Chenu, M. D. "Cur Homo? Le sous-sol d'une controverse au XIIᵉ siècle." *Mélanges de Science Religieuse* 10 (1953): 195–204.

————. *Nature, Man, and Society in the Twelfth Century: Essays on New Theological Perspectives in the Latin West*. With a Preface by Etienne Gilson. Edited and translated by Jerome Taylor and Lester K. Little. Chicago: University of Chicago Press, 1968.

Clausen, Wendell. "An Interpretation of the Aeneid." In *Virgil: A Collection of Critical Essays*, edited by Steele Commager, 75–88. Englewood Cliffs, N.J.: Prentice-Hall, 1966.

Close, Anthony. "A Poet's Vanity: Thoughts on the Friendly Ethos of Cervantine Satire." *Cervantes* 13, no. 1 (1993): 31–63.

Cohen, J. M., ed. and trans. *The Penguin Book of Spanish Verse*. Baltimore, Md.: Penguin, 1960.

Cornford, F. M. *Principium Sapientiae: The Origins of Greek Philosophic Thought*. Cambridge: Cambridge University Press, 1952.

Cotarelo y Mori, Emilio. *Bibliografía de las controversias sobre la licitud del teatro en España*. Madrid: n.p. 1904.

Davenant, Sir William. *Gondibert*. Edited by David F. Gladish. Oxford: Clarendon Press, 1971.

Dawson, Christopher. *The Dynamics of World History*. New York: Sheed and Ward, 1956.

Delumeau, Jean. *La Civilisation de la Renaissance*. Paris: Arthaud, 1967.

————. *Le Christianism va-t-il mourir?* Paris: Hachette, 1977.

————. *Sin and Fear: The Emergence of a Western Guilt Culture, Thirteenth–Eighteenth Centuries*. Trans. Eric Nicholson. New York: St. Martin's Press, 1990.

Derrida, Jacques. *Margins of Philosophy*. Translated by Alan Bass. Chicago: University of Chicago Press, 1982.

Di Cesare, Mario A. *The Altar and the City: A Reading of Vergil's Aeneid*. New York: Columbia University Press, 1974.

Dumont, Louis. *Essays on Individualism: Modern Ideology in Anthropological Perspective*. Chicago: University of Chicago Press, 1985.

Durkheim, Emile. *The Elementary Forms of the Religious Life*. Translated by Joseph Ward Swain. London: Allen and Unwin; New York: Macmillan, 1915.

Eliade, Mircea. *Le Sacré et le Profane*. Paris: Gallimard, 1967.

Eliot, T. S. *On Poetry and Poets*. London: Faber and Faber, 1957.

————. "Religion and Literature." In *The New Orpheus: Essays toward a Christian Poetic*, edited by Nathan A. Scott, Jr., 225–35. New York: Sheed and Ward, 1964.

Ellul, Jacques. *The New Demons*. New York: Seabury, 1975.

Else, Gerald F. *The Origin and Early Form of Greek Tragedy*. New York: Norton, 1972.

Elster, Jon. *Making Sense of Marx*. Cambridge: Cambridge University Press, 1985.

Epicurus. *The Philosophy of Epicurus: Letters, Doctrines, and Parallel Passages from*

Lucretius. Translated by George K. Strodach. Evanston: Northwestern University Press, 1963.

Ferguson, Wallace K. *The Renaissance in Historical Thought: Five Centuries of Interpretation.* Cambridge, Mass.: Houghton Mifflin, 1948.

Festugière, A. J. *L'astrologie et les sciences occultes.* 2d ed. Vol. 1 of *La révélation d'Hermès Trismégiste.* Paris: Gabalda, 1950.

———. *Le dieu cosmique.* Vol. 2 of *La révélation d'Hermès Trismégiste.* Paris: Librairie Lecoffre, 1949.

Fichter, Andrew. *Poets Historical: Dynastic Epic in the Renaissance.* New Haven: Yale University Press, 1982.

Fowler, W. W. *The Religious Experience of the Roman People.* London: MacMillan, 1911.

Frank, Erich. *Philosophical Understanding and Religious Truth.* Oxford University Press, 1945.

Fraser, Russell. *The War Against Poetry.* Princeton: Princeton University Press, 1970.

Galen. *On the Usefulness of the Parts of the Body.* Translated by Margaret Tallmadge May. Ithaca: Cornell University Press, 1968.

García Cárcel, Ricardo. *Herejía y Sociedad en el Siglo XVI: La Inquisición en Valencia, 1530–1609.* Barcelona: Ediciones Peninsula, 1980.

Gardner, Helen. *Religion and Literature.* New York: Oxford University Press, 1971.

Gauchet, Marcel. *Le Désenchantement du monde: Une histoire politique de la religion.* Paris: Gallimard, 1985.

Gernet, Louis. *Anthropologie de la Grèce antique.* Paris: François Maspero, 1968.

Gil Vincente. *Obras completas.* 4th ed. 6 vols. Lisbon: Sa da Costa, 1978.

Gilmore, Martin P. *The World of Humanism, 1453–1517.* New York: Harper and Bros., 1952.

Girard, René. *A Theatre of Envy: William Shakespeare.* New York: Oxford University Press, 1991.

———. *Deceit, Desire, and the Novel: Self and Other in Literary Structure.* Trans. Yvonne Freccero. Baltimore: Johns Hopkins University Press, 1965.

———. *Things Hidden Since the Foundation of the World.* Translated by Stephen Bann and Michael Metteer. Stanford: Stanford University Press, 1987.

———. *Violence and the Sacred.* Translated by Patrick Gregory. Baltimore: Johns Hopkins University Press, 1977.

Glover, T. R. *Virgil.* London: Methuen, 1923.

Granger, F. "Folklore in Virgil." *Classical Review* 14 (1900): 24–26.

Greene, Thomas M. *The Light in Troy: Imitation and Discovery in Renaissance Poetry.* New Haven: Yale University Press, 1982.

Guepin, J.-P. *The Tragic Paradox: Myth and Ritual in Greek Tragedy.* Amsterdam: Adolf M. Hakkert, 1968.

Gunton, Colin E. *The Actuality of Atonement: A Study of Metaphor, Rationality and the Christian Tradition.* Edinburgh: T. and T. Clark, 1988.

Haecker, Theodore. "Odysseus and Aeneas." In *Virgil: A Collection of Critical Essays,* edited by Steele Commager, 68–74. Englewood Cliffs, N.J.: Prentice-Hall, 1966.

Hägin, Peter. *The Epic Hero and the Decline of Heroic Poetry.* Bern: Francke, 1964.

Halliday, William R. *Lectures on the History of Roman Religion.* Liverpool: Liverpool University Press, 1922.

Hathaway, Baxter. *The Age of Criticism: The Late Renaissance in Italy.* Ithaca: Cornell University Press, 1962.

Heiserman, Arthur. *The Novel before the Novel: Essays and Discussions about the Beginnings of Prose Fiction in the West*. Chicago: University of Chicago Press, 1977.
Heliodorus. *Les Ethiopiques (Theagène et Chariclée)*. Edited by R. M. Rattenbury and the Reverend T. W. Lumb. Translated by J. Maillon. Paris: Les Belles Lettres, 1960.
Heller, Agnes. *Renaissance Man*. London: Routledge and Kegan Paul, 1978.
Heller, Erich. "The Hazard of Modern Poetry." In *Literature and Religion*, edited by Giles B. Gunn, 168–76. New York: Harper and Row, 1971.
Helton, Tinsley, ed. *The Renaissance: A Reconsideration of the Theories and Interpretations of the Age*. Madison: University of Wisconsin Press, 1961.
Henningsen, Gustav. *The Witches' Advocate: Basque Witchcraft and the Spanish Inquisition, 1609–1617*. Reno: University of Nevada Press, 1980.
Hudson, Winthrop S. "The Weber Thesis Reexamined." In *The Role of Religion in Modern European History*, edited by Sidney A. Burrell, 44–45. New York: Macmillan, 1964.
Huizinga, Johan. *Homo ludens: A Study of the Play-Element in Culture*. Boston: Beacon, 1955.
Ife, B. W. *Reading and Fiction in Golden Age Spain*. Cambridge: Cambridge University Press, 1985.
Jeanmaire, H. *Dionysos: Histoire du Culte de Bacchus*. Paris: Payot, 1951.
Johnson, Samuel. *Johnson's Lives of the Poets*. Edited by Mrs. Alexander Napier. London: n.p., 1890.
Johnson, W. R. *Darkness Visible: A Study of Vergil's Aeneid*. Berkeley and Los Angeles: University of California Press, 1967.
Jones, R. O. *Historia de la literatura española. Siglo de Oro: prosa y poesía*. Barcelona: Ariel, 1989.
Josephus, Flavius. *The Genuine Works of Flavius Josephus*. 6 vols. Translated by William Whiston. Bridgeport: M. Sherman, 1828.
Kamen, Henry. *The Spanish Inquisition*. London: Weidenfeld and Nicolson, 1965.
Kates, Judith A. *Tasso and Milton: The Problem of Christian Epic*. Lewisburg: Bucknell University Press, 1983.
Knight, William F. Jackson. *Roman Vergil*. London: Faber and Faber, 1944.
Lamy, Bernard. *Nouvelles réflexions sur l'art poétique*. Paris, 1678. Geneva: Slatkine Reprints, 1973.
Le Bossu, and Voltaire. *Le Bossu and Voltaire on the Epic*. Introduction by Stuart Curran. Facsimile reproductions. Gainesville, Fla.: Scholars' Facsimiles and Reprints, 1970.
Lebégue, Raymond. *La tragédie religieuse en France: Les debuts (1514–1573)*. Paris: Honoré Champion, 1929.
Leclercq, Jean. *Monks and Love in Twelfth-Century France: Psycho-Historical Essay*. Oxford: Clarendon Press, 1979.
Lewis, C. S. *A Preface to Paradise Lost*. New York: Oxford University Press, 1942.
Lienhardt, Godfrey. *Divinity and Experience*. Oxford: Clarendon Press, 1970.
Livy. *Ab urbe condita*. Translated by B. O. Foster. Loeb Classical Library 172. Cambridge: Harvard University Press, 1967.
Loukovitch, Kosta. *L'Evolution de la tragédie religieuse classique en France*. Paris: Librairie E. Droz, 1933.
Lucretius. *De rerum natura*. Translated by W. H. D. Rouse. Revised by Martin Fergu-

son Smith. Loeb Classical Library 181. Cambridge: Harvard University Press, 1975.

Lukács, Georg. *The Theory of the Novel*. Translated by Anna Bostock. Cambridge: MIT Press, 1971.

Marni, Archimede. *Allegory in the French Heroic Poem of the Seventeenth Century*. Princeton: Princeton University Press, 1936.

Marx, Karl. *Capital*. Vol. 3, *The Process of Capitalist Production as a Whole*. Edited by Frederick Engels. New York: International Publishers, 1967.

———. *Capital: A Critique of Political Economy*. Vol. 1, *The Process of Capitalist Production*. Chicago: Charles H. Kerr, 1909.

———. *Economic and Philosophical Manuscripts of 1844 and the Communist Manifesto*. Buffalo: Prometheus Books, 1988.

———. *Karl Marx: A Reader*. Edited by Jon Elster. Cambridge: Cambridge University Press, 1986.

———. *Pre-Capitalist Economic Formations*. Edited by E. J. Hobsbawm. Translated by Jack Cohen. New York: International Publishers, 1967.

———, and Friedrich Engels. *The German Ideology: Part 1*. Edited by C. J. Arthur. New York: International Publishers, 1970.

———. *On Religion*. Introduction by Reinhold Niebuhr. New York: Schocken, 1964.

Mazzeo, Joseph Anthony. *Renaissance and Revolution: The Remaking of European Thought*. New York: Pantheon, 1965.

Mazzoni, Giacopo. *On the Defense of the Comedy of Dante: Introduction and Summary*. Translated by Robert L. Montgomery. Tallahassee, Fla.: University Presses of Florida, 1983.

McKenna, Andrew J. *Violence and Difference: Girard, Derrida, and Deconstruction*. Urbana: University of Illinois Press, 1992.

McLellan, David. *Marx's Grundrisse*. London: Macmillan, 1971.

Menéndez Pelayo, M. *Historia de las ideas estéticas en España*. Edited by Enrique Sánchez Reyes. 5 vols. Santander: CSIC, 1940.

———. *Orígenes de la novela*. Edited by Enrique Sánchez Reyes. 2d ed. Vol. 1. Madrid: CSIC, 1962.

Milbank, John. *Theology and Social Theory: Beyond Secular Reason*. Oxford: Basil Blackwell, 1990.

Mittelstrass, J. "'Phaenomena bene fundata': From 'Saving the Appearances' to the Mechanisation of the World-Picture." In *Classical Influences on Western Thought, A.D. 1650–1870*, ed. R. R. Bolgar, 39–59. Cambridge: Cambridge University Press, 1979.

Moore, Leslie E. *Beautiful Sublime: The Making of Paradise Lost, 1701–1734*. Stanford: Stanford University Press, 1990.

Mulhern, Francis. *The Moment of "Scrutiny."* London: NLB, 1979.

Nelson, William. *Fact or Fiction: The Dilemma of the Renaissance Storyteller*. Cambridge: Harvard University Press, 1973.

Nethercut, William R. "Invasion in the *Aeneid*." *Greece and Rome* 15 (1968): 82–95.

Nilsson, Martin P. *Greek Piety*. Translated by Herbert J. Rose. Oxford: Clarendon Press, 1948.

Orgel, Stephen. *The Illusion of Power: Political Theater in the English Renaissance*. Berkeley and Los Angeles: University of California Press, 1975.

Otis, Brooks. *Virgil: A Study in Civilized Poetry*. Oxford: Clarendon Press, 1963.

Pagels, Elaine. *The Gnostic Gospels*. New York: Random House, 1979.

Parker, Alexander A. "*El médico de su honra* as Tragedy." *Hispanófila Especial* 2 (1975): 3–23.

Parry, Adam. "The Two Voices of Vergil's *Aeneid*." In *Virgil: A Collection of Critical Essays*, edited by Steele Commager, 107–23. Englewood Cliffs, N.J.: Prentice-Hall, 1966.

Peletier du Mans, Jacques. *L'Art Poétique de Jacques Peletier du Mans (1555): Publié d'après l'edition unique avec introduction et commentaire*. Paris: Les Belles Lettres, 1930.

Pelikan, Jaroslav. *The Growth of Medieval Theology (600–1300)*. Vol. 3 of *The Christian Tradition: A History of the Development of Doctrine*. Chicago: University of Chicago Press, 1978.

Pérez Villanueva, Joaquín, ed. *La inquisición española: Nueva visión, nuevos horizontes*. Proceedings of the First Symposium Internacional sobre la Inquisición Española. Cuenca, 1978. Madrid: Siglo XXI de España Editores, 1980.

Phillips, Henry. *The Theater and Its Critics in Seventeenth-Century France*. Oxford: Oxford University Press, 1980.

Pierce, Frank. "The Place of Mythology in the Lusiads." *Comparative Literature* 6 (1954): 97–122.

———. *La poesía épica del Siglo de Oro*. Madrid: Gredos, 1968.

Plato. *The Laws of Plato*. Translated by Thomas L. Pangle. Chicago: University of Chicago Press, 1988.

———. *The Republic*. Translated by B. Jowett. Vintage Books 128. New York: Random House, 1991.

———. *The Sophist and the Statesman*. Edited by R. Klibansky and E. Anscombe. Translated by A. E. Taylor. London: Thomas Nelson and Sons, 1961.

Po-chia Hsia, R. *The Myth of Ritual Murder: Jews and Magic in Reformation Germany*. New Haven: Yale University Press, 1988.

Poe, Edgar Allan. "The Poetic Principle." In *Essays: English and American*, edited by Charles W. Eliot, 371–92. Harvard Classics. New York: P. F. Collier and Son, 1938.

Popper, Karl R. *Objective Knowledge: An Evolutionary Approach*. Revised ed. Oxford: Clarendon Press, 1979.

———. *The Open Society and Its Enemies*. Princeton: Princeton University Press, 1950.

———. *Popper Selections*. Edited by David Miller. Princeton: Princeton University Press, 1985.

———. "Prediction and Prophecy in the Social Sciences." In *Theories of History: Readings from Classical and Contemporary Sources*, edited by Patrick Gardiner, 276–85. New York: Free Press, 1959.

———. *The Poverty of Historicism*. New York: Basic Books, 1960.

Rapin, René. *Reflections on Aristotle's Treatise of Poesie*. Translated by Thomas Rymer (1674). Reprint. N.p.: Gregg International, 1979.

Rapp, Francis. *L'Eglise et la vie religieuse en Occident à la fin du Moyen Age*. Paris: PUF, 1971.

Reiss, Timothy J. *The Meaning of Literature*. Ithaca: Cornell University Press, 1992.

Ridpath, George. *The Stage Condemn'd*. London, 1698. Reprint. New York: Garland, 1972.

Rose, H. J. *Aeneas Pontifex*. Vergilian Essays 2. London: Phoenix, 1948.

Sayce, R. A. *The French Biblical Epic in the Seventeenth Century.* Oxford: Clarendon Press, 1955.

Schmitt, Charles B. *Studies in Renaissance Philosophy and Science.* London: Variorum Reprints, 1981.

Sellar, W. Y. *The Roman Poets of the Augustan Age: Virgil.* Oxford: Clarendon Press, 1908.

———. *The Roman Poets of the Republic.* Oxford: Clarendon Press, 1905.

Serres, Michel. *La naissance de la physique dans le texte de Lucrèce: Fleuves et turbulences.* Paris: Editions de Minuit, 1977.

Seznec, Jean. *La survivance des dieux antiques: Essai sur le rôle de la tradition mythologique dans l'humanisme et dans l'art de la renaissance.* London: Warburg Institute, 1940.

Siebers, Tobin. "Violence and Philosophy." Paper read at the annual meeting of the Society for Phenomenology and Existential Philosophy. Boston, 1992.

Spingarn, J. E. *A History of Literary Criticism in the Renaissance.* 7th ed. New York: Columbia University Press, 1924.

Swedenberg, H. T., Jr. *The Theory of the Epic in England, 1650–1800.* Berkeley and Los Angeles: University of California Press, 1944.

Tasso, Torquato. *Discourses on the Heroic Poem.* Translated by Mariella Cavalchini and Irene Samuel. Oxford: Clarendon Press, 1973.

———. *Jerusalem Delivered.* Translated by Ralph Nash. Detroit: Wayne State University Press, 1987.

———. *Jerusalem Delivered.* Translated by Joseph Tusiani. N.p.: Associated University Presses, 1970.

Taylor, Charles. *Sources of the Self: The Making of the Modern Identity.* Cambridge: Harvard University Press, 1989.

Thomas à Kempis. *The Imitation of Christ.* Edited by Paul M. Bechtel. Chicago: Moody, 1980.

Tillyard, E. M. W. *The English Epic and Its Background.* London: Chatto and Windus, 1954.

Townend, Gavin. "Imagery in Lucretius." In *Lucretius,* edited by D. R. Dudley, 95–114. New York: Basic Books, 1965.

Turner, Victor Witter. *The Drums of Affliction: A Study of Religious Processes among the Ndembu of Zambia.* Oxford: Clarendon Press; London: International African Institute, 1968.

Virgil. *Aeneid VII–XII: The Minor Poems.* Translated by H. Rushton Fairclough. Loeb Classical Library 64. Cambridge: Harvard University Press, 1978.

———. *Eclogues. Georgics. Aeneid I–VI.* Translated by H. Rushton Fairclough. Loeb Classical Library 63. Cambridge: Harvard University Press, 1974.

Walzer, R. *Galen on Jews and Christians.* London: Oxford University Press, 1949.

Wasson, John. "The End of an Era: Parish Drama in England from 1520 to the Dissolution." *Research Opportunities in Renaissance Drama* 31 (1992): 70–78.

Weber, Max. *The Protestant Ethic and the Spirit of Capitalism.* With a Foreword by R. H. Tawney. Translated by Talcott Parsons. New York: Scribner, 1930.

Weinberg, Bernard. *A History of Literary Criticism in the Italian Renaissance.* 2 vols. Chicago: University of Chicago Press, 1961.

———, ed. *Trattati di Poetica e Retorica del Cinquecento.* Vol. 1. Bari: Laterza, 1970.

West, J. F. *The Great Intellectual Revolution.* London: Murray, 1965.

Willey, Basil. *The Seventeenth Century Background: Studies in the Thought of the Age in Relation to Poetry and Religion.* London: Chatto and Windus, 1957.

Williams, James G. *The Bible, Violence, and the Sacred: Liberation from the Myth of Sanctioned Violence.* San Francisco, Calif.: Harper Collins, 1992.

Wilson, Edward M. *Spanish and English Literature of the Sixteenth and Seventeenth Centuries.* Cambridge: Cambridge University Press, 1980.

Wormell, D. E. W. "The Personal World of Lucretius." in *Lucretius,* edited by D. R. Dudley, 35–68. New York: Basic Books, 1965.

Wright, T. R. *Theology and Literature.* Oxford: Basil Blackwell, 1988.

Young, Frances M. *The Use of Sacrificial Ideas in Greek Christian Writers from the New Testament to John Chrysostom.* Cambridge, Mass.: Philadelphia Patristic Foundation, 1979.

INDEX

death
life
├ undifferentiation
└ differentiation ┬ sacred (→victimization)
                  └ profane